MADE FOR EACH OTHER

BY THE SAME AUTHOR

Costume and Fashion

MADE FOR EACH OTHER
Fashion and the Academy Awards®

BRONWYN COSGRAVE

BLOOMSBURY

Published by Bloomsbury USA, New York
Distributed to the trade by Holtzbrinck Publishers

All papers used by Bloomsbury USA are natural, recyclable products
made from wood grown in well-managed forests. The manufacturing processes conform to the
environmental regulations of the country of origin.

Library of Congress Cataloging-in-Publication Data

Cosgrave, Bronwyn.
Made for each other : fashion and the Academy Awards /
Bronwyn Cosgrave.—1st U.S. ed. p. cm.
Includes bibliographical references and index.
ISBN 1-59691-087-9 (alk. paper)
1. Academy Awards (Motion pictures) 2. Costume—United States.
3. Fashion in motion pictures. I. Title.

PN1993. 92.C67 2007
391'.04791430973—dc22
2006032958

ISBN 1–59691–087–9
ISBN-13 978–1–59691–087–4

First U.S. Edition 2007

1 3 5 7 9 10 8 6 4 2

Typeset by Hewer Text UK Ltd, Edinburgh
Printed in the United States of America by Quebecor World Fairfield

For Elizabeth Cosgrave
and Peter C. Cosgrave

CONTENTS

Chapter One   Show Business   1

Chapter Two   The Getaway   18

Chapter Three *Gone With the Wind*   38

Chapter Four   Dark Victory   53

Chapter Five   Applause   70

Chapter Six   The Women   86

Chapter Seven Stepping Out   124

Chapter Eight The Bad and the Beautiful   158

Chapter Nine   The Only Game in Town   174

Chapter Ten   A Foreign Affair   186

Chapter Eleven What Price Hollywood?   207

Chapter Twelve The Greatest Show on Earth   226

Notes   261

Acknowledgments   293

Index   295

Chapter One

SHOW BUSINESS

Hollywood film mogul Louis B. Mayer launched the phenomenon of Academy Awards glamour. Short, squat, bespectacled Mayer was nothing to look at, but as the president of a leading studio, Metro-Goldwyn-Mayer, he was the filmmaking force of his time, and when in 1927 he founded the Academy of Motion Picture Arts and Sciences to unite the film industry's five branches—actors, directors, writers, technicians, and producers—Hollywood's bigwigs wanted in. The "Queen of Cinemaland," Mary Pickford, the single female among the Academy's original membership of thirty-six powerbrokers, hailed the Academy as the "League of Nations of Motion Pictures." Her husband, silent-screen action hero Douglas Fairbanks, suggested the organization should host an annual awards ceremony honoring outstanding contributions to the screen. By hyping Hollywood films, the Academy Awards would work wonders as a publicity stunt and thereby boost the already spectacular profits of the Big Five—that is, Paramount Pictures, Metro-Goldwyn-Mayer, Fox Films, Warner Bros., and Radio-Keith-Orpheum—the major studios that produced motion pictures, controlled vast stables of talent, and owned national movie theater chains. So L. B. Mayer set a May 1929 date for the first Academy Awards, which he funded. He also appointed Cedric Gibbons, the urbane New Yorker who operated as MGM's art director, to design a trophy. By August 1928 Mayer's handpicked Central Board of Judges gathered to determine the prizewinners.

Six months later the countdown to the first Academy Awards commenced with a front-page *Los Angeles Times* story heralding fifteen trophy winners. "There was more excitement than at a children's party when you played pin the tail on the donkey," confirmed scriptwriter Frances Marion.[1] But an undercurrent of fear laced the festive spring air. Hollywood geared up for the first Academy Awards just as "talkies," early sound films, had emerged as preeminent over traditional silent photoplays. New sound technology enhanced the total cinematic experience, but careers of silent-era legends capitulated as most cowered before microphones. "The demands of roles in which they had to use their voices were simply beyond their talent," observed academic Roy Liebman.[2] The pressure to shine in the Golden Age, as Hollywood's thirties heyday of sophisticated sound motion pictures became known, and the bleak possibility of failure shaped the route to the Academy Awards as well as the ceremonial dress adopted by Janet Gaynor, Mary Pickford, and Norma Shearer, three silent-screen stars who emerged as early actress nominees.

"It was a thrill to be chosen," said Gaynor, of receiving advance notice in a February 1928 telegram that she was the recipient of the first actress Academy Award. The Academy recognized three silent films in which Gaynor had starred at Fox Films, her studio, from 1927, including *Street Angel* and *Seventh Heaven*. The pair of hit, romantic dramas catapulted the diminutive, twenty-one-year-old redhead and former extra into becoming the "most important star on the Fox lot," noted Ephram Katz.[3] Gaynor's standout performance in the epic tragedy *Sunrise*, as Indre, a farmer's wife whose life is jeopardized by her scheming spouse, also contributed to her victory. "A distinguished contribution to the screen—a story as simple as it is human," raved *Variety* after the September 1927 premiere of *Sunrise*, which the French journal *Cahiers du Cinéma* later hailed as the greatest film of all time.[4] L. B. Mayer, all-powerful on the Academy's Central Board of Judges, argued the "merits of *Sunrise* deep into the night," when the panel of five tallied its winners, wrote Anthony Holden in *Behind the Oscar: The Secret History of the Academy Awards*. *Sunrise* also claimed the first cinematography Academy Award because, according to Holden, Mayer considered the film's director, F. W. Murnau, a Berlin art historian turned Fox Films cinéaste, "an internationally respected artist who would bring kudos to the Academy."[5]

Murnau was an uncompromising perfectionist. For one scene in *Sunrise*, he insisted a species of deciduous tree be transported hundreds

"It was a thrill to be chosen," said Janet Gaynor, right, after receiving advance notice in a February 1928 telegram that she won the first actress Academy Award. (Karl Struss/Courtesy of the Academy of Motion Picture Arts and Sciences)

of miles from Lake Arrowhead to the Fox Hollywood lot, where three hundred Mexican laborers glued new leaves to its withered branches. Once erected on set, it so displeased Murnau, he insisted more new foliage be manually applied while swarms of salaried extras hung about waiting for their cue. "It was nothing to have thirty, forty takes," said Gaynor, recalling Murnau's work ethic. "I was told by people who could understand German that he was very, very cruel to them in his language, but he was marvelous to me."[6]

When Gaynor put down the Academy's telegram, she swiftly went back to work with taskmaster Murnau on *Four Devils*, her first sound film. In the romantic circus tale she starred as Marion, a trapeze artist, but recording its dialogue proved as perilous for her as tight-rope walking. Initially Gaynor's speech pattern recorded unsatisfactorily high and thin. "It is a tiny sort of voice," she told the *Los Angeles Times*. "It seemed almost a baby voice when I first heard it. I couldn't believe it was mine."[7]

In the lead-up to the first Academy Awards, she devoted all of her

3

spare time to voice coaching and elocution lessons. So the day-in-the-life-of-Janet-Gaynor feature the *Los Angeles Times* published twenty-four hours before the ceremony contained no details of the dress she planned to wear to it. "She is up each day for breakfast at sunrise," began the story. "One and a half hours of vocal practice follows . . . motors to the studio, dons her make-up for work . . . lasting sometimes long into the night. Then home again, an hour with a trained masseuse, an hour of study on the next day's dialogue and so to bed."[8]

On Academy Awards day, Hollywood's prominent meticulously primed. "I shall never forget my personal preparations, the thrill of shopping for my gown, the last-minute visit to the beauty parlor," recalled influential gossip columnist Louella O. Parsons, motion picture editor for William Randolph Hearst's International News Service.[9] But in Gaynor's Hollywood Hills household, ceremony time was like any other in her six-day workweek. She rose at five A.M. and then drove off to Fox. By evening she slipped on a quick find—a knit, knee-length dress with a sweet Peter Pan collar. Its probable source was a children's shop, which was the only place that sold clothes fit for Gaynor's five-foot, ninety-six-pound frame. "I wanted to look grown-up and sophisticated," she lamented.[10] Her pint size, however, proved an obstacle. Yet at the Academy's inaugural banquet ball, Gaynor eventually hit the right note.

The First Academy Awards, May 30, 1929. A commotion erupted on a stretch of Hollywood Boulevard outside the Roosevelt Hotel just before eight P.M. as 270 film-industry silent-screen notables slipped from a convoy of luxury automobiles and into its cavernous event space, the Blossom Room. "Fans waving and shouting," wrote Louella Parsons of the clamor greeting her entrance.[11] "Diamonds sparkled," added Frances Marion of the opulent accessories on view. Potted flowering cherry trees and Japanese lanterns decorated the Blossom Room, and a big-band orchestra kicked off the festivities.[12] "As you danced, you saw most of the important people in Hollywood whirling past you," recalled Gaynor, who waltzed, wide-eyed, in her dress that stopped short on her knee.[13]

Ankle-grazing hemlines of chiffon and satin evening dresses swept past her on the dance floor. The Academy's prominent guests included Mary Pickford, Norma Shearer, and MGM starlets Marion Davies and Joan Crawford.[14] Lean and tanned, these actress lovelies looked as delicious as their sugar-spun party favor—a waxed-candy replica of Cedric Gibbons's golden Academy Award trophy. Among the thirty-six banquet tables, studio fat cats were bedecked in black tie, including L. B. Mayer. "Dad was always the first out on the floor— a tireless, straightforward dancer—he took them all on, plain or fancy, old or young, provided they were light on their feet," noted Irene Mayer Selznick, his daughter, who watched the action from an MGM table.

By ten P.M. emcee Douglas Fairbanks commenced the awards presentation. "The Academy had already announced who the winners were in its first [*Academy Bulletin*] of three months earlier—there was no surprise," recounted costume designer Edith Head, who listened from her perch alongside heavyweights from Paramount Pictures, where she worked in wardrobe, contributing her expertise to *Wings*, the studio's Great War romance nominated as the picture prizewinner. The first Academy Award Fairbanks bestowed went to Frank Borzage for directing *Seventh Heaven*. Next Joseph Franham received one for writing titles for a series of silent films. Then Janet Gaynor mounted the podium. Her vocal cords seemed exhausted. Later she claimed that stage fright prevented her from formally addressing the Academy. "I was in sort of a daze," she admitted. So, minimizing her time expressing gratitude, she declared, "Thank you very much."[15] Then she blew kisses, waved to the audience, and went back to her seat.

The night was young, and like any opener the Academy Awards experienced its first big glitch—specifically a series of ten boring speeches, which took the crackle out of the Blossom Room's air. "Long-winded— the audience sank back exhausted," wrote Frances Marion of the lectures delivered by a cross section of Academy grandees, the dean of the University of Southern California, and even a representative of the Federated Women's Club.[16] Some guests decamped to the Roosevelt's lobby, where they held up the bar.

Al Jolson, star of *The Jazz Singer*, the pioneering 1927 Warner Bros. musical, which claimed a special Academy Award, roused the somnambulant banqueters as he concluded the ceremony by lamenting he was going home empty-handed. "They didn't give me one," he said of the Academy Award. "I could use one; they look heavy and I need another paperweight." The crowd chuckled and clapped. But looking back on the night, Frances Marion claimed that Janet Gaynor received the "loudest" round of applause for delivering "the shortest unrehearsed speech."[17]

★   ★   ★

The clout the actress Academy Award delivered to Gaynor was carte blanche to select her Fox film projects and her artistic collaborators. So at the height of her fame as a million-dollar earner, she demanded that MGM's gifted costumer Gilbert Adrian create her wardrobe for the 1931 romantic comedy *Daddy Long Legs*. Adrian transformed Gaynor's innocent trademark look, shrinking the proportions of his swish costumes to fit her junior-miss size. "I designed grown-up clothes for her on a smaller scale—that's all I did, and she thought I was a genius," he recalled. Adrian also fell in love with Gaynor and they married in 1939. Seven years later as his muse, she received the fashion industry's highest honor when the U.S. Dress Institute elected her to its International Best Dressed List.[18] For six years she maintained her position on the list, alongside socialites and aristocratic fashion leaders. Of her brisk Academy Awards preparations she revealed little through her lifetime. "Being the first year, the Academy had no background or tradition, and it naturally didn't mean what it has come to mean," she explained. "Had I known then what it would come to mean in the next few years, I'm sure I would have been overwhelmed."[19] Gaynor's successors Mary Pickford and Norma Shearer intricately plotted their victory strategies and ceremonial wardrobe plans.

Pickford, Hollywood's queen, viewed the actress Academy Award as her divine right. Nevertheless she mapped out a strategic campaign to triumph at the second ceremony with *Coquette*, a hit Broadway play she acquired and adapted for the screen in the summer of 1928. She promised to deliver "the performance of [her] career," portraying *Coquette*'s lead character, Norma Besant, a Southern debutante whose torrid romance with a handsome hillbilly so shames her genteel father that he commits suicide. But striving for Academy greatness stretched Pickford's dramatic ability and nearly shattered her steely inner core.

Coquette marked the thirty-five-year-old's sound feature-film debut and also the first time she'd performed in an adult screen role. The stock-in-trade of the flaxen-haired, five-foot Canadian former child megastar was downtrodden adolescent heroines, which she played in 243 silent films from 1909, including *Little Annie Rooney*, *Little Lord Fauntleroy*, *Pollyanna*, *Rags*, and *Rebecca of Sunnybrook Farm*. Pickford's global fan base adored her as "Little Mary" and "America's Sweetheart," and as they spent nickels and dimes buying tickets for her latest tragedy or slapstick romp, she became the film industry's richest female mogul. "Though she looks almost helplessly feminine she makes every year a tremendous fortune," marveled *Vogue* of the savvy beauty referred to as "Bank of America's Sweetheart" by Charlie Chaplin, with whom, in 1919, she, Douglas Fairbanks, and pioneering director D. W. Griffith cofounded United Artists, Hollywood's first successful independent film studio.[20]

An impoverished childhood, however, made Pickford parsimonious, and though marriage in March 1920 to cosmopolitan, suntanned Fairbanks loosened her purse strings, department-store merchandise and Old Master fakes furnished Pickfair, the power couple's eighteen-acre Beverly Hills estate. "There were rumors of penny-pinching," noted biographer Eileen Whitfield of the impecunious manner in which Pickford conducted her domestic transactions. "Mary, gossips said, would wear a dress, then return it to the store with the claim that it didn't fit."[21]

Pickford steadfastly believed the publicity she generated modeling high fashion in films and frequent photo opportunities ("a tree planting, the unveiling of a statue, the dedication of a civic building," wrote journalist Dorothy Spensely, outlining some of Mary's myriad duties), equated to an advertising return for its maker and thereby entitled her to substantial discounts on whatever she purchased. So she stood firm in the Paris couture houses she patronized on annual continental sojourns with Fairbanks, confidently negotiating clothing markdowns (despite her weak grasp of French), and likely bought the gown she wore competing for the second Academy Awards at a hard-won reduction. According to Hollywood lore, so confident was Pickford of her Academy Awards victory that she purchased her ceremonial dress around the time she acquired *Coquette*. Just then newspapers also chronicled a cache of expensive haute couture she had obtained at dramatic price cuts. MARY PICKFORD'S DOZEN TRUNKS HELD IN CUSTOMS reported the first of a weeklong stream of June 1928 newspaper headlines charting the "gown row," as became known a fracas involving the seizure of twelve among thirty-two trunks "crammed with finery from Europe," and retained by customs agents, after Pickford and Fairbanks disembarked *Roma*, an ocean liner ferrying them back to New York from Europe. MARY PICKFORD GETS TRUNKS announced a June 20 headline, as the saga ceased. Pickford had agreed to pay duty heftier than on an original "undervaluation" of her possessions.[22] And after she explained couturiers granted movie stars concessions, the inspectors announced, "It was all just a big mistake."[23]

Academy Awards dress acquired, Pickford got on with *Coquette*.

Before it swung into action at Santa Monica Boulevard's Pickford-Fairbanks Studio in late summer 1928, the consummate professional first mastered the art of delivering dialogue with the help of the best voice coach, Constance Collier, the British thespian who later trained Katharine Hepburn. But Pickford grew impatient as members of *Coquette*'s crew fumbled with heavy, early sound machinery, significantly prolonging production. Director Sam Taylor, like all of his contemporaries, struggled with the camera, which was placed in a large wooden box to conceal its operating noise. Pickford, however, felt Taylor was unnecessarily distracted and consequently her performance suffered. "It was left up to me to make my role come alive," she reflected. "Mr. Taylor seemed to think the important thing was just to show me off in a sound movie as if to say, 'Look, everyone, Mary Pickford can talk!'"[24]

"You proved yourself long ago and beyond all our imaginations," scriptwriter Frances Marion reassured her best friend, Pickford, as she observed the signs of production strain set in. Marion also described as "distressing" the ruthless demeanor Pickford displayed on set. "I was out for the Oscar," admitted Pickford, recalling her impulsive dismissal of cinematographer Charles Rosher midway through *Coquette*.[25] Rosher had worked for a decade on seventeen Pickford films, but his harmonious liaison with the star ceased soon after he shut down his camera while she sobbed through an emotional *Coquette* sequence.[26] "Cut!" bellowed Rosher, startling Pickford.[27] "A shadow fell across your face that I didn't like," he patiently explained.[28] "I'm afraid I cannot get the mood back," she retorted imperiously, storming off *Coquette*'s set. Pickford refused Rosher entry to her bungalow dressing room where he promptly reported to settle the matter.[29] Then she terminated his employment by note, reflecting, "I didn't have the courage or the backbone to face him."[30] Two doctors eventually tended to Pickford as *Coquette* concluded so she could recover from what was later assessed as a nervous breakdown.

At the Rialto Theatre April 1929 world premiere of *Coquette*, the convincing Southern drawl Pickford delivered as flirty Norma Besant was initially inaudible to the elite New York audience gathered to experience her sound debut. "*Coquette* got off to a disastrous start," confirmed critic Alexander Walker. "A fuse blew two minutes after the start and the film had to be begun again. Even then the amplification system was so distorted that Pickford's voice sounded weak compared with the male players' voices and this made an accurate impression of her success impossible."[31]

Coquette was a very pretty picture thanks to the ultramodern costumes Los Angeles designer Howard Greer produced for Pickford, as well as her fashionable bob, coiffed by Nina Roberts, her personal hairstylist. (Getty Images)

Coquette was a pretty picture thanks to the ultramodern costumes Los Angeles designer Howard Greer produced for Pickford, as well as her fashionable bob, coiffed by Nina Roberts, her personal hairstylist. So despite mixed reviews, it played in one Los Angeles cinema continuously from ten A.M. until midnight. Pickford ensured *Coquette*'s continued commercial success, which was critical for a film to qualify for an Academy Award, by waging an effective publicity campaign. Driving it was a contest for a fan to win the film's standout costume—Howard Greer's "orchid dress" of silk organza. Its pretty, drop-waist skirt hung in petal-like tiers, while a silk orchid prettified its cummerbund. Pickford was photographed giving it away to the one among seven thousand contestants whose measurements matched her petite size four— Marie Hilkevitch, a grocery store checkout clerk.

On October 31, 1929, the Academy granted Pickford an actress nomination, but she had to clear a final hurdle before qualifying as winner. She faced a quartet of actress competitors, twice the competition Janet Gaynor had encountered, and received news she'd qualified just a day after the New York Stock Exchange crashed. Working the economic crisis to her advantage, Pickford invited the Academy's Central Board of Judges to Pickfair for tea, to lift their spirits. In the twenties, Pickfair was the most famous residence in the country, aside from the White House. So all five judges assembled at Pickfair, and as butler Rocher served tea from eye-popping gold china (formerly owned by Napoléon and Josephine), Pickford secured the actress vote by deploying her persuasive charm.[32]

Two days before the second ceremony, the Academy Award was

hers. On the ceremony's eve, Nina Roberts styled Pickford's locks into a smooth marcel wave. Then the winner Pickford stepped into chic haute couture. A flounced skirt, satin bodice, and tastefully feminine neckline inset with sheer, silk net defined Pickford's Academy Awards dress. Its look matched the *robe de style* innovated by the leading Paris couturier Jeanne Lanvin, whose trendsetting, feminine mother-and-daughter ensembles Pickford alternated in playing Pickfair's chatelaine and youngsters on-screen. The frock's Fragonard blue shade was Pickford's personal favorite and one among a number of trademark cerulean hues Lanvin concocted from her own specialist dyes. But its exact make remains unknown because

Mary Pickford accepted the second actress Academy Award in Fragonard blue haute couture she likely acquired at a hard-won reduction in price. (Courtesy of the Academy of Motion Picture Arts and Sciences)

Pickford left behind no clue related to her dress, possibly because her Academy Awards moment failed to proceed exactly as she'd arranged.

The Second Academy Awards, April 3, 1930. Recording a one-hour Academy Awards special, its first live broadcast, KNX, a local Los Angeles radio station, was on hand at the Ambassador Hotel's Cocoanut Grove nightclub, the MGM watering hole. Its desert-oasis decorative theme, complete with palm trees, waterfalls, and a trompe-l'oeil azure sky covering its ceiling, served as a decadent backdrop for the Academy's three hundred elegantly dressed guests. "Glittering with jewels," recalled an attendee of the women present, "you could scarcely believe there had ever been a depression."[33]

A few eminent film professionals made "short addresses," relieving the audience from the boredom induced by the first ceremony's lengthy orations. By ten thirty P.M. producer William C. deMille, the Academy's new president, got to the point, recapping contest rules before commencing the awards presentation. After five trophy winners delivered brief, polite "responses," Pickford was caught off guard when summoned to the podium.[34] "I've forgotten my prepared speech," she announced, burst into tears, and abruptly cleared off the stage, toting her cherished Academy Award. Winning the prize for which Pickford had so rigorously prepared flashed by in seconds.[35]

Norma Shearer was certain that portraying *Ex-Wife*'s lead character, a dynamic Seventh Avenue fashion executive and divorcée, Jerry Bernard, would deliver her an Oscar nomination. "Perfect for me!" thought Shearer when in late summer 1929 she unearthed the romantic drama from a pile of projects in MGM's script department.[36] As the wife of Irving Thalberg, MGM's all-powerful vice president of production, Shearer was the studio's "First Lady" and had an access-all-areas pass to its expertly equipped fifty-three-acre Culver City lot.[37] MGM, Hollywood's "studio par excellence," was an operation without equal, producing "top quality, first-class films for its urban, and urbane, customers," observed Peter Hay.[38] An estimated billion people annually viewed MGM's escapist fantasies. Its box office profits escalated as silent films gave way to sound pictures. So million-dollar sums were lavished upon production trimmings, including jaw-dropping leading-ladies wardrobes masterminded by the studio's costumer-in-chief, Gilbert Adrian. At MGM Adrian, as was known the twenty-seven-year-old former protégé of epic filmmaker Cecil B. DeMille, presided over a sweeping white, stucco wardrobe department. "Astonishing workrooms, embroiderers, drapers and tailors of couture-caliber," observed *Vogue*'s European editor-at-large Hamish Bowles, describing Adrian's territory.[39] It served as Shearer's walk-in closet, and when Academy Awards season arrived, she planned to clutch the actress trophy in a shimmering Adrian something.

Shearer remained focused on her goal even when, in autumn 1929, Thalberg dispensed with the notion that she headline *Ex-Wife*, after she suggested it over breakfast at their Sunset Boulevard home. "You're not glamorous enough," he told Shearer. The frank reply was typical of repartee the fiercely ambitious thirtysomething twosome exchanged. Their September 1928 nuptials were perceived as an arrangement hastening their professional advancement. "They were both too deeply involved in their careers to take time out for love, or even fun," confirmed Hollywood scribe Anita Loos, whom they both worked with at MGM.[40]

Thalberg's black-coffee sharp rebuttal should have ended talk of *Ex-Wife*. He had already cast Joan Crawford, then a twenty-four-year-old Texan stunner, former burlesque dancer, and Charleston champion, as Jerry Bernard. But Shearer was tired of perpetually playing the ingénue, realizing her typecasting was a holdover from the silent age. "I've got to play something more daring," she thought.[41]

Determined to evolve her range, Shearer devised a covert plan to clinch the lead in *Ex-Wife* and, with it, win an Academy Award. So on the sly she arranged a fashion shoot with George Hurrell, the most celebrated photographer of Hollywood's Golden Age. But back in 1929, Hurrell was an up-and-comer whose work Shearer had first noticed when, soon after she breakfasted with Thalberg, MGM actor Ramon Novarro dropped by her dressing room and displayed the result of his sitting with the legendary photographer. "You've never looked like this before!" said Shearer as she studied Novarro's contact sheets.[42] Their crisp, clear sex appeal intrigued her because, as the antithesis of the soft, grainy, staid style governing Hollywood portraiture, it could portray her transformation from MGM's First Lady to *Ex-Wife*'s Jerry Bernard. Deciding Hurrell's work was the black-and-white evidence she needed to prove to Thalberg she was right for the sought-after part, Shearer set an October 1929 shoot date with the photographer. Then she turned to Adrian, who provided a "stack" of filmy lamé gowns to heighten her metamorphosis.

Tenacious Shearer overcame every obstruction that threatened to impede her career path. Tedious, tiresome vision exercises tamed a cast that crossed her deep brown eyes. She eventually whittled her shapely five-foot-three frame to perfection, sacrificing her downtime to grueling workouts at the Torture Chamber, as was known the Los Angeles gym run by Eastern European fitness guru Madame Sylvia, whom *Los Angeles Times* columnist Alma Whitaker described as a "bantam blond with arms of steel and the chest of a lightweight champion."[43] Madame Sylvia's painful cellulite-busting massage was part of the regime to which Shearer adhered. "Right away we went into the bedroom and I started to pound her," recalled Sylvia of a home visit she once paid Shearer.[44]

The lemon-sherbet shade of Shearer's Buick limousine recalled the day when as a twenty-one-year-old dilettante she'd taken a beating from L. B. Mayer. "You are yellow! You are through!" hollered Mayer to Shearer, after Reginald Barker, the director of *Pleasure Mad*, her

At MGM Gilbert Adrian (background) presided over the studio's sweeping wardrobe department. It also served as the walk-in closet of Norma Shearer (foreground). (Getty Images)

1923 MGM debut, complained about her temperament. "I'll show you!" declared Shearer to Mayer, and she returned to Barker's set and stunned the director with a sincere performance.[45]

But when Shearer stepped before MGM's cameras, Thalberg dictated her look. Producing a screen wardrobe in early Hollywood was a collaborative process through which a costume designer's vision merged with ideas produced by a committee of studio executives, including a film director and producer. So Adrian interpreted Thalberg's preferences by designing costumes commensurate with Shearer's First Lady role. Think fluttery tulle, fusty tweeds, girl-next-door sportswear, prissy period looks, and the occasional fox fur stole. "Nice clothes; nice, but uninteresting—satisfactory but a little commonplace," admitted Adrian.[46] Shearer's session with Hurrell would, however, totally dispense with her prim MGM image.[47] "The idea was to get her looking real wicked and sirenlike," recalled Hurrell. "She was not *that* type. She didn't have any of it."[48]

With a white-knuckled grip Shearer clung to a wrought-iron balustrade as she descended a staircase that led from Hurrell's dressing room to his set, sparsely furnished with a brocade settee and fold-out screen. Shearer, a celebrity weaned on cushy, MGM luxuries, customarily inhabited backdrops like Manhattan penthouses laden with fluffy French carpets and shiny art deco fixtures. So she felt as if she were slumming it in Hurrell's bohemian studio, and also completely exposed, too, although a voluminous Adrian lamé gown edged with chocolate mink covered her taut limbs.[49] But on Hurrell's insistence she faced the camera for the first time makeup free. "A little oil on your face and that was all," recalled actress Loretta Young of minimalist Hurrell, who forged the otherworldly glow typifying Golden Age glamour by doing away with thick, feature-flattening, pan-stick "greasepaint" foundation customarily applied to stars before they stepped before the camera.[50] Hurrell mussed up Shearer's slicked-back mane. "Bushy—a down-over-the-forehead sweep," he said, explaining an untamed look necessary to transmit a believable brand of *Ex-Wife* sensuality.[51]

He also spun Dixieland jazz on his phonograph, hoping it would relax Shearer. But she stiffened. To Shearer, Hurrell's playlist was background noise. "She didn't like it," he remembered.[52] A mini-orchestra of classical session musicians worked her into a mood at MGM. Ignoring his superstar subject's haughty attitude, Hurrell sang and danced while working his camera. "I was mobile—bam, bam, bam, bam! Lots of activity," he recalled of the technique he used to prompt natural poses.[53] "He'd talk to you constantly and he'd get pictures while I was talking, asking for a cup of coffee—whatever," said Joan Crawford, who later became the photographer's favorite movie star model.

Disaster struck when, leaping before Shearer, Hurrell tripped over his tripod. Yet the slipup transformed his awkward sitter into an Academy Award contender. "She laughed and I could see she was starting to enjoy herself," remembered Hurrell.[54] Reclining languidly, Shearer became one with Adrian's gold lamé, smiling lustily for Hurrell. Tossing back her mussed-up chestnut curls, she fearlessly flashed bedroom eyes at his camera and never looked back. "She was beautiful," confirmed Hurrell. "She was not the old Norma Shearer any longer."[55]

Two days later, sixty portraits of the new Norma Shearer landed on Thalberg's desk at MGM. Shearer arranged the delivery. At first Thalberg was speechless examining the seductive results of the covert Hurrell session. "Astonished, then amused, then excited at the seductiveness of his wife in a variety of lamé wrappers," wrote Shearer's biographer Gavin Lambert.[56]

Immediately Thalberg reversed his casting call, granting Shearer the lead role in *The Divorcée*, as *Ex-Wife* was soon retitled. "The project screamed success from the word go," claimed Shearer's costar Robert Montgomery. "Everyone was feeling positive. I knew Norma was happy with her role; they had given her something she could really get her teeth into, and I could sense her elation."

"She worked very hard on it," added Robert Z. Leonard, director of *The Divorcée*. "She went over the dialogue again and again—she drove us all crazy wanting rehearsals, then endless takes. She would sit with me in the cutting room, muttering to herself. Knowing her anxiety, I would order even more takes to reassure her. Then she'd slap me playfully and hiss, 'Slave driver!'"

Meanwhile, Thalberg appointed George Hurrell to work as MGM's official publicity photographer, sparking a decade-long association for the portraitist with the leading studio. Viewing an advance print of *The Divorcée*, Louis B. Mayer was so impressed by Adrian's designs for Shearer that at the mogul's behest "Gowns by Adrian" splashed up prominently with the film's opening credits when it premiered in April 1930 and from then on until the costumer resigned from MGM eleven years later. "One of her best films," verified Adrian of Shearer in *The Divorcée*. "She became a striking individual. She changed."[57]

Critics noticed. So did Shearer's fans. *Photoplay* printed excerpts from adulatory letters sent in by her devotees. Some hailed Shearer as the silent-screen star set to be the leader of Hollywood's Golden Age.[58] By November 1930 four hundred Academy members voted in Shearer as one of three actresses competing for the third actress Academy Award. Two days before the ceremony as her victory was announced, Shearer contemplated her attire and concluded it had to be golden, just like the Adrian lamé gown she'd modeled the first time she'd played the divorcée on George Hurrell's set.

★　　★　　★

The Third Academy Awards, November 5, 1930. Six hundred guests jammed the Fiesta Room, the sweeping event space inside the downtown Los Angeles Ambassador Hotel. "The Awards had become so popular," reflected *Los Angeles Times* gossip columnist Hedda Hopper, acknowledging the capacity crowd. Shearer's victory moment was the highlight of the ceremony. When actor Lawrence Grant stepped into the spotlight to present her actress trophy, a velvet curtain was parted and Shearer emerged through it, shimmering in a gold lamé Gilbert Adrian evening ensemble trimmed with brown mink. As she graciously thanked the Academy as well as her colleagues, Irving Thalberg, observing from a banquet table, glowed. "The award brought great joy to Thalberg," wrote his biographer Bob Thomas. "It displayed to the world that Norma was an honored performer who achieved her position not merely because she was the wife of the studio boss."

Shearer's victory dress set a precedent. For three decades most actress nominees turned to studio costume designers for their ceremonial attire, although a lineup of her successors passed up the chance to showboat at the Academy Awards.

Norma Shearer, recipient of the third actress Academy Award, concluded her ceremonial attire had to be golden, just like the Adrian lamé gown she modeled the first time she played the divorcée on George Hurrell's set. (David Downton)

Chapter Two

THE GETAWAY

"My first Academy Award—I couldn't believe it!" wrote Katharine Hepburn in *Me*, her 1991 autobiography, recalling her elation upon discovering two days before the sixth Academy Awards that she'd won the actress prize for portraying thespian Eve Lovelace in the drama *Morning Glory*.[1] A hush fell over the Fiesta Room inside downtown Los Angeles' Ambassador Hotel when on March 16, 1934, Will Rogers, the ceremony's emcee, presented long-stemmed roses to her competitors—May Robson, star of the underworld comedy *Lady for a Day*, and Diana Wynyard, who headlined *Cavalcade*, the screen adaptation of Noël Coward's dramatic stage play. Radio-Keith-Orpheum's president, B. B. Kahane, accepted the Academy Award on Hepburn's behalf. At home in Manhattan, she turned in early and the next morning boarded the luxury ocean liner *Paris*. Before it set sail from New York for France, a pack of wily photographers camped outside Hepburn's stateroom, pleading with her to pose up on deck for an Academy Awards publicity shot. "Go away! I'm incognito!" she shouted, spurning their hearty congratulations.[2] "Upturned collar—hat pulled over eyes," noted biographer Barbara Leaming of the disguise Hepburn assumed aboard ship.[3] "Aw, let us take another picture!" implored a shutterbug.[4] "It'll be lousy!" cried Hepburn through her cabin-door keyhole, and as the *Paris* pushed off she stayed put.[5]

Hepburn deserved the holiday she'd organized just prior to the Academy Awards. Jed Harris, the producer/director who'd staged the Empire Theater production of *The Lake*, in which she had starred in the run-up to the ceremony, so browbeat her through its grueling, unsuccessful seven-week run that upon his announcing its cross-country tour, she bought her way out of the production by delivering to Harris the $13,675.75 deposited in her Chase National bank account. "Real disaster," reflected Hepburn of the temporary career crisis.[6] Her passage aboard the *Paris* was also arranged as an escape from her fraught love life. Suave Leland Hayward, Hepburn's lover and Hollywood agent, was pleading with her to divorce bookish Ludlow Ogden Smith ("Luddy"), her long-suffering husband, who paid for her cruise, hoping for their reconciliation. Above all, Hepburn's "attitude to awards ceremonies was that she didn't need to attend," observed Leaming. In thirties Hollywood the sentiment prevailed.[7]

Oscar—as actress Bette Davis christened the Academy Award back then because, she said, the statuette's shapely bottom resembled her husband Harmon Oscar Nelson's—came of age during Hollywood's thirties heyday, the Golden Era. Box office profits soared as Depression-weary Americans escaped their troubles and decamped in record numbers to movie palaces for the light relief offered by screwball comedies, gangster flicks, sophisticated literary adaptations, and costume epics then dominating the big screen. While households across the country penny-pinched, in Hollywood million-dollar sums were dropped on costumes that transformed stars like Hepburn and Davis into fashion icons. "Days were spent in wardrobe," observed costume expert Robert La Vine. "Hollywood fashion production and society flowered. It was a time when bias-cut crêpe-de-Chine gowns and satin pumps were worn for dancing to the wistful tunes of Cole Porter."[8]

Yet the Academy's annual shindig was the low point on Hollywood's frenetic social calendar. Academy membership plummeted as MGM's Louis B. Mayer, its founder, lorded over the affair. A spate of Metro-Goldwyn-Mayer victories—consecutive triumphs seemingly fixed by the studio boss—jeopardized Oscar's validity as the ultimate prize recognizing outstanding contributions to the screen. Reported *Photoplay*, "When you sign with Metro they hand you the award."[9] Actors within the Academy's ranks also began to decamp to the Screen Actors Guild (SAG), an organization representing their best interests. While *Screen Actor*, SAG's monthly magazine, advised its members to avoid the Oscars, Claudette Colbert, Bette Davis, and Luise Rainer qualified as front-running actress nominees. Like Hepburn, they each made Oscar-night escape plans and intended to relax in vacation casuals rather than sweat up their silken finery awaiting the actress category's outcome. But caught on the fly and involuntarily dragged to the ceremony, this errant trio sported garb revealing their getaway plans.

In February 1935, when Colbert received her Academy Award nomi-nation honoring her acclaimed role in *It Happened One Night* as Ellie Andrews, the spoiled daughter of a Wall Street tycoon who, deserting her blue-blooded fiancé, falls for Clark Gable's reporter Peter Warne as they travel on a slow-moving, dilapidated Greyhound bus, she notified Travis Banton, costume designer at Paramount Pictures, her studio, of her own impending cross-country trip. Aboard the luxury Super Chief train, Colbert intended to travel from Los Angeles' Union Station to Manhattan's Grand Central on the evening of the seventh Academy Awards. Banton, who'd dressed Colbert on- and offscreen since she'd joined Paramount in 1930, agreed to make her a fleet of new traveling clothes for the journey, but a dazzling Academy Awards' red-carpet duo they could have made. The black-eyed charisma of Paris-born, Manhattan-bred thirty-one-year-old Colbert first held New York's drama critics in thrall when in the late twenties she was a promising newcomer on the Broadway stage. Laudatory *Vanity Fair* and *Time* reviews brought her a Paramount contract, and at the studio she became a hot property after flamboyant director Cecil B. DeMille displayed her on a chariot as Empress Poppaea, the ruthless wife of Nero in *The Sign of the Cross*, his 1932 biblical epic. Prior to *One Night*, Colbert played Queen of the Nile in DeMille's *Cleopatra*. "Diamond-shaped," said Paramount's makeup artist Wally Westmore, describing Colbert's lovely face, which was framed by a distinctive fringed bob. He classified her leggy frame as in the "sex queen" league.[10] "The best figure of any actress in Hollywood," confirmed *One Night*'s director Frank Capra of Colbert, whom he cast as Ellie Andrews believing her physique alone would draw crowds.[11] But offscreen, instead of exploiting her natural assets in figure-hugging showstoppers, Colbert opted for Banton's timeless classics.[12] "Eighteen karat," wrote *Los Angeles Times* gossip columnist Hedda Hopper, rating the Oscar contender's innate chic.[13]

Silent-screen star Mary Pickford had spotted Banton's Midas touch. Reading *Vogue* in 1920, she noticed a while organdy gown trimmed in apple-green satin, which Texas-born Banton had conceived while assisting leading Manhattan dress designer Mme. Francis. Pickford wore the frilly frock marrying Douglas Fairbanks in March 1920. Five years later producer Walter Wanger enlisted Banton to apply his Euro-chic signature to the design of costumes at Paramount. By 1929, talented Banton controlled the studio's vast wardrobe department with its one hundred pattern makers, fitters, seamstresses, milliners, furriers, and embroiderers. "There was a sheen and glamour to much of Paramount's output," film critic Clive Hirschhorn noted of the studio through the Depression, even though it hovered close to bankruptcy.[14] All the while, Banton cut Paramount's costumes from couture-quality textiles including silks by Bianchini-Férrier, the Lyon mill employing fauvist painter Raoul Dufy as artistic director, and tweeds from Linton, the Scottish Borders knitwear manufacturer Coco Chanel utilized. He sourced embellishments such as bugle beads and sequins from the Paris supplier that surrealist couturier Elsa Schiaparelli patronized, and when Paramount's leading lady Marlene Dietrich needed packing cases as props for *Shanghai Express*, Josef von Sternberg's 1932 railroad caper, he dispatched her to the world's finest luggage maker, Hermès, in Paris, where her set was custom-made. "They had the most wonderful everything just stacked up, and if they didn't have it, they got it," recalled costume designer Bob Mackie, who in the sixties worked for Banton's former assistant Edith Head and discovered his legendary leftovers.[15]

Three months before the seventh Academy Awards, the cover of *Vogue*'s December 15, 1934, issue confirmed Banton's preeminence. The sunny Pacific Ocean–front scene displayed statuesque Paramount actress Miriam Hopkins enjoying a beach getaway in the costumer's exotica—a bedouin-inspired coffee wool cape. But when Colbert requested her traveling clothes, Banton knew better than to suggest she complete the Super Chief wardrobe with an Oscar dress. Like every Hollywood costume designer, gallant Banton played confidant to the actresses he worked alongside, and during a fitting she probably revealed her feelings about *One Night*. Colbert doubted that her character Ellie Andrews would deliver an Academy Award and agreed to make the low-budget film strictly for the money. A colossal return of fifty thousand dollars—twice Colbert's usual shooting salary and five times the money Clark Gable earned playing Peter Warne—came her way because Columbia Pictures' proprietor, Harry Cohn, *One Night*'s producer, paid the price she set. He was tired of searching for the perfect candidate to play Ellie after six leading ladies had passed up the part. The reason? Ellie's meager wardrobe amounted to a skirt suit, a pair of men's pajamas, and an evening dress, while a typical Golden Era Hollywood production demanded dozens of costume changes. Through the Depression, Hollywood's epics fed women's vicarious desires for *le dernier cri*. "Many, many more thousands of women went to the movies than studied high-fashion magazines," confirmed costume historian Caroline Rennolds Milbank.[16] Hollywood actresses outclassed models found on the stylish pages of *Vogue* and

Paramount's costumer Travis Banton, left, and nominee Claudette Colbert, right, could have made a dazzling Academy Awards red carpet duo, but instead he made her traveling clothes for a trip on the night of the seventh ceremony. (Corbis)

Bazaar. "People needed fantasy, they needed a dream of splendor and glamour, and here we were looking a little seedy riding our bus," recalled Colbert of *One Night.*

She felt dubious about the film's stark style, doubted Capra's ability, and regarded as "corny" its pivotal scene, an upbeat, spontaneous musical number through which Ellie, Peter, and their fellow Greyhound passengers burst into a sing-along of "The Man on the Flying Trapeze." "How could everyone in the bus know all the words to the song?" demanded Colbert of Capra after its first take.[17] According to Capra's biographer Joseph McBride, Colbert "remained skeptical [about it] until she noticed her black maid was 'beside herself watching the scene.'"[18] "*Then* I knew we had something," recollected Colbert.[19] But she "hated" the "abrasive" Capra, with whom she had made her 1927 screen debut, a soppy silent drama, *For the Love of Mike*.[20] Far worse than Capra for Colbert was the daily descent she made from her white, neo-Georgian mansion in exclusive Holmby Hills to work at Columbia. It was found on Beachwood Drive, or "Poverty Row," as the wrong turn off a far-eastern stretch of Sunset Boulevard was known in Hollywood, because its second-class B movies were mostly made there.[21] "[It] looked like a red light district," wrote Cohn's biographer Bob Thomas.[22]

Blue-chip treatment always came Colbert's way at Paramount. She was coddled by Banton, and studio directors put up with her quirks. Upon Colbert's insistence, directors captured her face from the left side, so as to conceal a bump on her cute, button nose. Though the facial flaw was invisible to the naked eye, a right camera angle inflated it to a proportion Wally Westmore described as "Mount Everest."[23] As she resisted the overtures of Columbia's beautifiers, *One Night*'s crew concluded Colbert was "bitchy, snooty, standoffish," and prone to "angry sulking."[24]

Paramount's leading lady wasted no time celebrating with the little people of Poverty Row when *One Night* earned five Academy Award nominations. The tally was a coup for fledgling Columbia Pictures. So was the film's box office take. Following its February 1934 premiere at New York's Radio City Music Hall, *One Night* played in cinemas across the country for a year. Depression-weary viewers were still getting a kick out of its comic vitality as Colbert's maid packed suitcases for her impending train trip and a hullabaloo enveloped the Academy.

Weeks away from the ceremony, Bette Davis, then a twenty-six-year-old Warner Bros. newcomer, caused a fuss because she failed to rank alongside Colbert and her two competitors for the actress prize, Norma Shearer and Grace Moore. Davis, however, outclassed them all with her bravura performance as Mildred Rogers, a scheming cockney waitress in *Of Human Bondage*, the haunting screen adaptation of Somerset Maugham's tragedy. "Probably the best performance ever recorded on screen by a U.S. actress," concluded *Life* of Davis's feat after the March 1934 New York premiere of *Bondage*, which concluded with a standing ovation. But Davis believed her boss, Jack Warner, Warner Bros.' vice president of production, passed on submitting her name to the Academy for consideration because her possible victory would publicize a film produced by a rival studio. She made *Bondage* at RKO on "loan out"—the practice of studio bosses who, like farmers trading cattle, trafficked between them performers from their talent stables in exchange for lucrative deals. As Davis's colleagues beseeched the Academy with telephone calls and telegrams contesting her snub, members were eventually advised to disregard the original actress ballot and "write in any name they preferred."[25] After write-in votes were tallied, a press leak confirmed Colbert was the actress front-runner. Colbert said she "never dreamed" of winning: "I [was] not even optimistic."[26]

So on Oscar night she dressed impeccably for takeoff in a toffee-colored Travis Banton skirt suit. As the Academy Awards festivities geared up at the Biltmore Hotel in downtown Los Angeles, Colbert was swathed in a lush brown mink coat in the backseat of a limousine bound for Union Station.

The Seventh Academy Awards, February 27, 1935. Deploying guerrilla tactics to rile Oscar-night revelers, the SAG had besieged the Academy's red carpet with aggressive picketers brandishing placards printed with anti-Academy slogans. As SAG's angry mob heckled Hollywood stars decamping from stretch limousines, platinum-blond MGM star Jean Harlow slipped out of the fray unscathed. A pale green corsage adorned the plunging neckline of Harlow's white, bias-cut crêpe Gilbert Adrian dress, noted Sylva Weaver, the first roving fashion reporter to cover the Academy Awards, for the *Los Angeles Times*. "Fresh-scented flowers everywhere," noted Weaver of the scene inside the Biltmore Bowl nightclub, "worn as bracelets, as hair ornaments, as neckpieces and as corsages."[27]

Six-year-old Shirley Temple, in a petal-pink petite, was set to receive the evening's final prize—a special, child's-size Oscar for her starring role in two box-office toppers—*Bright Eyes* and *Little Miss Marker*. She amused herself at the banquet table she occupied alongside her parents by crumbling bread rolls and furtively studying the seduction tactics of vivacious Harlow. Seated at a nearby table, Harlow tantalized handsome actor William Powell, her latest accessory, with an ermine wrap she wore beneath a white fox double-layer cape. "[It] seemed alive," marveled Temple of Harlow's stole, "first draped over one shoulder then another. Whatever her technique, it was proving effective."[28]

Host Irvin Cobb awkwardly clutched Claudette Colbert's Academy Award after he announced her victory in the actress category. The prize was the fourth so far received by *It Happened One Night*, a record number for a motion picture. Clark Gable had already claimed the actor trophy, and with Colbert's win, the prize combo made it the first time a film had received the Academy's pair of top performance honors. After Cobb upped *One Night*'s total to five Academy Awards with the picture prize, Columbia's Harry Cohn demanded that Colbert be located for a photo session. "Find her!" shouted Cohn to Academy publicist Leroy Johnston. "I'll miss my train!" bellowed Colbert after Johnston confronted her in a Super Chief compartment. The locomotive's departure time was imminent, but Johnston convinced the conductor to delay it so Colbert could make a quick trip to the Biltmore.[29] Colbert, however, refused to budge, shrieking, "I'm not dressed!"

Six-year-old Academy Awards presenter Shirley Temple noticed that Claudette Colbert, recipient of the seventh actress Academy Award, remained "quite dry-eyed" through her choked-up acceptance speech. (Courtesy of the Academy of Motion Picture Arts and Sciences)

"It's the Nobel Prize of motion pictures!" pleaded Johnston. Soon they were in a limousine heading for the Biltmore.[30]

Meanwhile, an Academy team had uprooted Shirley Temple from her banquet table to a backstage zone so she could present Colbert with her Academy Award. Instead of trooping up to the podium through the Biltmore Bowl, Colbert took a shortcut, discreetly accessing the dais via a door near the nightclub's dance floor. She felt ill at ease in the two-piece Banton had tailored for the Super Chief. "It was a very formal affair and there I stood in my traveling suit and hat," she recalled.[31] But as Temple bestowed the actress prize, Colbert, on cue, turned on the charm. "I'm afraid I am just going to be very foolish and cry," she whispered into the microphone. Temple, however, noticed that despite the choked-up delivery, the winner remained "quite dry-eyed."[32] Sniffling,

25

Colbert said that fatigue had prompted her vacation.[33] "And to take it," she explained, "I have to catch the train tonight in order to reach New York by Sunday."

After a four-minute photo session, Colbert made way for Union Station. Back at the Biltmore, the crowd roared as Cobb demanded, "Is Shirley Temple in the house?"[34] The sleepy Temple marched back to the podium and tried to snatch her tiny Oscar away from Cobb. "Thank you all very much," she announced. Then Temple yawned and, cuddling her Oscar, delivered a request into the microphone: "Mommy, can I go home now?"[35]

A year later, Bette Davis officially qualified for the actress prize, when in February 1936 she received a nomination for her role as alcoholic Joyce Heath, a washed-up Broadway thespian in *Dangerous*, a drama loosely based on the tragic life of the drug-addicted Hollywood silent-screen star Jeanne Eagels. "Critics raved," noted James Spada of the reception to Davis in *Dangerous*, after its January 1936 premiere.[36] The Academy nod made her the first Warner Bros. actress to receive the honor, but she disregarded it. *Dangerous*, Davis insisted, was typical of the lightweight films she was forced to make at Warner Bros. She said she toiled "like ten men" to deliver a standout performance from material she classified as "maudlin [and] mawkish."[37] During the two and a half years Davis had so far worked at Warner Bros., she had made sixteen films. Among them was box-office fluff she detested and considered an insult to her ability. "I am ambitious to become known as a great actress," she wrote in a memo to Jack Warner outlining her career objective. "In a business, where you have a fickle public to depend on, the money should be made when you mean something."[38]

To miserly Warner, cash was king. Artistic integrity never registered in the list of his production priorities. He ran the Burbank studio he'd cofounded with his three older brothers in 1920 "like a sweatshop." To maximize profits at Hollywood's "Ford automotive plant," Warner relentlessly drove its top ten box-office stars, including Davis, James Cagney, and Errol Flynn. "Actors often performed in two pictures at once, literally bicycling between sound stages," wrote Bob Thomas. "Actors frequently worked until midnight and were told to report back early the next morning."[39] Warner kept a particularly tight rein on Davis because he realized the sparky brunette was the studio's number one actress. "If I'd meet Jack Warner at a party," she remembered, "as he was leaving he would wag his finger at me like the father of a delinquent: 'Remember, Bette. You have to be at the studio at six o'clock. Get to sleep soon.'"[40]

Days before the eighth ceremony, Davis made big plans to recuperate from her Warner Bros. workload. She intended to set sail aboard a luxury ocean liner a day before the ceremony from Los Angeles to Hawaii with Ruth Davis, her mother. But then the ship pushed off with Ruth alone in Davis's stateroom. Bette was back in the Cape Cod cottage on Hollywood's Franklin Avenue, which she shared with her husband, the musician and big-band conductor Harmon Nelson. Discovering her vacation plans, Jack Warner had grounded his contract star, ordering her to appear at the Academy Awards. Davis realized she was powerless—every Big Five studio had sent eleventh-hour telegrams to their employees requesting their presence at the eighth ceremony as a display of solidarity against the Screen Actors Guild. A year after the seventh Academy Awards, SAG and two new film-industry labor unions, the Screen Writers Guild and the Screen Directors Guild, had attracted new members, decimating the Academy's ranks. Only forty actors remained Academy affiliates, down from its original count of six hundred.[41] "The odds were ten to one the Academy would fold and Oscar would acquire a patina of a collector's item," confirmed director Frank Capra, who, serving a five-year term from 1935 as Academy president, struggled to revitalize the ceremony.[42]

On Oscar day, Davis was a wreck, although competitive anxiety was not the problem. She was resigned to defeat—"certain" her competitor Katharine Hepburn would win the eighth actress prize for portraying the twentysomething social-climber title character in *Alice Adams*, RKO's romantic drama based on Booth Tarkington's 1921 Pulitzer Prize–winning novel.[43] Martin Gang, Davis's attorney, had induced her nervous exhaustion when, on Oscar morning, he'd delivered the news that Jack Warner had refused to grant a loan-out agreement so she could star as the British monarch Queen Elizabeth I, in RKO's biopic *Mary of Scotland*. Davis had hoped Warner would view her attendance at the Oscars as good behavior and reward it with the prime role. She had set her sights upon portraying a queen and in the lead-up to the ceremony had struggled through the final days of *Cream Princess*, a potboiler in which she played a cashier masquerading as a beauty mogul. The film was partially shot at Santa Monica Beach, and the hot sun and harsh stage lights induced headaches and eyestrain and burned to a crisp

Davis's pale skin. A month before the ceremony, she walked off the film's set. "[I'm] dead after five days and nights of work," read the cable she sent to Tenny Wright, Warner's studio manager, explaining her departure. "I cannot work. . . . I cannot do myself justice."[44] By Oscar afternoon, Ham Nelson had at the ready white tie and tails, but Davis avoided ceremonial preparations and took to her four-poster bed. "I felt my career was going downhill at a rapid rate," she recalled.[45]

After making *Of Human Bondage* at RKO, she longed to work there, or at any Big Five studio other than Warner Bros. By Oscar eve Davis felt so in "servitude" to Warner that she decided to dress "like the hired help," wrote James Spada.[46] Chronicling the nominee's preparations, Charles Higham noted Davis "struggled out of bed and discovered she hadn't a single dress worthy of the occasion."[47] Eventually her grasp fell on the perfect pieces—a navy-and-white coat and dress that would make her thoughts perfectly clear to Jack Warner.

Davis had purchased the coordinating ensemble from the Warner Bros. wardrobe department in late spring 1934, after modeling it in *Housewife*, an inconsequential love story in which Warner cast her as Patricia Berkeley, a destructive siren. The "trivial" romance was a comedown for Davis, assigned by Jack Warner after she'd made the monumental *Bondage* to keep her in check. Davis refused to report to work on set, delaying for two weeks the film's early-April shoot date. Customarily she operated faultlessly. "Never late on a set in my life," she claimed.[48]

Through *Housewife*'s standoff, Warner suspended her from the studio payroll, a move that sent her back to work quickly. With a $1,350 weekly salary, Davis supported two households—Franklin Avenue and the Lowell, Massachusetts, home her mother and sister, Barbara, shared. She completed *Housewife*, but the altercation with Warner marked a turning point as it set in motion a cycle of rebellion she maintained through her eighteen years at the studio.[49] As Barbara Leaming noted, "If Bette Davis disapproved of a project Warner Brothers was going to hear about it."[50]

At five foot three, petite, brunette Davis acquired the nickname Little Brown Wren, but she let nobody forget she was a Boston Yankee. After *Housewife* she fought Warner's inept casting calls. Camping outside his office, she waited to pester him for major screen roles. Denied access, she screamed at his secretaries. To escape Davis's wrath, Warner sent her scripts via emissaries, who bore the brunt of her verbal assaults. "Tell Mr. Warner I'm not going to do it!" she informed Tenny Wright

"I am ambitious to become known as a great actress," Bette Davis wrote in a memo to Jack Warner, her boss, outlining her career objective. Here, she models a suit made for her by Warner Bros. costume designer Orry-Kelly. (Corbis)

when in autumn 1935 he handed over *The Man with the Black Hat*, an adaptation of Dashiell Hammett's *The Maltese Falcon*. It was "so atrocious," Davis wanted to "throw up" after perusing its script.[51] *"Crap!"*

she labeled *The Case of the Howling Dog*, and passed it up.[52] "What a title!" she balked on *Cream Princess*.[53] (It was later released as *Golden Arrow*.) Declared Davis of *Housewife*, "What a horror! Terrible. [The] turkey."[54] Deigning to work on it plagued her. "*Housewife* was a picture Davis absolutely despised, before, during, and after appearing in it," confirmed Lawrence J. Quirk. "For many years thereafter, she took the name of *Housewife* in vain, along with the director and screenwriters."[55]

Davis's Academy Awards ensemble offered her the chance to holler "*Housewife!*" from the highest Hollywood peak—the Oscar podium, if she proved victorious. Jack Warner would surely get the message. The outfit was "her silent statement for the occasion," confirmed Leaming.[56] The dowdy semiformal would clash with the black-tie dress code to be observed by stalwart Academy members. Its two-tone color scheme and busy print were signatures Warner's costume designer in chief, Orry-Kelly, devised to make Davis stand out on screen. Through the thirteen years from 1933 that Orry-Kelly worked with Davis, he balanced her awkward, top-heavy figure by cloaking it with strong combinations of bolds on white. Flashy prints, like the pansies dappled upon the *Housewife* ensemble, added a hint of velocity to Davis's kinetic on-screen gestures. To set off her wild, wide blue eyes, the costumer swathed adornments around her long neck, tying bows, knotting cravats, dusting ruffles around it, and draping it with pearls. To the *Housewife* coat Orry-Kelly applied crisp, cotton piqué lapels that emphasized the scheming expressions Davis struck as *Housewife*'s Patricia Berkeley and then again at the Oscar podium.

The Eighth Academy Awards, March 5, 1936. The fancily dressed crowd inside the Biltmore Bowl greeted the arrival of Davis and Ham Nelson with murmurs and bewildered stares. The simple costume from *Housewife* "caused a commotion," according to an attendee.[57] A standing ovation erupted as pioneering silent-screen director D. W. Griffith escorted his wife, Evelyn Baldwin, into the nightclub. Academy president Frank Capra had lured Griffith from his home in Kentucky to receive a special Oscar for his contribution to cinema. As Griffith reveled in the glory and shared emcee duties with Capra, a "dispirited" Davis chatted quietly with Ham Nelson at a table near the dance floor.[58]

By one A.M. Griffith announced Victor McLaglen as winner of the actor prize for his role as a penniless stool pigeon in John Ford's drama *The Informer*. Accessing the podium, McLaglen looked sharp in white tie. Then Griffith thundered, "To Miss Bette Davis for her work in

Dangerous!" The houselights enveloping banqueters went low. A shout went up from Davis's table. As a spotlight swirled toward it, zeroing in on the winner proved impossible because she was lost beneath a scrum.

"Everybody was kissing me," recalled Davis. Released from Ham Nelson's arms, she followed a phosphorescent trail toward the podium. "It's a consolation prize," she thought en route. Davis still felt cheated by having lost the seventh Academy Award for *Of Human Bondage*. "This nagged me," she admitted. "It was true that even if the honor had been earned, it had been earned last year."[59]

Facing the crowd, Davis felt "ecstatic" but played it cool, smoking a cigarette. "You don't know how lucky you are, young lady," lectured Griffith. "At your age—to be where you are—making all that money. Fame—everything—"[60] "I do," interjected Davis. Then she exhaled a thick, gray cloud of cigarette smoke. Beaming at the audience, she delivered thanks to the Academy and the Screen Actors Guild. Signing off, she insisted, "Jack Warner stand up and take a bow!"

As Davis headed for the powder room, Ruth Waterbury, editor of *Photoplay*, followed her inside. Backing up Davis against the pink-and-black-tiled walls, Waterbury raged, "How could you? You don't look like a Hollywood star! You could be dressed for a family dinner. Your

On the night of the eighth Academy Awards in 1936, actress winner Bette Davis didn't look like a Hollywood star in the navy-and-white two-piece Orry-Kelly made for her to wear in *Housewife*. (Courtesy of the Academy of Motion Picture Arts and Sciences)

photograph is going round the world. Don't you realize? Aren't you aware?"[61] Davis pried herself away from Waterbury. A day later she changed her vacation plans. Leaving her mother to relax in Honolulu, she boarded the Super Chief for New York and traveled on to Boston, where she celebrated her Oscar victory with family and old friends.

Over breakfast inside their sprawling Summit Drive, Beverly Hills, mansion, Hollywood power couple Mr. and Mrs. David O. Selznick (the thirty-five-year-old hotshot independent producer and the daughter of Academy Awards founder L. B. Mayer, respectively) scanned the Oscar nominations the *Los Angeles Times* published on February 3, 1937. Irene Selznick lingered over the list of actress nominees. It included two MGM stars, the studio's First Lady, Norma Shearer, who qualified for leading George Cukor's splashy production of *Romeo and Juliet*, and its new Viennese import, Luise Rainer, who emerged as a contender for costarring in the musical extravaganza *The Great Ziegfeld*. Paramount's Gladys George figured she was the "dark horse" of the actress race with her impressive sound-feature debut—the drama *Valiant Is the Word for Carrie*. Irene Dunne factored in for headlining the comedy *Theodora Goes Wild*. But Irene Selznick paused at the boldface mention of Carole Lombard, the front-runner for her role as a zany heiress in Gregory La Cava's smart screwball comedy *My Man Godfrey*. "Carole might make a nice study in Technicolor," mused Selznick of Paramount's curvaceous, blond comedienne.[62]

In the works at David O. Selznick's eponymous Culver City, Los Angeles, studio was the megaproject *Gone With the Wind*, his monumental adaptation of Margaret Mitchell's 1936 best-selling Civil War romance. Like every A-list Hollywood actress, Lombard longed to play *Wind*'s heroine, Scarlett O'Hara. She wanted the Oscar just as much. Selznick was hoping to cast her boyfriend, Clark Gable, as Rhett Butler, the blockbuster's swaggering male lead. But as he put down the *Times*, picked up the telephone, and dialed his talent agent brother Myron Selznick, who represented Lombard, David Selznick realized she'd be perfect for another project—the satire *Nothing Sacred*. Commencing negotiations that ultimately clinched it for Lombard, Selznick demanded, "All right, Myron—let's talk."[63]

A month later, as the countdown to the ninth Academy Awards commenced, Lombard was the talk of Hollywood. Initially bets were placed that the actress Oscar would go to Shearer on the strength of the sympathy vote. Irving G. Thalberg, her thirty-six-year-old husband, had passed away on February 14, 1936. Then a "Norma already has one" backlash set in. "Carole intercepted a rumor that the smart money had switched," noted Lombard's biographer Larry Swindell. "Soon a lot of people were saying they 'just *knew* she was going to win!'"[64]

Lombard was "thrilled" to receive an Oscar nomination, and it came at the right time. Frank Capra spent 1936 revamping the Academy and placated the SAG by making the acting Oscar competition a leveler playing field. He set the list of nominees at five and introduced new categories for supporting cast members. Gable and Lombard were appointed to an esteemed committee of fifty Academy members selecting preliminary nominations. As Mason Wiley and Damien Bona wrote in *Inside Oscar*, the duo failed to show at a meeting to determine the nominees for song, score, and sound prizes.

But Lombard was off to the ceremony. She intended to journey there by limousine with a glamorous entourage including Gable, who would don black tie custom-made by Eddie Schmidt, his Sunset Boulevard tailor. Hitching a ride was Hollywood's most bankable and best-dressed actor, handsome William Powell. Lombard remained on such good terms with Powell, her ex-husband and longtime leading man, that he "insisted" she play Irene Bullock in *My Man Godfrey* to his Oscar-nominated character Godfrey Parke, a down-and-out Harvard grad Irene employs as a butler and eventually marries. Powell's Oscar night date was Jean Harlow, his fiancée of two years, Gable's "favorite" costar ("sometimes bedmate," noted Swindell), and Lombard's close friend. Harlow had a case of the "sniffles," as well as a Gilbert Adrian Oscar satin that was at the ready because she "had no intention of missing the big night."[65]

As Lombard planned her ceremonial attire, she "vacillated between two new evening gowns," wrote biographer Warren G. Harris.[66] Eventually she plucked her Oscar frock from a flotilla of diaphanous evening dresses Paramount's Travis Banton had made for her to wear in *My Man Godfrey*. The connoisseur costumer had designed all of Lombard's clothes after they'd first worked together in 1931 on *Ladies' Man*. The romantic drama was the second Lombard/Powell pair-up, and midway through its making their engagement was announced. Sophisticated Powell's courtship had refined the athletic tomboy formerly known as Jane Alice Peters. "It was a limousined, tuxedoed romance," observed Swindell.[67] *Ladies' Man* also proved Lombard and Banton's *coup de foudre*. Her penchant for wisecracking and dropping four-letter words went down a storm in the expansive office occupied by the feisty Texan costumer. So did her patience through grueling, eight-hour costume fittings. But ultimately Lombard's nonchalance made her Banton's muse, according to Edith Head, his assistant, who testified, "Some girls never learn how to wear elegance naturally, but it seemed Carole had always known how."[68]

Lombard's Oscar dress—one of many known as a Lombard Gown—

followed a rigorous blueprint. "Straight lines and stark simplicity," wrote Hollywood historian Larry Carr, outlining it.[69] "Bias cut—always molded tightly against her thighs," added costume expert David Chierichetti.[70] Rendered in lush, Bianchini silks and often embellished with Gallic bugle beads, the figure-flattering silhouette of a Lombard Gown seductively clung to her toned, five-foot-four-and-a-half-inch, pale frame.

On Oscar morning as the Banton lay waiting in Lombard's plum-colored boudoir, MGM's Luise Rainer sported jeans and sneakers as she navigated her car through lush Santa Barbara toward Los Angeles, after a two-week motoring jaunt to San Francisco with her boyfriend, Group Theater playwright Clifford Odets. Rainer made a roadside stop to check in over the telephone with her housekeeper and was surprised when she insisted, "You must come home right away. Tonight is the Academy Awards. They expect you there!"[71]

Twenty-four-year-old Rainer, an Austrian, a former Berlin stage star, improved her "broken English" by studying scripts for three films she made in the eighteen-month period following her 1935 arrival in Hollywood. She never read film-industry trades.[72] So as her maid implored her to return home, she was completely unaware that she had factored onto the Academy's short list of five actress nominees. There was little Oscar buzz about Rainer, although she had earned critical raves for her nominated portrayal of French chanteuse Anna Held, the first wife of Broadway impresario Florenz Ziegfeld, in the big-budget MGM musical biopic *The Great Ziegfeld*. During production on the 180-minute epic, "case-hardened electricians shed a volume of tears" watching Rainer perform. "Tops," concluded *Variety* of her work after *Ziegfeld*'s April 1936, Broadway premiere.[73] But Rainer's on-screen time was brief compared to that of her fellow leading lady, MGM brunette Myrna Loy, who portrayed Ziegfeld's second wife, showgirl Billie Burke. Loy classified her performance as "self-conscious," but also maintained that *The Great Ziegfeld* was "Bill Powell's picture."[74]

The Academy bypassed Powell's role as Florenz Ziegfeld, but mastering the role strengthened his actor bid with *My Man Godfrey*. Rainer, it was said, would lose the ninth actress Oscar but win the tenth for her starring role as O-Lan, a Chinese wife of a peasant farmer in the soon-to-be-released *The Good Earth*, MGM's blockbuster adaptation of the 1931 Pearl S. Buck Pulitzer Prize–winning best seller. Three directors worked on *The Good Earth*, whose filming was described as "jinxed and interminable," after George Hill, its original driving force, committed

CAROLE LOMBARD
in Paramount Pictures

Oscar nominee Carole Lombard was Travis Banton's muse,
according to Edith Head, his assistant. (Getty Images)

suicide.[75] As long production delays separated Rainer from the tempera-
mental Odets, who divided his time between Hollywood and Connecticut,
their yearlong relationship proved rocky. The couple's San Francisco
sojourn afforded them some necessary downtime. "I was tired from

35

making three major films and more than tired from the emotional turmoil of my private life," reflected Rainer. "I was hating the phony film world of Hollywood and its cigar-eating executives."[76]

By Oscar eve, Rainer and Odets retreated to her Brentwood home. As she padded around in slippers, the telephone rang. It was MGM boss Louis B. Mayer. "Put on some makeup and get downtown!" he ordered. Rainer hastily complied. "They owned me completely," she said of MGM.[77] Few dresses hung in her mostly casual wardrobe. "So I wore my nightgown," said Rainer in 2003. "It was the nicest dress I owned. And I often wore it as an evening gown."[78]

The Ninth Academy Awards, March 4, 1937. A gridlock of haute couture jammed the polished marble steps leading down from the Biltmore's lobby into its buzzing nightclub hosting the Oscars. A lavish crystal-beaded white crêpe by Jean Patou adorned Ouida Bergere, the socialite wife of MGM's Basil Rathbone, a supporting actor nominee for *Romeo and Juliet*. MGM's starlet Loretta Young followed on, shimmering in an Edward Molyneux copper-sequined sheath. Louis B. Mayer "waved off photographers," escorting Norma Shearer into the Biltmore Bowl.[79] Shearer modeled stylish widow's weeds—a black fox coat and a flowing charcoal velvet gown by Manhattan's Hattie Carnegie. Then the "glittering foursome"—Lombard in Banton, black-tied Gable, Adrian-clad Harlow, and Powell in tails—stole the limelight. "Press photographers had a field day," observed Warren G. Harris of their arrival.[80]

Following the four-course banquet dinner, Gable and Powell knocked back postprandial whiskeys. Lombard and Harlow decamped for the powder room, where they happened upon nominee Gladys George in a drunken stupor. "Luise Rainer won," slurred George. "Mayer's trying to build her up and thought an Oscar might help." Lombard applied lipstick and brushed off the suggestion. "You're full of shit and gin," she told George. "Anyone can win."[81]

By ten thirty P.M., as Academy president Frank Capra geared up for the awards ceremony, Luise Rainer was circling the Biltmore, trying to regain composure after a blistering row with Clifford Odets. "He wanted to go [to the Oscars] with me, but I didn't want him to come," she reflected. "He made me so unhappy. He made me cry all of the time."[82]

After eleven P.M., actor George Jessel, the Academy's emcee, announced *The Great Ziegfeld* as winner of the picture prize, and Victor McLaglen quashed Powell's hope to win the actor prize, bestowing it on Paul Muni, for immortalizing scientist Louis Pasteur in *The Story of Louis Pasteur*. McLaglen lingered so long over the actor presentation that Jessel hastily commenced the actress presentation, enraging Bette Davis, who was scheduled to do the honors. Halting the suspense, he revealed the winner. "Miss Rainer," he began, "I want to present you with the token of the finest acting in the 1936 season among Hollywood women stars."[83]

Rainer arrived at the podium with windswept hair and ruddy, tearstained cheeks. In her nightgown she commenced a brief acceptance speech. "Thank you very much," she said, holding her Oscar. "I am very glad to get it. And I thank everybody who made me capable of getting it."[84] Carole Lombard joined the hearty round of applause. She smiled,

At the ninth Academy Awards, actress winner Luise Rainer appeared with windswept hair, tearstained cheeks, and in her nightgown. (Courtesy of the Academy of Motion Picture Arts and Sciences)

noted Swindell, and "burned inside."[85] Her hope of playing Scarlett O'Hara was soon dashed, too.

At the tenth Academy Awards, Rainer set an Academy record by receiving her second Academy Award for *The Good Earth*. She was the first performer to consecutively receive a pair of trophies. "Don't ask me what I wore!" said Rainer, looking back on the tenth Oscars.[86] Pictures reveal that as she clutched her prize in a cloak of white ermine, a smiling Louis B. Mayer looked on from the sidelines.

Chapter Three
GONE WITH THE WIND

The *Times*, the daily London newspaper to which Vivien Leigh subscribed, carried no news of the Academy Awards, although from 1937, as she followed its ongoing report of the epic, two-year global casting search David O. Selznick conducted to find the right actress to play Scarlett O'Hara in *Gone With the Wind*, she acquired the necessary characteristic to clinch the part—blind ambition. I HAVE NO ENTHUSIASM FOR VIVIEN LEIGH, wrote Selznick in a February 1937 cable he sent to Kay Brown, his New York production executive, initially rejecting Leigh.[1] John Gliddon, Leigh's agent, relayed the news, but she took it in stride. Leigh, obsessed by Margaret Mitchell's fictional Southern-belle heroine, was convinced the role was hers.

RADA-trained Leigh's film career was minor, but she was a member of London's Old Vic theater troupe and could hold her own onstage with her lover, the actor Laurence Olivier. A *Vogue* regular (Cecil Beaton often photographed her for the British edition), she had bright green eyes that lit up her face just like Scarlett O'Hara's. Leigh's piercing beauty prompted Myron Selznick, Olivier's agent, to arrange for her to meet his brother, David. So in December 1938 Leigh crossed the Atlantic, and through the stormy passage aboard the *Queen Mary* she practiced Scarlett's feline expressions into a makeup mirror and made notes on the tumultuous era through which she'd lived. On December 10, Leigh, Myron, and Olivier arrived at Selznick Studios to watch the first night of *Wind*'s production—the pivotal burning-of-Atlanta scene. "Before the fire had died down, Vivien had stepped, phoenixlike out of the embers and presented herself to David O. Selznick," wrote Alexander Walker in *Vivien: The Life of Vivien Leigh*.[2] Legend has it that just as Leigh uttered, "Good evening, Mr. Selznick," a breeze blew open her chocolate brown mink coat, revealing her slight frame clad in a becoming beige silk dress that clung to her Scarlett O'Hara–narrow waist. A professional makeup artist had also beautified Leigh to resemble Scarlett. "Her eyes were lined with deep green shadow, making them seem more catlike than usual," noted biographer Anne Edwards.[3] Gruff, thirty-six-year-old Selznick was a snob and not easily impressed. But Leigh walked off his studio lot with the part she so longed for. "I took one look and knew she was right," recalled Selznick, who soon authorized Leigh's winning screen test. "Her tests showed that she could act the part right down to the ground, but I'll never recover from that first look."[4]

By February 1939, two weeks into work on *Wind*, Leigh regretted her careerist determination. Selznick had abruptly fired *Wind*'s director, George Cukor, with whom he ceaselessly argued, appointing Victor Fleming as his successor. Fleming and Selznick agreed a heaving cleavage would be necessary for Leigh to effectively portray Scarlett. The pair envisioned a "tougher, bitchier, and more dangerous" Scarlett than the "tender wanton" Cukor had imagined.[5] Trouble was, Leigh's flat chest had gone undetected during her screen test and preproduction. But before Fleming's cameras, the tops of Scarlett's antebellum gowns caved in, most especially the long, burgundy velvet dress her husband, Rhett Butler, in a jealous rage, forces her to wear to the birthday celebration of her beloved Ashley Wilkes. "Wear that!" Rhett orders Scarlett, removing it from her bedroom wardrobe and tossing it at her. "For Christ's sake, let's get a good look at the girl's boobs!" bellowed Fleming from behind the camera when Leigh appeared in it on set.[6] So on Selznick's command, Fleming insisted that Walter Plunkett, *Wind*'s costumer, bind Leigh's breasts together with adhesive tape. "Dear Vivien stood patiently while we pushed her breasts together and a fitter strapped adhesive tape to keep them in that uncomfortable position," recalled Plunkett.

Talented Plunkett, Hollywood's leading authority on period costume, could have whipped up Leigh's Oscar fashion dream in the "garment factory" he operated on the back lot of Selznick Studios, where over two years his team produced the fifty-five hundred costumes that made up *Wind*'s wardrobe. "It took countless people," he recalled. "I had two women to assist me, cutters and fitters, each of whom had their own crew of seamstresses, plus a crew of milliners. Almost everything was made from scratch."[7] Experts skilled in corset making, hoopskirt

It has long been assumed that *Gone With the Wind*'s costumer, Walter Plunkett, designed Vivien Leigh's Oscar dress, but when production ceased, she stepped out of his work for good. Because her flat chest made the tops of Plunkett's Scarlett O'Hara gowns cave in—particularly in this long burgundy velvet dress—Leigh grew resentful of the attention her upper proportions generated on the film's set. (Corbis)

production, and pleating fashioned Scarlett's wardrobe from bolts of pretty calico, jewel-toned silk velvets, and French petticoat lace—textiles explicitly produced in small, costly quantities by obscure mills Plunkett discovered, after intensive research. It has long been assumed that Plunkett designed Leigh's Oscar dress, but when *Wind* ceased, she stepped out of his costumes for good. Leigh and Plunkett's relationship was based on mutual adoration, but she grew resentful of the attention her upper proportions generated once clad in his work, as well as Selznick's exacting standards.

Intensifying Selznick's perfectionism was his propensity to ingest energy-inducing artificial stimulants, principally the prescription drug Benzedrine, which Evelyn Keyes, who played Suellen, Scarlett's younger sister, watched him swallow "like popcorn."[8] Consequently *Wind* became a nightmare project for its cast and crew, but most especially for Leigh.

"I have perfectly good ones of my own!" she protested to Plunkett's assistant, claiming the adhesive tape cut off her circulation. On set Leigh complained that she could not breathe in Scarlett's wardrobe and grew to loathe the man who on Selznick's orders orchestrated her daily torture— Victor Fleming. Leigh had become a fast, lifelong friend of George Cukor, who protected her from the barrage of production memos Selznick wrote. In them he frequently mentioned the "breast work situation" and the "chest experiment," pondering matters relating to its size, shape, and position in costume.[9] A veteran Broadway stage director, Cukor, said Leigh, "was after all, like Olivier—first of the theatre."[10] Macho Fleming finished his day on set drinking whiskey with his pal Gable, whom Leigh loathed kissing because his false teeth left his breath reeking. "Ham it up!" Fleming told her when she approached him for guidance.[11] Outraged by Cukor's dismissal, Leigh threatened to resign, but relented after a meeting with her new agent, Myron Selznick. He told Leigh, "If you quit this film, you will be in court till your last day on earth. You will never work again on stage or screen. You will never be free. David will see to that. And so, too, Miss Leigh, will I."[12]

Venting her rage about the trials of film acting, Leigh wrote letters to her mother, Gertrude, and her husband, Leigh Holman, with whom she remained on amicable terms despite their impending divorce. Shooting, she related to Holman, operated "at a snail's pace" and was "exhausting and miserable." She compared the rules and regulations that governed her life in Hollywood to those she'd endured at the string of boarding schools she'd attended in England and on the Continent. She felt like a prisoner in the North Camden Drive, Beverly Hills, home Selznick rented for her and arranged for it to be watched by a twenty-four-hour guard so that her relationship with Olivier could be kept top secret. In London, Leigh and Olivier lived together openly. In Hollywood, Selznick feared a similar domestic setup might prove gossip fodder and create a scandal that could jeopardize *Wind*'s success. So after filming *Wuthering Heights*, Olivier moved to New York to appear in a Broadway production of S. N. Behrman's *No Time for Comedy*, an assignment Leigh's biographers claimed Selznick arranged to keep the lovers apart.[13]

With Olivier gone, Leigh grew intensely lonely. She made tearful, long-distance telephone calls to him, suffered from exhaustion, hysteria, and what was later classified as a minor nervous breakdown.[14] On set her emotional strain became apparent as she experienced radical mood swings. "For God's sake, leave me alone!" she shouted at Lydia Schiller, a continuity assistant, after she attempted to adjust the fringe on Scarlett's green velvet bonnet.[15] "She whacked me," Evelyn Keyes wrote, recalling the force Leigh applied to slapping her face during a cotton-picking scene. "My cheek wore the imprint of Vivien's fingers for the rest of the afternoon."[16]

Dealing with volatile Leigh pushed Victor Fleming to the breaking point. One morning on his way to Selznick Studios, he nearly drove his dove gray Cadillac off a cliff near Malibu. He took two weeks off to recuperate. Sam Wood took over as *Wind*'s director, but the production spun out of control. Selznick shifted his obsessive attention from Leigh's chest to her eyes, pressuring Monty Westmore, his head makeup artist, to apply excessive amounts of green eye shadow to her lids, to enhance the color of her hazel irises. Studying the rushes, Selznick concluded that Leigh's eyes looked "violet, gray, blue, tan, and nearly every other color in the spectrum" other than the requisite green, which he explained during the first of a series of nocturnal telephone calls he made to Westmore.[17] "Monty, I hope I'm not disturbing you," Selznick usually began their late-night conversations. "Why, no, Mr. Selznick," Westmore customarily replied. "What would make you think you were disturbing me? It's only three in the morning."[18]

Fueled by more than adrenaline, Selznick was binging on methedrine and barbituates. "Whatever was handy," noted Patrick McGilligan, George Cukor's biographer. Though not embittered by his dismissal, Cukor was repulsed by Selznick's habit of "crushing up Benzedrines and licking the pieces from the palm of his hand, a grain at a time."[19] For a week, Selznick forced Leigh and some of *Wind*'s cast and crew to wake at two thirty A.M. to reshoot the daybreak scene during which she uttered, "As God is my witness, I'll never be hungry again." Her delivery was perfect. Selznick, however, was displeased with the look of the sunrise in the background. On June 27, 1939; *Wind*'s final shooting day, Olivia de Havilland, who costarred as Melanie Hamilton, walked straight past Leigh, failing to recognize her. "She looked so diminished by overwork," remembered de Havilland. "Her whole atmosphere had changed. She gave something to that film which I don't think she ever got back."[20]

Selznick made up for his bad behavior on *Wind*'s set by picking up the tab for the wardrobe custom-made by Irene Gibbons for Leigh and all the women appearing at the series of gala premieres and after parties feting *Wind*'s December 1939 release in Atlanta, New York, and Los Angeles. "Irene" was the couturier who operated the French Salon, the exclusive ladies' dress department at Bullock's Wilshire, the downtown Los Angeles luxury department store. While Irene fitted Leigh with an ermine-tipped, black velvet gown and golden tulle ensemble for *Wind* premieres, Leigh discovered in the designer's spring 1940 collection what became her Oscar dress. Leigh's Oscar bid—one among an unprecedented total of thirteen nominations *Wind* received—factored onto a list made up of box office draws, including Bette Davis, Greta

Garbo, Greer Garson, and Irene Dunne. Vying for her third Oscar with her laudatory performance in *Dark Victory*, Davis was considered Leigh's only challenger.

No actress contender had yet modeled an Irene gown at the Academy Awards. But Dolores Del Rio and Ginger Rogers as well as Paramount stars Claudette Colbert and Carole Lombard had already sashayed in her featherweight floating gowns on Hollywood's social scene and across the big screen. "I've designed clothes for everyone in Hollywood, really everyone," Irene claimed in 1939. She refused an offer to head up the costume department at Paramount Pictures after Travis Banton decamped to work freelance for Twentieth Century–Fox's wardrobe department in 1938. Edith Head, his right hand, assumed Banton's position at Paramount, but the studio's leading ladies viewed the bespectacled former schoolteacher as "the assistant" and insisted that their costumes be made by tall, tawny-haired Irene, who had acquired a decade of experience operating her own Sunset Boulevard boutique after a stint studying fashion design in Paris. Marriage in January 1937 to Elliot Gibbons, the scriptwriter brother of Cedric Gibbons, MGM's art director who conceived the Oscar trophy, increased Irene's stature. "Believe me, she was as good as the best," claimed the finicky Colbert. "Irene was the only woman at the time who could be compared to Coco Chanel."

Beneath the swaggering crystal chandeliers in Bullock's art deco–accented French Salon hung Irene's evening gowns. Cut from exotic Bianchini printed silk, adorned with fourteen-karat gold buttons, and generously slit, they carried the fashion industry's highest price tags. At $450 each, her gowns were over twice the price of a Paris couture model. But cost seemed irrelevant to Irene's customers. "I should have ordered more dresses!" wrote Marlene Dietrich on the back of a Paris postcard she sent Irene after a Bullock's shopping spree. "Every star and social butterfly who could afford her prices went to Irene," recalled fashion photographer John Engstead.[21] Every piece of clothing owned by Edie Goetz, David Selznick's discerning sister-in-law, came from Irene's atelier, including the skirts she wore playing tennis on the court behind her Bel Air mansion. Carole Lombard tied the knot with Clark Gable in March 1939 in an Irene gray flannel skirt suit. She planned to attend the early fall 1940 show the couturier staged in September 1939 to scout for pieces for *Wind*'s premieres, but she was busy working. "I'm damn mad that I can't get to the show," wrote Lombard, who sent regrets by a note typed on her

"Irene" was the couturier who operated the French Salon, the exclusive ladies' dress department at the luxurious Bullock's Wilshire, in downtown Los Angeles. (Courtesy of the Academy of Motion Picture Arts and Sciences)

emerald-green-embossed personal stationery. "You better save a lot of good things for me or we will have to do originals." Irene, however, set aside the best dress for Leigh.

Irene's show commenced in Bullock's lounge with a whisper: "Doesn't she look smart?" Edna Woolman Chase, *Vogue*'s editor, had just arrived, eliciting the comment of approval from someone among the crowd of about one hundred well-dressed Hollywood wives. Chase's visit to Bullock's also marked a turning point for the Los Angeles fashion scene because it was the first time she traveled to the West Coast to view fashion produced by a Los Angeles designer. Leigh, on her way back to Los Angeles from London to shoot retakes of *Wind*'s opening scene, wasn't there. So aside from silver-haired, sixty-three-year-old Chase, the show's guest of honor was MGM leading lady Greta Garbo. Reclusive Garbo, clad in slacks and a floppy sun hat, rarely ventured beyond MGM's lot. The presentation of Irene's collection was the only L.A. fashion show she attended. By her side was the man with whom the *L.A. Examiner*'s Louella Parsons reported she was swiftly moving "that-away" toward marriage—her nutritional guru, Gaylord Hauser, who later penned the best-selling raw-food diet book *Look Younger, Live Longer*. Outside Bullock's a pack of reporters waited on the pavement to capture Garbo and Hauser's exit. The pair refused to sit alongside Irene's audience assembled in Bullock's lounge. So just before the dimmer switch flipped the chandelier light low, signaling showtime, French doors were swung back to create a private enclave for the VIPs.

Irene's program described Leigh's Oscar dress, which debuted as look fourteen on a pale blond model, simply as "Red Poppy Evening Gown." Green-stemmed red poppies exploded like fireworks upon the long chiffon gown. Its vibrant floral print carried on a theme Irene had been exploring for a while. She produced sexy gowns drenched with big, bold blooms including a frisky white dance dress dotted with perky black-eyed Susans in which Ginger Rogers boogied alongside Fred Astaire in 1937's *Shall We Dance*. A year later, at a San Francisco hotel party, Marlene Dietrich caused a sensation in a low-cut, spaghetti-strapped Irene frock of white silk enlivened with purple hydrangeas. "The bigger, the better" was Irene's pattern philosophy

Leigh adored flowers. They brought to mind fond childhood memories of times spent with her mother in the vast garden behind their family mansion in Calcutta. Leigh had lived there happily until her parents sent her off to a string of continental boarding schools.

Irene's October 1939 fashion show program described Vivien Leigh's Oscar dress, here worn by an unknown model, as "Red Poppy Evening Gown." Green-stemmed red poppies exploded like fireworks on chiffon. (Courtesy of the Academy of Motion Picture Arts and Sciences)

Throughout her life, gardens and wildflowers brought her comfort. "A garden for her had qualities of beauty and tranquillity," observed Alexander Walker. "In whichever parts of the world she later found herself, 'the garden' was present or re-created in the bouquets on first nights, in vases arranged to welcome her to strange hotel suites, in

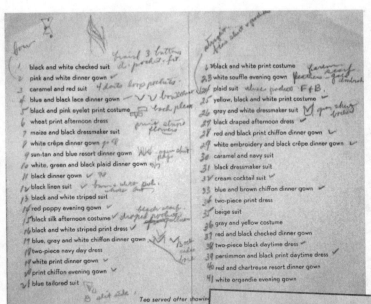

1. black and white checked suit
2. pink and white dinner gown
3. caramel and red suit
4. blue and black lace dinner gown
5. black and pink eyelet print costume
6. wheat print afternoon dress
7. maize and black dressmaker suit
8. white crêpe dinner gown
9. sun-tan and blue resort dinner gown
10. white, green and black plaid dinner gown
11. black dinner gown
12. black linen suit
13. black and white striped suit
14. red poppy evening gown
15. black silk afternoon costume
16. black and white striped print dress
17. blue, gray and white chiffon dinner gown
18. two-piece navy day dress
19. white print dinner gown
20. print chiffon evening gown
21. blue tailored suit

22. black and white print costume
23. white souffle evening gown
24. plaid suit
25. yellow, black and white print costume
26. gray and white dressmaker suit
27. black draped afternoon dress
28. red and black print chiffon dinner gown
29. white embroidery and black crêpe dinner gown
30. caramel and navy suit
31. black dressmaker suit
32. cream cocktail suit
33. blue and brown chiffon dinner gown
34. two-piece print dress
35. beige suit
36. gray and yellow costume
37. red and black checked dinner gown
38. two-piece black daytime dress
39. persimmon and black print daytime dress
40. red and chartreuse resort dinner gown
41. white organdie evening gown

Tea served after showing

Bullock's-Wilshire
requests the honor of your presence
at a showing of the
Early Fall Collection
by
Irene
on Thursday, the twenty-fifth of August
at three o'clock in the afternoon
in the Lounge-fifth floor

Daily showings from two until five thereafter
in the Irene Salon-second floor

Life captured Vivien Leigh placing the Academy Award she received for *Gone With the Wind* atop the mantel in her Beverly Hills home. (Getty Images)

flower paintings by French Impressionists which traveled with her in her luggage and were then stood on bedside tables or hung on the walls of rented apartments to turn them into a reminder of home, the minute she opened her eyes."[22] As Leigh's travails with Selznick and Fleming intensified on *Wind*'s set, she retreated to the rambling, terraced garden behind George Cukor's Beverly Hills mansion. Surrounded by its high, wisteria-and-ivy-covered walls, Cukor and Leigh reclined side by side on padded pool loungers most every Sunday, her day off, commiserating about *Wind*'s chaos. Cukor's garden became Leigh's haven, and on Oscar night, Irene's dress was its equivalent rendered in silk.

Within its bodice was a light, inner support necessitating that nothing need be worn beneath it. "[Irene's] soft crêpes and chiffons were meant to be worn without a brassiere—a discreet construction underneath them lifted the breasts delicately," wrote Hollywood costume expert David Chierichetti of the frocks Irene built for maximum comfort because so many of her movie star clients, like Leigh, spent long days on film sets bound in tight-fitting, corset-topped period costumes.[23]

On the night of the twelfth Academy Awards, between Red Poppy Evening Gown and Leigh's skin mingled merely the rose and jasmine scent of Jean Patou's Joy, her favorite perfume. She splashed it on and fastened an aquamarine pendant. Olivier had purchased the semiprecious piece in New York from Van Cleef & Arpels, the Fifth Avenue jeweler, and sent it to Leigh in Los Angeles as a token of his affection as she suffered through *Wind*. On Oscar night it hung from a long gold chain and drew attention to the plunging bodice of Irene's dress. Like a trophy medallion, it displayed that after a tough seven months of portraying Scarlett O'Hara, Leigh was finally free. She and Olivier set off by limousine to a pre–Academy Awards cocktail party at David Selznick's sprawling home on Summit Drive. "Everybody was keyed up—they all came in limousines," recalled Irene Mayer Selznick, David's wife.[24] Celebrating at Selznick's lofty abode, Leigh discovered she had won an Academy Award. In banner headlines, the *Los Angeles Times*' early edition published results it was meant to print the following day —*Wind* had set an Academy record, winning an unprecedented nine Oscars. Supercharged by the news, Selznick hustled Leigh, Olivier, Clark Gable, and Olivia de Havilland into the back of a limousine bound for the ceremony at the Ambassador Hotel's nightclub, the Cocoanut Grove.

The Twelfth Academy Awards, February 29, 1940. Veiled in stardust, gowned by Irene, Leigh was ushered into the Ambassador's lobby by David Selznick as a "near riot of admirers" rushed toward them, wrote *Variety*'s Alta Durant. Leigh, noted the columnist, was the "star" of an illustrious Academy Awards. "Every name of note in the industry was either a guest or host," observed the *Hollywood Reporter*. Bob Hope was debuting as master of ceremonies, a post he would mostly maintain over the next thirty years. Actor Spencer Tracy had arranged to be discharged from the hospital so that he could be on hand to present the

Oscar to Leigh. After MGM's teen queen Judy Garland, recipient of a special juvenile Oscar for her outstanding performance as Dorothy in *The Wizard of Oz*, sang "Over the Rainbow," its Academy Award–winning theme, Hope entertained the crowd. "What a wonderful thing this benefit for David Selznick," he cracked.

It was just after midnight. Selznick had traveled back and forth from his seat to the podium to personally claim most of *Wind*'s nine Oscars.[25] "Hallelujah!" proclaimed Hattie McDaniel, who, for portraying Mammy, Scarlett's governess, received the best supporting actress Oscar—which made her the first black actor to win an Academy Award. At one fifteen A.M. it was Spencer Tracy's turn at the podium. "Need I say this is a privilege and an honor to announce this winner: Miss Vivien"—[26] Deafening applause drowned out the rest of Tracy's preamble. Having anticipated the victory moment, Leigh glided gracefully to the podium. "She looked beautiful and glowing, her chiffon gown billowing, her head tossed back, hair loose," noted her biographer Anne Edwards.[27] Beaming before the crowd, Leigh relied on her theatrical skills and succinctly delivered an eloquent speech. "Ladies and gentlemen," she began, "if I were to mention all those who have shown me such wonderful generosity through *Gone With the Wind*, I should have to entertain you with an oration as long as *Gone With the Wind* itself."[28] Before departing the rostrum she thanked "Mr. David Selznick, all my coworkers, and most of all Miss Margaret Mitchell."[29]

Back at one of *Wind*'s two tables, Leigh was as bubbly as the flowing Lanson champagne. Later she claimed to be unnerved by the experience of departing from the podium and making her way through the Cocoanut Grove with her Oscar. She likened the route to the perilous journey she'd witnessed on the night she'd landed her part in *Gone With the Wind*—Scarlett and Rhett's harrowing horse-drawn-buggy ride through burning Atlanta. "Only instead of flames," she said, "it was people reaching out to touch me."[30]

Journeying home by limousine was no pleasure cruise. Laurence Olivier qualified as an actor Academy Award nominee for *Wuthering Heights*, but he lost out to *Goodbye, Mr. Chips*' Robert Donat.[31] In the back of the limo, as Olivier sat next to Leigh, he grabbed her Oscar and later admitted, "I was insane with jealousy. It was all I could do to restrain myself from hitting her with it."[32] *Life* captured Leigh arriving home, where she placed her Oscar atop the mantel above her fireplace.

★   ★   ★

Leigh's successor, *Kitty Foyle*'s star Ginger Rogers, appeared at the thirteenth Academy Awards in an Irene stunner combining layers of gray peau de soie with black American-made lace. Like every American designer, Irene had been encouraged to produce collections from domestic fabrics while the U.S. government's L-85 emergency measure prevented the use of materials necessary for the oncoming war effort, including wool, silk, and metal.[33] At the start of World War II, the Academy instituted its own rules, stipulating that service people temporarily stationed in Los Angeles bound for South Pacific combat zones were welcome at the Oscars, while Academy members were to opt for dark, semiformal red-carpet attire in keeping with the solemn, conflict-ridden times. "White tie, tuxedos and décolletage," according to the Academy's memo, were "very definitely out."[34]

In the run-up to World War II, Irene, like every American designer, was encouraged to make her creations from domestically produced fabrics. So in 1941, for *Kitty Foyle*'s Oscar-winning star, Ginger Rogers (foreground), Irene incorporated black American-made lace into Rogers's dress. (Courtesy of the Academy of Motion Picture Arts and Sciences)

Chapter Four

DARK VICTORY

"Malarkey!" balked gossip columnist Hedda Hopper after the Academy's dress-code memo touched down on her desk in 1942. Hopper made it her personal mission to revive the practice of flaunting formal attire at the Oscars, where she ritually preened. Studio costume designers Adrian, Banton, and Orry-Kelly all slavishly custom-made clothes for slim "worldly, lovely, beautifully groomed" Hopper (as MGM actress Kitty Carlisle Hart described her friend), and their services were usually paid for by studio bosses as gift-bribes to keep their actors appearing boldface in "Hedda Hopper's Hollywood," her *Los Angeles Times* column.[1] Hopper claimed battling the Academy's dress code was on behalf of the boys at war. For troops stationed abroad, news and photos of Academy Awards guests decked out in black tie could work as a moral booster, she reasoned. "Servicemen were starving for glamour—they're hungry for gay clothes and bright colors," she went on.[2] "If clothes, no matter how lavish, cannot create glamour they can and do create morale."[3]

Hopper was too proud to wave a white lace handkerchief and surrender operation "guerrilla warfare," although it was soon in retreat. World War II brought fierce political correctness to Hollywood, and consequently attendance at the Academy Awards became viewed as a patriotic duty. Actors once reluctant to attend the Oscars now showed up in force, donning dark, semiformal attire. As a fashion spectacle, the Academy Awards was in a holding pattern as reports of tragedies from war-ravaged Europe replaced Oscar style news in the *Los Angeles Times*.

The Academy's war-era dress code should have simplified Oscar-night preparations. But behind the scenes, assembling the requisite dark semis proved complicated for a trio of leading ladies represented by producer David O. Selznick—Joan Fontaine, Jennifer Jones, and Ingrid Bergman. Nerve-racked by their competition, Selznick's stars floundered dressing up for the affair. Heightening their anxiety was the media's increasing fascination with the ceremony, which, two decades from its inception, had become the main event on Hollywood's social calendar.

Fontaine attempted to ignore the gossip and fanfare surrounding her 1942 actress Oscar bid for playing Lina, a timid newlywed in Alfred Hitchcock's gripping thriller *Suspicion*. But on Oscar morning, her downtime between takes of *The Constant Nymph*, the Warner Bros. romantic drama in which she played Tessa, a fourteen-year-old experiencing first love, was interrupted by a telephone call from producer Walter Wanger, the Academy's new president. Wanger had just discovered twenty-five-year-old Fontaine had no plans to appear at the fourteenth ceremony. "Surely you are attending," he inquired. Shrewdly Fontaine refused to offer herself up as banquet sweetmeat and politely begged off his invitation to the Oscars, explaining that a hectic shooting schedule made her attendance impossible. Wanger had hoped to maximize the drama at the ceremony by seating Fontaine across from her main challenger—Olivia de Havilland, her twenty-six-year-old sister.

Fontaine and de Havilland, the first siblings to compete for an Academy Award, dominated talk in Hollywood in the lead-up to the ceremony because it was assumed one sister would triumph over the other. The press had long portrayed them as bitter rivals, chronicling their every move as they frequently struggled to win the same film roles and romantic partners, including Howard Hughes. While brunette de Havilland was briefly engaged to the notorious aviation mogul/playboy/movie producer, Fontaine made her aware of how hotly Hughes simultaneously pursued her, too. "Sparks flew," she recalled.[4]

She admitted that competitiveness tainted her sisterly love. Fontaine narrowly lost the Oscar in 1941 for mastering the timid lead role in Selznick's masterly production of Daphne du Maurier's *Rebecca*. The first Hollywood film directed by Alfred Hitchcock, *Rebecca* established her as the British director's blond leading lady and eradicated her former career as a B-movie actress. But Hitchcock's *Suspicion* was "not the classic that *Rebecca* was," she admitted. "I felt my chances of winning this time were negligible."[5] Like her competitors Bette Davis and Greer Garson—who both sent regrets to the Academy and embarked on cross-country war-bond selling tours—Fontaine expected de Havilland to win the Oscar.

"She is excellent," confirmed the *New York Times* of de Havilland's nominated performance in the political thriller *Hold Back the Dawn* as Emmy Brown, an American schoolteacher who discovers her engagement to a Romanian immigrant is a ploy to facilitate his entry to the United States.[6] Grittier than the costume epics in which Jack Warner habitually cast de Havilland, *Hold Back the Dawn* displayed her flair for leading a contemporary drama.

"You're an Academy *member*—the contestants in all of the categories are expected to be there," explained de Havilland, who early on Oscar afternoon reached Fontaine by telephone.[7] "I haven't anything to wear!" wailed Fontaine. Clutching the receiver of her dressing-room telephone, she broke down in tears.[8]

Fontaine usually possessed a disciplined approach to maintaining her soigné. Her wardrobe was personally fit inside Hattie Carnegie, the plush East Forty-ninth Street, Manhattan, fashion boutique to compliment the immaculate Savile Row–tailored suits co-opted by her British husband, MGM actor Brian Aherne. Socializing with a haughty Brit pack of film professionals, Fontaine and Aherne were part of forties Hollywood upper echelon. "We dressed to the teeth for everything," claimed Ouida Bergere, wife of MGM's Basil Rathbone, the group's ringleader.[9] To dine à deux inside their white, rose-covered Rodeo Drive cottage, the Ahernes customarily donned black tie. Unfortunately, on Oscar afternoon there was no appropriate ceremonial attire in Warner's costume department for Fontaine to commandeer. The government's L–85 restrictions meant that screen costumes were utterly basic, including the tattered dress and tennis shoes she sported shooting *The Constant Nymph*.

But late in the day a sea of chic semiformals from the exclusive department store I. Magnin & Co. surrounded Fontaine. Supervising an impromptu fitting to find her an Academy Awards ensemble were the women who masterminded her rescue—de Havilland and Magnin's dress-salon director, Stella Hanania, or Miss Stella as she was known to loyal clients like Fontaine and de Havilland, who informed her of her sister's predicament. *Vogue* labeled Magnin's dress department a

West Coast "landmark," and Hollywood's stylish shopped there from 1942, after Irene Gibbons left Bullock's French Salon, assuming Gilbert Adrian's position as chief costume designer at MGM. Between Magnin's frescoed walls Fontaine found the gown she wore to marry Brian Aherne in August 1938, as well as her trousseau. For her consideration, Miss Stella pulled together potential Oscar ensembles in a matter of minutes, ordering a troupe of assistants to lift from display every item appropriate for the ceremony in size six.

Miss Stella traveled down the department store's sweeping, pink marble staircase and out its door, leading a procession of delivery boys who carried tan and white boxes containing the merchandise and deposited them in the trunk of de Havilland's waiting delivery wagon, a Warner Bros. limousine. Together the pair traveled on to the studio, seeing out Oscar afternoon with Fontaine inside her dressing room. Between takes of *The Constant Nymph* they helped her decide which black ensemble looked best. As Fontaine settled on an onyx, silk, ankle-length skirt and a midnight lace mantilla, de Havilland explained it was a gift, wished her sister well, and left her in the hands of a Warner grooming team. As they set to work brushing out the pigtails Fontaine wore playing Tessa in *The Constant Nymph*, de Havilland went back to her Los Feliz home to slip on a black chiffon dress.

Her display of good sportsmanship concealed a burning desire for the Oscar.[10] As for the Magnin's shopping expedition, it was likely a stress-relieving bout of retail therapy for which de Havilland found time because she was on a recuperative break, overcoming a series of maladies that had resulted from the stress of working overtime on back-to-back film projects at Warner Bros.[11] On Oscar morning she was in the "worst possible mood," according to Charles Higham, after she received the news that her next Warner project would be the slapstick comedy *George Washington Slept Here*.[12]

The Fourteenth Academy Awards, February 26, 1942. By evening de Havilland had regained composure as her actor boyfriend Burgess Meredith escorted her inside the Biltmore Hotel. Outside on the red carpet Brian Aherne and a placid Joan Fontaine posed for photographers. "They looked like a page out of *Harper's Bazaar*," observed Louella Parsons, who monitored the sisters' arrivals. "Joan, so fragile. Olivia—beautifully gowned, had many admirers rooting for her."[13]

Hollywood heavyweights, black-clad leading ladies, servicemen and -women in freshly pressed army uniforms, mingled at banquet tables spreading into the Biltmore Bowl nightclub's orchestra pit. "The room was in a hubbub over the fact that the two sisters were in direct competition," noted Higham.[14] But swarming photographers staking out optimum angles to best capture both winner and loser at the final hour obstructed the view of Fontaine and de Havilland at David Selznick's banquet table. Despite the intruders and bet-placing background chatter, the pair remained calm but exchanged stilted conversation through the four-course dinner. "Hardly anyone touched the meal," recalled Fontaine.[15] She and her sister sat on their seat edges awaiting the result of the actress prize, which according to tradition would be announced last, by Ginger Rogers, the previous year's winner. The buxom blond entertainer wanted to avoid the duty because as a mutual friend of both Fontaine and de Havilland she couldn't face denying one the prize. Awkwardly she mounted the podium at midnight. "Both sisters leaned forward, each one eager to hear the news," chronicled Parsons. "I've never been present at a more dramatic moment. The air was tense. You could have heard a pin drop."[16]

Outside the Biltmore Hotel at the fourteenth Academy Awards, Oscar nominee Joan Fontaine posed alongside her husband, actor Brian Aherne. (Courtesy of the Academy of Motion Picture Arts and Sciences)

Rogers's apprehension was compounded by her sapphire blue evening gown, which she wore at Hedda Hopper's behest. Alongside black-clad Academy members inside the Biltmore, bead-bedecked Hopper claimed she and Rogers "stuck out like the observatory on Mount Wilson."[17]

"The envelope, please," said Rogers, requesting a new, suspense-

At the fourteenth Academy Awards, photographers staked out optimum angles to capture Joan Fontaine and Olivia de Havilland, the first siblings to compete for an Oscar. (Courtesy of the Academy of Motion Picture Arts and Sciences)

inducing element Walter Wanger had introduced. A Price Waterhouse representative accidentally delivered the envelope to Rogers upside down, so she tugged at its stiff bottom instead of easing open the seal. "The mike amplified the sound of the ripping of paper," remembered Fontaine.[18] "Olivia and Joan tried not to look at each other," added Higham.[19] Then Rogers realized the ballot was the wrong way up. Flipping it, she revealed the competition's result: "And the winner is— Joan Fontaine for *Suspicion!*"

Fontaine sat rigidly, listening to the gasps, whistles, and resounding applause that greeted her victory. Shocked, she stared blankly across the table. De Havilland swiftly leaned across it, frightening Fontaine as she whispered, "Get up there, get up there."[20] A nudge from Brian Aherne forced Fontaine out of her seat, but she sobbed moving toward the podium. "I was appalled that I'd won over my sister," she later wrote.[21] Despite years of childhood diction lessons, Fontaine had trouble making a speech. "I tried to find my voice," she added. All she managed was a quick "Thank you."[22]

"What Olivia's feelings were can only be imagined," noted Higham.[23] Two years earlier at the twelfth Academy Awards, de Havilland had fled the Cocoanut Grove, bursting into tears after Hattie McDaniel, her costar in *Gone With the Wind,* beat her for the supporting actress prize. As photographers swarmed around de Havilland as the fourteenth ceremony concluded, she clung to Burgess Meredith's hand. When Fontaine took a seat, she clasped hers. Expertly improvising a happy ending to their Oscar night, de Havilland raised her arm and Fontaine's into the air, declaring a joint victory: "We've got it!"[24]

Sibling rivalry gave way to friendly fire when, in 1944, the Oscar came between two chummy twentysomething Selznick Studios stars, Ingrid Bergman and Jennifer Jones, who received nominations for their acclaimed roles in screen adaptations of best-selling novels, respectively, *For Whom the Bell Tolls,* a Paramount Pictures production of Ernest Hemingway's Spanish Civil War adventure romance, and *The Song of Bernadette,* Twentieth Century–Fox's biopic adapted from Franz Werfel's story of Bernadette Soubirous, a peasant from Lourdes, France, canonized as Saint Bernadette in 1914. Jones turned twenty-five on Oscar day, but certain that Bergman would claim the prize, David Selznick advised her not to expect the actress trophy as a birthday gift. "As I have told you I hope that Ingrid will win the Academy Award this year," read the memo he sent Jones four months before the ceremony. "You are young and have plenty of time. Let's keep our fingers crossed and not be too sure."[25]

Bergman revered the Academy and regarded the Oscars as an event to honor cinematic talent, but she kept her preparations to a minimum. "I think the Academy Awards is a great one for the film industry— something that will be built up through the years, something with a tradition behind it," she told *Photoplay*. In May 1939, when she arrived in Hollywood from her home in Stockholm, Sweden, she avoided dressing up in "Hollywood fashions," as Bergman described studio-manufactured red-carpet glamour. "Mother was way too practical to be considered a fashion victim," claimed Isabella Rossellini, Bergman's daughter. "To begin with, her Protestant upbringing made her feel guilty about spending too much money on dresses. She thought carefully and bought few."[26]

At five foot nine, Bergman was approximately a half foot taller than most of her colleagues and found it difficult to fit her large frame into shop-bought clothes. Her wardrobe was mostly composed of tailor-made, mix-and-match skirt-and-blouses she purchased from studio wardrobe departments after wearing them on-screen. She planned to wear one of her trusty combos to the sixteenth Academy Awards. But Selznick had another idea.

Prior to the Oscars he secretly commissioned costumer Travis Banton to design a black evening suit for Bergman. Together with designers Irene Gibbons and Barbara Karinska, Banton had recently produced Bergman's wardrobe for *Gaslight*, a period drama she shot at MGM during Oscar season. Just prior to the ceremony an item in "Hedda Hopper's Hollywood" revealed the Banton suit. The news so angered Bergman when she read about it that she informed Banton she planned to wear her *"oldest"* dress to the Academy Awards.[27] "She would not stand for being exploited," recalled Joseph Henry Steele, her publicist.[28]

Bergman was no show pony. However, her heated declaration seemed prompted by a state of high anxiety she customarily experienced during Oscar season. Her nomination for the sixteenth actress prize came five years after her 1939 Hollywood debut—an eternity because most of Selznick's discoveries received the honor after appearing in their first major feature. Fiercely ambitious and competitive, Bergman longed to win an Oscar. "I never want to hear the words Academy Award until I have the prize in my hands," she wrote in her acting diary, after she discovered that her critically acclaimed performance in *Dr. Jekyll and Mr. Hyde* failed to register with Academy voters in 1942.[29]

Banton's ensemble was, in fact, the finishing touch of a Selznick-supervised grooming procedure to which Bergman willingly submitted, hoping that it might help her clinch the Oscar for her role as Maria in *For Whom the Bell Tolls*. With its three-million-dollar budget, *Bell* was produced to rival *Gone With the Wind*—shot in Technicolor, it was the most expensive film Paramount Pictures had yet made, and when studly Gary Cooper was cast as its lead, Robert Jordan, a college professor turned Spanish Civil War freedom fighter, a Scarlett O'Hara–style casting search ensued to find his object of love, Maria, a peasant girl he meets roaming near his mountain hideaway. For two years Selznick waged negotiations with Paramount executives to win Maria for Bergman, but discovered that she was a tough sell.

"Very un-made-up, very simple," said Bergman, explaining her low-maintenance look, which she insisted be maintained when she joined Selznick Studios in May 1939.[30] Selznick agreed to Bergman's demands and shooed away Wally Westmore, his makeup man, when he came at her wielding tweezers to tame her bushy eyebrows. Selznick believed a "natural" actress would be a novelty in Hollywood and in keeping with the realistic style of pictures made during World War II.[31] But Paramount's Edith Head, who conceived *Bell*'s costumes, claimed that studio executives considered "un-made-up" Bergman too frumpy to play Maria. "Just a big, hefty Swede—wooden and dull and not at all suited to their conception of the Spanish miss who went a-bundling in a sleeping bag with Gary Cooper in the battlefields of the Spanish Civil War," wrote Head of the executive view.[32] Cooper and Ernest Hemingway, *Bell*'s creative forces, considered Bergman to be an ideal Maria, but to keep production costs down, Paramount awarded the part to its unknown contract star Vera Zorina, a former prima ballerina from Norway and wife of choreographer George Balanchine. But for delicate Zorina the film's rugged wilderness location, Sonora, the foothills of Northern California's Sierra Nevada, proved difficult terrain. When Cooper grew frustrated by Zorina's fragility, she was replaced by Bergman. Advance good word on Bergman's role in the 1942 romance *Casablanca* as Ilsa, a World War II refugee torn between her resistance-leader husband and her old flame, nightclub impresario Rick Blaine (Humphrey Bogart), convinced Paramount that she could play Maria.

Wanting nothing to diminish her chance at winning an Academy Award for *Bell*, Selznick insisted that she beautify herself to play Maria, and Bergman played ball. She traded in a costume she'd cobbled together with a man's shirt and pair of trousers from Paramount's old wardrobe stock, for a new wardrobe Selznick insisted Edith Head create from scratch. "It was not a fashion picture," recalled Head of *Bell*. "Her scenes called for nothing but dirty old pants and shirts."[33] But Selznick was "furious" when he discovered Bergman was making her color-film debut hiking around Sonora's foothills before director Sam Wood's camera in wardrobe castoffs.[34] Bergman also acquired the most expensive haircut in Hollywood history, after Selznick paid MGM's Sydney Guilaroff, the film industry's top stylist, the unprecedented sum of three thousand dollars to shape her long, sandy blond hair into a "Maria cut" of chin-length ringlets.[35] Its staggering cost was due to Bergman's fear of being groomed, wrote Guilaroff: "Bergman was so nervous about having her hair worked on that I decided to proceed very gradually."[36]

Much to Selznick's satisfaction, Bergman became a beauty icon following *Bell*'s August 16, 1943, premiere. Across America women went to hair salons demanding the "Maria cut," although Guilaroff was disappointed by its look on-screen and claimed that Selznick "ruined it" by demanding that he shape tight curls when, for the sake of credibility, he felt that mountain-roaming Maria should wear a loose, wavy hairstyle.[37] "All of those pretty curls, she was strictly Elizabeth Arden out of Abercrombie and Fitch," a disgruntled Hemingway said, dismissing what he considered a glossy, Hollywood hatchet job of his epic novel.[38] But *Bell*, wrote Bergman's biographer Donald Spoto, became a commercial hit, attracting "enormous crowds nationwide," and the talk of her sure shot at the actress Oscar began with its release and continued unabated after it received eight Academy Award nominations.

Selznick assured Bergman that the sixteenth actress Oscar was hers. "David Selznick promised her that she would win an Academy Award," confirmed Edith Head.[39] But buzz about *The Song of Bernadette* sent Bergman to its late-December 1943 screening. "Jennifer was so moving," admitted Bergman to Joseph Steele. She cried all the way through the two-and-a-half-hour tragedy. Perhaps she realized Jones posed a direct threat to her chance at the Oscar.[40]

Intensifying Jones's Oscar stake was the first Golden Globe actress prize she received in January 1944 from the Hollywood Foreign Press Association. But Jones recoiled from the scrutiny that came with sudden fame, although the former B-movie star, Phylis Isley Walker, was rigorously coached for her moment in the spotlight. Signing a seven-year Selznick Studios contract in the summer of 1941, she spent eighteen months leading up to work on *Bernadette* in New York receiving voice, posture, and diction training as well as Group Theatre drama coaching. "Like a Tiffany jewel," said an insider on *Bernadette*'s set, describing the preferential treatment Jones received throughout production.

Retreating from Hollywood as rumors swirled about her tumultuous love affair with Selznick (whose fourteen-year marriage was acrimoniously unraveling), Jones avoided *Bernadette*'s December 27, 1943, Carthay Circle Theater Hollywood premiere. Following her Oscar nomination, she refused to participate in a campaign to help boost her victory chances. Red-carpet events, though now obligatory for an Oscar contender, terrified Jones. "It's about fucking time, she hasn't done a goddamn thing to publicize the movie!" Twentieth Century–Fox's William Goetz, *Bernadette*'s executive producer and Selznick's brother-in-law, exclaimed after Jones agreed to attend the film's February 25, 1944, premiere in Tulsa, Oklahoma, her hometown.[41] Confronted by a friendly *Tulsa Tribune* reporter, Jones clammed up. Beseeched by autograph seekers, she struggled to produce a legible signature. "I never could make a decent *J* and now I have to make two of them," she admitted.

To make Jones picture-perfect for Oscar night, Selznick lavished on her red carpet accoutrements—including a sable coat and diamond earrings by his friend Harry Winston. He also hired fashion stylist Anita Colby to help her find a dress. "Colby knew makeup, publicity pictures, clothes . . . and how to behave," noted Selznick's biographer David Thomson of the confident thirty-year-old. Colby, "The Face," was a former top fashion model whose image had fronted innumerable advertising campaigns and *Harper's Bazaar* covers in the thirties.[42] Selznick preferred her sharp-suited, Upper Manhattan–manicured blond beauty to what he called the "fan magazine glamour girl" standard Hollywood studios manufactured. Awarded the prestigious title "feminine director" of Selznick Studios in 1943, Colby received a yearly six-figure salary to coach Selznick's actress stable. Much of her work focused on Jones. "Because Jennifer was so insecure about clothes," claimed Joan Fontaine.[43]

For the sixteenth Academy Awards, Colby suggested Jones play it safe in a black taffeta cocktail dress dusted with a white ruffled collar, although selecting it was trying. "Jennifer, behave as if you are beautiful and you'll be beautiful," said Colby, reassuring her diffident charge during a ceremonial coaching session she conducted in her studio office. She showed Jones how to confidently meet the press.[44] "Just raise your

In sable, Harry Winston diamonds, and a sharp, black dress, Jennifer Jones, here with Henry Wilson, made a phalanx of photographers go wild outside Grauman's Chinese Theatre at the sixteenth Academy Awards in 1944. (Courtesy of the Academy of Motion Picture Arts and Sciences)

eyebrows . . . and say: 'Well, how have *you* been?'"[45] She taught her how to stride along the red carpet like a top model conquering a runway. "Don't run with your hands and folding your hips into the fetal position," explained Colby. "Be an actress—perform! Come in and *want* people to notice you."[46]

Colby considered the rigorous preparatory work necessary, given Jones's acute nervousness and the poor quality of war-era clothes tailored from man-made fibers. "If you don't have the kind of dame who can give a fourteen-dollar dress a hundred-dollar look," she concluded, "you have to do something drastic about it."[47]

The Sixteenth Academy Awards, March 2, 1944. In sable, Winston diamonds, and Colby's little black dress, Jennifer Jones made a phalanx of photographers go wild outside Grauman's Chinese Theatre, the Academy Awards' new venue on Hollywood Boulevard. "Photographers had a field day when Miss Jones arrived," confirmed Academy Awards historian Robert Osborne.[48] A studio publicist protected Jones from the chaotic throng. Fans heckled complaints about the poor view from bleacher seats erected outside Grauman's, while scenes of road rage played out on Hollywood Boulevard. The Academy's planning committee forgot about valet parking. So with no attendants to move along the limousines, cars backed up while chauffeurs unleashed their frustration on steering-wheel horns. Bergman stepped out of the racket and flashed photographers a winning smile. Instead of her oldest dress, she wore a black Persian-lamb coat, a recent Christmas gift from Selznick, and a white, ruffled blouse and black skirt—the two-piece she sported at the fifteenth ceremony. Before the sixteenth commenced, Selznick posed next to her with his hands stuffed into the front blazer pockets of his pinstripe suit.

Midway through the three-hour ceremony, it was impossible to predict who would claim the actress prize. First Greek actress Katina Paxinou, who played Pilar, Bergman's costar in *Bell*, was named supporting actress. Next, *Bernadette* collected three trophies—cinematography, art direction, and song. Then the cast and a crew of *Casablanca* claimed two major awards for screenplay and direction. To ease the stress spreading along his front row, Selznick cracked jokes. "Somebody did a great embalming job on Pickford," he muttered as silent legend Mary Pickford departed from the stage and made way for Greer Garson to present the actress prize.[49] As the room fell silent, Jones and Bergman fixed their gaze on the stage where Garson stood before a towering, twelve-foot golden Oscar. Jones bit her lip. Bergman sat upright. Then Garson opened the envelope and announced, "Jennifer Jones for *The Song of Bernadette*!" Shouts of "Bravo!" sent Jones bounding down the theater aisle and up a short flight of steps to the podium. "I am thrilled. I am grateful," she began. Then her voice quivered. She sobbed so uncontrollably that host Jack Benny escorted her backstage. Jones rested her head upon his shoulder. "I felt like a starving person sitting down unexpectedly to a sumptuous banquet with no warning—then all of a sudden—wham! I had success in my hands," she said, looking back on the moment.[50]

"Don't worry, you're going to win one, too," Selznick whispered into Bergman's ear. But she was inconsolable.[51] Rushing backstage to congratulate Jones, a *Photoplay* reporter spotted Bergman throwing a tantrum. "They promised me I would win!" she allegedly raged, and stamped her foot.[52] She was "jolted," confirmed publicist Joseph Steele.

Shouts of "Bravo!" sent Jennifer Jones bounding down the theater aisle and up to the podium, where she collected the sixteenth actress Academy Award (Courtesy of the Academy of Motion Picture Arts and Sciences). Later she smiled backstage. (Corbis)

"I am deeply grateful," said Ingrid Bergman as she accepted the seventeenth actress Oscar wearing the requisite war-era black semiformal attire: a dirndl skirt, billowy peasant blouse, and embroidered cummerbund by Los Angeles designer Howard Greer. (Courtesy of the Academy of Motion Picture Arts and Sciences)

A year later Bergman received the seventeenth actress Oscar for *Gaslight*. Critics believed her trophy was yet another consolation prize, making amends for her losing the Oscar to Jones. "I am deeply grateful," said Bergman, accepting her prize from Jones. She wore requisite black—a dirndl skirt, billowy peasant blouse, embroidered cummerbund, and ballet slippers. "Very simple," approved the journalist Frances Scully of the ensemble.[53] "A glorified peasant costume," winced Howard Greer, its designer, who matched his tailoring to Bergman's specifications.[54] "I'm not the 'chic' type—I may as well stick to clothes I feel well in," confessed Bergman at the start of their fitting sessions.[55]

A few months after Bergman's victory, World War II ended and the Academy lifted its semiformal dress code. The postwar era marked a return to lavish costume epics and the start of economic turbulence in Hollywood as television decimated box-office ticket sales. Another staggering setback was the U.S. government's forcing Hollywood's big five studios to sell their national movie-theater chains so as to break the monopoly those film corporations had long enjoyed over struggling independents. The popularity of Hollywood's costume designers—to whom most nominees turned for Oscar dresses through the tumultuous late forties—abated. Though Olivia de Havilland claimed her second Academy Award for *The Heiress* in 1949 in a pretty Orry-Kelly sequined, white organdy dress, there were signs of a sea change on her winning night. As she swept into the Pantages Theatre amid a fusillade of flashbulbs, the word PARIS was emblazoned in neon on a marquee high above. And in the French fashion capital, Hollywood's discerning soon found groundbreaking Oscar attire.

Amid a fusillade of flashbulbs, Academy Award winner Olivia de Havilland swept into the Pantages Theatre while a marquee hanging high above flashed PARIS, the French fashion capital, where Hollywood's discerning soon found groundbreaking Oscar couture. (Courtesy of the Academy of Motion Picture Arts and Sciences)

Chapter Five
APPLAUSE

Marlene Dietrich brought down the house at the twenty-third Academy Awards in 1951, effortlessly working its stage in a Christian Dior cocktail gown. "Airbrushed on," marveled film critic Alexander Walker, recalling the slink of Dietrich in her Oscar Dior.[1] The original piece of postwar haute couture specifically tailored for the Academy Awards, Dietrich's Dior Oscar dress was the first to steal headlines and one of countless commissions from Hollywood that allowed the newly revived French fashion industry to flourish in the fifties. Haute couture was the shape of things to come at the Oscars, as Audrey Hepburn soon demonstrated at the twenty-sixth Academy Awards, where her spontaneous moves in an original by Hubert de Givenchy got huge, good-natured laughs, exactly the ballyhoo needed as the ceremony went live on TV.[2]

Dietrich spent the lead-up to the twenty-third ceremony, at which she was set to present the foreign-language film prize, in her Park Avenue, Manhattan, apartment. Over a series of long-distance telephone calls with Dior, she thrashed out her Oscar dress. There was no need for face time or even a fitting. Dior understood Dietrich's needs. The movie star and the master couturier had worked side by side producing costumes for feature films, starting with *Stage Fright*, in which Dietrich portrayed Charlotte Inwood, a jaded London performer implicated in the murder of her manager/husband. Though not an Oscar contender, the 1950 Alfred Hitchcock murder mystery established Dietrich's close creative bond with Dior and resurrected her career after what had proved a fallow postwar period.

With peace declared after World War II, Dietrich had become the first woman to receive the United States Medal of Freedom (the highest

A "twentieth-century Venus," concluded Michael Wilding of Marlene Dietrich, whom he encountered on the set of Alfred Hitchcock's *Stage Fright* "draped" in Christian Dior haute couture. (Getty Images)

suffered no rivals for absolute authority on his productions," wrote biographer Donald Spoto, verifying Dietrich's victory.[10] Warner, however, demanded and received a twenty-five percent discount on the cost of Dietrich's *Stage Fright* Dior couture. In exchange, Dior insisted upon and clinched his first Hollywood screen credit. Dietrich kept Dior's *Stage Fright* couture wardrobe, and she contributed her considerable expertise to its design.

During her Paramount glory days Dietrich studied every aspect of filmmaking. To perfect her on-screen look, she devoted herself to costume design. Maria Riva spent her childhood observing her mother's sessions with Travis Banton. "Day in, day out, they worked," she wrote. "My mother never tired, had a bladder of astounding capacity, could fit for hours without moving a muscle, and as she was perpetually starving herself, such normal things as food, bathroom and rest did not exist while Dietrich prepared clothes for a film."[11] "I was amazed at her stamina and determination," continued Edith Head, recalling a thirty-six-hour session through which she worked alongside Dietrich as she selected a hat for a scene of the 1936 Paramount thriller *Desire*. "We sat up for hours trying on dozens of different hats," recounted Head, "changing them, tilting them, taking off this one and trying that one, snipping off a veil or a brim, switching ribbons and bows—finally we got what she wanted." While Dior diligently sketched during *Stage Fright*'s preproduction, Dietrich was by his side, selecting expensive textile swatches—gleaming satin, fur pelts, fluffy marabou, and feather-weight chiffon—and sending them on to London for Hitchcock's approval.

"Marlene Dietrich looks too good in the close-ups," Hedda Hopper reported in the *Los Angles Times* during *Stage Fright*'s production at London's Elstree Studios. Hopper was hinting at an on-set love affair between Dietrich and Michael Wilding, the thirty-seven-year-old British actor cast as police inspector Smith. "A twentieth-century Venus," concluded Wilding of Dietrich, whom he encountered on set "draped" in Dior white fox, defying her forty-nine years. Viewing *Stage Fright*'s rushes, Jane Wyman, who starred as RADA student Eve Gill, broke down comparing her college-girl screen garb to seductive Dietrich swathed in formfitting Dior. "She couldn't accept the idea of her face being in character while Dietrich looked so great," confirmed Hitch-cock.[12] Dietrich "walked off," with *Stage Fright*, wrote biographer Steven Bach, noting the positive reviews hailing her comeback after its February 1950 premiere.[13]

As the twenty-third Oscars rolled around in 1951, Dietrich and Dior's second joint effort, *No Highway*, an adaptation of Nevil Shute's aviation saga, was already in the can. "The clothes they conceived were so perfect, so utterly Dietrich, that throughout the film she looks as though she is doing a portrait sitting for *Vogue*," wrote Maria Riva.[14]

To aid Dior's design of a limelight-stealing Oscar dress, Dietrich conducted preliminary research from Manhattan. Contacting her "intel-ligence unit," as she collectively described her Hollywood allies, she extracted strategic information relating to the looks bound for the twenty-third Academy Awards.[15] "Springtime ball gowns," Dietrich explained to Dior of the ceremony's theme.[16] If hemlines were to hit the floor, Dior decided Dietrich's would halt just below the ankle, so as to optimally reveal her shapely "million-dollar" legs. "What about the colors?" he asked.[17] "Pale carnation pink, champagne, silver-blue, mauve, white, and pastels," continued Dietrich. Bugle beads and embroidered sequins were also set to shine at the annual glitter-fest. So Dior opted for subtle.

Next he inquired about the décor planned for the Pantages Theatre's stage set. "Red, white, and blue," confirmed Dietrich, of the color scheme selected to express the ceremony's patriotic theme. A giant Academy Award trophy flanked by a pair of Roman columns would also command center stage. "So Mama had better be slinky, nice, slinky," added Dietrich.[18] "Satin," responded Dior with finality. Dietrich agreed. But before Dior got the chance to suggest its optimum shade, she said, "Black," completing his sentence as close partners often do.

A sleeveless bolero jacket and saucy hip-swaggering side bow, both of black silk velvet, added subtle drama to the slim-fit, ankle-grazing satin cocktail dress Dior designed for Dietrich's Oscar moment. It probably took a few weeks for it to be executed, but no record of the design process remains in the couturier's Paris archive. Its finishing touch might have been applied at Dior's New York flagship, after Dietrich's dress rehearsal at the Pantages. Academy presenters, today, spend Oscar weekend in run-through sessions. At the time of Dietrich's appearance, practice for a presenter was rare and unnecessary because small film crews sporadically captured the ceremony, until 1953, when it went live on television. But Dietrich considered her every performance epic, and while she ensured that the stage lights best displayed her presence, Dior waited patiently to hear the angle from which she would access the stage. This vital information would reveal the optimum point where he would cut a vertical slit on the gown's skintight skirt. The incision allowed for a "'now you see it, now you don't' flash of calf as she moved," noted Alexander Walker.[19] Dior's pattern cutter applied the last-minute magic, after Dietrich relayed news that she would make her "entrée" from stage left.

The Twenty-third Academy Awards, March 29, 1951. By eight P.M. the Academy's audience of eighteen hundred notables were on their feet inside the Pantages Theatre. Front and center were political dignitaries, including California's Governor Warren; the mayor of Los Angeles; Mogens Skot-Hansen, the UN representative and documentary-film producer; and the best-picture presenter, UN delegate Dr. Ralph J. Bunche, the scholar, diplomat, and first African-American to receive the Nobel Peace Prize. Everyone stood silent as the Academy's symphony orchestra launched into "The Star-Spangled Banner." As the song wafted from speakers outside the Pantages, hundreds of fans rose from bleacher seats pitched up on Hollywood Boulevard. Parking attendants and valets with caps in hand were rendered motionless as the

A sleeveless bolero jacket and saucy hip-swaggering silk velvet side bow added subtle drama to Marlene Dietrich's slim-fit, ankle-grazing, satin Christian Dior cocktail dress at the twenty-third Academy Awards in 1951. (David Downton)

national anthem swelled to a crescendo. "The Oscars are something people yearn for, fight for, and cry for, and there is never an end to the competition until the tributes are finally won," stated Fred Astaire, the Academy's master of ceremonies, delivering the keynote speech.[20]

In the Pantages' wings, Dietrich abstained from the backstage catering laid on by the Hollywood Brown Derby coffee shop and removed herself, too, from a scrum of starlets and posse of Academy attendants fussing over twenty-five-year-old Marilyn Monroe, supporting cast member of *All About Eve*, the Joseph Mankiewicz black comedy sweeping away the Academy Awards. Monroe was set to present just before Dietrich. But she was in tears, having discovered a rip in her borrowed wardrobe-department black bouffant gown. "I can't go on!" insisted Monroe. In minutes her dress was mended. Then in a sulk she presented the Academy's sound-recording prize.

Charles Brackett, the Academy's president, welcomed Dietrich onstage to present the foreign-language film prize. He paused, delivering his regrets that the Academy bestowed no "medal for glamour." Dietrich, he said, "would have earned it." Propelling Dietrich from the Pantages' wings to its stage was her famous, confident, quickstep stride—otherwise known as the "Dietrich strut."[21] "A vision in black," confirmed a source that witnessed her entrance amidst a standing ovation. At the podium Dietrich bowed, acknowledging the audience's admiration. "She was moved," recalled a spectator.[22] Grasping the envelope from Price Waterhouse's attendant, Dietrich's platinum and ruby Cartier wrist cuff sparkled in the crystal glow of the stage lights. As she broke the envelope's seal, her diamond ring twinkled. *"Walls of Malapaga,"* said Dietrich, announcing the Oscar-winning foreign-language film, a drama directed by René Clement. "Which up to that moment nobody around here had ever heard of before," admitted *Los Angeles Times* reporter Philip Scheuer. But as Dietrich spread the word, Hollywood took note.[23]

A day later banner headlines celebrating Dietrich's Oscar moment matched those fêting the final take of six Academy Awards by *All About Eve*. GLAMOROUS MARLENE STEALS SPOTLIGHT! raved the *Hollywood Examiner*. "Dietrich's dress stole the show," confirmed Academy historian Robert Osborne.[24]

Stage Fright was the first of eight Hollywood film productions for which Dior provided costumes. In 1953 as he commenced work on his third, David O. Selznick's *Indiscretion of an American Wife*, advance news circulated about an Oscar nomination honoring Audrey Hepburn's portrayal in William Wyler's *Roman Holiday*. Hepburn mastered *Roman*

Edith Head, Paramount Pictures' chief costume designer, was a "grande dame," according to her friend Audrey Wilder. (Getty Images)

Holiday's lead role—Her Royal Highness Princess Ann—an adventurous European monarch who goes temporarily AWOL with dashing Joe Bradley, an expatriate journalist played by Gregory Peck.[25] "We even began to talk off-camera about the chance that she might win an Academy Award," said Peck, recalling the film's location shoot in Rome over the summer of 1952.

By March 1953, Paramount Pictures had acquired the rights to adapt *Sabrina Fair*, Samuel Taylor's hit Broadway stage play, as Hepburn's next megaproject. A romantic comedy, *Sabrina*, as it was retitled for the screen, recounted the travails of Hepburn as its lead character, Sabrina Fairchild, the daughter of Thomas Fairchild, chauffeur to New York tycoon Oliver Larrabee. After she is packed off to a Paris cooking school where she flops soufflés, Sabrina meets an aging baron. His etiquette coaching refines her, and when she returns as a sophisticate to the Larrabee compound on Long Island's salubrious South Shore, Larabee's two sons, playboy David and business mogul Linus, fight to win her heart.

Billy Wilder, *Sabrina*'s director/producer, rounded out a first-rate cast and crew for *Sabrina*, recruiting Oscar winners William Holden and Humphrey Bogart to play David and Linus Larrabee, respectively. Edith Head was set to costume the production. "It was the perfect setup," she recalled. "Three wonderful stars and my leading lady looking like a Paris mannequin."

Belgian-born Hepburn was long and lean, just like the ivory holder from which she puffed Gold Flakes, her preferred brand of cigarette. She radiated a potent, kittenish sex appeal that relied on her natural attributes, including wide hazel eyes and a playful singsong saturating her poised speech pattern—a result of her continental upbringing. Her regal bearing (from classical ballet training by the legendary choreographer Marie Rambert), physique, and polished charm were unique to fifties Hollywood, where studios scrambled to lure back to the movies fans who'd rather watch TV. As an overabundance of vehicles were churned out for pinups Marilyn Monroe, Betty Grable, and Jane Russell, and the charm of such sweater girls wore thin, lacing the air was Oscar talk about the Euro beanpole who, since landing a seven-year contract with Paramount in 1953, eschewed the limousine service shuttling megastars from their dressing rooms to film sets. Instead Hepburn padded around the Paramount lot in ballet slippers or peddled a bike Wilder gave her during preproduction on *Sabrina*. "Flat-chested, slim hipped and altogether un–Marilyn Monroe–ish," reported *Life* of her unorthodox appeal. "Her measurements are: bust, 32"; waist, 20½"; hips, 34". Nothing sensational there, is there? And yet, Hollywood standards or no, Audrey Hepburn is the most phenomenal thing that's happened to the film capital since Marilyn Monroe!" "What impressed me was her body," added Head. "I knew she would be the perfect mannequin for anything I would make."[26]

Head designed the breathtaking brocade imperial-court gowns Hepburn wore in *Roman Holiday* as well as a striking pedestrian ensemble in which, as Princess Ann, she tours Rome with Peck's Joe Bradley. For a time, Hepburn wore Head's designs offscreen, too. "I've come to know Edith Head and we've worked out a few little numbers," she revealed to *Photoplay*'s Pauline Swanson.[27] No longer viewed with disdain by Paramount's leading ladies, Head was a bespectacled "grande dame," as Audrey Wilder, Billy Wilder's wife, called the costumer, who controlled the studio's wardrobe department from the "big, beautiful, superelegant," office she had inherited from Travis Banton.[28] It was painted dove gray, just like Christian Dior's Avenue Montaigne atelier, enhanced by perky draperies printed with California wildflowers and floor-to-ceiling mirrors. French Provençal bric-a-brac was scattered throughout the space, while a shelf behind Head's antique desk displayed confirmation of her expertise—a quartet of gleaming Oscar trophies she claimed from 1950, a year after the Academy introduced two new categories honoring the contribution of costume designers to both color and black-and-white motion pictures. "It was paradise on earth—not unlike anything I've seen in legendary ateliers in Paris or Rome," costumer Donfeld remembered of Head's expansive setup.

During preproduction on *Sabrina*, Head traveled to San Francisco, where Hepburn was completing the smash-hit cross-country tour starring in *Gigi*, the coming-of-age tale based on the best seller by French novelist Colette. "I took with me pages and pages of 'little Audreys'— the Hepburn face and figure in miniature—on which Audrey could doodle dresses," she recounted. "We worked as a team on the *Sabrina* clothes."[29]

Hepburn adored fashion and between takes on film sets devoured glossy European magazines. She appeared in *Monte Carlo Baby*, a 1951 French comedy, because its producer allowed her to keep the strapless, lace Christian Dior ball gown she wore performing a walk-on part. "That was reason number one," she admitted. "Like Dietrich, Audrey's fittings became the ten-hour not the ten-minute variety," recalled Head. "She was never arrogant or demanding. She had an adorable sweetness that made you feel like a mother getting her only daughter ready for her first prom."

But after viewing Head's *Sabrina* sketches, Hepburn went above Head, suggesting to Billy Wilder that Paramount could "commission a genuine French couturier" to provide the wardrobe her character wears upon returning from Paris.[30] "To make the metamorphosis evident," she reasoned.[31] *"Bien sûr!"* responded Wilder, who fired off a memo to studio executives requesting permission to acquire a "particularly *Frenchy* suit" for Hepburn and some "extreme French hats."[32] Hepburn was thrilled to learn that to curb the expense of paying custom duties, she would embark on a solo Paris shopping mission and personally select couture for *Sabrina* at the Paris *maison* Hubert de Givenchy, operated from a Gothic mansion on rue Alfred Vigny. Head was "furious" and according to Hepburn's biographer Diana Maychick "almost quit" *Sabrina* when she discovered from Billy Wilder and Hepburn that her task was to complete the backdrop of *Sabrina*—a wardrobe for Holden, Bogart, the rest of *Sabrina*'s cast, but only two ensembles Hepburn sports as a teenage Sabrina in its opening scenes.[33] "The director broke my heart," wrote Head, recalling the episode in her memoir.

The "costume crisis" was later classified as a classic case of an actress pulling rank.[34] "Hepburn realized she was a star and wanted more say about what she wore," noted Paddy Calistro in *Edith Head's Hollywood*.[35] But Wilder claimed that *Sabrina*'s script motivated Hepburn. "She knew the character," he insisted. "You can't fake it," Hepburn often said, citing wisdom William Wyler shared with her on the set of *Roman Holiday*.[36] Audrey Wilder, it is said, bent her husband's ear about Givenchy. The attractive brunette and former Paramount actress embarked upon "legendary shopping trips to the Parisian couture houses," noted Ed Sikov in *On Sunset Boulevard: The Life and Times of Billy Wilder*. Audrey Wilder, "one of the few Hollywood women to whom other Hollywood women turned when they wanted a living definition of the word 'chic,'" wrote Sikov, "discovered Givenchy during one of her Paris shopping sprees."[37]

In February 1952, Givenchy, a former assistant to Elsa Schiaparelli, presented his debut collection of breezy couture made entirely of white percale. The crisp, slim-fit, lightweight separates introduced a modern sportswear's ease to the formerly rigid haute couture

The fit-and-flare silhouette of Audrey Hepburn's white Givenchy Oscar frock followed the figure-flattering line of the black cocktail dress she modeled in *Sabrina*. (David Downton)

realm and interpreted the concepts of freedom expounded by philosophers then inhabiting the bohemian Saint-Germain-des-Prés cafés he frequented. Fashion editors hailed his inventive spirit, delivering the "biggest ovation" witnessed since the debut of Dior's New Look.[38]

"*Mademoiselle?*" Givenchy's doorman politely inquired when Hepburn turned up on the couturier's threshold on a June afternoon in 1953. Unaware that Paramount money burned a hole in the pocket of Hepburn's well-worn ped pushers, he mistook her for a tourist. *Roman Holiday*'s London premiere was a month away, and though Hollywood tipped Hepburn to win an Oscar, she was totally unknown in Paris. But she piped up and announced, "I'm here to see Monsieur Givenchy."

Ushered inside the *maison*, she brushed past the Casablanca lilies perfuming its foyer and took two steps at a time ascending the curvaceous marble staircase leading to Givenchy's office. Mannerly, aristocratic, and handsome, Givenchy had just returned from a jaunt to Ravello, where, with *Harper Bazaar*'s Carmel Snow, he'd visited director John Huston on the set of *Beat the Devil* and pitched in tweaking the costumes Gina Lollobrigida and Jennifer Jones wore in the slapstick comedy. He disguised his disappointment at meeting "Miss Audrey Hepburn." Gladys de Segonzac, the wife of Paramount's French production head, had arranged Givenchy's meeting with "Miss Hepburn," and he was awaiting the MGM legend Katharine Hepburn, not Paramount's star ingénue. Politely he cut short discussing *Sabrina*. "I told her the truth: I was in the midst of putting together my next collection and didn't have the time to spend with her," he recalled.[39] "Please, please, please—there must be something I can try on," insisted Hepburn. So he acquiesced, suggesting she "could choose anything she liked from my current collection."

Givenchy escorted Hepburn to a clothing rack erected inside his salon. Dreda Mele, his *directrice*, stood by. But Hepburn required no assistance. "She knew exactly what she wanted," recalled Givenchy. Hepburn quickly seized ensembles for three *Sabrina* scenes, lunged behind a screen to change, and emerging, delivered a knockout performance. A suit of pencil-gray flannel floated upon a pirouetting Hepburn as though it were made from tulle. Its glove fit confounded Givenchy. He'd cut the skirt and jacket so small that "only one model in Paris could get into it," noted the costume expert David Chierichetti.[40] "Something magic happened," confirmed the couturier. "The way she moved in the suit, she was so happy. She gave life to the clothes—she had a way of installing herself in them. The suit just adapted to her."[41]

Next Hepburn put on a strapless, white organdy ball gown. "[It] gave her a very flattering line," admitted Givenchy.[42] A cocktail dress of ribbed, black piqué cotton effortlessly adapted to her, too. Fitted at the waist, its skirt flared. Bows at each shoulder disguised fasteners, while buttons descended down its plunging V-back. The slash across its neckline followed the horizontal shape of a traditional Breton sailor's shirt collar and was then aptly referred to as a boat neck or *décolleté bateau*. "Audrey loved this neckline because it disguised her skinny collarbone but emphasized her very good shoulders," confirmed Givenchy.[43] And so it became known as décolleté Sabrina, while Givenchy's little black dress became an indispensable staple after the smash-hit September 1954 premiere of *Sabrina*.

Before Hepburn returned to Hollywood, it was up to Billy Wilder to approve Givenchy's couture. He questioned the necessity of the black, $560 Givenchy frock. Edith Head told Wilder to avoid "dead black." Hepburn persisted and left Paris with the three outfits she'd modeled for Givenchy. Actor Mel Ferrer, Hepburn's fiancé, presented her fourth piece as a gift after she received an Oscar nomination for *Roman Holiday*. Made of crisp white organdy, the cocktail frock was quintessentially Givenchy. Its fit-and-flare silhouette followed the figure-flattering line of the black cocktail dress Hepburn had acquired for *Sabrina*.

On Oscar night, Hepburn and Ferrer were at work at New York's Forty-ninth Street Theater costarring in *Ondine*, the Jean Giraudoux stage play based on a German fairy tale. Because so many Oscar nominees performed on Broadway, the Academy staged two ceremonies, at New York's NBC Century Theater and in Hollywood at the Pantages. *Ondine*'s curtain call came midway through the ceremonies. So after Hepburn and Ferrer took their bows, together they dashed out the stage door and climbed into a Rolls-Royce that sped uptown toward the Century. Hepburn's swingy Givenchy tent coat concealed her risqué *Ondine* costume Manhattan's Valentina had designed under her watchful eye. Hepburn "immersed herself totally in the minutest details" of the mesh bodysuit she wore playing a water sprite. According to Alexander Walker, the flimsy costume "gave the impression that Audrey was naked except for a few strategically positioned wisps of seaweed."[44]

The Twenty-sixth Academy Awards, March 25, 1954. "Hepburn's coming!" went up a cry from a rowdy paparazzi pack that shifted from the lobby at the Century outside onto the pavement as the Rolls ferrying Hepburn and Mel Ferrer pulled up. Shadowing Hepburn for the night was *Life* photographer Leonard McCombe. He followed her out from the limo, kept close backstage, and clicked his shutter in Hepburn's dressing room as a groomer removed *Ondine*'s stage makeup. When the time came for Hepburn to slip into Givenchy, the space was off-limits. Was she nervous? Absolutely. "I thought it was a joke," she said of her Oscar nomination.

Inside New York's Century Theater, Oscar contender Audrey Hepburn nervously chewed her nails as she waited to hear the result of the Academy's twenty-sixth actress race. (Leonard McCombe/Time & Life Pictures)

An hour and thirty-five minutes into the Pantages' ceremony, the audience stifled laughter as a costume fashion show commenced and an Audrey Hepburn look-alike, starlet Marla English, nearly toppled over in Princess Ann's *Roman Holiday* brocade court gown. As sleek Gene Tierney passed Edith Head the costume-design prize for *Roman Holiday*, Hepburn remained inside her dressing room fastening on good-luck charms—the diamond and pearl earrings she wore as Princess Ann. "Hey, skinny, come on out!" bawled McCombe, banging on the door of her dressing room.[45]

Ferrer led Hepburn inside the dark auditorium. Cutting through its sea of black tie and a fog of chinchilla, Hepburn attempted to tiptoe quietly to her seat. But moving down the aisle, she was greeted by appreciative smiles. "Everybody's rooting for you," whispered Ferrer.[46] Next to her mother, Ella van Heemstra, just in from London, Hepburn nervously chewed her nails and hardly noticed as Frank Sinatra won the supporting actor Oscar for his role as Private Angelo Maggio in *From Here to Eternity*. As the Pantages' emcee, actor Donald O'Connor, arrived at the podium to present the actress prize, it was as if a bolt of lightning struck Hepburn. She sat up dead straight. O'Connor opened the envelope and declared, "The best film actress of 1953 is Audrey Hepburn for her performance in *Roman Holiday*!"

An astounded Hepburn remained seated and shielded her beautiful face with her hands. "I was so surprised when they called my name, I didn't know what to do," she said later. Mel Ferrer kissed his girlfriend's cheek and said, "There you are!"[47]

Jumping up, Hepburn made a swift dash for the podium. Onstage awaited the Century's emcee, Fredric March, but for much longer than he expected. The deafening applause so unnerved Hepburn that, racing down the aisle, instead of ascending the stage steps, she made a wrong turn, landing in the Century's upper box seats. The audience burst out laughing as the cameras captured the winner clowning around and cracking a comic frown. "Very effective and greatly appreciated," recalled spectator David Niven of the moment, which made great TV for the forty-three million watching the Oscars.[48]

"It's too much," said Hepburn, catching her breath at the podium. "I want to say thank you to everybody who through these past months and years has helped, guided, and given me so much. I'm truly, truly grateful and terribly happy."[49] Then she dashed into the wings and, besieged by reporters and photographers, disappeared backstage. Somewhere, between the podium and the pressroom, Hepburn misplaced her Academy Award. But it turned up later that night in the Century Theater's ladies' room.

The twenty-sixth Academy Awards was the first time Hepburn was seen in Givenchy. For the rest of her life, he remained her image maker. By 1956, a clause in Hepburn's contract stipulated that the couturier would produce wardrobes for her movies with a contemporary setting. Subsequently Hepburn and Givenchy collaborated on six hit films. She always wore Givenchy to the Oscars. "I felt so good in his clothes," reasoned Hepburn. "She remained—absolutely, unbelievably loyal to me," confirmed Givenchy. "They were made for each other," concluded Givenchy's diretrice, Dreda Mele.

Chapter Six
THE WOMEN

Heady opulence typically hails the end of a grand era, and so it was in Hollywood on Oscar night as the studio system declined and eventually capitulated over thirteen years from 1955. Through the turbulent times, nominees Grace Kelly, Elizabeth Taylor, Julie Andrews, and Faye Dunaway opted for Oscar gowns masterminded by female Hollywood studio costume designers. The handiwork Hollywood's designing women masterminded for this quartet of contenders pushed Academy Awards glamour to an unprecedented zenith and defined the meaning of dressing up for the affair by capturing their idiosyncratic style as well as the spirit of box-office hits impelling them to Oscar greatness.

Kelly, Taylor, Andrews, and Dunaway each possessed radically different fashion philosophies. Separating them, too, was a revolutionary time that produced seismic social change heralded by political upheaval, scientific discovery, space travel, and sexual liberation, as well as the ascendance of rock music, pop art, and television. While TV predominated as the number one form of entertainment, the studio system crumbled. By the midfifties, movies were rarely shot entirely on the back lot of Hollywood's studios, and the nominees who experienced the nadir of the studio system each discovered during costume fittings and between takes a wardrobe expert who not only knew their measurements and how best to manipulate their physical curves, but one who was also a friend and trusted confidante, prepared to go beyond the call of duty when it came time to dress them for the Academy Awards.

By February 1955, as the Academy released its list of contenders competing in the twenty-seventh actress Oscar race, Grace Kelly was an instant front-runner thanks to her assured performance as Georgie Elgin, a rurally raised, subservient wife of an alcoholic actor in the Paramount Pictures' adaptation of *The Country Girl*, Clifford Odets's stage drama. Competing with Kelly were former actress Oscar winners Audrey Hepburn and Jane Wyman, while Dorothy Dandridge ranked as the first African-American to qualify for a chance at the prize. Kelly's main challenger was Judy Garland, for her role as big-band singer Esther Blodgett in *A Star Is Born*, George Cukor's tour-de-force remake of William Wellman's 1937 classic on the perils of Hollywood fame. According to the Associated Press, Garland was "virtually a lead-pipe cinch" to win the actress Oscar.[1]

But Kelly's portrayal of Georgie Elgin was considered the finest yet delivered by the twenty-five-year-old MGM star, and one that displayed an entirely new range of her dramatic abilities. Prior to her nomination she was known as a Hitchcock blonde. She had played a series of ice-cool society girls in *Dial M for Murder, Rear Window*, and *To Catch a Thief*—a trilogy of stylish thrillers the director made over one year from 1953. But Kelly exchanged Hitchcock's au courant Paris couture-inspired wardrobes for drab skirts and blouses, an old cardigan, and a thick pair of horn-rimmed spectacles necessary to play *The Country Girl*, reasoning, "There was a real acting part in it for me."[2] Her professional conduct and effortless transition from Hitchcock's sophisticate to domestic victim was so admired on the set of *The Country Girl* that on its final shooting day the crew presented her with a commemorative plaque. "To our Country Girl," read its inscription, "this will hold you until you get next year's Academy Award."[3]

Months later, Paramount's top brass splurged so as to make memorable Kelly's moment at the ceremony.[4] Director Cecil B. DeMille, the studio's cofounder, enlisted his chauffeur to motor her to the Pantages Theatre. Joining Kelly in the backseat of DeMille's Rolls would be Don Hartman, Paramount's head of production. As for her Oscar night attire, she settled on a road-tested Paramount classic—a cloak and slim, floor-length column suspended from spaghetti straps, which Paramount's Edith Head had originally made from a costly bolt of aquamarine French duchesse satin for Kelly's apperance at *The Country Girl*'s January 1954 New York Criterion Theatre premiere.

Head's Oscar dress epitomized the contender's glacial glamour. It was also the sartorial pinnacle of a harmonious, two-year relationship she'd forged with Kelly. By the time Head made the premiere satin

Kelly wore to the Oscars, her fifth Academy Award, for *Roman Holiday*, sat atop her office shelf. The unrivaled collection of trophies symbolized Head's prestige as Hollywood's uncontested style leader. Delegating most of the design work for Paramount's costumes to her staff of fifty, Head pursued innumerable ventures, including a gig as the Academy's official fashion consultant, a post she reverently described as "governor of hemlines and bodices" and occupied for a consistent stretch of sixteen years from 1953, ensuring that nominees, presenters, and performers were respectably clad before they faced Oscar night's TV cameras. On daytime TV she hosted a regular spot delivering dress advice to the eight million women who watched *House Party*, Art Linkletter's CBS afternoon show. She produced a teenage fashion line inspired by costumes from Paramount's box-office toppers that became best sellers at department stores nationwide. Head also made house calls, visiting the estates of Barbara Stanwyck and Loretta Young, where she conducted "clothes clinics" during which she patiently styled their *"entire"* personal wardrobes. Back at Paramount she played den mother to A-list stars like Kelly, who regularly dropped by her office, familiarly known to leading ladies at Paramount as Edie's Room.[5]

Kelly and her "dear Edith" worked together on *The Bridges at Toko-Ri* before *The Country Girl*. William Perlberg and George Seaton, the sharp Paramount producer-writer/director team, made both dramas, and though Kelly's actress Oscar nomination for *The Country Girl* came as a result of their tutelage, neither film project, claimed Head, was a "costume picture" that afforded her the opportunity to bond with the actress she instantly considered her "favorite."[6] Head and Kelly got acquainted during the making of Hitchcock's *Rear Window* and became firm friends in May 1954. At Hermès, the luxury goods Paris boutique at 24 rue du Faubourg Saint-Honoré, Hitchcock permitted the pair to acquire accessories for Kelly's star turn as Frances Stevens, the oil heiress vacationing in Cannes at the Hotel Carlton in *To Catch a Thief*. "People dress here," explained Hitchcock to Head of the film's ritzy, Côte d'Azur location. "It's the place where style is created. So do it." And at some point as Kelly peeled off her trademark white cloth gloves, slipped in and out of the butter-soft suede models and hand-embroidered leathers offered up to her on a silver tray at Hermès, Head discovered a new model-perfect actress muse—a suitable replacement for Audrey Hepburn, whom she lost to Hubert de Givenchy in the summer of 1953. "Like two girls in an ice cream shop we fell in love with everything we saw," recalled Head of that fateful spring afternoon she and Kelly whiled away at Hermès, marveling over gloves, handbags, silk print scarves, and expensive porcelain knickknacks. "Grace got more and more excited—she had this rather charming, childish exuberance about her when it came to shopping. Grace was tops."[7]

"Grace Kelly and I were her pets," confirmed Arlene Dahl, the Paramount actress, describing their relationship with Head.[8] "Edith taught us everything from the bottom up, from the inside out, how to stand and how to hold the train of a dress."[9] And though Kelly was confident and poised (not to mention financially secure, due to an endowment bequeathed to her at age twenty-one by Jack Kelly, her wealthy Philadelphia businessman father), she "hated" Hollywood and distanced herself from its prying gossip columnists by commuting to work there from an apartment on New York's Upper East Side. She refused to release to the press the measurements of her model-perfect figure and, during an arranged interview, frankly told one inquiring reporter, "I don't think it's anybody's business what I wear to bed."[10]

Kelly's antipathy toward Hollywood's media stemmed from frequent reports of the passionate love affairs she conducted with the leading men on most every film she made—a roll call that included Gary Cooper, Clark Gable, Ray Milland, Bing Crosby, and William Holden. But Kelly was, in fact, more of a girl's girl than a "nymphomaniac," as Hedda Hopper described her to Crosby.[11]

At work in Hollywood, she kept close by her a cadre of female friends, including Rita Gam, the actress with whom she shared a rented one-bedroom North Hollywood apartment; Virginia D'Arcy, the noted MGM hairstylist; and Head, whom she monopolized during lunch, the only break during the costume designer's fifteen-hour day at Paramount. Kelly often appeared unannounced at her office for late-night soul-searching sessions during which she let off career-related steam and cooled her heels doing laps in the swimming pool at Casa Ladera—or "House on the Slope" as was known the hacienda set within five acres at 1700 Coldwater Canyon, Beverly Hills, that Head shared with Hollywood art director Bill Wiard Ihnen, her husband. Head, wrote Sarah Bradford, Kelly's biographer, was part of a "discreet, loyal personal bodyguard, which Kelly developed around herself," as a coping mechanism while she experienced the highs and lows of Hollywood fame, including the controversy that followed her Oscar nomination.[12]

Kelly's accolade was a triumph—the "climax of a long period of harried expectation and excitement," wrote biographer Steven Englund—but she achieved it while facing adversity at MGM, her studio.[13] She clinched *The Country Girl* by chance, after the advancing pregnancy of Jennifer Jones, its original star, made it impossible for her to commit to the project. William Perlberg offered Kelly the part she recognized as a "once in a lifetime" career opportunity, but she soon discovered that Dore Schary, her boss, who'd succeeded Louis B. Mayer as MGM's production head in 1948, promptly turned down Paramount's request for her services. Schary had signed Kelly to a long-term MGM contract in 1952. He considered her "stunning" in her first major role as Amy Kane in *High Noon*, Fred Zinnemann's 1951 Academy Award–winning western, but his interest soon dwindled.

MGM, the once leading Big Five Hollywood studio that produced Oscar-winning musicals such as *An American in Paris*, *Show Boat*, and *Singin' in the Rain*, was no longer a "great machine," observed studio expert Thomas Schatz.[14] Kelly regretted signing her MGM contract and regarded as antiquated the studio's methods of star grooming and the willful submission of its contract stars to executive whims. By early winter 1954, when she commissioned Edith Head to make her *Country Girl* premiere satin that did double duty at the Oscars, Kelly had retreated to the East Coast to reconsider her career. *The Country Girl* was the fourth in a series of five films in which she starred that were released in 1954, a twelve-month stretch *Life* magazine heralded as the "year of Grace."[15] By October *Vogue* declared she possessed "the quality that may be a new standard for queens of the silver screen—quality."[16]

Kelly considered inferior a series of three action-adventure scripts sent to her for consideration by MGM. She rejected each script and was looking for work on the Broadway stage, dividing her spare time between Manhattan and her family's Ravenhill mansion, from where she wired Head requesting the ensemble for *The Country Girl*'s premiere. Head spent four thousand dollars acquiring its French satin, an astronomical sum considering Kelly was not a Paramount contract star, and made the ensemble on a cotton torso built to replicate the exact measurements of her muse. The creation was both exquisite and commemorative. Like a fond picture postcard, the cloak and dress recalled the fun they had had in Paris prepping *To Catch a Thief*. Its light aquamarine satin dusted with mother-of-pearl beads matched the color of Kelly's eyes. It was also the sort of delicate shade Hitchcock felt best suited his ideal blonde and evoked the spirit he requested Head capture in Kelly's *Rear Window* wardrobe. "Make her look like a princess," Hitchcock told Head,[17] "a piece of Dresden china."[18]

That Kelly settled on Head's premiere-wear to be her Academy

Awards night look was testament to the costumer's skill but also a force of circumstance. Three weeks before the twenty-seventh Academy Awards, Kelly discovered that MGM's wardrobe department—which customarily produced dresses for studio actress-Oscar nominees—was off-limits to her. Paramount's golden country girl was by now considered an "outlaw" by MGM—a persona non grata on the studio's lot. She had been suspended from its payroll for passing up the chance to appear in *Something of Value* and *Jeremy Rodock*, properties considered "top-notch" by Dore Schary. Declining his offers brought the total of MGM projects Kelly had rejected within a year to five—much to MGM's embarrassment. "MGM announcements of Grace Kelly's next movie appeared regularly in Hollywood's trade papers only to be retracted when the star, whom the studio had not consulted before-hand, refused to make the picture," observed Kelly's biographer James Spada.[19]

Dore Schary believed Kelly's latest refusals "smacked of simple insubordination" and withheld her salary, a hostile gesture that usually forced cash-strapped actors to accept studio demands and return to work.[20] Not Kelly. The trust-fund twentysomething retreated to the comfort of a new Manhattan luxury zone, a sweeping Upper East Side apartment she'd purchased just prior to her suspension. From there she delivered a statement to the press. Disguising her feelings of distress, she said, "I'm afraid I'll have to stop decorating my new apartment for the present."[21] The remark, added Spada, "galled MGM bigwigs" because it was "hardly a hardship compelling enough to force Grace into acquiescing to her studio's demands."[22]

As the Academy Awards approached, Kelly remained the presumed Oscar winner and maintained a dignified silence in "ladylike seclusion," reported *Life*, while MGM appeared to be guilty of exerting highly aggressive employment tactics—or of "playing the part of heavy," as Steven Englund observed.[23] All the while, MGM executives scurried in and out of crisis meetings wondering what to do about their absentee Oscar nominee. "MGM didn't relish the embarrassment of having that year's Oscar winner on suspension from the studio," noted Spada of the decision made by a studio committee nine days before the ceremony to lift Kelly's suspension and reinstate her salary.[24] It was a coup for the actress, but in the week leading up to the Oscars it seemed as if it might be her sole conquest. Just as Edith Head rushed Kelly's handmade champagne blue ceremonial evening slippers to a downtown L.A. leather expert—having discovered they were "too small and had to be stretched"—*A Star Is Born*'s Judy Garland emerged as a leading contender for the twenty-seventh actress Oscar.[25]

An eleventh-hour crisis boosted her chances. Forty-eight hours before the Oscars, Garland was rushed to Beverly Hills' Cedars of Lebanon Hospital, where she delivered by emergency cesarean section Joseph Wiley Luft, her third child. Born a month premature, a Cedars' obstetrician estimated the infant's likelihood of survival as "fifty-fifty" and placed him in an incubator.[26] A day later, Garland was "weak and exhausted." But she and Sid Luft, her husband/manager, allowed an NBC crew to set up in her hospital room and film her if she won the actress Oscar. The sentimental moment would add to an Academy Awards spectacular the network produced at the cost of five hundred thousand dollars—the highest budget yet devoted to the three-year-old telecast.[27] "If she won, Lauren Bacall [Garland's close friend] would run up onstage to accept the Oscar, the circuits would open up between the Pantages and the hospital, and Judy and Bob Hope would banter with each other and she would make her little acceptance speech," wrote Gerold Frank, Garland's biographer, outlining NBC's game plan.[28]

"We were praying for her—it was the peak of her career and she knew it was then or never," wrote Bacall of the moral support offered to Garland by close friends including Humphrey Bogart—Bacall's husband—Frank Sinatra, and columnist Sheilah Graham.[29]

On Oscar morning Bacall visited Garland at Cedars and discovered a media circus: "Men were hanging outside her window, placing cables, lights, God knows what."[30] Sid Luft, preparing for his wife's imminent victory, set up at the foot of her hospital bed a cocktail bar to rival Chasen's, stocking it with king prawns and beluga caviar. While NBC technicians tramped through the maternity ward, outside Garland's window a construction crew swung hammers and wielded heavy equipment, as the contender recalled, "I was lying in bed and three men came [in] with three huge television sets and I said, 'What's this for?' and they said, 'When you win the Academy Award, you've got to be able to talk back and forth to Bob Hope.' And I said, 'You can't just bring a whole crew and lights and all that stuff in here; there are other women in here having babies,' and they said, 'Don't worry about that,' and they pulled up the Venetian blind and they had built a four-story-high tower outside the hospital for the camera to point into my room."[31]

Beverly Hills sleepwear—a new peignoir and feathery bed jacket—replaced a black velvet maternity Oscar dress costume designer Michael Woulfe originally made Garland. As a grooming team prepped her for the imminent on-camera spot, she motioned NBC's crew to two big buckets filled with chilled champagne, asking, "Boys, wouldn't you like a drink?"[32] And though the boys refused Garland's offer, she ordered in coffee and sandwiches. Smiling during run-throughs, she moved from left to right across her hospital bed, although her cesarean stitches were still fresh. Then NBC detected sound trouble. "So they strung wires all over the room and put a microphone under my nightgown and taped it to my chest," she added.[33] Garland grew hopeful as Oscar afternoon turned to evening and NBC's crew continued rehearsals. "They got me all worked up," she admitted. "I was positive I was going to win."[34] But due east of Cedars on Hollywood Boulevard a high-octane scene unfolded, as C. B. DeMille's Rolls-Royce pulled up outside the Pantages and from it Grace Kelly emerged in ice blue satin with her Paramount entourage, including Edith Head, her date for the Oscars.

The Twenty-seventh Academy Awards, March 30, 1955. "This is Oscar night!" roared NBC's announcer as the third annual telecast went live across the nation's airwaves. "Celebrities arrived in dress even more glamorous than usual," confirmed *Life*.[35] Actor presenter Bette Davis paraded in a gold lamé and black velvet, off-the-shoulder Oscar dress by Charles Le Maire, the costume designer with whom she then worked on *The Virgin Queen*, a biopic of Elizabeth I. Davis had shaved her head to portray Elizabeth, so Le Maire made her a golden turban, too. "A sort of jeweled space helmet," a gobsmacked *New York World Telegram* reporter wrote, describing the curious headgear.[36] Supporting-actress nominee Katy Jurado marched past the press in a red Christian Dior gown adorned at its plunging neckline with a row of silk roses. "The bra and the panties that came with it are flame-colored, too" she revealed.[37] But Kelly drew "the biggest fusillade of flashbulbs of the night," wrote her biographer Robert Lacey.[38] "I was longing to win and wanted to so badly," she confessed.[39] But according to a reporter, Kelly "looked cool" and before a pack of paparazzi aptly played the country girl. Halting before an urn of yellow roses, set up inside the Pantages' imposing neo-medieval foyer, she dipped her white opera gloves deep into the mountain of flowers, plucked two buds, and tucked them neatly into her chignon. Turning on the heel of her satin evening slippers, Kelly made way for the auditorium, leaving Head to face the reporters. "Some people need sequins—others don't," said Head, and followed on.[40]

Inside Garland's hospital room, Leonard Gershe, her friend and contributing lyricist to *A Star Is Born*, arrived to watch the Oscars. Jovial Bob Hope kicked off the ceremony's telecast and it flew by due to the Academy's decision to announce only the name of each category winner, rather than the usual roll call of five nominees. *On the Waterfront*, Elia Kazan's romantic drama, was midway through its sweep of eight Oscar trophies just as a message from Oldsmobile, the telecast's sponsor, gave way to a Hope gag introducing actress presenter William Holden. "To present the award for best actress, the fellow from Paramount to whom I give all the parts I turn down," joked Hope, "last year's award winner Bill Holden."

Hope and Holden's playful banter increased the anxiety of Kelly and Garland. "Flat on my back trying to look cute—I was ready to give a performance," recalled Garland of the moment. "Hold me down if it isn't my name," whispered Kelly to Don Hartman.[41] Onstage, Holden maximized the tension by laconically checking his wristwatch. "Well, time is running short," he proceeded drolly. "So, the award for the best performance by an actress." He paused to open the envelope, then announced smoothly, "Grace Kelly for *The Country Girl*."

"*Whaatt??*" went Garland. Her anguished cry echoed from her hospital room down through Cedars' maternity-ward corridor.[42] "Are you sure? Are you sure?" Kelly asked Don Hartman, and as he confirmed the prize was, indeed, hers to keep, she swished up to the Pantages' podium in Head's champagne blue satin. The crowd cried, "Bravo! Bravo!" At the podium, Kelly calmly faced the Academy's audience and exhaled one line into the microphone: "The thrill of this moment prevents me from saying exactly what I feel."[43] She looked down and then out to the audience, adding, "I can only say thank you, with all my heart, to all who made this possible for me. Thank you." The three TV sets at the foot of Garland's bed captured Kelly floating offstage, and then NBC's crew abruptly drew their off-site production to a close. "Okay, wrap it up," the network's director announced to his team of technicians. "Take it down!" he hollered out the hospital window to a construction team waiting on the ground to dismantle the camera platform.[44] "Nobody said good-night, nobody said good-bye, nobody said, 'We're sorry,'" recalled Leonard Gershe of NBC's brusque departure.[45] "Baby, fuck the Academy Awards, you've got yours in the incubator," said Sid Luft, repairing to his makeshift bar.[46] Garland lay silent in her hospital bed and then dissolved into laughter.[47] "I have my own Academy Award," she agreed. "Forget it—open the champagne!"[48]

Backstage at the Pantages, Kelly negotiated her way through a jungle of TV apparatus. "Cameras all over the place," recalled Greer Garson of the scene, "hundreds of young men dashing in and dashing out, six different monitors to watch, director's arm wagging frantically."[49] Amidst the chaos, the winner "got completely out of control and cried like a baby," reported a witness.[50] With Oscar in hand and yellow rosebuds nestled in the back of her upswept blond hair, she dominated the Academy's victory dinner at the Beverly Hills restaurant Romanoff's.

Two weeks later Kelly appeared on the cover of *Life*, posing in her blue satin, Edith Head Oscar dress, kick-starting for the costume designer yet another thriving sideline designing ceremonial attire. Over the five years following Kelly's Academy Awards victory, Head dominated the craft, annually producing originals for an average of three actress nominees and presenters, including Eva Marie Saint,

With Oscar in hand and yellow rosebuds nestled in the back of her blond chignon, Grace Kelly dominated the scene at the twenty-seventh Academy Awards in 1955. (George Silk/Time & Life Pictures)

Sophia Loren, Shirley MacLaine, Jane Wyman, Anna Maria Alberghetti, Greer Garson, and Janet Leigh, most spectacularly. At the thirty-second Academy Awards, Leigh presented the writing awards, clad in a sleeveless, floor-length Edith Head incorporating twenty-eight thousand silver-lined crystal bugle beads. Weighing twenty-three pounds, the frock

At the thirty-second Academy Awards, presenter Janet Leigh modeled an Edith Head original with twenty-eight thousand silver-lined crystal bugle beads. Weighing twenty-three pounds, the frock cost Tony Curtis, Leigh's husband, three thousand dollars.
(Courtesy of the Academy of Motion Picture Arts and Sciences)

cost Tony Curtis, Leigh's husband, three thousand dollars. Edith Head's originals for Oscar night followed a carefully worked-out formula, devised to play to the TV cameras. Most were cut from satin and, like Kelly's aquamarine ensemble, were often completed with an evening coat. "The dresses couldn't overwhelm the actress inside," revealed Head of her design strategy. "I did a lot with back panels, so that a grand exit could be made."[51]

Kelly's departure from Hollywood became imminent as Rainier III, Prince of Monaco, announced their engagement in January 1956. Head hoped to make her wedding dress, but instead Kelly commissioned her to design her going-away honeymoon ensemble. "Edith was livid," confirmed David Chierichetti, Head's biographer.[52] But the royal bridal gown came with a lucrative package Kelly negotiated with MGM. In exchange for terminating her contract, she granted the studio exclusive film rights to produce *The Wedding in Monaco*, a half-hour documentary chronicling her nuptials. As part of the deal the studio also paid for her regalia and assigned Helen Rose, MGM's chief costumer, to make her wedding dress. The lavish confection of antique rose point lace, twenty-five yards of silk taffeta, and thousands of pearls catapulted Rose from a behind-the-scenes MGM player to a renowned Hollywood fashion force. By 1958, Rose devoted much of her time to attiring Elizabeth Taylor, who as MGM's biggest box-office attraction had assumed the mantle of Hollywood's queen.

But in February of that year, when the Academy announced its list of Oscar nominees, Taylor, twenty-six, was viewed as the long shot in an actress contest with an outcome that was impossible to predict. A trio of contenders vied for the prize including Deborah Kerr, Lana Turner, and Joanne Woodward, whom *Variety*, the film-industry trade paper, expected to emerge victorious for her role as Eve White, a housewife suffering from a multiple-personality disorder in drama *The Three Faces of Eve*.[53] Twenty-eight-year-old Woodward, however, remained doubtful of victory, cast her vote for competitor Deborah Kerr, and two weeks before the ceremony dropped one hundred dollars on a few yards of emerald green satin. Setting to work in the Westport, Connecticut, converted barn she shared with Paul Newman, her husband, she hunkered down at the sewing machine and made her Oscar ensemble, composed of a long, strapless dress and evening coat.[54]

"I thought Liz Taylor would walk off with the award, so I didn't invest a lot of money in a dress," admitted Woodward. "I was convinced nobody would see it."[55]

Taylor was equally uncertain about winning. She considered her Oscar-nominated role as Southern belle Susanna Drake in *Raintree County* "interesting" but admitted the film was "bad." *Raintree*, a three-hour, five-million-dollar adaptation of Ross Lockridge's 1948 Civil War history of Indiana State, was ambitiously produced by MGM to be an epic to match *Gone With the Wind*. MGM's Dore Schary hoped that *Raintree* would spearhead a new era of superproductions delivering "size and wallop" to the screen, drawing America's youth away from their TV sets and back into movie theaters.[56] But *Raintree* proved disastrous. "Money was spent recklessly," confirmed Edward Dmytryk, its director.[57] On location near Danville, Kentucky, as the cast and crew worked through an intense August heat wave, Taylor suffered an attack of hyperventilation, collapsing under the strain of her costume—a seventy-five-pound, corseted, petticoat-lined antebellum gown. "It was about a week before Elizabeth was able to return to work," added Dmytryk.[58]

At the time, Taylor was involved with wheeler-dealer Mike Todd, the forty-nine-year-old mogul producer and innovator of Todd A-O, a high-tech projection process he pioneered with the American Optics Company. Todd utilized the technique for *Around the World in Eighty Days*, the big-budget adventure comedy he worked on as he romanced Taylor. As their passion intensified during *Raintree*'s production, Taylor's heart belonged to Todd, not Susanna Drake. "I'm so sick of all this I feel like screaming," she confessed on set in Danville, where, between takes, she talked to Todd on the telephone five times a day.[59] Come Fridays, she boarded a private plane for New York so she and Todd could weekend together at his Park Avenue penthouse.

Critics dismissed *Raintree* as "rambling"[60] following its December 1957 premiere, while the *New York Times* classified Taylor's performance as "vain, posey [and] shallow."[61] By then, Todd and Taylor were married, and undeterred by the film's poor reviews, he launched an aggressive Oscar campaign on her behalf, purchasing prominent advertising space in Hollywood's trade papers, where her performance was favorably publicized.[62] Todd was also suspected of circulating a form letter to Academy members to solicit votes for Taylor, although when news of it surfaced in a Los Angeles newspaper he denied involvement. Taylor was running on "merit alone," he said.[63]

Two weeks before the thirtieth Academy Awards, Taylor commenced *Cat on a Hot Tin Roof*, MGM's screen adaptation of Tennessee Williams's domestic drama. She hoped her role in the film, as Mississippi housewife seductress Maggie Pollitt, would be her farewell to the screen—a triumphant conclusion to her fourteen-year MGM career. She intended to retire after the film's release and raise her three children with Todd at their Westport, Connecticut, estate. "I'm far more interested in being Mrs. Mike Todd than in being an actress," she admitted.[64] As Todd talked up *Cat on a Hot Tin Roof* as Taylor's sure bet for a thirty-first Oscar, he also commissioned Helen Rose to make her Oscar dress.

Fifty-four-year-old Rose, a two-time Academy Award winner, was the only Hollywood-studio costume designer whose profile rivaled Edith Head's. According to an MGM insider, Rose "hated" Head. At the thirtieth Academy Awards, while Taylor was set to compete for the actress prize, *Designing Woman*, an MGM comedy starring Lauren Bacall as Marilla Hagen, a Hollywood fashion designer its scriptwriter George Wells based on his friend Rose, was in competition for a screen-play award. David Chierichetti noted that an advantage Rose enjoyed during her MGM tenure was that the studio "had a virtual monopoly on Hollywood's beautiful women," including Ava Gardner, Lana Turner, Deborah Kerr, Esther Williams, Cyd Charisse, and Taylor, with whom Rose had worked with closely for a decade on ten films.

Such an uncanny resemblance marked dusky, beautiful Taylor and attractive Rose that some said that they could pass for sisters. But like a mother, the costume designer doted upon her star charge, easing her out of an adolescent uniform of blue jeans and sweaters, transforming her from the twelve-year-old who shot to global fame in 1944 as Velvet Brown, an equestrian show jumper, in MGM's *National Velvet*, into the teen queen star of a string of light, early-fifties romantic comedies that cemented her unchallenged reign at the box office. "She could play Dracula's daughter and still draw crowds," said Louis B. Mayer of Taylor's unrivaled allure.[65]

But at five feet two inches, Taylor was "short, extremely curvaceous [and] not as easy to dress as Grace Kelly or Audrey Hepburn," admitted Edith Head.[66] Rose, however, devised slimming coats with cowl-neck collars, cinch-waist jackets, and fit-and-flare skirts as costume staples that accentuated Taylor's triple assets, a chiseled face set off by large, piercing lavender-blue eyes, a voluptuous bust-line, and an egg-timer narrow, twenty-two-inch waist.[67] Rose's expertise delivered the illusion that Taylor possessed "physical perfection," complimented one film critic. "I had to keep her clothes simple and dramatic," revealed Rose of her designs for Taylor. "If you have a magnificent jewel, you put it in a simple setting—you don't distract from it with a lot of detail."[68]

"You do the dress, I'll take care of the diamonds," Mike Todd told Rose a few weeks before the thirtieth Academy Awards, and then he purchased a six-thousand-dollar diamond tiara for Taylor to wear to the ceremony.[69] The pricey headgear was part of a renowned jewelry collection he began to amass for Taylor weeks after they met, presenting her initially with a thirty-thousand-dollar black, baroque pearl friendship ring ("For weekdays," he wrote on its gift card),[70] then a Cartier emerald bracelet ("I love you," read its accompanying telegram),[71] a 29.7-carat diamond engagement ring ("as big as a hard-boiled egg," noted biographer Kitty Kelley), and, later, a Cartier tiara that Taylor wore to the twenty-ninth Academy Awards at which Todd claimed the picture Academy Award for *Around the World in Eighty Days*.[72] "Doesn't every girl have one?" Todd asked Hedda Hopper just before the ceremony commenced, acknowledging the gift, which Rose claimed Taylor stowed with the rest of her jewels in a large brown paper bag, collectively referring to her hoard as "the loot."[73]

Like *Raintree County*, the "Mike Todd Oscar Dress," as her husband publicized Rose's finery, was produced to be MGM mega—if not the costliest couture piece yet made for the ceremony, it was inimitably stylish. The modish, knee-length, formfitting white frock featured a deep-dip cowl décolleté and plunge back. Ashen mink trimmed the Oscar dress of snow-white French silk chiffon jersey, the textile from which Rose made most of MGM's leading-lady costumes because its buoyancy best suited the prosperous postwar era.[74] To accentuate Taylor's narrow waist, Rose adorned the bodice and skirt with a hand-embroidered crystal bead pattern incorporating two birds in midflight beneath a diamond-studded coronet, a symbol best representing the bond showman Todd shared with his imperious lady love.

Rose packed away Taylor's ceremonial stunner four days before the Oscars when invincible Mike Todd plunged to his death. Midflight on his way to Manhattan aboard the *Lucky Liz*, Todd's leased Lockheed Lodestar passenger plane, it crashed into the Zuni Mountains, twelve miles southwest of Grants, New Mexico.[75] Devastated by Todd's death, Taylor was heavily sedated by Dr. Rex Kennamer, her personal physician, while Rose remained by her bedside. She dressed Taylor in a dark broadtail suit, sat next to her on Howard Hughes's plane bound for Chicago, and stood by her through Todd's hastily arranged funeral.[76]

Back at home in Los Angeles as Oscar day dawned, Rose reached Taylor by telephone at the Coldwater Canyon mansion she had shared with Todd. "Elizabeth, what about that white dress you meant to wear tonight?" she asked, referring to the Mike Todd Oscar Dress.[77] "Forget it," replied the distraught Taylor, and put down the receiver.[78]

Later that night Taylor watched the Academy Awards at home on TV with MGM publicist Bill Lyon and Howard and Mara Taylor, her brother and sister-in-law. She wore a hostess gown ("one of those magnificent gowns Mike liked to see her in," revealed Lyon),[79] accessorized solely with Todd's mangled gold wedding band, which was retrieved from the crash wreckage.[80] Through the Oscars telecast, Taylor stared blankly at the TV screen and, muffling sobs, murmured, "Joanne Woodward is going to win. Nothing is going right for me—nothing will go right for me from now on because Mike is gone."[81] As John Wayne arrived at the Pantages' podium to present the actress prize, she admitted defeat. Watching Woodward dash from the arms of Paul Newman and then to the stage, Taylor went into crisis mode, instructing Lyon to send Woodward a white orchid corsage. "Tell the florist to have the card read, 'I am so happy for you. Elizabeth Taylor Todd and Mike, too," said Taylor. Then she collapsed.[82] "We had to carry her back upstairs," recalled Lyon[83]

Three years later, Taylor was making *Cleopatra* at Britain's Pinewood Studios and sharing a London Dorchester Hotel double penthouse with Eddie Fisher, her fourth husband. She discovered the dress she planned to wear to the thirty-third Academy Awards by viewing photographs of the first couture collection Marc Bohan produced for Christian Dior in January 1961. Collating an extensive shopping list, Taylor dispatched it to Dior, while Fisher paid the hefty bill.[84] "I had bought her almost the entire collection," confirmed Fisher of Taylor's sizable Bohan-Dior cache, from which she selected twelve dresses, including her sleeveless chiffon Oscar gown.[85]

Taylor first met Bohan while touring Europe in the summer of 1957, promoting *Around the World in Eighty Days* with Mike Todd. They had stopped in for a power shop at Dior's British headquarters, a vast Georgian town house on London's Conduit Street, over which Bohan helmed. By 1959, debonair Bohan made Dior's couture modern, lending

This Cartier tiara, which Elizabeth Taylor wore at the twenty-ninth Academy Awards in 1957, was part of a renowned jewelry collection her husband, Mike Todd, who won best picture for *Around the World in Eighty Days*, began to amass for her weeks after they met. Taylor stowed her pricey headgear with the rest of her jewels in a large brown paper bag, referring to it collectively as "the loot." (Courtesy of the Academy of Motion Picture Arts and Sciences)

to its unabashed femininity what he described as a "casual fit" and relaxed spirit. He had assumed total creative control of the international fashion empire when Yves Saint Laurent struggled to establish a comeback for the couture house after Christian Dior suffered a fatal heart attack in 1957. Bohan's first collection of fifty-four pieces could be folded and packed into the suitcases of the jet set, rather than stored in the steamer trunks once necessary to preserve Christian Dior's delicate, elaborate creations. "Extreme elegance or formality in dress is not for our active life," said Bohan, speaking on behalf of his clientele, which after his first show counted the world's most stylish women, including Babe Paley, Gloria Guinness, the Duchess of Windsor, Her

Royal Highness Princess Grace of Monaco, as well as Dior's devotee celebrities—Taylor, Dietrich, Olivia de Havilland, Sophia Loren, and Brigitte Bardot.[86]

Detailing Bohan's dazzling Dior debut, where *Soirée à Rio*, Taylor's pretty lime-and-white Oscar dress, appeared amid couture rendered in pleasing Provençal shades like lemon and apricot, Eugenia Sheppard, the all-powerful fashion editor of the *International Herald Tribune*, confessed that she felt "like a cat before a saucer of cream."[87] Meanwhile, the *New York Times* recounted as front-page news the glory and chaos of its grand finale: "The shouting, clapping—M. Bohan was pushed up against the *boiserie*, kissed, mauled and congratulated. Chairs were toppled. Champagne glasses were broken. People were knocked down."[88]

Taylor had declined her invitation. "It was a simple, sexy look," reflected Bohan of Taylor's Oscar gown—the first of "hundreds" of pieces he said she acquired from his collections over the successful twenty-nine years he reigned at Dior.[89] "She was animated, attractive, seductive, cordial, polite, easy to please," he described Taylor.[90] "She favored décolleté dresses, with tightly cinched belts around the waist as well as short dresses." But fashion critics disdained Taylor's preferred flirty Dior style.[91] "Elizabeth Taylor looked dreadful in Christian Dior," believed Hebe Dorsey, Sheppard's successor at the *IHT*. "She resembled a call girl attempting to impersonate a princess."[92]

Taylor's new image seemed apt for Oscar night, given that she, as Hollywood's sovereign, was set to compete for the Academy's crown with a confident performance as Gloria Wandrous, the lady-of-the-evening lead character of *Butterfield 8*. Director Daniel Mann's adaptation of John O'Hara's novel recounted the escapades of Starr Faithful, an infamous jazz-age New York prostitute upon whom Wandrous was based. But her Dior Oscar dress epitomized feminine refinement. With a high neckline and long, bell-shaped skirt, the dress proved functional, disguising her bandaged left leg, which had become inflamed from a blood clot a month before the thirty-third Academy Awards. Taylor's health crisis was prompted by a bout of pneumonia she contracted on the damp, cold *Cleopatra* Pinewood set six weeks before the Oscars. Rushed from the Dorchester to the London Clinic, she was treated for severe breathing complications. Headlines reported a "life-death struggle," inspiring an outpouring of support while Taylor's obituary splashed across page one of some newspapers.

The illness, however, was also said to be induced by "health shots"—

Christian Dior
30. AVENUE MONTAIGNE
PARIS.8ᵉ

"I had bought her almost the entire collection," confirmed Eddie Fisher of the twelve dresses he acquired for Elizabeth Taylor from couturier Marc Bohan's February 1961 Christian Dior debut, including this sleeveless chiffon gown, Soirée à Rio, which she wore to the thirty-third Academy Awards. (Christian Dior)

regular injections of liquid vitamins and methamphetamine, a prescription speed, regularly administered to her over three years from June 1958 by Dr. Max Jacobson, Fisher's personal physician—or Dr. Feelgood, as he was known to his celebrity patients. Fisher admitted he was usually "flying" on Jacobson's speed shots.[93] And by *Cleopatra*'s making, Taylor, he said, grew "dependent on every pill on the market—

pills to help her sleep, pills to keep her awake, pills to dull her pain, pills and more pills."[94] Taylor, later admitting to self-destructive tendencies, claimed Todd's loss proved impossible to overcome and that life became empty with Fisher, his former best friend. "We called him the Bus Boy," said Truman Capote, Taylor's friend, who through Oscar season occupied a Dorchester Hotel room neighboring the Taylor-Fishers' suite. "But I felt sorry for him," Capote went on. "He was so much in love with her and she was so rude to him."[95]

As reporters reached Taylor by telephone to comment on her fourth bid for an Oscar, she hurled invectives, deeming *Butterfield 8*'s script "pornographic—the worst ever written" and referred to Gloria as a "sick nymphomaniac."[96] "I had been ordered to do it even though I thought it was dreadful," Taylor reflected of *Butterfield 8*. MGM threatened to sue Taylor if she refused to delay her million-dollar deal for making *Cleopatra* and accept a comparatively modest salary of $375,000 to make *Butterfield 8*, which as her last project at the studio would amicably terminate her contract. She loathed every aspect of the film, including the nifty night-stalking gear Helen Rose made for lusty Gloria. Taylor always considered Rose to be a "super lady," a "super designer" and her "super friend." She wore Oscar dresses made by Rose at two Academy Awards ceremonies she attended following her defeat for *Raintree County*, but she was consistently trounced competing for the actress prize, although her successive nominated performances are still recognized as her finest—*Cat on a Hot Tin Roof*'s Maggie Pollitt and Catherine Holly, a sensitive young woman unjustly institutionalized after witnessing a gruesome murder in *Suddenly, Last Summer*, the Columbia Pictures masterpiece Gore Vidal adapted from Tennessee Williams's domestic drama.

Neither ill will toward MGM nor Taylor's delicate condition in any way changed her plan to attend the thirty-third Academy Awards. "She was determined to go—even though she was certain she would lose again," confirmed Fisher.[97]

Three weeks before the Oscars on March 27, Fisher accompanied his sable-clad, wheelchairbound wife to London's Heathrow airport, and together they boarded a transatlantic flight for New York. From there they traveled to Palm Springs, for a recuperative break before their trip to the Academy Awards. "Her legs were so swollen that she was on crutches and had to be lifted on and off the plane," recalled Fisher of Taylor's perilous condition.[98] By now, she was the strongest contender in the actress Oscar race—the "odds-on favorite" to win, due to a "mammoth" Oscar campaign MGM launched into overdrive during her near-death experience at the London Clinic.[99] As Academy members delivered Taylor their sympathy vote, her public forgave her for breaking up Fisher's marriage to MGM actress Debbie Reynolds. "Hell—I even voted for her," admitted Reynolds. Most of Taylor's competitors waved the surrender flag instead of breaking out their finest eveningwear. Nominee Shirley MacLaine canceled her trip back to Los Angeles from Tokyo where she was filming, and by Oscar morning the *Herald-Examiner* printed in Louella Parson's column an admission by competitor Deborah Kerr: "The Oscar should go to Elizabeth— her performance in *Butterfield 8* is superb."[100]

From their station at the Beverly Hills Hotel the Taylor-Fishers departed for the ceremony in a gleaming chariot—a brand-new stretch limousine Twentieth Century–Fox bestowed upon *Cleopatra*'s star as an Oscar-night gift.

The Thirty-third Academy Awards, April 17, 1961. A towering, twenty-five-foot, shiny Academy Award statue held court outside the Santa Monica Civic Forum as twenty-five hundred frenzied fans camped out on bleacher seats, hollering for Hollywood's queen: *"Where's Liz? We want Liz! We want Liz!"* A bank of klieg lights illuminated three hundred feet of plush red carpet, but crossing it kicked up minimal fuss for supporting actress nominee Shirley Jones, swathed in a sweeping gold-sequined Don Loper, or Edith Head–clad presenter Janet Leigh. Nominee Greer Garson made a regal decamp from a limo, her ginger bouffant topping a flattering Edith Head–draped eggshell chiffon, but she was perturbed by immediate questions about Taylor, her competitor. "I don't feel that I'm in competition with anybody but myself," sniffed Garson.[101] Meanwhile, a topless, Bermuda-shorts-bedecked teenager emerged from the bleacher-seated throng and breezed past the Academy's tight security force of two hundred police. Barreling up to forecourt emcee Johnny Grant, the bare-chested teen wondered into his micro-phone, "Is Liz here? She's well, isn't she?"[102] The crowd cheered and then fell silent realizing they'd mistook starlet Marla Massey for Taylor, who was the last of twenty-five hundred Oscar guests to arrive.

Fans surged toward the contender. A deep Palm Springs suntan offset Taylor's Dior couture. Her accessories—a mink capelet and diamond chandelier earrings—were her signature dazzlers. Taylor's gait was unsteady. Close by were Fisher and Dr. Rex Kennamer. "We all love

Elizabeth Taylor, seen here with fourth husband Eddie Fisher, eventually modeled the Mike Todd Oscar dress at the 1959 Academy Awards. (David Sutton/Hulton Archive)

you!" yelped a fan.[103] "Thanks," whispered Taylor, and then she collapsed. Fisher caught Taylor before she hit the pavement and then reassured the crowd, "She's in great shape!"[104]

By seven thirty, as emcee Bob Hope warmed up the crowd, police cleared the way so Taylor, Fisher, and Dr. Kennamer could proceed from a lounge off the lobby to their middle-row auditorium seats.

"Now, to a more pleasant aspect of the show—the collection of the outstanding actress of the year," announced Hope midway through the ceremony. "Presenting this Oscar will be the distinguished dramatic artist and performer Mr. Yul Brynner!" Like a black cat, Brynner pounced onstage, the tails of his dinner suit flapping in his wake. A flurry of applause and cheers punctuated his athletic lunge toward the podium. "Now this year, there were many magnificent performances by actresses," he began in a low baritone. Then he belted out the actress nominee list: "Greer Garson, Deborah Kerr, Shirley MacLaine, Melina Mercouri, and Elizabeth Taylor." As Brynner retrieved the envelope from Price Waterhouse's man, a camera focused on Taylor. Aware of its gaze, her charcoal-lined, sexy violet eyes, rendered onyx by the black-and-white film footage, conveyed nothing. Bravely she stared down the camera, but as Brynner wrestled with the envelope, she turned to Fisher. "I know I'm not going to get it," she sighed.[105] Glancing at the ballot, Brynner smirked, working the palpable tension. Then he purred, "*Eeee-liz-a-beth Tay-lorrr.*"

With her white-gloved hands Taylor smacked her rose-red lips, remaining speechless amidst what was later calculated as the longest standing ovation in Oscar-night history. "I don't believe it! Take me down the aisle!" she begged Fisher. And so together, Hollywood's queen and her trusty footman made the ascent. "Both of us holding on to each other every step of the way," recalled Fisher.[106] Arriving at the staircase that led up to the stage, she stopped. "Walk me to the podium," she instructed Fisher. "This is your moment—you take it from here, kid," he said, exiting stage right.[107] "Oh," sighed Taylor into the microphone as she clutched her Oscar, gazing at it appreciatively. "I don't really know how to express my gratitude for this. And for everything—I guess all I can do is say thank you. Thank you with all my heart."[108]

Backstage, *Variety* columnist Army Archerd saw Taylor collapse into Fisher's arms.[109] "I'm just putting on an act," she said to *Cleopatra*'s hairstylist Sydney Guilaroff, dismissing her display of heartfelt gratitude.[110] Taylor "didn't care about winning," wrote Guilaroff.[111] *Butterfield 8*'s Oscar was another of the Academy's consolation prizes, amending its dismissal of Taylor's fine performances in *Cat on a Hot Tin Roof* and *Suddenly, Last Summer*. Or so she thought.[112] Nevertheless, Taylor basked in her victory moment. She refused Fisher's offer to carry her Oscar on to the Beverly Hilton's Governor's Ball, where she regaled friends recounting their mount to the podium. "That's the most walking I've done since I left the London Clinic!" she said.[113]

Julie Andrews dug her size-eight heels into a messy patch of wet concrete outside Grauman's Chinese Theatre, leaving an imprint beneath a star emblazoned with her name spelled out in shiny gold letters along Hollywood Boulevard's Walk of Fame. It was March 1966, three weeks before the thirty-eighth Academy Awards, and branding the turf was a "routine" publicity stunt, but one necessary for Andrews to mark her

Mayhem erupted when Elizabeth Taylor and Eddie Fisher made a late red carpet entrance at the thirty-third Academy Awards. Audrey Hepburn and Mel Ferrer, her husband, watch from the sidelines. (Courtesy of the Academy of Motion Picture Arts and Sciences)

front-running position in the actress Oscar race.[114] Andrews's nomination honored her portrayal of Maria, the Catholic governess who tames Captain Georg von Trapp's rowdy brood of seven by teaching them to sing along with her as she strums an acoustic guitar in *The Sound of Music.* Following the March 1965 premiere of the smash-hit musical, it broke attendance records in twenty-nine countries, mostly from receipts of repeat viewers, surpassing *Gone With the Wind* as the most profitable film of all time. Rare was the musical talent possessed by British Andrews, a result of a five-octave singing voice she'd honed working for eight years on Broadway and in London's West End from 1955, headlining stage musicals *My Fair Lady* and *Camelot*. Her bid for the thirty-eighth actress Oscar with *The Sound of Music* brought the film's total number of nominations to eleven and also offered Andrews a chance to set an Academy record. The nomination followed her 1965 actress victory at the thirty-seventh Academy Awards for playing the title character in *Mary Poppins*, the Walt Disney live-action and animated musical that marked her screen debut. Not since MGM's Luise Rainer received the ninth and tenth Academy Awards had an actress enjoyed a successive winning streak. "As long as it goes to a Julie," said Andrews diplomatically, uttering a cordial statement referring to the intensifying competition she faced from her "chum" from London, Julie Christie.[115]

Petite, blond Christie received a thirty-eighth actress Oscar nomination for her role as Diana Scott, a scheming fashion model in John Schlesinger's drama *Darling*. She also impressed critics with her portrayal of Lara, the starring role in *Doctor Zhivago*, director David Lean's big-screen magnum opus, which with ten Oscar nominations challenged the supremacy of *The Sound of Music*. News of her Oscar nomination sent the naturally nervy nail biter into paroxysms of anxiety. "I didn't want to go and get up in front of that Hollywood crowd," recalled Christie, who, in the run-up to the ceremony worked at London's Pinewood Studios on *Fahrenheit 451*, François Truffaut's adaptation of Ray Bradbury's futuristic novel. "I was overcome," she added, "terrified."[116] So Christie made no trip to source something edgy for the Oscars at Biba (the swinging emporium off Kensington High Street that provided her *Darling* costumes), Ossie Clark, or Mary Quant, where London It Girls like her bought everything.

Andrews, however, scrupulously prepared to play a prominent role in a momentous Academy Awards—the first transmitted in Technicolor over ABC-TV's airwaves. After receiving a letter from Edith Head requesting that actress nominees and presenters opt for vibrant ceremonial attire to perk up the upcoming telecast, Andrews turned to Dorothy Jeakins, *The Sound of Music*'s Oscar-nominated costume designer and Hollywood's leading expert on color.

"You give Dorothy a piece of cloth and she will strip it, redye it, and overdye it until she gets just the color she has in mind," claimed

Head, validating the expertise of Jeakins, who at the twenty-first Academy Awards in 1949 triumphed in the color costume category, claiming its first prize for her screen debut, *Joan of Arc.* "My life was altered in an instant," remembered Jeakins of her good fortune.[117] From then on she operated as a highly sought-after freelance costumer, combining lucrative Hollywood assignments (including a lasting professional partnership with director John Huston) with work on Broadway and at the Stratford Shakespeare Festival. From 1953, she served a ten-year term running the Los Angeles Civic Light Opera Company's wardrobe department.[118]

"Feminine without frippery," added Anjelica Huston, Jeakins's long-time friend, describing the costumer's spare touch, which was defined by a 1961 trip to the Orient, where she traveled on a Guggenheim Fellowship to research the dress art involved in Noh, the form of dance-drama that had evolved in the fourteenth-century Japanese royal court. The pencil drawings, textile collages, and watercolors Jeakins produced in Japan were later exhibited and contributed to her February 1967 appointment as the curator of the costumes and textile department at the Los Angeles County Museum of Art. Jeakins's affinity for Japanese arts and dress also proved inspirational as she settled on the shape of Julie Andrews's Oscar dress, a sexy twist on a kimono.

Amidst the Zen calm of the sewing room on the second floor of her minimalist modern redwood cabin set on a lush acre in Santa Barbara, Jeakins conceived the Andrews Oscar kimono. But instead of cutting it from silk, the material traditionally used to make the long Japanese robe, she worked with lightweight wool broadcloth, selecting the textile because it had the strength to withstand the harsh glare of TV spotlights while its rich, passionate shade, matching the ripe flesh of a vine tomato, honored a request made by Andrews, who wanted to wear a red dress to the Oscars. "I've always wanted one—all my life," she said.[119]

Once the slim-fit kimono wrapped around the slender, five-foot-seven Andrews, its deep V-neck worked as the yin to the yang of its "discothèque back."[120] From behind, it fanned out slightly at the nape of the nominee's neck, displaying a hint of the garment's shocking pink silk lining—a provocative touch sure to tantalize the Academy's cameras.[121]

Generating heat on-screen was a specialty of Jeakins, who memorably emblazoned Marilyn Monroe in magenta for her role as sexy Rose Loomis in the romantic drama *Niagara,* then painted the blond bombshell in an R-rated shade of baby blue for her turn as Amanda Dell in *Let's Make Love*. Heat, however, was the one thing missing from Andrews's image. "My problem is everyone thinks I'm square," she lamented to *Vogue*'s Gloria Steinem, as they shared brandy and sodas at a New York nightclub just prior to *The Sound of Music*'s premiere.[122] Walt Disney's *Mary Poppins* had made Andrews's persona interchangeable with the storybook nanny. "Look, dear, there's Mary Poppins!" said a mother to her child, pointing out Andrews at a Los Angeles department store.[123] "It's like being hit over the head every day with a Hallmark card," said Christopher Plummer, cringing at the thought of performing with his perpetually sunny *Sound of Music* costar.[124] As freezing rain and icy winds plagued its five-and-a-half-month shoot in the Austrian Alps, between takes, Andrews, bundled in a brown mink coat, played her guitar, entertaining her shivering colleagues with witty renditions of the "Hawaiian War Chant" and the "Indian Love Call." Jeakins admired Andrews's positive spirit, "purity [and] zeal," raving, "She's ethereal, yet down-to-earth—everything she does is fresh and impromptu."[125]

Late during Oscar week, publicists representing Andrews and Christie quashed their spontaneous plan to share a limousine to the Santa Monica Civic Forum. Arriving together might, the nominees thought, kill a planted rumor of mounting tension between them.[126] "It may turn out to be kind of funny," said Christie to Andrews over the telephone thirty minutes after she arrived at the Los Angeles airport with boyfriend Don Bessant.[127] Christie had stitched together a funky Oscar ensemble—a shiny gold lamé trouser suit. "Pants are great, great gear," she asserted.[128] Her pants also proved practical. Plunging temperatures made for the coldest Oscar night in the ceremony's history.

The Thirty-eighth Academy Awards, April 18, 1966. "And now for the first time in color . . .," announced ABC, commencing the Oscars at seven P.M. Meanwhile, the "two Julies" sat at opposite ends of the Santa Monica Civic Forum. As *Darling* and *Doctor Zhivago* claimed successive costume design Academy Awards, defeating *The Sound of Music*'s Dorothy Jeakins, Christie was captured smiling in gold lamé. She clapped her hands while perched on a fifth-row seat next to black-tied Don Bessant. "In that enormous theater, with all of those famous people, stars—I felt out of place, ridiculous," she later confessed.[129] She was jet-lagged but animatedly giggled through much of the ceremony. "Oh, boy!" declared Andrews from her ninth-row seat. *The Sound of*

Julie Christie stitched together a funky Oscar ensemble—a gold lamé trouser suit.
"Pants are great, great gear," she said. (David Downton)

Music had just collected the editing prize, and the excitement sent her
white mink wrap flying from the lap of her kimono.[130]

"Great dress—I love your dress," enthused Oscar presenter Shirley
MacLaine as Andrews arrived at the podium to accept the director

The Sound of Music's Oscar-contending star, Julie Andrews, scrupulously prepared for her arrival at the thirty-eighth Academy Awards in 1966. Dorothy Jeakins, the film's nominated costumer, master-minded Andrews's Oscar kimono. (Courtesy of the Academy of Motion Picture Arts and Sciences)

trophy on behalf of *The Sound of Music*'s Robert Wise. "I know he's heartbroken not to be here, but he's filming in Hong Kong," Andrews told the crowd, although Wise was actually in Taiwan.

At the ceremony's three-hour-and-thirty-two-minute mark, British actor Rex Harrison, who'd played Henry Higgins to Andrews's Eliza Doolittle through *My Fair Lady*'s Broadway run, arrived at the podium. "For the best performance of an actress the Academy has nominated these five gifted ladies," announced Harrison, crisply proceeding. "Miss Samantha Eggar in *The Collector*; Miss Simone Signoret in *Ship of Fools*; Miss Julie Christie in *Darling* . . ." The camera cut to Christie as she clutched Don Bessant. "I wanted to win," she admitted.[131] Harrison

"With all of those famous people, stars—I felt out of place, ridiculous," confessed Julie Christie of the thirty-eighth Academy Awards. Her boyfriend Don Bessant (left), escorted her inside the Santa Monica Civic Forum. (Courtesy of the Academy of Motion Picture Arts and Sciences)

concluded the list of nominees announcing, "Miss Julie Andrews in *The Sound of Music.*"

A stealthy cameraman located Andrews in the Civic Forum's wings and transmitted an image of the keyed-up contender hoping to make Academy history. Her brow appeared sweaty. Her lips were pursed. "May I have the results of the ballot please?" asked Harrison politely. Slipping open the envelope, he announced, "Julie . . ." The camera lingered on Andrews as Harrison proclaimed, "Christie, for *Darling!*"[132] Clapping her hands to her mouth, Christie remained seated through "a great roar of applause," recorded director David Lean.[133] "I thought, 'Oh, well, that's it. It's not me. Maybe some other time,'" recounted Christie.[134] Then realizing her victory, she bounded toward the stage. "I didn't know where to go or what to do," she added.[135] Sobbing and laughing, she embraced Harrison, who seemed flustered by the spontaneous affection. "I don't think I can say anything except thank everyone concerned, especially *my darling* John Schlesinger, for this

115

great honor—this is the most wonderful thing on earth," said Christie, fighting back the tears, clutching her trophy.[136]

Andrews remained backstage and soon jumped for joy in her kimono as presenter Jack Lemmon revealed *The Sound of Music* as winner of the picture prize. "We did it!" she cried. "Now, I'm happy."[137] Christie concluded her night of glory at the Governor's Ball and then sped off in a rented Cadillac with Don Bessant to catch a gig by the Four Tops.

In March 1968, Faye Dunaway returned to Los Angeles, relaxed and invigorated after a two-month winter vacation in Paris, Bombay, and Moscow, a journey upon which she'd embarked after discovering the Academy had honored her with a fortieth actress nomination for her role as gangster's moll Bonnie Parker in *Bonnie and Clyde*—Warner Bros. crime thriller charting the escapades of the Barrow gang, a notorious band of bank robbers who swept Texas and Oklahoma at the height of the Great Depression. Dunaway's holiday luggage was loaded with traditional Indian saris and fine, hand-tooled silver jewelry—talismans that might have made for an inventive Oscar ensemble, as well as one totally in sync with hippie-deluxe late-sixties L.A. But to discuss ceremonial fashion she contacted Theodora Van Runkle, the costume designer who'd become her best friend and style guru after they'd worked together on *Bonnie and Clyde*. "What am I going to wear to the Academy Awards?" Dunaway asked Van Runkle, who quickly consulted her collection of Renaissance art-history books to contemplate an Oscar gown that was a modern masterpiece just like *Bonnie and Clyde*.[138]

In February 1968, *Bonnie and Clyde* received a total of ten Academy Award nominations, more than any of its competitors, including one for Dunaway, a brainy, Basom, Florida, brunette-turned-blonde who, during the film's preproduction period, hard-bargained its producer, Warren Beatty, shaving $25,000 from her $60,000 salary to receive above-the-title billing. Her negotiations proved a wise move, contributing to her front-rank position in an actress Oscar race dominated by legends including Anne Bancroft, Audrey Hepburn, and Katharine Hepburn. While Van Runkle's costume designs made the Academy's cut of five, a pair of nominations acknowledged Beatty's performance as gang leader Clyde Barrow as well as his debut producing a film that paved the way for a new era of counterculture Hollywood cinema.

Intent on making his own movie, then a novel venture for an actor, Beatty followed a tip by French New Wave director François Truffaut and tracked down Robert Benton and David Newman, two New York journalists who wrote *Bonnie and Clyde*'s script. And though Benton and Newman hoped that Truffaut, their hero, would direct a film based on their work, they sold it for ten thousand dollars to Beatty and, with writer Robert Towne, adapted it for the Hollywood screen. Jack Warner reluctantly agreed to fund and distribute *Bonnie and Clyde*, delivering to Beatty a slim, two-million-dollar budget, which forced the neophyte to personally bankroll part of the production. Warner loathed the rough cut—completed by director Arthur Penn in merely six weeks on remote, small-town locations north of Dallas, Texas—although it was revolutionary. The first Hollywood film to display scenes that would traditionally be left on the cutting-room floor, *Bonnie and Clyde* juxtaposed graphic violence with comedy and portrayed a hopeless love story between antiheroes—Dunaway's sexually voracious Bonnie and Beatty's impotent Clyde. But disavowing himself of it, Warner referred to it as "Warren's picture" and authorized a limited box-office run, opening it in two New York cinemas that screened B movies, the Murray Hill and the Forum, at the worst possible time in the summer of 1967—August 13, the month then known as the "graveyard" for film releases.[139] But by word of mouth and Beatty's relentless promotional efforts, *Bonnie and Clyde* hit third position at the American box office and in Europe became a cinematic phenomenon. Hundreds cued for its September 15, 1967, opening at Warner's Leicester Square, London, cinema, where ticket sales quickly escalated to a thirty-five-year high. *Bonnie and Clyde* polarized film critics, but its renegade spirit caught the disaffection of the time brought on by the U.S. government's participation in the Vietnam War from March 1965.[140]

The Bonnie Parker outlaw-ensemble Van Runkle created for Dunaway became iconic, blending a calf-length "maxi" skirt, a cable-knit sweater (beneath which she daringly wore an undershirt rather than a bra), and a beret, the flat French-peasant cap the real Bonnie Parker favored. "Offbeat boutiques sprang up everywhere with reproductions of the film's poor-people wardrobe for sale at highly inflated prices," observed costume expert W. Robert La Vine of the *Bonnie and Clyde* fashion craze that commenced in autumn 1967.[141] At Cartier's Manhattan flagship, its Fifth Avenue windows were decorated with fake bullets and Bonnie berets. In Pau, the French Pyrénées site of beret manufacture, an additional seven thousand hats were made weekly to keep up with a new demand. Valentino Garavani, the Italian couturier today known as Valentino, and then a darling of *Vogue*'s editor Diana Vreeland, presented at his Rome atelier a *Bonnie and Clyde*–inspired couture collection. Edging the red carpet stretched out before the Paris Cinématèque, fêting the film's French premiere in autumn 1967, were Bonnie Parker clones. "Young girls, teenagers, all wearing berets," marveled Dunaway.[142] In December, a photographer snapped Dunaway on London's King's Road wearing a beret, maxiskirt, and belted sweater. "A few days later a photo showed up in a story about how the Bonnie look was all the rage," remembered Dunaway.[143] When she and Van Runkle modeled maxis on the streets of Beverly Hills, the costumer admitted, "People looked at us as if we were out of our minds."[144]

But Van Runkle was a logical choice to create Dunaway's Oscar gown. "She is the only close girlfriend I've ever had," Dunaway owned up of Van Runkle, during an interview she conducted in her suite at the Paris Hotel George V after the French premiere of *Bonnie and Clyde*. "Theodora feeds my spirit. She is a very brave girl—all instinct and emotion, combined with a marvelous intelligence and great insight. She's something very rare."[145]

A one-off on the Hollywood costume-design scene, bubbly redhead Van Runkle dropped out of Beverly Hills High School. The former department-store fashion illustrator became an on-the-spot hire for *Bonnie and Clyde* after Dorothy Jeakins, her former boss, recommended her to Arthur Penn, the film's director. As Van Runkle reflected, "Arthur just threw my portfolio down and grabbed me and danced me around and said, 'If our movie is as good as the drawings, then we'll have a hit!'"[146]

"Pretty much, a hippie," she added, describing herself back then, while she called home base a "shack." Actually, it was a cozy cottage found along a woodsy trail in Laurel Canyon, a hip Hollywood Hills enclave where high-living rock stars set up decadent residences.[147] "Joni Mitchell was down the street writing *Ladies of the Canyon*," said Van Runkle of her environs, referring to the classic folk-rock album eventually recorded in 1970 by her neighboring guitar-strumming songstress. "I'd go to the mailbox and either the Rolling Stones or the Beatles were in every car that passed by. I spent a weekend with the Beatles in Devonshire. We all smoked weed. We all got up in the morning and lit a doobie before we even got out of bed."[148]

Bonnie and Clyde's hit status kept Van Runkle on the move. "I had limousines take me everywhere," she recalled. "Every single morning reporters called me from all over the world. I was *the* designer—it was my fifteen minutes of fame and fortune."[149]

She was the driving force behind Dunaway's glamour squadron. "When Faye came in for her first fitting at Warner Brothers, she was wearing an avocado jersey sheath dress—so *ugly*—and scuffed avocado pumps, with no stockings, and a floppy, avocado green fur felt hat," recalled Van Runkle of first viewing Dunaway in August 1966, during preproduction on *Bonnie and Clyde*.[150] Seventeen months later Dunaway had made the 1967 International Best Dressed List, thanks to Thea. Meanwhile, Jerry Schatzberg, Dunaway's fashion-photographer fiancé, who produced portraits of the Rolling Stones, the Beatles, and Bob Dylan, among others, working for *Vogue, Glamour*, and *Esquire*, translated his cool factor, masterminding thoroughly mod concepts for *Bonnie and Clyde*–themed magazine-cover shots of Dunaway.

Leading up to the Academy Awards in the winter of 1968, as Schatzberg's photos of Dunaway appeared in *Life* and *Newsweek*, they effectively composed her Oscar campaign because Warner Bros. devoted no resources toward it. Beyond Jack Warner's aversion to *Bonnie and Clyde*, Hollywood's studios no longer employed teams to manufacture Oscar-publicity glamour for up-and-coming nominees. Just as acting talent worked for studios on a freelance contractual basis in the late sixties, so, too, did hairstylists, makeup artists, publicity photographers, and costume designers. Assembling a team of image manipulators and an Oscar dressmaker became responsibilities for an actress to independently manage.

"Let's go very short, this woman doesn't do anything by half measures," said Dunaway to Van Runkle of the costumes she envisioned for her character, Vicki Anderson, a sophisticated, Fifth Avenue–shopping insurance investigator in *The Thomas Crown Affair*, the super-cool heist film directed by Norman Jewison, which the pair worked on just prior to the fortieth Academy Awards.[151] "Fine—let's do," agreed Van Runkle, accepting a suggestion Dunaway later claimed introduced the micromini to modern fashion.[152]

Hemlines were back on Van Runkle's design agenda as she next set to work on Dunaway's Oscar dress, because there were ceremonial dress-code rules to abide by. Gregory Peck, elected the Academy's president in June 1967, was on a mission to restore "dignity" to the Oscar ceremony, and so on his behalf Edith Head circulated a letter outlining a series of stipulations to the twenty-five hundred guests attending the ceremony.[153] Everyone was asked to don "white tie."

Banned from the ceremony were turtlenecks, love beads, and minis due to a surprise appearance at the thirty-ninth Academy Awards by Julie Christie, who presented the actor trophy in a black-and-silver chiffon baby doll that was considered risqué by the telecast's censors. "Formal evening gowns either Maxi or floor length," read Head's missive. "No Mini or day length."[154]

Variety heaped scorn upon the Academy's new dress code, which denied its members rights in the liberated late sixties, claiming the organization was out of sync with "the times."[155] Its leader, Peck, had nothing against the mini. In 1966 the City of Los Angeles elected as Woman of the Year Veronique Peck, his stylish Parisian wife, because she'd persuaded André Courrèges, the couturier who innovated the miniskirt, to stage his first North American fashion show as a Hollywood charity event. Embarking on the first phase of a two-part plan to revitalize the Oscars' look and rejuvenate the Academy's membership, Peck also replaced longtime inactive board members with a new generation of those under thirty-five to ensure that the organization and its voting procedure remained "responsive to contemporary attitudes."[156] He telephoned every nominee, personally inviting them all to attend the Oscars, and scored big as Her Royal Highness Princess Grace of Monaco agreed to be beamed in from her Monte Carlo palace. Over the airwaves from London would come Katharine Hepburn, who, though an Oscar winner and a thirty-five-year Hollywood resident, had yet to turn up.

In Laurel Canyon, Theodora Van Runkle moved with the changing times, accepting the Academy's dress code rules. *Thomas Crown* would introduce her micromini. *Bonnie and Clyde* had trailblazed with the maxi. So floor-length, she reasoned, was the best way for Dunaway to go to the Oscars. And just as Beatty and Arthur Penn had cobbled together *Bonnie and Clyde*, Van Runkle picked up pieces left on her cutting-room floor—leftover yards of black satin-mohair she'd acquired for *Thomas Crown* from textile emporium Beverly Hills Silk and Wool—and with them made Dunaway's Oscar dress.[157] The *Birth of Venus*, Sandro Botticelli's late-fifteenth-century portrait of legendary Renaissance beauty Simonetta de Vespuci, proved its initial inspiration. "I called Faye's dress the Simonetta de Vespuci Dress, although the title had nothing to do with anything—I was just in love with Botticelli, at that point," revealed Van Runkle.[158]

Embodying an aesthetic Van Runkle classified as a "murky pond," Dunaway's gown was more directly inspired by the costume designer's

For Faye –
Story

Black Satin –
backed crêpe
avec
Lilys Roses
grasses &
frogs, all in
black silk

Theodora Van Runkle's dress for Faye Dunaway's appearance at the fortieth Academy Awards in 1967 was inspired by the costumer's leafy Laurel Canyon environs. neighborhood. Down the front of its slinky, slim-fit silk-wool bodice, edging its train and neckline, were handcrafted black satin calla lilies, toads, and frogs. (Theodora Van Runkle) leafy green Laurel Canyon surroundings. Down the front of the gown's slinky, slim-fit silkwool bodice, edging its train and neckline, were calla lilies, toads, and frogs she handcrafted from black satin. Commingling with the flora and fauna were wispy offshoots. "Long, black, shiny grasses," explained Van Runkle of the fringe. "It was so far-out."[159]

Butterflies fluttered away inside Dunaway's stomach. "The Oscar represented the epitome of what I had struggled for and dreamt about since I was a young child," she confessed.[160] Wide-eyed, she patiently stood motionless as Lily Fonda, an expert fitter at Western Costume, finished Van Runkle's Oscar dress. Fonda diverted the anxious actress nominee with stories of disciplined Marlene Dietrich. "That was a different era, when stars were pampered and petted by the studios so that they would feel like great, exotic creatures," reflected Dunaway. "I was lucky enough to be on the tail end of it."[161]

Dunaway held her breath when Gregory Peck rescheduled the Academy Awards for April 10, two days after its original date and twenty-four hours following the funeral of civil rights leader Dr. Martin Luther King Jr., who had been assassinated in a Memphis hotel. The *Los Angeles Times* Oscar morning edition delivered good news for Dunaway, predicting a victory for *Bonnie and Clyde*'s gang in the "Academy Forecast," as Joyce Haber's gossip column was headlined.[162]

The Fortieth Academy Awards, April 10, 1968. "We love you! We love you!" shouted teenage girls as their idol Dunaway, on the arm of Jerry Schatzberg, slinked past in her funky, black, eco-chic Van Runkle. "Nobody wore a minidress—that is nobody who was anybody," wrote Shirley Paul, the *Citizen News'* fashion reporter, confirming that Gregory Peck's white-tie dress code was mostly observed.[163] "We must unite in compassion if we are to survive," said Peck, delivering the Academy's address. Then Bob Hope kicked off the awards presentation with habitual wit: "Last year Hollywood made its first movie with dirty words, and this year we made the pictures to go with them!"

Camelot's costumer John Truscott defeated Van Runkle, who was already resigned to the loss, after experiencing a "psychic premonition." *Bonnie and Clyde*'s Estelle Parsons, wearing a little, black thrift-shop dress, picked up the supporting actress Oscar. Warren Beatty lost the actor prize when Audrey Hepburn passed the trophy to Rod Steiger, star of *In the Heat of the Night*, a Deep South–set crime thriller exploring prejudice. Two hours in, actress Oscar presenter Sidney Poitier, costar of *In the Heat of the Night* and *Guess Who's Coming to Dinner*, the ten-times nominated comedy about interracial marriage, approached the podium and "relieved the tension" by announcing a surprise winner, noted Dunaway's biographer Allan Hunter.[164] It was a second victory for Katharine Hepburn, who in *Guess Who's Coming to Dinner* portrayed Christina Drayton, the California WASP housewife whose daughter Poitier weds. He also accepted the Oscar on Hepburn's behalf.

Dunaway magnanimously admitted defeat. "Martin Luther King had just been assassinated—it was no time to worry about a piece of gold statuary," she reflected.[165] "It was an important night for me. I was a young actress, and I knew there were other roles for me to play."[166]

A decade later Dunaway went back to the Oscars, as part of a group of nominees whose ceremonial casuals put paid to the Academy's white-tie decree.

Chapter Seven
STEPPING OUT

Rapturous reviews hailed the 1966 debut of evening pantsuits on couturier Yves Saint Laurent's Paris runway. "The cat's pajamas," raved *Time* of YSL's flared trousers, three years later confirming that such mannish apparel was once uncommon in the fashionable female wardrobe. But by 1969 pants were "everywhere—in all sorts of styles and at all sorts of places," including the Oscars.[1] The shift to a new, chic casual feminine dress code at the Academy Awards happened as a relaxed, free-spirited modernity ruled style and realism defined Hollywood cinema. A young, liberated bell-bottom-clad generation shook up the traditions of movie production as the sixties gave way to the seventies and as they established thriving, independent film companies, ownership of major studios changed hands. Conglomerates such as Paramount and MGM were helmed by corporate executives concerned with the bottom line rather than what an actress wore on-screen or to the Oscars.

Liberated from grip of the studio system, actress nominees determined their own ceremonial attire and arrived on the red carpet with their husbands or family, instead of paternalistic studio moguls. No longer was the podium a flyby zone where a winner timidly expressed gratitude and then fled backstage. For some, the rostrum became a confessional; for others, a pulpit to dispatch sanctimonious protest calls. The two-decade phase through which individuality and self-expression ruled the Oscars was set in motion by entertainer Barbra Streisand when in February 1969 the Academy announced her actress nomination for her debut screen role—Fanny Brice in *Funny Girl*, William Wyler's musical romance recounting the life story of the legendary twenties Ziegfeld

Follies star. "She wanted to look good—glamorous, sexy, but she also wanted her appearance to in some way convey 'I don't give a damn' kind of irreverence, even though she did care, greatly," wrote Randall Riese in *Her Name Is Barbra*, outlining the nominee's ceremonial agenda.[2]

Fiercely driven yet deeply insecure, twenty-seven-year-old Streisand was known as a "chronic worrier," who strove maniacally to perfect her image on stage, screen, at premieres, and even Hollywood cocktail parties. Thespians admired her perfectionism, but she alienated members of *Funny Girl*'s crew. She thought that expertise gleaned from starring in its original, smash-hit musical Broadway-stage production entitled her to share her opinions on all aspects of its motion-picture production. "You leave the film to me—you just take care of the acting," Harry Stradling Sr., the Oscar-winning cinematographer, told Streisand during preproduction on *Funny Girl*. "With excessive and often incoherent talkativeness, she expressed her opinions freely and endlessly about everything," claimed an irked Irene Sharaff, the leading costume designer who created the wardrobe for the Broadway and Hollywood productions of *Funny Girl*, but resigned from *Hello, Dolly!*, Streisand's follow-up, after engaging in heated disagreements with Streisand.[3] Sharaff had earned five Academy Awards and operated like a "powerful general," said her former assistant Tzetzi Ganev, master dressmaker at Western Costume. "Nobody could say no to her—there was no such thing."[4] Streisand did. However, she remained unusually tight-lipped about her plans for the forty-first Oscars when gossip columnist Dorothy Manners dropped by the set of *On a Clear Day You Can See Forever*, the musical comedy she was shooting at Paramount. "I've made up my mind just not to think about the awards," confessed Streisand. "Somehow I can't believe I'm going to get it. I can't win—not me."[5]

Las Vegas odds validated Streisand's pessimism, predicting that she would place third in the actress race, trailing competitor Joanne Woodward for her role as Rachel Cameron, a thirty-five-year-old spinster in *Rachel, Rachel*, a drama produced and directed by Paul Newman, her husband. Sixty-one-year-old Katharine Hepburn was an expected runner-up for her interpretation of Eleanor of Aquitaine, the French wife of Britain's Henry II in *The Lion in Winter*, a masterly period drama based on James Goldman's historical play about the destructive relationship of the twelfth-century monarchs. While Woodward received three prestigious accolades for *Rachel, Rachel*—the New York Film Critics prize, a Golden Globe, and an award from London's Royal Academy of Dramatic Arts—Hepburn's "instinct" upon landing *The*

Lion in Winter was that she would "win the Academy Award," wrote Barbara Leaming, her biographer.[6]

Funny Girl, however, earned eight Academy Award nominations, two more than the six received by *The Lion in Winter*, and it was long talked up as the pet project of Ray Stark, who'd emerged in sixties Hollywood as an independent filmmaking force. "The last of the great old-world Hollywood producers," the *New York Times* described Stark, a mogul mentored by Golden Era figureheads Louis B. Mayer, Harry Cohn, and Sam Goldwyn.[7] He was also the son-in-law of Fanny Brice, and from 1953 his screen project of her life story languished in development. So ten years later he announced his intention to stage *Funny Girl* on Broadway, casting Streisand in the lead after Jule Styne, its lyricist, and the Oscar-winning choreographer Jerome Robbins, a behind-the-scenes creative force, convinced him she possessed the requisite star quality.

Twenty-two-year-old Streisand had dreams of Oscar gold but was a rough diamond. An "awkward, skinny girl with [a] distractingly large nose and crooked teeth and eyes that seemed to watch each other," wrote biographer James Spada.[8] She was a self-taught singer who first performed solo on an open-air, makeshift stage—the rooftop of the Newkirk Avenue, Brooklyn, housing project where she grew up. But by 1961, Streisand's gigs at Bon Soir Club, a Greenwich Village gay nightspot, had an Uptown Manhattan following, earning her a six-figure recording contract with Columbia Records as well as TV guest spots on the *Tonight Show Starring Johnny Carson* and the *Dinah Shore Show*. A captivated Styne successively witnessed twenty-seven of Streisand's Bon Soir performances, through which she slipped from wisecracking comedy to her own renditions of poignant ballads and up-tempo show tunes. Between numbers in a cramped, backstage dressing room, she changed costumes she assembled from an eclectic mix of thrift-shop finds—pairing Venetian glass bangles and T-strap shoes with twenties, bias-cut dresses or Victorian negligés.[9] Bon Soir regular Baron Nicholas de Gunzburg, the refined French aristocrat who worked as *Vogue*'s editor at large, was combing Manhattan for a fashion designer to polish his discovery, who he accurately predicted would rise to be a "tremendous star."[10]

So de Gunzburg approached Arnold Scaasi, the Montreal-born, Paris-trained couturier who operated an exclusive atelier at 26 East Fifty-sixth Street in Manhattan. Fashion critics then considered Scaasi to be "an American Christian Dior" and the "United States rival to Yves

Saint Laurent." Along with Geoffrey Beene, Bill Blass, Oscar de la Renta, and Pauline Trigère, he was part of a generation of international designers who by the midsixties established Manhattan, their base, as a world-class fashion capital. He caught Streisand at Bon Soir and enjoyed the show, but passed on the chance to play her Pygmalion. Scaasi had a business to run and Streisand's vintage stage costumes failed to translate that she had a big enough bank account to pay three figures for one of his made-to-order dresses.

Scaasi and Streisand became collaborators two years later, when in May 1964 at the height of her fame as *Funny Girl*'s star, she appeared at his buff-colored headquarters to view the presentation of his first complete couture collection. Scaasi's sharp-suited, blue-blooded American socialite clients, including Brooke Astor, Mrs. William Randolph Hearst Jr., and Mary Rockefeller, sat in the front row next to "The Girl," as *Time* magazine headlined Streisand in a six-page, April 1964 cover story charting her overnight success. In Scaasi's showroom she lounged in a characteristically funky black poncho and floppy felt hat, but appreciated his gift for manipulating color and luxury textiles. "Extravagant styles—coats of feathers, elaborate creations of satin, dramatic evening clothes, lavished with fur and intricately cut—he definitely does not believe in the 'Less is more' dictum," wrote Bernadine Morris of the *New York Times* describing the couturier's flamboyant signature.[11]

Soon after the presentation, Streisand wooed Scaasi over the phone as she enthused about the final piece in his collection—a wedding dress. "It was made of stiff white faille and had a hood and tiny buttons down the front, and she asked if we could make it for her in black!" recounted Scaasi.[12] "She wanted to wear it as a coat for evening. My staff thought it was a wild idea, but I felt she had great flair and a strong sense of personal style. We just clicked. I knew she had something."[13]

Scaasi and Streisand shared an inspired knack for reinvention. Scaasi hit his stride in 1954, reversing the spelling of his surname, from ethnic Jewish *Isaacs* to *Scaasi* because of its continental connotations. "Italian names being very big in the design world," remarked *Vogue* of the switch.[14] By 1968, Streisand factored in among the Best Dressed List's roll call of the ten Most Imaginative Women in Current Fashion, due to her own deft styling of Bergdorf Goodman couture with cheap finds from Loehmann's, the Bronx designer outlet toward which she frequently steered her Bentley in pursuit of bargain-priced labels. Flashing Scaasi eveningwear she "stopped traffic" at *Funny Girl*'s 1968 autumn premieres in New York, London, and Los Angeles. "She looked like a fairy princess," wrote Scaasi, recalling the shimmering, nude tulle gown and cape Streisand modeled at the film's New York opening.[15]

In March 1969, Scaasi was in the running to dress Streisand for the forty-first Academy Awards. By then he commuted weekly from Manhattan to Los Angeles, where at Paramount he worked alongside Cecil Beaton as part of a two-man team producing her extensive wardrobe for *Clear Day*. A few weeks before the ceremony Scaasi turned up unexpectedly on the set of *Clear Day* as she conferred with Howard W. Koch, the film's producer. "What do you think, Scaasi?" asked Streisand, rising from her seat and twirling in a long, black taffeta hooded cape—part of a Paramount-devised Oscar ensemble.[16]

Paramount's wardrobe department, like many at major studios, was shut down as a budget-slashing exercise amid the restructuring of Hollywood's film industry. By the late sixties screen wardrobes were mostly purchased at department stores by skilled hunter-gatherers known as shoppers, while leading costume designers were assigned to work freelance on prestige projects. Edith Head had decamped to run the costume department at Universal. And to Scaasi's trained eye, Streisand's Paramount ceremonial attire did not cut the swath of Head's former Oscar-night knockouts. "You must be kidding," he responded, and, turning to Koch, said, "She looks like a character out of *Gone With the Wind*! We have to do something modern—really of *today*—I think the cape is all wrong."[17]

Period costume defined Streisand's look in *Funny Girl*, *Hello, Dolly!*, and in zany *Clear Day*, in which she played Daisy Gamble, a downtown New Yorker who, imbued with psychic powers, time-travels back to eighteenth-century London, where she lived as the noble seductress Melinda Tentrees. While Scaasi admired Streisand's appreciation for vintage, he believed that historical screen dress aged her prematurely. "On Oscar night she could be her own person, youthful and current," he thought. "She was good-looking—a size six—and she was tall. So I said to her, 'Let's get you into the modern world.'"[18] So Oscar contemporary evolved on Scaasi's sketchpad into an evening pantsuit. "Bell-bottoms were all the rage," he added. "I wondered why Barbra couldn't wear some kind of pants to the awards. It was a thought that kept germinating in my head."

The eveningwear Yves Saint Laurent had produced in 1966, introducing Le Smoking, a seductive, black trouser suit inspired by and named after the tuxedo, also impressed Scaasi. Two years later Saint

Laurent debuted a risqué variation of Le Smoking, pairing black Bermuda shorts with a dark, sheer blouse. It was an immediate critical hit. *Vogue*'s Richard Avedon captured society-girl model Penelope Tree in YSL's shorts and see-through blouse. So Scaasi made Streisand's bell-bottom trouser suit from similar sheer black tulle dusted with iridescent sequins, but lined the combo with nude silk to prevent it from appearing transparent. "The bell-bottoms were exaggerated—flaring out widely from the knee down, almost giving the appearance of a trumpet-shape evening skirt when she stood still," he explained. "The top was a straight overblouse with two patch pockets. It was finished with a basic white collar and cuffs and black satin bow at the neckline. There was nothing overtly sexual about the outfit. Young girls were wearing things like that all over the world."[19,20]

A week before the Academy Awards, Streisand reconsidered her plan to touch down on the Academy Awards red carpet in Scaasi.[21] By then a "hate Streisand cult" had developed in Hollywood as stories of her forthright manner circulated, jeopardizing her shot at the Oscar. Joyce Haber, the influential *Los Angeles Times* gossip columnist, claimed that through the making of *Funny Girl*, "monster" Streisand treated sixty-seven-year-old William Wyler like a "butler."[22] Devoting little energy to *Funny Girl*'s Oscar campaign, she remained "reclusive" as the forty-first ceremony neared, wrote Shaun Considine in *Barbra Streisand: The Woman, the Myth, the Music*.[23] She reneged on an agreement to meet Academy members at one of an ongoing series of *Funny Girl* screenings followed by a casual, Columbia-hosted dinner. The last-minute decision pissed off a studio publicist, who huffed, "Barbra ordered her own menu for a party of five and then never showed."[24]

But on Oscar Monday, Streisand went all out, commencing ceremonial preparations six hours in advance of the event, retreating to her dressing room with personal hairstylist Frederick Glaser and an impromptu technical adviser—Howard Koch, who sent the cast and crew of *Clear Day* home early. "She seemed to take to me as, like, her father image," said Koch.[25] In doubt about what to wear to the Oscars, Streisand sought Koch's opinion—should it be Scaasi's trousers or a Dior gown? Surveying the options, Koch advised her to wear the trousers. "She kept changing back and forth," recalled Glaser. "When she asked my advice, I said, 'Wear the Dior,' so naturally, she chose the Scaasi number."[26] Next Glaser set to work styling Streisand's chin-length bob wig. She wanted it teased. "I kept telling her it looked overdone, phony," he added, "and she said, 'Good! This whole town is phony, and if I lose, they'll know I don't give a damn!'"[27] Glaser, however, succeeded in styling the hairpiece sixties mod smooth.

Actor Elliott Gould, Streisand's estranged husband, donned a dark dress suit to accompany her to an Academy Awards preparty at Ray Stark's Holmby Hills estate and then on to the ceremony. But Gould was no dream date, later admitting he was "flying high" on marijuana.[28] "It was a difficult night for me—a trauma," reflected Gould. "I was terribly self-conscious about being with a woman from whom I had just separated and about being among people I felt weird about, people who thrive on the dramatic implications of that kind of situation."[29]

By late afternoon Streisand and Gould arrived on Stark's stately property, a rambling, green expanse of expensive real estate dominated by a museum-worthy collection of modern sculpture by Alexander Calder, Alberto Giacometti, Ellsworth Kelly, Henry Moore, Aristide Maillol, and Gaston Lachaise. But all eyes fixed upon the trouser-clad Streisand as she made her way across the Starks' manicured lawn, and the consensus of guests in the garden was that Scaasi's Oscar-night trouser suit was a real work of genius. "She was the epitome of elegance, carrying white kid gloves and a black satin clutch that matched her evening pumps," affirmed Scaasi, who was on hand that night. Unusually high praise for Streisand came from hostess Fran Stark. The daughter of Fanny Brice, Stark was renowned in Hollywood for her grace, style, faultlessly applied makeup, and extensive couture wardrobe. "I'll never let that girl play my mother," she'd vowed in 1963, after she and her husband had seen Streisand perform at Bon Soir.[30] According to biographer Anne Edwards, Fran Stark "hated" Streisand upon first sight, later called her a "nut," and felt she lacked "class."[31] But on Oscar eve, her attitude reversed. "Arnold, you *are* brilliant," Stark whispered to Scaasi, "she looks ravishing."[32]

Streisand had realized a long-cherished fantasy as her stretch limousine led a motorcade descending from the Starks' mansion en route to the Dorothy Chandler Pavilion, the imposing white marble complex in the recently built Los Angeles Music Center selected as the Oscars' new venue by Gower Champion, the Tony Award–winning stage director and choreographer whom Gregory Peck had persuaded to produce the forty-first Oscars. "No Pavilion, no Champion," Champion told Peck, insisting the Oscars be held at the Music Center, which he classified as the "theatrical mecca of the West."[33] He also stipulated that ten hosts would preside over the proceedings, rather than the single master of ceremonies Bob Hope, who was placated at being usurped with the promise of receiving the Irving Thalberg Award. So Champion reeled in an extraordinary lineup of emcees—"Oscar's Best Friends"— including Diahann Carroll, Tony Curtis, Jane Fonda, Burt Lancaster, Walter Matthau, Sidney Poitier, Natalie Wood, and Ingrid Bergman, who was scheduled to present the actress Oscar. Streisand had fantasized about winning the prize since childhood. Aged twelve, she devoured *Life*'s April 1954 story recounting Audrey Hepburn's victory. "[Barbra] had read a lot about how actresses behave, and she had got all the clichés and put them into a pattern for herself," confirmed Irene Sharaff. "She would turn up at costume fittings impersonating other stars. The best was when she came as Garbo, in full dress, and gave a complete performance."[34] Working Scaasi's kicky two-piece, Streisand stole the show at the Oscars.

The Forty-first Academy Awards, April 14, 1969. "You'll make it in time," reassured the chauffeur behind the wheel of Streisand and Gould's limo as they approached the Music Center complex at dusk.[35] In the backseat a stressed-out Streisand surveyed bumper-to-bumper traffic— a lumbering pile-up of approximately three hundred dark luxury auto- mobiles. "Nearly everybody was late," recalled an Oscar guest.[36] The three thousand attending the forty-first ceremony had received advance warning that latecomers would be locked out of the Music Center after the prompt six P.M. ceremonial start time as ABC cameras were then set to roll. Streisand was "agitated—her voice high-pitched, strained. Elliott attempted to calm her," wrote Anne Edwards.[37] The sight of guests exiting their limos, sprinting toward the Chandler, frazzled the nominee because making the dash was impossible due to Scaasi's fluffy tulle bell-bottoms. With merely two minutes to spare Streisand crossed the Chandler's threshold with Gould escorting her down the long aisle to the front row. As a posse of seated Academy voters cheered them on, Edwards wrote that "shocked faces" also stared as Streisand shimmied by in sequined bell-bottoms flickering in the honey glow emanating from the Chandler's crystal chandeliers.[38]

Gower Champion's slick, two-hour Oscar ceremony ran at breakneck pace due to a clever innovation by its art director, James Trittipe, who eradicated the "long walk" to the podium for winners, installing a T- shaped ramp of steps that extended from the stage out into the audience. To its left sat Streisand, who clutched Gould as *Funny Girl* lost six Academy Awards, defeated in the score, art direction, and director categories by *Oliver!*, the musical adaptation of Charles Dickens's *Oliver Twist*. After a

Actor Elliott Gould donned a dark dress suit to accompany his wife, Oscar nominee Barbra Streisand, to the forty-first Academy Awards. Gould later admitted he was "flying high" on marijuana at the time. (Courtesy of the Academy of Motion Picture Arts and Sciences)

commercial break a classy prelude to the actress Oscar presentation commenced on a giant, split-screen panel looming above the Chandler's stage, which displayed a series of large-scale moving images—sequences of Oscar-clinching scenes delivered by the five first-rate nominees: Katharine Hepburn, Patricia Neal, Vanessa Redgrave, Streisand, and Joanne Woodward. There was no voice-over from an announcer through the film clips. Rather, wild applause from the audience accompanied the images of skilled performances fading in and out on the big screen. Cheers greeted Streisand's turn as *Funny Girl's* Fanny Brice. Soon she and Gould rose to their feet, joining a standing ovation greeting presenter Ingrid Bergman as she made her way across the stage in a gown of flowing white chiffon trimmed with shimmering silver bugle beads. "There they are," began Bergman, "the best actresses of 1968." As regal Bergman expressively worked her way through the list of nominees, the TV cameras caught Streisand reclined in a red velvet seat chewing gum, possibly to ease the tension, and next captured a wide-eyed Gould, who released his wife's hand and tugged twice on his earlobe—a covert signal to alert a friend watching the ceremony that he was stoned.

"The winner is . . .", said Bergman, but then, having studied the ballot, she looked up, beat her left hand to her chest, grasped her chin in astonishment, again gazed out toward the audience, and gasped, "It is . . . it's a tie! The *winners* *are* Katherine Hepburn"—a cry went up from the audience—"and . . . Barbra Streisand!" The tie—an Academy first since Fredric March and Wallace Beery shared the fifth actor Oscar in 1932—flabbergasted the audience, and Streisand, too. "I wasn't sure it was mine until Elly turned to me and said, 'It's you!'" she recalled.[39] Anthony Harvey, the director of *The Lion in Winter*, accepting the prize on behalf of Katharine Hepburn, leaned forward in his seat behind Streisand, offering to walk her to the podium. The camera remained fixed on Streisand as she cocked a coy expression, refrained from kissing Gould, calmly rose to her feet, but paused on her way to meet Harvey. Before thirty million TV viewers she hitched up her Scaasi bell-bottoms from the backside of their waistband while the zone just below, her butt cheeks, was rendered totally sheer

On her way to the podium at the forty-first Academy Awards, Oscar winner Barbra Streisand lost her footing and tripped on the stairs to the podium. (Corbis)

due to the powerful glare of the auditorium's 153 hot, beaming klieg lights. So flashing on TV screens across the country was an "ample view of her near-naked, sequin-covered derrière," wrote Randall Riese.[40]

Gracious Harvey navigated the route toward the Academy's stage, but mounting the T-shaped ramp, Streisand lost her footing as one of her vertiginous heels caught and ripped the trailing hem of her bell-bottom pant leg. She stumbled momentarily. The *Los Angeles Times* reported the seams of her pantsuit actually split. But the actress winner

Bemused Oscar presenter Ingrid Bergman moved backstage as winner Barbra Streisand strutted in swirling Arnold Scaasi bell-bottoms. (Corbis)

never let on. At the podium as Harvey thanked the Academy for Hepburn, Streisand regained composure in the background, silently running through in her mind the acceptance speech prepared by Columbia's publicist Jack Brodsky. Her delivery proved perfect, despite a technical complication. She was totally unaware that her trouser suit was by now "very see-through," confirmed Joyce Haber of her view from the audience.[41] But Streisand had the Oscar and the crowd in the palm of her hand as she commenced her speech with the first line of *Funny Girl*: "Hello, gorgeous!" Then she made a bittersweet admission: "Somebody once said to me—asked me if I was happy, and I said, 'Are you kidding? I'd be miserable if I was happy.' And I'd like to thank all the members of the Academy for making me really miserable. Thank you."

A bemused Bergman made the move backstage with Streisand, who strutted along as her elaborate bell-bottoms swirled. "We just never realized what would happen!" confessed Scaasi of the transparency of his tulle trouser suits. The day after the Oscars, newspapers featured damning reviews of his creation. STREISAND NUDE declared a headline, while another critic deemed the pantsuit "a monumental salute to bad taste." One columnist wrote that *Funny Girl*'s winner resembled "a fugitive from a harem."[42] "Haute tackiness," concluded the *Los Angeles*

Times. Despite the reprimands, Scaasi remained Streisand's preferred couturier, as he reflected of the morning after the ceremony: "Barbra was on the phone to me laughing about the whole episode."[43]

"As Oscar time drew near, everyone was telling me I would win, and this time I felt they were right—it was in the air," wrote Jane Fonda, reflecting upon the "favorite" position she occupied in the forty-fourth actress race by February 1972, as the Academy announced her nomination for the crime thriller *Klute*, in which she played Bree Daniels, an aspiring New York actress who turns tricks to pay for drama lessons and then becomes involved in a murder investigation led by dishy Donald Sutherland's detective John Klute.[44] Merely two Oscar nominations came *Klute*'s way, but unanimous praise hailed the performance of thirty-four-year-old Fonda, placing her far ahead of Academy running mates Julie Christie, Glenda Jackson, Vanessa Redgrave, and Janet Suzman. "She's Bree, not Jane Fonda—there isn't another young, dramatic actress in American films who can touch her," confirmed Pauline Kael, the country's leading film critic, at the *New Yorker*.[45]

Mastering Bree, Fonda relied on Method acting skills gleaned from training in 1959 with New York Actors Studio founder Lee Strasberg, who advocated his students seek inner truth and human fullness to conquer a role. Accordingly, for motivation, Fonda tapped into ménages à trois encounters she shared with director Roger Vadim, her estranged husband, and call girls he'd enlisted from the pricey Paris escort agency Madame Claude. Through *Klute*'s two-week preproduction period, she also shadowed the film's "technical adviser"—a twenty-three-year-old hooker hired to navigate the New York underworld by Alan Pakula, *Klute*'s director. Pakula, forty-three, was at the forefront of an esteemed group of seventies directors who transformed the "hired help" status once associated with their profession amid the conveyor-belt culture of Old Hollywood studio moviemaking to the rank of artistry by "developing personal styles that distinguished their work from that of other directors," noted film expert Peter Biskind of the approach.[46] Considering Fonda "extraordinary," Pakula gave "full rein" to the feminist ideals harbored by his leading lady, forgoing exploitative nudity to convey the reality of prostitution, upon her suggestion.[47] Championing Fonda's aesthetic vision, he let her play set decorator, too, and so she furnished Bree's bohemian digs with authentic touches such as a faux

Tiffany lamp shade (similar to one she'd spied on a visit to a New York call girl's pad) and stocked its shelves with popular paperbacks she figured a streetwalker might read, including romance novels, self-help books, and *Sun Signs*, the astrology manual.

"Hollywood princess," *Vanity Fair* described an adolescent Fonda.[48] Daughter of upstanding American actor Henry Fonda and Frances, his first wife, as well as sister to the renegade millionaire filmmaker Peter Fonda, producer of *Easy Rider*, she divided her childhood between an East Coast boarding school and Tigertail, a Pennsylvania farmhouse built to Henry Fonda's specifications and set amid nine pastoral acres of Brentwood, California. Dropping out of Vassar, she worked as a model, represented by Ford, the top New York agency, while simultaneously studying with Lee Strasberg. *Vogue*'s July 1959 cover first displayed Fonda's magnetism. While the points of a glittery starfish pin adorning her saffron shift dress balanced the flip of a Salon Antoine bouffant in this pristine Irving Penn beauty photo, the touch of Fonda's Saks Fifth Avenue lipstick-pink, gloved right hand softened her prominent chin. Promoting the 1960 romance *Tall Story*, her first Hollywood feature, in which she played a cheerleader, she cooperated with the publicity department at Warner Bros., its producer. "She was put on the gossip-column circuit and showed up carrying balloons that were color-coordinated with her girlish outfits," noted Peter Collier in *The Fondas*.[49] Married to Vadim and living in Paris by 1965, she went hippie-chic barefoot on their Saint-Tropez vacations.[50] Smooth Vadim, a force within the French New Wave filmmaking movement who'd played Svengali to his former movie-star wives Brigitte Bardot and Catherine Deneuve, transformed Fonda from a "gauche American" to a "dazzling, disquieting and ethereal beauty," noted the *London Express*.[51] As a Bardot blonde, Fonda headlined three films Vadim directed from 1965, including *Barbarella*, an adaptation of Jean-Claude Forest's futuristic comic strip in which she played the title character— an intergalactic nymphomaniac. *Barbarella*, released in 1968, made five-foot-eight Fonda, reed-slim at 120 pounds, the "most fantasized-about woman in the world," as well as a permanent fixture in the front row at couture presentations staged by Chanel and Yves Saint Laurent. Come fashion-show time, she shuttled to Paris from Saint-Ouen-Marchefroy, a salubrious hamlet thirty-seven miles west of the city where she and Vadim occupied a rambling farm.[52] But by Oscar season in 1972, Fonda and Vadim's separation was headed toward divorce, and she displayed a new allegiance to the feminist sisterhood by adopting a wash'n'go brunette shag. She ceased applying makeup and decided to "no longer dress for men—I would dress so that women weren't uncomfortable around me. My wardrobe was pared down."[53]

So was her Oscar-night look—a four-year-old, black Saint Laurent trouser suit she brought to Los Angeles from Paris, two months before the Academy Awards, after filming *Tout Va Bien*, a leftist political drama made by French New Wave director Jean-Luc Godard. Fonda's Saint Laurent ensemble came from Rive Gauche, his 21 rue de Tournon boutique, which derived its name from its trendy Left Bank, Saint-Germain-des Prés locale. It sold Rive Gauche, the directional ready-to-wear line Saint Laurent debuted in 1966. "Expensive but not as expensive as couture," fashion historian Katell Le Bourhis, classified Rive Gauche ready-to-wear.[54] The boutique also served as the head-quarters for a Euro-cool tribe who surrounded dashing Saint Laurent. "Everyone went to Rive Gauche, absolutely everyone," claimed Susan Train, *Vogue*'s Paris bureau chief.[55]

Though a confirmed Saint Laurent fan, Fonda never ran with the designer's hedonistic crowd. In 1970, she became a radical activist, developing the new persona over the spring and summer of 1968, through which she was pregnant with Vanessa Vadim, her first child. On visits to her Paris obstetrician, she witnessed the May 1968 uprisings as Sorbonne university students and leading intellectuals took to the streets of the Latin Quarter protesting government repression and media censorship. "Paris was up in arms," she recalled.

French TV, which broadcast unedited footage received from the Vietcong, North Vietnam's communist regime, made a profound impact on Fonda, too. Deep into her pregnancy, she retreated to her farmhouse, watching gruesome war reports as the U.S. government escalated to unprecedented historical levels bombing attacks against the Vietcong, hoping to halt the spread of communism throughout Southeast Asia. Scenes of American unrest were broadcast throughout the momentous time, including the assassinations of Martin Luther King Jr. and Robert Kennedy as well as reports on race riots outside Miami's convention hall when in August at the Republican National Convention Richard M. Nixon was announced as the party's presidential candidate. "I watched women leading marches," she recorded. "I watched women getting beaten up. I watched women walking up to the bayonets—and they were not afraid."[56]

Fonda became a fearless opponent of the right-wing Nixon admin-istration from 1970, using her celebrity as a platform to increase awareness

Nominee Jane Fonda's Oscar night
look—this black Yves Saint Laurent Rive
Gauche trouser suit—reflected her casual
counterculture cool. (David Downton)

of an array of causes including the militant civil rights group the
Black Panthers, to whom she granted access to her Visa card after
meeting Huey P. Newton, the organization's defense minister, following
his release from prison in July 1970. She also joined nonviolent

demonstrations at Fort Lawton and Alcatraz to aid displaced Native Americans. After a two-year hiatus from screen acting, interrupting a self-financed lecture tour through which she spoke out against the Vietnam War, she agreed to make *Klute*, because activism had exhausted her personal funds. On its set, she was "*always . . . on the phone hustling people for money for one cause or another,*" recalled Pakula. "I'd wonder if she knew her lines. But I'd say, 'We're ready, Jane.' Then she'd stop what she was doing, stand still, and concentrate. When she'd . . . walk into the scene, she was totally involved in the film. When the scene was right, she'd just go back to the phone calls—and the *other* world was total."[57]

As *Klute*'s filming ceased, there was rumbling on set of an Oscar for Fonda, but no best wishes from the cast or crew. Relentlessly fundraising for radical causes, she acquired a reputation as a communist sympathizer. She railed against the media, conservative America, and the FBI. "One day Jane arrived on the set to find it decorated with American flags—the crew's silent response to Fonda's militancy," noted her biographer Christopher Andersen.[58] After *Klute*, she was arrested at the Cleveland airport, returning to Los Angeles from a November 1970 speaking engagement on a London, Ontario, college campus. Catching a connecting flight, Fonda was stopped by a customs agent, who seized vials containing suspected narcotics, and during an ensuing scuffle she branded a police officer a "pig." Released after a night in the Cuyahoga County jail, charges against Fonda were eventually dropped as the pills in her luggage were discovered to be vitamins B, D, and L, as well as prescription drugs Dexedrine, Valium, and Compazine. But officially she became an enemy of the U.S. government as her name went down on a list of radicals to be stopped by border patrols. "Ordered surveillance, ordered the opening of her mail, the checking of her bank records—the whole bit," revealed Steve Jaffe, Fonda's publicist, of the FBI monitoring of his client.[59]

"Demonizing the U.S. government was a very fashionable thing to do," observed academic Kenneth S. Lynn, referring to political activism in seventies Hollywood.[60] While Marlon Brando campaigned to increase civil liberties for Native Americans, actress Candice Bergen and producer Bert Schneider, her boyfriend, journeyed to Oakland, California, where they met Huey Newton. Actor Warren Beatty took a sabbatical from filmmaking in 1972, devoting a year to defeat Richard Nixon by fundraising for Senator George McGovern of South Dakota, who on a propeace platform ran for president on the Democratic Party ticket. Beatty, claimed his friend Gary Hart, then McGovern's campaign manager, "invented the political concert" by recruiting his friends Carole King, James Taylor, and Barbra Streisand to sing at a Democrat Los Angeles fund-raiser, while Mike Nichols and Hart persuaded Elaine May, Peter, Paul & Mary, Dionne Warwick, and Goldie Hawn to take part in the Madison Square Garden extravaganza benefit "Peace Can Bring Us Together."[61]

A political performance at the Oscars, Fonda realized, offered the chance to speak out about continuing atrocities in Vietnam, to address the "masses" tuning in on television and an unprecedented number of media, as the Academy announced plans for a grand finale at the forty-fourth ceremony—a tribute to eighty-two-year old Charlie Chaplin, the pioneering cinéaste. From 1952, Chaplin had lived in self-imposed exile in Corsier-sur-Vevey, Switzerland, fleeing America after being suspected a communist by the U.S. government at the height of the Cold War. Though confined to a wheelchair, he agreed to fly to Hollywood with Oona O'Neill, his wife, and personally accept an honorary Oscar, after attending a career retrospective at New York's Lincoln Center Film Society. "I was touched by the gesture," he said of the Academy's plan.[62]

As one hundred reporters gave Chaplin a hero's welcome when he arrived at New York's Kennedy Airport on April 2, 1972, simultaneously Hollywood was "abuzz with rumors about what Jane would do" at the Oscars, wrote Peter Collier. "Would she spit in the face of the Hollywood establishment? Would there be a nasty, five-minute rant against American imperialism?"[63]

Beneath her tough, tatty, secondhand-clad exterior, Fonda, however, yearned for the Oscar. Wanting the symbol of acceptance from Hollywood's establishment was part of a conundrum that was Fonda, a movie star who at the Academy Awards in 1965 modeled white Chanel haute couture but on the red carpet thrust a clenched fist in the air, displaying the Black Panther's power-to-the-people allegiance sign. Though she had "systematically" rid herself of what radicals termed her "ruling-class privileges," she hung on to her expensive Louis Vuitton handbags, toting one on *Life*'s April 23, 1971, cover.[64] "Please call me Jane—there are no more stars—just equals," she told a production hand on the set of *Steelyard Blues*, a hapless comedy she made after *Klute*, but within a nanosecond bellowed, "Where's my dresser?"[65]

"If you win an Oscar, what happens to your career is not to be believed—your price goes up, you get offered all kinds of things," she told the *New York Times* Rex Reed while puffing on a joint she rolled to celebrate New Year's Eve in 1969, two months before she received her first actress Academy Award nomination for the role of Gloria, a suicidal dance-marathon contestant in *They Shoot Horses, Don't They?* Then she was "bitterly disappointed" to be defeated by *The Prime of Miss Jean Brodie*'s Maggie Smith.[66]

Hollywood figured Fonda's stunt at the 1972 Golden Globes—where a decorated Vietnam veteran she recruited accepted her actress prize to publicize opposition to the ongoing conflict—foreshadowed an inevitable protest at the Oscars. But the Academy was prepared for an onslaught. If Fonda won the forty-fourth actress Oscar and then went on the attack, the stage microphone would be cut and a message from a commercial sponsor would fill the extra airtime.[67] Hollywood had had enough of her relentless proselytizing. "You'd say to somebody, 'I'm working with Jane Fonda,' and eyes would roll," admitted Alan Pakula.[68] "An ego trip," stated folk musician Country Joe McDonald, quitting Fuck the Army (FTA), a touring performance troupe Fonda organized with Donald Sutherland, her activist cohort and then lover, to be a riposte to the patriotic USO and therefore entertain American GIs with countercultural cabaret.[69] Six hundred pieces of hate mail addressed to Fonda had recently arrived at Los Angeles radio station KABC-AM after Steve Jaffe had spoken up for his client on a talk show. "One letter really flipped me out," he recalled. "It was unsigned— a very specific warning that she would be assassinated by sniper-rifle fire on a street in Los Angeles."[70]

"I was afraid she might be in danger from some maniac," reflected Henry Fonda, to whom his daughter made an appeal at the eleventh hour before venturing to the Oscars.[71] "Should I make a statement about the war? If I didn't, would it be irresponsible of me?" she asked her dad in despair.[72] Henry Fonda supported the war effort upon returning from a USO "Handshake Tour" through which he met servicemen stationed around Southeast Asia. Denouncing Method acting as "crap," he also didn't vote for his daughter for the forty-fourth actress prize.[73] But fearing grave consequences, he pleaded with her not to "turn her acceptance speech into a pro-Hanoi harangue."[74] "They called her a traitor, they wrote unsigned letters urging me to send her back to Moscow," he reflected. "I stewed a lot about her."[75] So Fonda advised his daughter to remain neutral. "Tell 'em there's a lot to say," he suggested, "but tonight isn't the time."[76]

Jane Fonda and boyfriend Donald Sutherland took their seats inside the Dorothy Chandler Pavilion at the forty-fourth Academy Awards in 1972, leaving politicking to the actors preening outside on the red carpet. (Frank Edwards/Hulton Archive/Getty Images)

On Oscar day, a bout of flu left Fonda weak, but she soldiered on, departing from her San Fernando Valley home with Donald Sutherland. Before hitting the Oscars, they decamped to a Chinese restaurant near the Dorothy Chandler Pavilion. There, Richard Rosenthal, Fonda's attorney, helped shape Henry Fonda's advice into an acceptance speech that proved elegant and sharp, just like the concise cut of her black Saint Laurent Rive Gauche pantsuit. Fonda's detractors could not fault her Oscar-night fashion, including Henry Fonda's Old Hollywood cronies ("If it's pants, it's Yves's," declared Lauren Bacall, his good friend), or members of the Black Panthers, who called her a "rich white bitch."[77] Fonda's Oscar night pantsuit lacked ornament, save for silver buttons atop its jacket's four patch pockets and another single row that worked as fasteners descending down the front from a Maoist collar. Though stylish, its jet-black sobriety recalled the somber dress adopted by the Oscar-bound during World War II. In YSL, Fonda faded into the background at a convivial Oscars, dominated by the Hollywood homecoming of Charlie Chaplin.

★   ★   ★

The Forty-fourth Academy Awards, April 10, 1972. Placard-waving protesters besieged the Chandler, as an anti-Vietnam organization and the Gay Community Alliance marched round a fountain in front of the Department of Water and Power, just across from the Music Center Mall. But for Fonda, this time there was no display of solidarity. She and Sutherland swiftly made way for the auditorium, leaving politicking to the actors preening on the red carpet. While Jack Nicholson displayed a George McGovern badge on his velvet jacket lapel, master of ceremonies Sammy Davis Jr. raised his hands in the air, flashing a peace sign to the throng spilling from bleacher seats, while another one rendered in silver dangled from a chain atop his ruffled tuxedo shirt. Bypassing the red-carpet protest chaos, Chaplin slipped into the Dorothy Chandler Pavilion via a stage door and awaited his grand finale in the green room.

"I remember the booming silence. I remember my fear that I would black out. I felt so small all alone on the stage looking out into the cavernous theater," wrote Jane Fonda about her 1972 Oscar victory moment. (Courtesy of the Academy of Motion Picture Arts and Sciences)

"I read that line wrong," admitted a jovial Walter Matthau, giggling as he stumbled through a speech introducing the nominees competing for the forty-fourth actress Oscars. Hearty applause egged on Matthau. "For the best performance by an actress, the nominees are Janet Suzman, Julie Christie, Jane Fonda . . ." Caught on-screen, Fonda, twitchy in a front-row seat, maintained an animated conversation with Sutherland, until Matthau declared her the actress winner. A mix of angry booing and warm cheers greeted the result. "I somehow managed to make the endless march to the stage without falling," remembered Fonda, although her front-row seat was just steps from the podium.[78] Audience members on the edge of their

143

seats awaited a hostile speech. But as Fonda cradled the Oscar, her knees went weak beneath her Saint Laurent flares. "I remember the booming silence. I remember my fear that I would black out. I felt so small all alone on the stage looking out into the cavernous theater," she wrote, describing the moment.[79] She worked up her courage and finally began, "Thank you. Thank you very much. There's a great deal to say, but I'm not going to say it tonight. I would just like to really thank you, very much."

Skipping the Governor's Ball at the Beverly Hilton, Fonda went home to sleep off her flu. So Charlie Chaplin was the main attraction. "He appeared promptly—partook of the lavish spread and drank at least two Zombies without visible effect," wrote Chaplin's biographer.[80] Exiting the Hilton at one thirty A.M. the merry film pioneer encountered comedian Groucho Marx. "Stay warm, Groucho," advised Chaplin, "you're next!"[81]

A year later Diana Ross and Liza Minnelli vied for the forty-fifth actress prize. They shared a preference for modern "expensive casuals" as Oscar attire, and like Oscar nominees Julie Andrews and Julie Christie, the competitors were friends. "Am I supposed to treat you like the enemy?" joked Minnelli to Ross at a Hollywood function during Oscar season in 1973.[82] Just as pals Ingrid Bergman and Jennifer Jones were nominated on the strength of headlining the same type of genre picture, Ross and Minnelli also received nominations for leads in two groundbreaking period musicals. In *Lady Sings the Blues*, episodes of the tragic and triumphant life of forties jazz songstress Billie Holiday were immortalized onscreen with great prowess by Ross, the twenty-eight-year-old former lead singer of the Supremes, the hit sixties female supergroup launched by Motown Records. Following the Supremes acrimonious bustup in 1970, Berry Gordy Jr., Motown's founder and Ross's former lover, remained her manager/mentor, establishing Hitsville, a West Coast production operation based on Sunset Boulevard, to mastermind her transition from the concert stage to the screen. With Paramount Pictures he produced *Lady* as the studio's first big-budget musical performed by an entirely African-American cast. Stylishly the biopic merged grit with glamour. Ross as Holiday struggles through life as a New York prostitute and emerges as Lady Day, an itinerant jazz singer who becomes hooked on heroin. *Lady* depicted Holiday clean at the end of the cinematic journey. After a triumphant Carnegie Hall performance, newspaper

inherited as a signature from Edith Head, his former boss whom he'd assisted at Paramount in 1964. For Ross's inevitable ascent to collect the actress Oscar at the podium, he made a lean-tailored, floor-length gown from black chiffon embellished with beads clustered into the shape of tiny rosettes, finishing it with wrist cuffs and a collar, both made from white chiffon. "It was very demure," he added.[104] The second-skin glamour recalled the spirit of Jean Louis, Columbia Pictures' legendary costume designer, who dressed Rita Hayworth and Marilyn Monroe, as well as Marlene Dietrich, and for whom Mackie worked following his tenure with Head.

From 1969, Mackie concentrated on television, flitting between sets as the twenty-nine-year-old boy-wonder costume designer behind two colossal CBS hits—*The Carol Burnett Show* and *The Sonny and Cher Comedy Hour*, while Aghayan operated as the silent-partner business brain keeping their ventures afloat. Together they produced Mackie-Aghayan, an eponymous, elaborate dress line for Bonwit Teller. "Enjoy me" defined its feeling.[105] As the Academy Awards' fashion consultants, the pair conceived special-order couture for presenters Greer Garson, Cher, Natalie Wood, Diahann Carroll and cohost Carole Burnett. But Mackie's intention was that Ross would stand out from the crowd. So he applied brash finishing touches on her trouser suit, dusting sequins on its waistcoat, attaching a keepsake to the ascot—a stickpin of a black man savoring a slice of watermelon—while he tossed in a black fox-fur fling to adorn the neckline of her gown, confirming it was "made for her to win in. They had her believing she was winning," said Mackie, who considered it risky creating two Oscar outfits for Ross, although he had complete admiration for the contender, after working on *Lady*.[106] "Anyone she wanted to be, she could be," he went on. "Anything she wanted, she could have. And she wanted to change. Nobody changed back then at the Oscars, but Diana wanted to."[107]

The dual Oscar-night strategy indeed worked a trick, but left Ross exhausted. The high spirits she displayed at her birthday party seemed motivated by relief that a trying Oscar season had nearly ceased. Vincente Minnelli claimed the month leading up to the forty-fifth ceremony had been "agonizing" for both Ross and his daughter due to excessive Oscar campaigns waged by Allied Artists, *Cabaret*'s producer, and Gordy, *Lady*'s driving force.[108] Fearful that Bob Fosse's avant-garde *Cabaret* might alienate mainstream moviegoers, Allied launched a "promotional blitz" following its release to ensure that the film proved a commercial hit.[109] Meanwhile, Berry Gordy believed he could buy

Ross an Oscar by acquiring advertising space in the *Hollywood Reporter* and *Variety* to promote her nominated performance as Billie Holiday. So through Oscar season he spent thousands on full-page pictorial color ads, noted J. Randy Taraborrelli, Ross's biographer. "Whereas ads for other motion pictures boasted the accomplishments of the supporting actors in the films, the ads for *Lady* only cheered on Diana."[110]

Gordy also plied Academy voting members with gifts and dinners. He conspired against a columnist who devoted favorable coverage to Cicely Tyson, Ross's competitor, who received an actress nomination for her portrayal of Rebecca Morgan, the wife of an imprisoned sharecropper in *Sounder*, Martin Ritt's Depression-era domestic drama. Motown's success had established Gordy as a modern music legend, but in Hollywood his Oscar campaign for *Lady* branded him an arriviste. The resulting publicity was so overt some feared it might inhibit Ross's victory shot. "It was like every day in the trades—huge ads, pushing and pushing and pushing," confirmed Mackie. "In those days you ran a couple of ads. Maybe once a week or something."[111]

Ross seemed embarrassed by the media exposure. "I want to win it, grab it, and run," she confessed to gossip columnist Dorothy Manners,

"Anything she wanted, she could have and she wanted to change," recalled designer Bob Mackie of Oscar contender Diana Ross. So for the forty-fifth Academy Awards in 1973, Mackie made Ross two outfits, including this satin trouser suit. (Bob Mackie)

referring to the actress Oscar.[112] "I'm going to get up early tomorrow and not worry—just being nominated on my first picture, I'm so lucky," she assured her champion Joyce Haber as they bid each other farewell at her pre-Oscars birthday party. But at four A.M. on Oscar morning, Ross remained wide-awake, fretting about the long night up ahead. "Do you think I'll get it?" she asked Ron Miller, the straight-talking Motown composer, who was one of the last of Ross's birthday party guests.[113] "Creatively you definitely deserve it," explained Miller. But his hunch was that Minnelli would win the actress prize and he told her so: "They never gave one to her mother and it would be Hollywood's way of appeasing its own guilt."[114] But Miller joked with Ross, "Promise me that whatever happens—you won't change the name of your dog. Call him Oscar anyway."[115]

The Forty-fifth Academy Awards, March 27, 1973. Outside the Dorothy Chandler Pavilion a valet sporting a crimson jacket peeled opened the door of Ross's Rolls-Royce, and she slipped gracefully from the vintage automobile looking every inch a champion. Moving onto the red carpet, she puckered her lips into a wide, confident smile, painted in a shade of scarlet matching the carnation pinned to the lapel of her Mackie-Aghayan silver-gray trouser suit. Beaming, Ross strode confidently through a chaotic media horde flanked by husband Bob Silberstein, Berry Gordy, and her parents. She threw her hands up in the air and waved through the "confusion of spotlights," smiling to hundreds of fans filling the bleachers. "Diana knew she was a winner and her family knew it as well," wrote J. Randy Taraborrelli of the upbeat entrance.[116]

Liza, sunny in yellow Halston cashmere, remained on the red carpet with her boyfriend Desi Arnaz Jr., speaking to the Academy's press corps for about an hour. "If I don't win, I can think of it as just a nice party," said Minnelli philosophically to a TV reporter, as teenage fans in the bleachers unleashed "frantic squeals. Half of them yelling for Lisa—with an *s*—while the other half called more properly for Liza with a *z*," noted a member of the Oscar-night media pack.[117]

Thirty minutes before showtime, Minnelli reclined in an auditorium seat flanked by her dad and Desi Arnaz Jr., while across the way was Ross's posse. Inching both nominees closer to their moment of truth was "Make a Little Magic," a showstopper commencing the Oscars. "Squadrons of chorus boys and showgirls, glittering costumes, sweeping staircases, a splendidly robust tap dance number, not to mention Angela Lansbury singing and dancing up a storm," wrote *Los Angeles Times*

Diana Ross greeted fans at the forty-fifth Academy Awards, flanked by her husband, Bob Silberstein, and mentor, Berry Gordy. (Courtesy of the Academy of Motion Picture Arts and Sciences)

columnist Cecil Smith, summing up what he classified as a "smashing" opening number.[118]

Backstage there was trouble. Charlton Heston was nowhere to be seen, but with Rock Hudson and Carole Burnett, he composed the trio sharing the Oscars' master-of-ceremonies duty. As news came in that Heston was on his way in a taxi, while his broken-down car was towed from a freeway ramp, Clint Eastwood was corralled into taking over as emcee. But cowboy actor Eastwood stumbled through a prepared speech laced with witty, biblical references to Heston's iconic role as Moses in *The Ten Commandments*. "Flip the card, man, this is not my bag," Eastwood growled into the microphone, advising the production hand to forgo the teleprompter. Then he awkwardly ad-libbed his way through the opening address.[119]

By the time James Coburn and Ross came onstage to present the

"We did it!" declared Julie Andrews after *The Sound of Music* earned the picture prize at the thirty-eighth Academy Awards. Here, she admires the film's trophy at the 1965 Governors Ball. (Courtesy of the Academy of Motion Picture Arts and Sciences)

Cher made her debut as a presenter at the Academy Awards in 1973 wearing a sexy Bob Mackie chiffon two-piece, which was inspired by Dorothy Lamour's trademark exotic style. (Ron Gallela/Wire Image)

"We love you! We love you!" shouted teenage girls as their idol Faye Dunaway left the theater at the fortieth Academy Awards in 1967. (Corbis)

At the sixty-eighth Academy Awards, nominee Susan Sarandon appeared cool and copper-coated from the tips of her Louis Licari–tinted crop to a glossed metallic pout by makeup artist Laura Mercier to the toes of her Dolce & Gabbana evening slippers. (Corbis)

To boost her shot at winning the fifty-eighth supporting actress Oscar in 1986, Anjelica Huston tapped into her Celtic family history, deciding her dress would be emerald green, Ireland's national shade, known for lending good fortune to those who wear it. (Corbis)

"It takes guts to wear chartreuse to the Academy Awards," TV reporter Laurie Pike remarked of Nicole Kidman's 1997 Christian Dior Oscar dress by John Galliano. (Corbis)

Flinging her yoga-toned arms into the air, Versace-clad Courtney Love basked in the shower of 250 flashbulbs at the sixty-ninth Academy Awards in 1997. (Corbis)

The fashion press marveled at the perfect Italian workmanship of Uma Thurman's Prada Oscar gown, although it was designed in Los Angeles by Barbara Tfank. (Alex Berliner)

At the seventy-first Academy Awards in 1999, a relaxed Gywneth Paltrow breezed across the red carpet as though it was her front lawn. "I just wanted to look very sweet," she said of her pink paper taffeta Ralph Lauren gown. (Alex Berliner)

"I'm Cinderella! My Van Cleef diamonds go very well with my Gap T-shirt!" nominee Sharon Stone told TV host Joan Rivers after she arrived at the sixty-eighth Academy Awards in 1997. (Corbis)

"My husband's jaw dropped," recalled nominee Hilary Swank of the reaction that persuaded her to wear Randolph Duke's strapless dress to the Oscars in 2000. (Alex Berliner)

A jubilant mood and Mexican suntan made vintage Valentino couture a glove fit upon seventy-third actress Oscar winner Julia Roberts. (Alex Berliner)

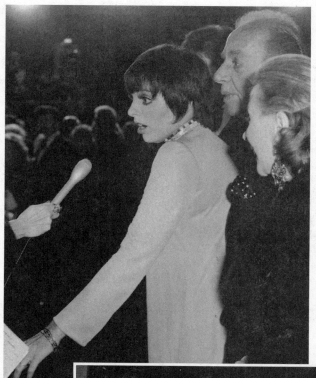

"If I don't win, I can think of it as just a nice party," said Oscar nominee Liza Minnelli to the Hollywood press corps gathered outside the Dorothy Chandler Pavilion at the forty-fifth Academy Awards. Her boyfriend, Desi Arnaz Jr., her father, Vincente Minnelli, and her stepmother, Denise Hale, were on hand for moral support. (Courtesy of the Academy of Motion Picture Arts and Sciences)

supporting actor prize, *Cabaret* had already claimed two technical Academy Awards, for sound and editing. "They must be a nervous bunch," quipped Coburn of the five supporting actor nominees. Joked Ross, "Uh, let's not talk about nerves, okay?" Ripping open the envelope, she revealed the supporting actor prize went to *Cabaret*'s Joel Grey. "Don't let anyone tell you that this isn't a terrific thrill!" cried Minnelli as Grey bolted for the podium. Next came a *Cabaret* sweep of four Academy Awards—art direction, score, cinematography, and direction, a victory for Bob Fosse that drew a gasp from the audience because *The Godfather*'s Francis Ford Coppola was expected to be the winner.

Vincente Minnelli considered Fosse's prize a "good omen" for Liza. But she was convinced that Ross would triumph, spying her competitor take a seat in Bob Mackie's black chiffon gown after presenting the supporting prize. "When I saw her change her dress, I felt she knew something I didn't know," admitted Minnelli. "So I thought she would win. She did a really good job."[120]

Apache Sacheen Littlefeather, in beaded braids and fringed buckskin, stalled the move on to the actress prize, making a surprise appearance to refuse the actor Academy Award on behalf of Marlon Brando for his performance as *The Godfather*'s mob boss Don Vito Corleone. Paramount's production head, Bob Evans, was set to accept the prize, but activist Brando sent on Littlefeather (an actress otherwise known as Maria Cruz), to protest the media's stereotypical treatment of Native Americans. But as Littlefeather delivered a rally cry, hissing and boos greeted it. "Liza's hand squeezed even harder," recorded Vincente Minnelli of Littlefeather's lurching the ceremony into overtime.[121]

Towering Rock Hudson swaggered across the stage, curbing the torrent of abuse as the Academy's crowd rose and cheered, delivering a "huge" standing ovation that roused millions of weary TV viewers as the clock neared midnight, East Coast standard time.[122] "Actors can get on a soap box, but I think often to be most eloquent is to be silent," began Hudson, hushing the audience and commencing the showdown between Ross and Minnelli. Rapt in silence, the seated industry power brokers intently listened to Hudson, whose smooth delivery of the actress presentation made it seem as though he were bantering with cohorts over Polo Lounge cocktails at the Beverly Hills Hotel. "People are always surprised singers can act," offered Hudson with his back to a big screen, introducing a polished sequence from *Lady Sings the Blues*. "They shouldn't be though—singing is just acting with a tune thrown in. She may have made her film debut with *Lady Sings the Blues*, but Diana has been an actress for a very long time."

Rounds of hearty handclapping greeted the sight of Ross lighting up the screen in magnificent white Mackie-Aghayan as she melodiously warbled "My Man," *Lady*'s hit tune. The applause ceased as Hudson turned to Minnelli. "She made her film debut when she was two and a half, clinging to her mother's hand, and even today it's hard not to think of one without the other." Then Garland came on-screen, walking hand in hand with toddler Liza, in the final scene of *In the Good Old Summertime*, unleashing a feral burst of cheers. "Wherever we go, whatever we do, we're gonna go through it together," harmonized sprightly Garland and teenage Minnelli as a ten-year-old clip from TV special *The Liza Show* displayed mother and daughter performing a catchy rendition of "Together." Then Hudson picked it up: "Judy Garland won a special Academy Award when she was seventeen—Liza won Broadway's Tony when she was nineteen." And there Hudson left off, as fading in on-screen came the virtuosic *Cabaret* solo in which Minnelli's Sally Bowles, bathed in a spotlight, sporting a jet-black bowler, garters, and stockings, gave everything to the jaded regulars at the Kit Kat Club: "Life is a cab-a-ret, old chum . . ."[123]

Whistles, cheers, and frenzied handclapping composed the sustained voluble praise that hit the Chandler's rafters before Hudson quieted the house. "In a horse race like tonight," he concluded, "bloodlines count, and Liza's got the bloodlines." Then actress presenters Raquel Welch and Gene Hackman announced Liza Minnelli as the winner of the forty-fifth actress Oscar. "Daddy let out a yell in my ear . . . enough to deafen me for life. It was just the *sha-reek* of the century and so hysterically funny," recollected Minnelli. "Desi let out a yell, but it didn't compare to Daddy's."[124] Diana Ross tossed her head back against her seat, breathed deep, and reached for Bob Silberstein's hand. "I cried," she admitted. "I was looking forward to being up there and getting it, looking gorgeous and saying all of the right things."[125] "Shock waves" shattered Berry Gordy as he absorbed the result.[126] Minnelli was steady on five-inch heels and in a flash of yellow Halston shot to the podium and there said what she felt was necessary. She resented the reference to "bloodliness" in Hudson's preamble. "That performance was *mine*," she told reporters a day later.[127] At the podium she conveyed her feelings eloquently: "Thank you very much," she said, clutching the forty-fifth actress Oscar. "Making the film of *Cabaret* was one of the happiest times of *my* entire life. Thank you for giving *me* this award. You've made *me* very happy."[128]

Faye Dunaway regretted accepting the forty-ninth actress Academy Award—for portraying Diana Christensen, a bullish TV executive in the black comedy *Network*—in a "karate-styled" pantsuit she'd borrowed from Manhattan designer Geoffrey Beene. "I had been determined to find something very simple to wear," she wrote. "It was an impulse that was not all bad, but I had yet to find the right balance."[129] Leggings peeped from beneath a heap of casuals in which Diane Keaton maneuvered herself to the podium accepting the fiftieth actress Oscar for playing the title character in *Annie Hall*, Woody Allen's romantic comedy. "So Fonda doesn't have to worry about underwear," said designer James Reva, explaining the lemon yellow silk he used as an underlay for an off-the-shoulder, shimmering silk crêpe chiffon gown he made for Jane Fonda, who as Keaton's successor received her second actress Oscar in 1979.[130] "Wear-your-own-thing," wrote Timothy Hawkins in the *Los Angeles Times*, describing the trend for laid-back Oscar attire, which carried on until the ceremony got a complete makeover in 1986.[131]

"Thank you for giving *me* this award. You've made *me* very happy," said Liza Minnelli upon receiving the forty-fifth Academy Award from Raquel Welch and Gene Hackman. (Courtesy of the Academy of Motion Picture Arts and Sciences)

Chapter Eight

THE BAD AND THE BEAUTIFUL

Venerated film director Stanley Donen, the Academy Awards' new producer, accelerated his overhaul of the fifty-eighth Oscars when in February 1986, over a late-night dinner in Beverly Hills, he popped a question to costumer Nolan Miller. "How would you like to be the fashion consultant of the Academy Awards?"[1] Sandy blond Miller, the golden boy of Hollywood fashion, was the perfect man for the job. But with the Oscars a month away, factoring it in would be tricky. Christened "TV couturier" by Andy Warhol's style bible, *Interview*, Miller earned thirty-five thousand dollars a week masterminding flamboyant wardrobes for six hit ABC-TV series, including *Dynasty*, *Hotel*, and *The Love Boat*. Intensifying the ninety hours he worked weekly was Elizabeth Taylor, who steadily acquired Miller's made-to-order, five-thousand-dollar one-offs. Regardless. "Be still my heart—of course!" Miller told Donen, agreeing to collaborate. "I had always fantasized about being the designer of the Academy Awards," he confessed, reflecting on the goal he'd nurtured since the sixties, toiling in Paramount's wardrobe department, observing Edith Head do the job.[2]

Taking charge, Miller revived Head's practice of dispatching a dress-code letter. "The whole world watches the Oscars—it is the night that Hollywood shows its face. So everybody should be elegant. Everybody should look like a movie star," he said, paraphrasing the communiqué he sent to nominees, presenters, and guests.[3] Once it was posted, Miller hoped Hollywood's finest would don their best. "A lot of good that did," he grumbled.[4]

Cher upstaged Miller's stylish contribution to the Oscars, appearing in what remains the most controversial ensemble ever to grace its stage—a black, beaded, Bob Mackie twelve-piece. "Las Vegas," said Miller, naming the place he viewed as appropriate for Cher's exuberant Mackie.[5] "That *ridiculous* letter," countered Cher, recalling the dictate she thwarted by taking the stage in the notorious feathery costume.[6] She had reason to play renegade. But Oscar-night jitters gripped the seasoned performer when she set out for the ceremony. Bravely Cher pushed on, contributing to an Academy Awards that, epitomizing eighties glitz, was classified by the *New York Times* as the "best Oscars show in years—perhaps ever."[7]

Stanley Donen masterminded an entertaining Old Hollywood theme to dominate the affair, honoring an array of modern blockbusters, including Steven Spielberg's *The Color Purple*, Sydney Pollack's *Out of Africa*, Peter Weir's *Witness*, John Huston's mobster yarn *Prizzi's Honor*, and the low-budget drama *Kiss of the Spider Woman*. The episode of event television would be star-studded and stylishly memorable as Donen's best films, including *Singin' in the Rain*, the greatest musical ever made, as well as a trio of Audrey Hepburn movies—*Funny Face*, *Charade*, and *Two for the Road*. So presenting Oscars alongside celebrated trophy winners, including Hepburn, were Molly Ringwald and Ally Sheedy, newcomers from the "Brat Pack"—the group of in-demand young actors featured in romantic comedies directed by John Hughes—as well as Michael J. Fox, star of the hit sci-fi comedy *Back to the Future*, and Angelina Jolie, the eleven-year-old daughter of Jon Voight, whose role as an escaped convict in the drama *Runaway Train* earned him an actor nomination. While Russian ballet star Mikhail Baryshnikov was set to perform a solo homage to Old Hollywood heroes Fred Astaire, Gene Kelly, and James Cagney, legendary cinéastes Billy Wilder, Federico Fellini, and Akira Kurosawa agreed to present the picture prize.

Miller was charged with gowning presenter Barbra Streisand in white and silver sequins, and costuming performer Melissa Manchester as well as the Oscars' hundred-strong troupe of singers and dancers. "I had a month to pull it all together and I was absolutely nuts," he confessed. "Every TV show that I was doing was at a different studio. So I would run to Warner Bros. for *Hotel. The Love Boat* and *Dynasty* were [shooting] at the old Goldwyn studios, and I had a miniseries going at Twentieth Century–Fox."[8]

After crisscrossing L.A. in his vintage '65 Rolls-Royce Silver Shadow, Miller retreated to his baronial Beverly Boulevard design headquarters,

To Nolan Miller
oh how glamorous
you made me!
Leslie Caron

Thinking "splashy," Nolan Miller made a flowing gown and cape from rippled blue chiffon for Esther Williams, shaped lilac silk into a wrap dress for Leslie Caron, and created this jade-beaded column for Ann Miller. The trio of Old Hollywood beauties were among nine former Metro-Goldwyn-Mayer leading ladies at the fifty-eighth Academy Awards performing "Once a Star, Always a Star," a song-and-dance tribute honoring the rich screen style pioneered by the once great film studio. (Nolan Miller) where he plotted the look of the Oscars. Inside his workspace—a series of interconnecting zones including his antiques-furnished office, a rose-pink silk-paneled fitting room, and a humming atelier—his team of forty translated his ideas. First came a batch of cupcake-cute satin bathing suits, slim-fit bomber jackets, and fluffy marabou chubbies, all rendered in a rainbow array of Betty Crocker pastels for a chorus line of flight-attendant cancan girls backing up comedienne Teri Garr. Thanks to high-tech special effects, Garr and her shimmying flight crew would land a prop airplane onstage at the Dorothy Chandler Pavilion, head-lining the Academy Awards madcap opening number, "Flying Down to Oscars"—a song-and-dance homage to *Flying Down to Rio*, the 1933 Fred Astaire–Ginger Rogers musical romantic comedy. Thinking "splashy," Miller's team made a flowing gown and cape from rippled blue chiffon for Esther Williams, shaped lilac silk into a wrap dress for Leslie Caron, and, cutting red silk crêpe at sharp angles, produced a slit, floor-length shift that optimally displayed Cyd Charisse's lean, long-legged frame. The trio of Old Hollywood beauties were among nine former Metro-Goldwyn-Mayer leading ladies performing "Once a Star, Always a Star," a song-and-dance tribute honoring the rich screen style pioneered by the once great film studio. A jade-beaded column for Ann Miller, another fabled MGM actress in the performance lineup, was fit on a bust made to replicate her measurements because she was on the road, starring in the touring musical *Sugar Babies*. She promised to stand for a personal fitting on Oscar morning. In the interim, the switchboard at Nolan Miller Inc. was jammed. "Everybody was calling asking me what to wear to the Oscars," recollected Miller, although supporting actress nominee Anjelica Huston and supporting actor presenter Cher enlisted other costume designers to interpret their own concepts into finery for the annual Hollywood ritual.[9]

As Cher contemplated hers in New York with long-standing collaborator Bob Mackie, Huston settled on an inspiration that harked back to her childhood growing up at St. Cleran's, the 110-acre Galway, Ireland, estate owned by director John Huston, her father. Her pastime back then was playing dress-up, assembling looks from a stash of exotic costumes Enrica Somer, her mother, preserved in a trunk. "There were saris and Afghan robes and clothes from the last two centuries," recalled writer Joan Juliet Buck, her best friend.[10] Huston's toys included the director and screenplay Academy Awards John Huston had won in 1949 for Mexican western *The Treasure of the Sierra Madre*, for which Walter Huston, her grandfather, also earned the supporting actor trophy. So by February 5, 1986, when the thirty-four-year-old actress received an Oscar nomination, for her role as interior designer Maerose Prizzi, a member of a prominent Brooklyn mobster clan around which revolved black comedy *Prizzi's Honor* (for which John Huston received a director nomination and Jack Nicholson, her boyfriend, competed for the actor prize), her accolade offered her the chance to qualify as the first third-generation Oscar winner. So to boost her victory shot, Huston decided her Oscar dress would be emerald green, Ireland's national shade, known for lending good fortune to those who wear it. "Anjelica does not normally wear green, but she said for luck, this time, she would," confirmed Tzetzi Ganev, master dressmaker in the women's couture department at reputed Hollywood wardrobe house Western Costume, whom Huston recruited to devise her gown while they worked together on her next starring role, in *The Dead*, a screen adaptation of the James Joyce short story, directed by John Huston and written by his son Tony.[11]

"Extraordinary—a beautiful Oscar dress," added Ganev, whom Huston left free to experiment. So the costumer splurged on hundred-dollar-a-yard, four-ply silk—a weave known to be particularly lustrous, supple, and weighty. "It hangs like a dead body, takes shape, and clings," explained Ganev.[12] On a bust made to match Huston's shapely proportions, she liberally draped the costly fabric. The result was an unusually beautiful, bias-cut, off-the-shoulder gown, displaying Huston's taut left arm, while its floor-length hem fanned out to form a slithery fishtail train—a rare accoutrement on an Oscar dress because most contenders fear tripping over excess material marching to the podium. "She could handle it," confirmed Ganev of poised Huston, who as a late-sixties top model played muse to her New York photographer boyfriend Bob Richardson.[13] By the seventies she was a *Vogue* regular, factored into the lineup on Halston's runway, while her intrinsic grace recalled her mother, a former Balanchine ballerina. "How to sit, how to pose, how to cross her legs, and how to make an entrance—Anjelica knew all the tricks," continued Ganev. "When she walks into a room, I mean, everybody turns to look at her. And she looked like royalty in her Oscar dress. She was like the queen of England."[14]

Cleopatra, Carmen Miranda, Lady Godiva, and thirties Paramount movie queen Dorothy Lamour were among myriad characters Cher impersonated on the Vegas stage and on TV. Bob Mackie had created costumes for them all. Since Cher and Mackie had first teamed up in 1971 to work on the hit CBS series *The Sonny and Cher Comedy Hour*, Mackie had stylishly mined Cher's Native American heritage, too. He created an immense red, white, and yellow headdress, which she wore with a beaded halter gown, for a solo TV performance of "Half-Breed," the hit single about her struggle growing up in sixties L.A. as Cherilyn Sarkisian LaPierre, a raven-haired misfit with Cherokee and Armenian blood. By 1976, Cher possessed eleven hundred Bob Mackie costumes. Ten years later, their joint effort for the fifty-eighth Academy Awards represented their seventh Oscar-night collaboration, dating back to the first time she'd presented at the ceremony in 1973. Their infamous seventh effort together mixed his opulent Native Americana with punk rock music, of which Cher was a fan.

Just as British punks adopted the aggressive spiked Mohawk hairstyle to display their disaffection with the country's monarchy and its elitist Conservative government, Cher intended to don a Mackie Oscar punk ensemble that would translate the enmity she harbored toward the Academy because it had ignored her compelling performance as Florence "Rusty" Dennis, a biker mom to a deformed teenager in *Mask*, a drama directed by Peter Bogdanovich. She'd tied with Argentine film star Norma Aleandro for the Palme d'Or actress prize at the Cannes Film Festival in May 1985. The recognition validated a momentous decision Cher had made in 1980, shifting her career from the Vegas stage to the Hollywood screen. Studying at New York's Actors Studio, she honed her talent and won a 1984 Golden Globe for her second major screen role as Dolly Pelliker, a lesbian power-plant worker in the biographical drama *Silkwood*, but Linda Hunt trumped Cher in the fifty-sixth supporting actress Oscar race.

Film critics perceived *Mask* as Cher's second shot at the Oscar she so longed for. But it received merely one nomination, for the makeup prize. Sheila Benson of the *Los Angeles Times* attributed Cher's Academy slight to a high-profile eleven-million dollar lawsuit Bogdanovich waged against Universal Studios, *Mask*'s producer, because of its decision to replace the film's Bruce Springsteen score with a Bob Seger sound track and cut two scenes that he considered crucial.[15] Universal also refrained from promoting Cher's performance. "They didn't know what to make of me," she reflected.[16]

A series of fifteen-second TV commercials promoting fitness guru Jack LaLanne's health clubs jeopardized Cher's credibility. In them, the thirty-nine-year-old displayed her jaw-dropping, model-perfect 32B–24–36 measurements. Gossip fodder, too, were her back-to-back relationships with younger men, including a rotating trio of twenty-four-year-old actors—Tom Cruise, Val Kilmer, and Eric Stoltz (who played her son in *Mask*)—as well as twenty-nine-year-old ABC-TV executive Joshua Donen, Stanley Donen's son. In today's Hollywood such romantic liaisons are the norm. So are commercial endorsements by actors. But Hollywood castigated Cher because her moves were two decades ahead of the curve. "The reasons people gave had nothing to do with my acting," she wrote of her Oscar shutout. "They said I wasn't serious enough—that I dated young men and I didn't dress like a serious actress. I wasn't going to go at all."[17,18]

Steven Spielberg declined an offer to present the fifty-eighth actor prize, a move he made to spite the Academy, according to speculation, because although *The Color Purple*, his epic adaptation of Alice Walker's Pulitzer Prize–winning novel received eleven nominations, his name was absent from the director category. But Cher acquiesced, concluding Mackie's comic spin could make clear her discontent to the Academy as well as the billion watching the ceremony on TV. "I was doing a big joke, but there was a serious undertone to it, because I was really hurt," she said.[19] Customarily Cher transforms low points into positive situations by applying a dash of humor.[20] In 1976 she discovered the demise of her brief marriage to rock star Gregg Allman. "My publicist called and said, 'Do you know Gregory is divorcing you?'" she recalled. "And I said, 'No. Hum a few bars.' You know, sometimes in my most painful moments, that's my reaction. That's the way I say, 'Fuck you.'"[21]

Independently she devised a catchy one-liner preamble to her presenter's script that would convey to the Academy her feelings and let everyone know exactly what she thought of Nolan Miller's dress-code letter. To heighten the visual impact of the Bob Mackie she planned to wear, Cher decided its details would remain secret until Oscar night. Until then, Mackie's team and Cher's network of beauty professionals were in on it. So was Tom Cruise. During Oscar season, Cher and the *Risky Business* star were still involved. So Mackie reported to Cruise's East Thirteenth Street, New York, loft apartment, where they first discussed ideas for her presenter's costume. "I want to look like a Mohawk," revealed Cher. "It was all about fun," she added. "Bob and I have said that a million times: 'Oh, this will be fun!'"[22]

This time a straight-faced Mackie hesitated. "Bob kept saying, 'Are you sure you want to do this? Are you sure you want to do this?'"[23] Mackie said he was considering the task at hand: "She was presenting an award for best supporting actor, and I said, 'Don't you think this is kind of upstaging the person you are giving the award to?'"[24]

He had his own reputation to consider. In 1982, Mackie established Bob Mackie Originals, an ambitious yet struggling Seventh Avenue, New York, fashion venture. During New York Fashion Week in the early eighties, as he displayed wild flights of fantasy like sparkly wet suits, jackets embroidered with Japanese sushi, and fifteen-thousand-dollar bejeweled serapes, alongside Calvin Klein's minimalist urbanity as well as Ralph Lauren's western denims, his wit fell flat. Possibly he anticipated the potshots if he, the "sultan of sequins," the "rajah of rhinestones," and onetime costumer to The Captain and Tennille, riffed punk rock. Mackie eventually gave in because he felt for Cher. "She was quite wonderful in *Mask*, but nobody in the Academy went to see it," he said. "They heard what it was about and they didn't want to."[25] Cher was also his muse—a woman whose beauty he found irresistible. "She was like this big Barbie doll I could dress up," he reasoned. "'If I'm going to go,' she told me, 'let them see that everything still looks good.'"[26]

So he set to work, suspending a skimpy bejeweled bikini from a grid-patterned breastplate choker. Cascading from second-skin, low-riding, licorice-whip-sexy, black Lycra leggings was a torso-skirting, beaded loincloth he'd originally made as part of an Indian-warrior costume Cher wore in the early seventies on *The Sonny and Cher Comedy Hour*. While the black top and bottom would frame Cher's ripped abdominals, or what Mackie reverentially described as the "best tummy in the business," a cashmere cape was draped to fall from her shoulders. Handmade were jet bead accessories, including earrings precisely measured to swing from Cher's lobes to collarbone, a pair of armbands, and two wrist cuffs. Mackie's pièce de résistance was a towering, two-foot, feathered headdress. Manipulating its eight hundred black-dyed rooster plumes, his expert milliner toiled for fourteen days. The grand total on the costume was twelve thousand dollars, and though it was more Mohawk Indian than punk rock, Cher didn't mind when, during Oscar week, she first set eyes on it in L.A. "It was *so* beautiful," she remembered. "I mean, if you could have seen the headdress, with the most beautiful feathers and the cashmere blanket. Bob is the best costume designer that ever lived."[27]

"Wait till you see what I'm wearing!" she gushed to Roy Christopher, the Academy's stage set designer.[28] It was two days before the Oscars, and Cher tried to play it cool when she showed up for rehearsal at the Dorothy Chandler Pavilion, dressed "way down" in a man's white undershirt, floppy hat, and dark sunglasses.[29] She had a tough time keeping a lid on it, realizing she would be framed like a prized painting by the slick black, white, and silver art deco archway Christopher had built as a passage for presenters to access the stage.

Behind the scenes, chaos reigned in Donen's Oscar production. From Rome, Fellini sent regrets that he was unable to present the picture prize because he'd slipped strolling along Via Margutta and fractured his leg. John Huston agreed to replace Fellini, but the frail seventy-nine-year-old was recovering from open-heart surgery and suffered from emphysema, which required he breathe with the help of an oxygen tank. Mikhail Baryshnikov was nursing an injured knee, so his dance solo was canceled—news that transformed Ron Field, the Academy's Tony Award–winning choreographer, into a "wild animal," claimed Nolan Miller.[30]

The *Los Angeles Times* reported Miller was "frantic" by Oscar weekend. A jade green gown was too small for the "Once a Star, Always a Star" suddenly stout performer Ann Miller, and yet to be fit for ceremonial attire were Debbie Reynolds and Ginger Rogers. While Anjelica Huston confirmed to *Variety* columnist Army Archerd that her partner Jack Nicholson would wear a sling at the Oscars because he'd broken his left arm skiing in Aspen, Cher attempted to prepare on/off boyfriend Josh Donen, who was escorting her to the ceremony his father, Stanley, was producing. "'No matter what I look like, you're not going to be embarrassed to go with me?'" she said, recalling the conversation she had with Donen. "I said it numerous times: 'Joshua, will you be happy to go with me, no matter what I wear? No matter what I look like?' I said this to him over and over again: 'Will you be okay?' And he said, 'Yes, sweetheart—no matter what you wear.'"[31]

On Oscar afternoon a relaxed Cher took a shower in the bathroom just off the master bedroom inside her Moorish, Mulholland Drive estate, and there, after an eighty-minute session with her makeup artist Leonard Engleman and hairstylist Renata Leuschner, Mackie's glossy black regalia went on in about five minutes. The loincloth was precisely fixed to her black Lycra leggings. "I had worn it before," said Cher of the panels. "I just had not worn pants underneath it. I just didn't wear anything underneath it, actually."[32] From her wardrobe came optimum footwear—a pair of black, satin, knee-high boots. "I had danced in them so they were really comfortable," she added.[33] Experimenting with newfangled color contact lenses, she mixed shades. "One blue eye and one brown eye," confirmed Cher of her choice.[34] "When I put in one blue eye, I thought, 'Oh, that will be a lot more fun. And you know what? If these people don't like the way I dress, and my boyfriends are not acceptable,' I thought, 'you know what? If you don't think that's acceptable, wait till you see this!'"[35]

Cher's beautifiers opened the bathroom door, releasing the superstar to a Gothic habitat—her bedroom styled with asp andirons, python-carved mirrors, and swaggering black velvet drapery. Donen was ready to go in a white dinner jacket. But as she finally faced him, Cher was more frightened chick than phoenix landing. Beneath the barely there Mackie, a cold sweat broke out on her buff limbs because the first sight of its plumage sent Donen into a complete tailspin. His shock shook Cher so much to the core that not until exiting the Academy's stage after presenting the supporting actor Oscar did her tension subside.

"I came waltzing out and I think he just about shit," she recalled.[36] "Jesus Christ, Cher," said Donen, falling backward onto her bed.[37] "That was my first moment of 'Oh my god! Have I gone too far?'" confessed Cher. "You have to realize, I was about seven feet tall."[38]

In the back of the limousine ferrying the couple to the Chandler, Cher felt like a baby sparrow tossed out of its nest. Because Mackie's headdress hit the car's roof, she squatted on the floor so as not to ruffle its quills. "I was so crouched down," she remembered. "I was so uncomfortable. Joshua kept looking at me and I said, 'You said, *"No matter what."*'"[39]

The Fifty-eighth Academy Awards, March 24, 1986. "Good evening, movie fans!" boomed the Academy's forecourt emcee, *Variety*'s bow-tied columnist Army Archerd. Nolan Miller was backstage amid "bedlam—it was a nightmare," he recalled. "Everybody was nervous. Everybody was in each other's way."[40] As he searched for Ann Miller's lost earring, Cher swooped through a stage door with Mackie and Donen, landing with a thud amid the star-studded commotion. "So much for my letter," said Miller to Mackie, who laughed and shrugged his shoulders.[41] "Isn't she swell? She is just the best, Joshua," enthused Stanley Donen.[42] "People were looking at me like I just stepped off Mars," confessed Cher.[43] She had no choice but to hold her head up high due to Mackie's crown of feathers. "Even though it was not that heavy, it

Cher — Academy Awards

Bob Mackie 1986

"If you could have seen the headdress and the cashmere blanket—Bob is the best costume designer who ever lived," recalled Cher about her first look at the black feathery costume Bob Mackie made for her appearance at the fifty-eighth Academy Awards in 1986. (Bob Mackie)

Arriving at the fifty-eighth Academy Awards, a nervous Cher made a crash landing on the red carpet with her date, ABC-TV executive Joshua Donen. (Ron Galella/Wire Image)

was so uncontrollable," added Cher of the top-off. "It had a mind of its own. I was so terrified and thinking, 'You have made *such* a terrible mistake.'"[44]

"Hello, Hollywood! You look great tonight!" roared vivacious Teri Garr, who in white Ginger Rogers–style chiffon opened the ceremony with "Flying Down to Oscar." Though the bouncy number flopped, Anjelica Huston swiftly came on to accept the supporting actress prize, eliciting praise from the audience of two thousand as well as the "beau monde of Tinseltown," as *Interview* columnist George Christy described the crowd celebrating at the Oscar-watching party hosted by Swifty Lazar at Spago, Sunset Boulevard's "be-seen" restaurant.[45] "This means a lot to me since it comes from a role in which I was directed from my father. And I know it means a lot to him," said a beaming Huston, firmly clutching her Oscar while flashing a bare arm from her glistening emerald green Tzetzi Ganev. Thanking *Prizzi's Honor*'s cast and Peggy Feury, her acting coach, Huston then spontaneously veered off the usual podium-to-pressroom route, working her train as she descended from the stage down its polished black steps to meet Nicholson in the aisle. There, he embraced Huston, despite his aching broken arm. "I never had a greater moment," recalled Nicholson. "Thank God it came early in the evening—I was legitimately stoned on pain pills."[46]

Backstage, Cher collided with Oscar cohost Jane Fonda. "I remember coming around the corner and running into Jane, and Jane just looking at me and just getting completely hysterical—laughing. Jane made it better."[47] At the one-hour-and-six-minute mark, Fonda paid tribute to Cher: "To present the Oscar for supporting actor is one of the most glamorous people in this, or any other, business. And you better believe it. Wait till you see what's going to come out here. Ladies and gentlemen, in a word, Cher."

Strutting Mackie's stuff through the Chandler's archway, Cher appeared onstage with insouciance. "Like she had jeans and a T-shirt on, no matter what it was," confirmed Mackie of the carefree attitude she customarily adopted.[48] Cher's stride to the podium seemed no big deal, although she quaked beneath her feathers, cashmere, jet beads, satin, and Lycra. Reflecting on the journey, she admitted, "It was step-by-step. To take a huge step like that to an audience you want to join but doesn't really want you—I went into some sort of out-of-body experience. I thought, 'This is kind of crazy because this could go terribly pear-shaped.' I had seen people at the Oscars—you know, when Barbra Streisand went up and her butt was showing. I knew that

Anjelica Huston's Oscar dress by costumer Tzetzi Ganev seductively displayed her taut left arm. Her boyfriend Jack Nicholson's was in a sling because he broke it skiing in Aspen. (Courtesy of the Academy of Motion Picture Arts and Sciences)

this could ruin a career—either momentarily or for a long time—because what you do at the Oscars, everyone sees."[49]

Cher, however, delivered an effective opening remark: "As you can see, I did receive my Academy booklet on how to dress like a serious actress." Laughter enveloped the auditorium. "Everyone got the joke," she confirmed.[50] Even after she announced seventy-eight-year-old Don Ameche, costar of *Cocoon*, as winner of the supporting actor prize, Cher had not yet exhaled a sigh of relief. Ameche bounded to the stage, amid a standing ovation, but stopped short at the podium. "Like a cat in a thunderstorm—a deer in the headlights," said Cher, describing his bewilderment while she handed on the Oscar.[51] Right then "Oh, fuck!" went through her head one last time.[52] "I thought, 'This is *his* big night. And look at him.' Because it's the best of your dreams and the worst of your nightmares—all at the same time. But he was very generous and a gentleman. So I tried to step out of his way."[53]

"Once a Star, Always a Star" evoked MGM's former glory. Lionel

171

Richie warbled "Say You, Say Me"—the theme from *White Nights*, for which he received an Academy Award from legends Gene Kelly, Donald O'Connor, and Debbie Reynolds. Thespian Geraldine Page claimed the actress prize for the drama *The Trip to Bountiful*—in a red velvet cloak, her third-act costume designed by Gail Cooper-Hecht for the Broadway production of Somerset Maugham's *The Circle*, in which she was then appearing.

Post-Oscar chatter was split three ways between the triumph of *Out of Africa*, Sydney Pollack's epic chronicling novelist Karen Blixen's life story, which collected seven Academy Awards, *The Color Purple*'s eleven "Oscarless" nominees, and Cher's Bob Mackie. In the Chandler's press-room, *Village Voice* columnist Michael Musto claimed from his close-up view that her towering headdress resembled a dead cockatoo.[54] "I thought it was beautiful, but I wouldn't want to sit behind her—all those feathers," said Audrey Hepburn after the ceremony at Spago.[55] "A monstrosity—suitable for Darth Vader's funeral!" opined David Letterman a day later on *Late Night*, his CBS-TV show.[56] *People* weekly called it "bonkers." *Time* commended as "epic" Cher's humor. "What's Cher to wear? How other stars might dress is nowhere near as interesting a subject," wrote *Los Angeles Times* fashion editor Mary Rourke in April 1988, two days before the sixtieth Academy Awards, where Cher claimed the actress Oscar for *Moonstruck* in a black, beaded, skin-baring Mackie gown.[57] "Beautiful," Cher classified her Oscar dress.[58] "The biggest thing in my life was winning that award," she added. "The second-biggest thing that night was shaking hands with Audrey Hepburn and having her say, 'I'm so happy you won.' I was thrilled and delighted, but my feet were killing me. You know how you get an outfit together and you get brand-new shoes and you don't go around walking in them? I never walked in my shoes and they killed me."[59]

Cher... Academy Awards
1988

Bob Mackie

"Beautiful," said Cher, recalling this beaded Bob Mackie in which she claimed the sixtieth actress Oscar for *Moonstruck*. (Bob Mackie)

Chapter Nine
THE ONLY GAME IN TOWN

The sixty-second actress Oscar race in 1990 was no contest. Jessica Tandy, the eighty-one-year-old star of the feel-good movie *Driving Miss Daisy*, was expected to win the trophy. But there was Oscar buzz about two fashion professionals vying for red-carpet recognition. "Oscar de la Hayman," the *Los Angeles Herald-Examiner* trumpeted, heralding the appointment of one—Rodeo Drive retailer Fred Hayman—as the Academy Awards' new fashion consultant. "I have big plans," announced Hayman. Among them was halting negative headlines like LOSER and WORST OUTFIT that dogged freewheeling, experimentally clad actress contenders who showed up at the Oscars in the late eighties. Hayman's solution was an "Oscar closet" styling service he operated in an enclave off the shop floor at his 237 Rodeo Drive boutique. Stocked with event couture produced by a list of international designers, which he personally selected as fitting for the occasion, Hayman invited nominees and presenters in to browse. "They can buy or borrow, and we'll fully accessorize them, from furs to whatever," he explained. "A rack of drop-dead, entrance-making gowns from the world's most extravagant designers," reported the *Herald-Examiner's* fashion writer Gaile Robinson, after trawling through Hayman's forest of Bob Mackie, Valentino, and Gianni Versace.[1]

"My goal was to dress the younger generation in Hollywood," explained Giorgio Armani in 2003, thinking back to the eveningwear loaning service he simultaneously ran from his 436 Rodeo Drive boutique.[2] Armani's mission served to heighten the brand recognition he achieved producing a wardrobe of superlative suits for Richard Gere's lead role as Hollywood hustler Julian Kaye in *American Gigolo*,

Paul Schrader's slick 1980 romance. Its sleeper hit status is today part of the Armani legend. Through the eighties and nineties, it established worldwide his signature relaxed suiting for men and women—"slouch chic"—as the preeminent luxury mode. After *Gigolo*, Armani became the first fashion designer since Christian Dior to make the cover of *Time*. His Milan atelier operated a thriving sideline producing movie costumes, and while his suits replaced crisp Savile Row tailoring as the uniform of Hollywood power brokers, his film-industry following motivated the August 1988 opening of his luxurious Beverly Hills flagship. "We used tons and tons of white gold," said the boutique's designer, international restaurateur Michael Chow, recalling the precious metal leaf that lined backlit wall panels climbing from a polished marble floor to a one-hundred-foot cathedral ceiling.[3] Gold lamé draped cardboard shipping cartons and served as soft furnishings on opening day of Giorgio Armani Beverly Hills because its faux art deco wrought-iron and ebonized-wood fixtures were still under construction. But the last-minute hitch was no major setback. The sweeping, thirteen-thousand-square-feet boutique made neighboring Polo Ralph Lauren, a third of its size, look like a quaint, corner store and the tradition of afternoon shopping seem square. Grand-scale megashops that alternated after hours as party spaces like Armani's soon mushroomed along Rodeo Drive.

The competition between Armani and Hayman as they vied to dress Hollywood during 1990's Oscar season spared women the expense of buying dresses, so the practice of commissioning great costume designers to make them halted. The rivalry between Armani and Hayman also established fashion competition as integral to the buildup heralding the Academy Awards. But inside Hayman's Oscar closet hung a few evening-wear samples from Borgonuovo, Armani's ladies' eveningwear line. As for suntanned Armani, he respected eminent, silver-haired Hayman, who'd originally operated the Rodeo Drive boutique Giorgio from 1962, establishing it as a retail landmark, due to the model-beautiful salesgirls who offered its merchandise, a mix of covetable continental and American ready-to-wear in perky yellow-and-white-striped paper. A '52 Silver Wraith Rolls-Royce served as Giorgio's delivery van until 1987, when Hayman cashed in, selling his mini-empire to Avon for $165 million, along with its signature floral fragrance.[4] During Giorgio's seventies heyday, it was a clubhouse meeting point where yesteryear stars like Norma Shearer and Loretta Young mingled at its cappuccino bar alongside now-girls Raquel Welch, Jacqueline Bisset, and Candice Bergen.

By 1990 Rodeo Drive retailer Fred Hayman, as the Oscars' fashion consultant, was part of a new regime producing the Academy Awards. "I have big plans," announced Hayman, accepting the post. (Fred Hayman)

By 1990 Hayman, as the Oscars' fashion consultant, was part of a new regime producing the Academy Awards, including TV and feature-film director Gil Cates, who commenced a nearly uninterrupted sixteen-year stint as the Oscars' producer. Strategizing about a new approach for the sixty-second ceremony, Cates settled on festive, international "companion ceremonies" staged via satellite linkup in Moscow, Tokyo, Sydney, London, and Buenos Aires.[5] Celebrating global unity, the Oscars telecast was a response to the November 1989 fall of the Berlin Wall, as well as a bevy of foreign films within the Academy's competition lineup. The leading contender was *My Left Foot*, Dubliner Jim Sheridan's take on the life story of Irish artist, poet, and author Christy Brown's against-the-odds triumph over cerebral palsy. The gripping, low-budget feature, adapted from Brown's autobiography, clinched four top nominations including picture, actor, direction, and supporting actress. Another overseas contender was Parisian Isabelle Adjani, thirty-five, who, as the title character of French romance *Camille Claudel*, received an actress Academy Award nomination for her portrayal of the late-nineteenth-century sculptress and tortured lover of master Auguste Rodin. Adjani had no need for Hayman's Oscar closet because she planned to wear white, ruffled couture by Christian Dior's Gianfranco Ferre. But fifty-year-old British actress Pauline Collins, her competitor, put Hayman to work. After Collins's role as a bored, middle-aged Liverpool housewife in the comedy *Shirley Valentine* earned her the Academy's actress cut, she rejected Polaroids of potential Oscar dresses Hayman sent on to her in London. So he sourced Collins an ensemble from Wilshire Boulevard's Saks Fifth Avenue.

A vanload of Hayman's evening dresses was dispatched to a remote location outside L.A., to the presenter of the cinematography prize, Melanie Griffith, whose intense shooting schedule on *Pacific Heights* prevented a trip to Rodeo Drive. Hayman quickly proffered an Oscar-night maternity dress for Rita Wilson, the five-and-a-half-months preg-nant wife of Tom Hanks, after her first choice—a black, sequined trapeze gown—went missing while it was shipped to L.A. But his fashion winning streak came to an abrupt end when well before Oscars, the *Los Angeles Times* published details of the floor-length, bugle-beaded, and sequined Bob Mackie that *Enemies, A Love Story*'s actress nominee Anjelica Huston found inside Hayman's Oscar closet. "Rankled" Huston shopped elsewhere for an Oscar dress. Meanwhile, front-runners were gravitating to Giorgio Armani, where, all year in a back office adjacent to the menswear department, Wanda McDaniel, Armani's West Coast representative, had been cultivating nominees.

"My goal was to dress the younger generation in Hollywood," explained Giorgio Armani, thinking back to the sixty-second Academy Awards in 1990. (Giorgio Armani)

Equipped to tackle the task, McDaniel, a former *Herald-Examiner* society columnist, had an enviable Rolodex laden with the private telephone numbers of every recent top box-office star. Enlisting this totally connected Beverly Hills trophy wife (whose husband, Albert S. Ruddy, produced classic Oscar-winning motion pictures including *The Godfather*) was among Armani's best Hollywood moves. "I've cut a wide swath. It's a real Armani swath—the kind of people who *get it*," admitted McDaniel, owning up to her social-butterfly status after joining forces with the designer in 1988.[6]

Brunette McDaniel made Armani's four-hour boutique launch a scene as three hundred shoppers dropped seventy thousand dollars while rubbing shoulders with her "pals," who received a special thirty percent discount—Mrs. Frank Sinatra, mogul Jeffrey Katzenberg, ABC-TV's Maria Shriver, her husband, Arnold Schwarzenegger, as well as starlet Sharon Stone, his costar in the forthcoming action-adventure blockbuster *Total Recall*.[7] "Studio 54, Rodeo Drive–style—we'd invite some people to a trunk show and five hundred would turn up," said McDaniel, describing the action at champagne-fueled evening fashion shows she organized at the boutique to build up Oscar momentum.[8]

Though rich enough to pay retail for the twenty or so double-breasted Armani suits that came wholesale with her job, Missouri-born, thirty-five-year-old McDaniel was a rare, down-to-earth breed apart from most fashion professionals—an executive with whom an Oscar contender could entrust her needs and know that everything would fit just right. Mastering celebrity dressing, she pioneered the type of Beverly Hills Oscar-fashion professional that *Premiere* later classified as a "point person"—that is, a well-connected emissary who on behalf of a designer recruits the right people to wear their latest to the Academy Awards. From Bottega Veneta to neighboring Dolce & Gabbana, Gucci, and Versace—today every Rodeo Drive megaboutique that launched in the wake of Armani's is ruled by teams of point people—many of whom McDaniel trained. "Months of phone calls, special orders, fittings, fallout, deadlines, last-minute additions, and last-minute subtractions," she remembered of forging the role in 1990.[9] McDaniel flew by the seat of her front-pleated Armani's and played translator, too, because the designer's minimalist *alta moda* was a foreign concept to the lineup of Academy nominees and presenters she wooed.

Some emerged headline-bruised after recently pulling up to red-carpet galas in "oversize this, thrift-shop that," as Graydon Carter summed up Hollywood style in 1989.[10] "Bosom-baring, hip-hugging," noted *People*, writing off the aqua, knee-length, strapless taffeta cocktail gown overloaded with a voluminous backside bow in which Jodie Foster collected the sixty-first actress Academy Award that year for her role as rape victim Sarah Tobias in *The Accused*, a drama produced by Paramount Pictures.[11] Foster's *People* Worst Dressed placer was a spur-of-the-moment purchase she'd made after spotting it in a Rome boutique window, following a press conference held there for *The Accused*, just prior to the Academy's announcement of her nomination. Along with the billion TV viewers that witnessed her Academy Awards victory, McDaniel noticed its poor fit, as ABC-TV's cameras twice caught Foster hiking up its plunging strapless bodice before shimmying to the podium. So a week after the ceremony McDaniel made her first phone call to Foster, suggesting she opt for a tailored Armani when she went back to the Oscars presenting the actor prize.

Yale graduate Foster, twenty-eight, made an ideal Armani movie-star muse. She spoke Italian, starred in *Alice Doesn't Live Here Anymore* and *Taxi Driver*, a pair of seventies dramas directed by Armani's close friend Martin Scorsese. She also showed signs of appreciating European fashion. Opting for the alternative she had for the sixty-first Academy Awards—a minidress version of Le Smoking, Yves Saint Laurent's inspired take on the classic tuxedo—she might have topped the International Best Dressed list. Foster also possessed a style instinct that was quintessentially understated Armani. "Not fashion! Very elegant, very simple, and very natural," said Armani to models backstage at a Milan fashion show, describing his approach. "I'm not interested in having bleached-blond hair, a big beauty mark, or bright red lipstick—a look that would make me conspicuous," explained Foster in a feature that accompanied a September 1989 *Harper's Bazaar* cover story celebrating her status as number one among America's ten most beautiful women. "My clothes have to be classic. Quality textures and cuts appeal to me—things that hold up to time. I much prefer being comfortable to standing out."[12]

Even better for Armani, Foster's arduous kickboxing sessions whittled down her figure to a petite sample size, and she was totally open to suggestion after McDaniel reached her by telephone. "Praise the Lord! Hallelujah! He will dress me for the rest of my life. You've just taken the greatest burden off of me," effused Foster to McDaniel, who arranged a private viewing of a special fleet of Oscar Armanis, including six- and ten-thousand-dollar taupe, rose, emerald green, and steel-gray evening dresses, pearl-encrusted sheaths, crystal-drenched columns, and formfitting whispers of dark jersey.[13] Armani plucked the eveningwear from his spring/summer 1990 collection, inspired by the illustrious geometric set design artist Léon Bakst made in 1909 for the Ballets Russes, the Russian-émigré dance troupe. "Totally directional," declared Kal Ruttenstein, Bloomingdale's influential fashion director, after joining the standing ovation greeting its debut at Milan's seventeenth-century Palazzo del Senato in October 1989.[14] "Incredibly beautiful," stated Tina Turner, who also witnessed it, from a front seat facing Armani's runway.[15] "What do you think would look good on me?" Foster asked McDaniel a month before the Oscars, admiring an abridged version of the Ballets Russes magnificence on a rolling rack set up inside a VIP showroom at Giorgio Armani Beverly Hills.[16]

Immediately she appreciated its sleek-cut, luxury textiles—which Armani sourced from Turin specialists Groupo GFT—and, no doubt, McDaniel's guidance. "I really just put myself in Mr. Armani's hands," reflected Foster on the session.[17] "She was the greatest," confirmed McDaniel. "She said, 'Tell me what I'm going to wear,' because, she figured, that's our job, and her job is to walk out across the Oscars' stage. And she walked in here with madras shorts and her mismatched shirt. But I knew we were going to the Oscars."[18, 19]

So was Julia Roberts. But two weeks before the event, the twenty-three-year-old supporting actress nominee for her role as Shelby Eatenton Latcherie, a Southern belle newlywed afflicted with diabetes in the drama *Steel Magnolias*, confessed she had nothing to wear to it, nor any time to shop. But in January 1990, the lanky superstar from Smyrna, Georgia, had strolled through Armani with her actor boyfriend Kiefer Sutherland. She'd bypassed the thousand-square-foot space devoted to Borgonuovo, and intrigued by an undulating jet-black steel staircase Michael Chow had specifically designed to entice discerning shoppers up to Armani's second-floor men's department, Roberts landed up there and stayed put, admiring the last of its winter collection including gray, brown, and tan, three-button sack suits. "Why do they get to dress so comfortably? I want to wear a man's suit," she told McDaniel.[20] "I'm sitting there thinking, 'I'm going to be fired,'" remembered McDaniel of the moment she contemplated a red-carpet train wreck of Roberts in Armani menswear at the Golden Globes.[21]

But off in matching, chocolate brown, tweed Armani men's suits went Roberts and Sutherland to the ceremony, where she claimed the supporting actress prize for *Steel Magnolias*. Clutching it, the sleeves of Roberts's gigantic suit jacket grazed her knuckles. Her slapdash style irritated aesthete Herb Ross, *Steel Magnolias'* director, who insisted the week before its rehearsal that she lose weight and groom her thick eyebrows. Then in September 1988, when the production ceased, Ross suggested Roberts pursue acting lessons, "now that you have some time on your hands."[22]

Vogue, however, celebrated quirky, beautiful Roberts. "She wears odd hats, five earrings, and Jean-Paul Sartre eyeglasses, and carries a purse that looks like a steamer trunk and an eyeball key chain," reported its April 1990 issue, published during the week leading up to the sixty-second Oscars.[23] By then, Roberts had made four films in quick succession following *Steel Magnolias*, including Joel Schumacher's supernatural drama *Flatliners* (where she met Sutherland), and *Pretty Woman*, a fairy-tale romance in which she played Vivian Ward, a Hollywood Boulevard hooker who falls in love with Richard Gere's billionaire-businessman character, Edward Lewis. Set to premiere three days before the Oscars, *Pretty Woman* shot up Roberts's customary six-figure salary into the million-dollar-per-picture bracket, generated talk of a sixty-third actress Academy Award, and landed her inside *Vogue*, where Helmut Newton captured her modeling skimpy Armani eveningwear—a sneak preview of what she'd soon debut at the sixty-second Academy Awards.

Four hours before showtime, McDaniel steered her Mercedes station wagon to her friend Michelle Pfeiffer's place in Santa Monica, personally delivering a navy Armani jersey dress to the thirty-two-year-old actress front-runner nominated for her role as Susie Diamond, a torch singer in the romantic musical comedy *The Fabulous Baker Boys*. "Star for the Nineties—current cinema's reigning object of desire," *Newsweek* christened Pfeiffer, whom *Driving Miss Daisy's* Jessica Tandy (another Armani recruit) bet her agent one hundred dollars she would claim the prize. Skeptical Pfeiffer, "certain" of Tandy's victory, viewed as "terrifying" the prospect

Giorgio Armani's West Coast representative Wanda McDaniel pioneered the type of Oscar fashion professional *Premiere* later classified as a "point person"—that is, a well-connected emissary who on behalf of a designer recruits the right people to wear their latest to the Academy Awards. (Giorgio Armani)

For the consideration of Jodie Foster, Julia Roberts, and Michelle Pfeiffer, Giorgio Armani plucked Oscar night eveningwear from his spring/summer 1990 collection, seen here debuting on his runway at Milan's Palazzo del Senato. (Giorgio Armani)

of competing at the Oscars.[24] "I'm not real social—it's just not my strong point," she admitted.[25]

McDaniel found Pfeiffer totally unprepared to face the competition. As she worked a hairdryer through her just-shampooed sandy blond mane, she admitted to be bereft of jewelry necessary to embellish her Armani. So thinking fast, McDaniel unhinged the clasp on her own double strand of pearls, twisted off the Bulgari knuckle-duster diamond with which her husband, Albert Ruddy, had proposed, and slipped the keepsakes to Pfeiffer. "We were playing dress-up," recalled McDaniel of the hasty handover.[26] "It was personal."

Jessica Lange—who also placed as an actress contender for her performance as lawyer Ann Talbot in the political thriller *Music Box*—made equally brisk moves as a limousine parade "began in earnest" outside the Dorothy Chandler Pavilion. Lange considered McDaniel's offer of an Oscar Armani, but by five P.M. her limo had halted curbside outside Fred Hayman's. Decamping from it, the lean, blond forty-one-year-old made tracks for the Oscar closet. She was ninth on the list of women making use of it during Oscar season. "Bought gown, got dressed, and left for the Awards!" said an astonished Hayman of the nominee's swift change. But the label inside Lange's gold-flecked, ivory chiffon cocktail dress was Armani, she confessed when she arrived outside the Chandler.[27]

The Sixty-second Academy Awards, March 26, 1990. Things were looking good for Armani at Swifty Lazar's Oscar party inside Sunset Boulevard's Spago. He was hotter there than the crispy, golden caviar pizzas slipping in and out of the brick oven as socialite revelers clad in colorful Oscar

At the sixty-second Academy Awards, nominee Michelle Pfeiffer appeared polished in Wanda McDaniel's pearls while her Giorgio Armani navy jersey dress turned heads. (Courtesy of the Academy of Motion Picture Arts and Sciences)

de la Renta ruffles and froufrou Saint Laurent held forth on his red-carpet debut. "I got a lot of congratulations," recalled McDaniel of the instant feedback coming at her as she took a seat to watch the Oscars on TV monitors set up beneath Spago's bleached-oak beams.[28] Down on the red carpet, Pfeiffer's domestic blow-dry went totally undetected. She appeared polished in McDaniel's pearls, while her Armani navy jersey dress turned heads. "It said, 'I'm beautiful—I don't need to make a statement,'" recalled entertainment fashion writer Merle Ginsberg, who, reporting from the red carpet, talked to Pfeiffer as she arrived with her boyfriend Fisher Stevens. "It was a breath of fresh air after years of Oscar-night taffeta—so modern, wearable, and soft."[29] Admitted Pfeiffer to Ginsberg, "I'm not excited—the Oscars make me nervous."[30]

"I don't know about *that* dress," some socialite said, choking back chilled champagne at the Oscars' forty-minute mark. Julia Roberts had

The racer back of the taupe chiffon Giorgio Armani slip dress that supporting actress nominee Julia Roberts wore to the sixty-second Academy Awards revealed her tattooed left shoulder and also clung to her ample, unsupported bosom. (Courtesy of the Academy of Motion Picture Arts and Sciences)

just introduced Randy Newman's rendition of *Parenthood*'s nominated song, "I Love to See You Smile," but the racer back of her taupe chiffon Armani slip dress revealed her tattooed left shoulder and also clung to her ample, unsupported bosom. "Misconstrued of lingerie," reported McDaniel of the consensus on Roberts from the Spago jamboree. "The slip dress hadn't hit yet. It was controversial. She got—not the best dressed."[31]

From the waist up Jodie Foster looked neat in a three-piece, knee-length Armani skirt suit, but her black, opaque tights were better for a stroll on Yale's campus than the strut she made across the stage come count-down time, presenting *My Left Foot*'s Daniel Day-Lewis with the actor prize. Though the black-stitched, white Armani leather gloves in which Foster ripped open the envelope lent her a magician's air, the faux pas faded into the background when amid a standing ovation ebullient Day-Lewis bounced to the stage in an Edwardian frock coat and peg-leg dandy trousers.

"It was a total triumph," said McDaniel, looking back on Armani's first appearance at the Oscars, which Pfeiffer closed by introducing Diana Ross. Glittery in a white, crystal-drenched Bob Mackie, Ross led a sing-along of "Over the Rainbow," *The Wizard of Oz* theme.[32] As the finale concluded, Mel Gibson flashed up on TV screens world-wide "wolfing food into his mouth," instead of harmonizing with Ross.[33]

Along with Pfeiffer, Foster, Roberts, and Lange, six leading men commanded the stage in Armani black tie that night, including Denzel Washington, supporting actor winner for the Civil War drama *Glory*, and *Born on the Fourth of July*'s Oscar nominee Tom Cruise, who waged a valiant fight with Day-Lewis to win the actor prize. A

day after the cere-
mony, *WWD* splashed
"sheer Ecstasy" across
a front-page photo of
Pfeiffer, elegant in navy
Armani, commending
the designer's effort.[34]

"We were the only
game in town,"
reflected McDaniel on
the clout Armani
enjoyed in Hollywood.
As his Milan atelier
produced costumes for
feature films, it also
made sophisticated red-
carpet eveningwear. In
it, Pfeiffer, Foster, and
Roberts are among the
litany of Hollywood
professionals who in
Armani continue to
detonate paparazzi
flashbulbs at the cere-
mony. Fred Hayman
maintained his position
as the Academy's
fashion consultant until
2000. He delivered an
honest opinion of
Armani's Oscar debut
soon after the sixty-
second ceremony. "I'm

Jodie Foster looked neat in a three-piece Giorgio Armani skirt suit as she announced Daniel Day-Lewis's actor Oscar victory at the sixty-second Academy Awards. (Courtesy of the Academy of Motion Picture Arts and Sciences)

not sure they were glamorous enough," he said of Armani's actress
tribe.[35] Hayman reversed judgment in 2002, when he officiated a ceremony honoring Armani as the original recipient of a gold star on the
Walk of Style—a Rodeo Drive route commemorating outstanding
contributions to Hollywood fashion—telling journalist Rose Apadaca
Jones, "It takes guts to wear something that breaks ground."

Chapter Ten
A FOREIGN AFFAIR

"With Mira I spent four hours—*four hours*—because she couldn't make up her mind. It was 'No.' Then it was 'Yes,'" recalled Armani of a trying 1996 Oscar dress fitting with *Mighty Aphrodite*'s supporting-actress contender Mira Sorvino. Armani put in the time, ensuring the session with Sorvino concluded harmoniously, because the Oscars had evolved from a cinematic showdown to a modern style spectacular, and the reigning king of its red carpet now vied with twenty rivals intent on usurping his place.[1] For a designer, the publicity reaped on Oscar night—globally circulated photographs of a couture-clad contender captured at parties hosted by glossy magazines *In Style* and *Vanity Fair* or talking to Joan Rivers, the boisterous blond comedienne fronting *Live from the Red Carpet*, which aired in March 1995 as a two-hour Oscar-style cable-TV special—was considered equivalent to launching a twenty-five-million-dollar advertising campaign.

So PR executives working on behalf of the biggest luxury dress labels ardently pursued Oscar contenders from nomination day, dispatching gift baskets bearing congratulation notes, exotic fruits, rare flowers, and dress sketches. Calvin Klein sent three-hundred-dollar sunglasses to every Academy Awards nominee; Valentino gifted Sharon Stone with a fleet of pricey couture and first-class plane tickets for her to view up close potential Oscar eveningwear. Dolce & Gabbana courted Susan Sarandon, and weeks before the sixty-seventh Academy Awards, Uma Thurman emerged as one half of a celebrated ceremonial fashion partnership, or so it seemed judging by the sound reverberating from the front row at a Milan fashion show staged by luxury accessories mogul Miuccia Prada, whose atelier was then producing her Oscar

"With Mira I spent four hours—*four hours*—because she couldn't make up her mind. It was 'No.' Then it was 'Yes,'" recalled Giorgio Armani of a trying 1996 Oscar dress fitting at his Milan atelier with *Mighty Aphrodite*'s supporting actress nominee Mira Sorvino. (Giorgio Armani)

dress. "Prada, Prada, *Pradissima*!" began murmurs that rose to an appreciative crescendo as retro-modern autumn/winter fashions passed down her runway.[2] The chant echoed the roar of French film fans who had recently cheered Thurman. "Oo-mah! Oo-mah! Oo-mah!" they cried as the statuesque, blond twenty-four-year-old gracefully emerged from a convoy of black limousines and glided up the steps of the Palais du Festival at the May 1994 Cannes Film Festival premiere of *Pulp Fiction*, the black comedy intertwining the escapades of her character, femme fatale Mia Wallace, an ice-cool, doped-out gangster's moll, with the exploits of hapless small-time crooks and a pair of hit men.[3]

Eight months later, as Thurman received a supporting actress nomination for *Pulp Fiction*, it was the high-profile film of the sixty-seventh Academy Awards. Coauthored and directed by Quentin Tarantino, a thirty-year-old former clerk at a Manhattan Beach movie-rental emporium, the film made him a bona fide Hollywood player after *Pulp* beat twenty-three others to win Cannes's prestigious Palme d'Or picture prize and followed the surprise victory there by collecting seven Oscar nominations.

Thurman's Academy nod fêted her comeback because she'd hit a rocky patch following her 1991 divorce from actor Gary Oldman and a disastrous starring role two year later in the box-office flop *Even Cowgirls Get the Blues*, Gus Van Sant's adaptation of Tom Robbins's best-selling road novel. Done up as *Pulp Fiction*'s Mia Wallace in a jet-black bob wig (Tarantino's homage to Louise Brooks), bloodred nails (MAC Dubonnet mixed with OPI matte-finish polish), and improvised pedal pushers ("We couldn't find a pair of pants that were long enough for Uma, so I said [to her], 'Know what? I'm just going to cut [a pair] to a length that I think would be great on you,'" recalled *Pulp*'s costumer, Betsy Heimann), Thurman became the iconic representative of Tarantino's aggressive brand of hip Hollywood filmmaking as her macabre screen garb was instantly commandeered by the fashion world. In it she dominated *Pulp Fiction*'s notorious scene—a twist contest at Jack Rabbit Slim's nightclub during which Mia wins the trophy, next slips into a heroin-induced coma, and is soon revived as her dance partner, hit man Vincent Vega (John Travolta), plunges an adrenaline-filled hypodermic needle into her chest.[4]

Thurman's Oscar Prada eventually proved resonant like her *Pulp Fiction* costume, but a week before the sixty-seventh Academy Awards, it landed dead on arrival in Los Angeles while Barbara Tfank, a freelance design consultant working as conduit between the Milanese fashion label and the supporting actress Oscar nominee, was left to resuscitate it. "It was the wrong color—it was way too small, and it was twelve inches too short," confirmed Tfank of Prada's nonstarter.[5]

Thurman's six-foot height confounded Prada's design team. Gussying up the subtle Prada signature for the Oscars' red carpet also stretched the atelier's ingenuity. The garment's fabric was stiff like Pocono, a durable, dark nylon Miuccia Prada utilized to make inconspicuous, costly, deluxe casuals like foul-weather gear, backpacks, as well as functional footwear, collectively known as *anonymous luxury*, a fashion-industry term then applied to the discreet look transforming into a two-hundred-million-dollar fashion corporation the eponymous leather-goods brand founded by Mario Prada, Miuccia's grandfather, in 1913.[6]

The starting point of Thurman's Oscar Prada was the label's look-book—a compilation of photographs capturing its spring/summer 1995 collection. Alongside Tfank, the contender flipped through it for inspiration but deemed its prevailing innocent sex appeal inappropriate for the Academy Awards. "The Prada look-book featured very sheer chiffon, lingerie-type dresses," explained Tfank. "Uma was adamant against wearing anything see-through. So I said, 'How would you like to look? Like a femme fatale? Or a fairy princess?' And she chose fairy princess."[7]

Unlike her eighties forerunners, Thurman was well versed on matters of style. Before breaking into Hollywood, she worked as a New York top model. She had a "low opinion" of her former profession, claimed director Terry Gilliam, with whom she worked early in her career on the fantasy *The Adventures of Baron Munchausen*, but the West Village–residing supporting actress nominee was a power shopper, like most downtown, nineties Manhattan girls.[8] "When I met Uma, she was buying my clothes—she really liked my style," confirmed designer Alberta Ferretti, at whose early-nineties Milan fashion shows Thurman appeared. (In 2000, Thurman wore a red jersey Ferretti column to the seventy-second Academy Awards.) "Uma has a strong personality," added Ferretti. "So she really knows what she wants."[9]

Ultimately, Thurman wore a Prada gown to the sixty-seventh Academy Awards, although Barbara Tfank proved its mastermind. A week before the ceremony, with Prada's dud on her hands, she convinced Miuccia Prada that on the company's behalf in Los Angeles she could make Thurman's attire. Tfank, a former New York fashion stylist turned Hollywood costume designer, was known for putting a fashionable spin on screen wardrobes she produced. For her fourth feature film, *Dream Lover*, a mystery directed by Nicholas Kazan, she mixed sleek Prada ready-to-wear with her own custom-made pieces and Tahitian pearls on loan from Harry Winston. Customarily, she shod actresses in pricey Manolo Blahnik footwear, while, personally, she lived in Prada. "Exclusively Prada," Tfank explained of her own wardrobe. "I loved the fit. I loved the fact that it wasn't superflashy. There was a modesty to Prada's clothes."[10]

A team of seamstresses worked under her direction, making two Oscar dresses for Thurman—one in a lavender shade the nominee originally requested after spying it in the Prada look-book, and a pastel yellow backup gown. After Thurman settled on the lavender, opalescent sequins were applied to its hemline in dawn-till-dusk sewing sessions.

In 1995, on behalf of Miuccia Prada, Los Angeles designer Barbara Tfank designed two Oscar dresses for *Pulp Fiction*'s supporting actress nominee Uma Thurman—one in lavender (left), and a pastel yellow backup gown. (Barbara Tfank)

A cream organza wrap completed the look. To ensure the pieces would hold up beneath the paparazzi's glare, Tfank tested them as though they were movie costumes. "We lit [her dress] from the front and the back, to make sure Uma's legs wouldn't show through the lining, and looked at it in several kinds of light, so I knew the color would be fine both indoors and out, both on film and in photographs," explained Tfank. "The fabric was chosen so that no wrinkles would show, and we had Uma walk, sit [and] stand—to make sure it always fell perfectly."[11]

The fashion press soon marveled at the fine, Italian workmanship that perfected Thurman's Prada gown, although Tfank's team, based in a Hollywood costume workshop, utilized textiles from Eastern Silk Co., a garment-industry supplier in Korea Town, a rough patch of Los Angeles off Wilshire Boulevard. So it was said. "Come on—this all happened in about five days," said designer John David Ridge, proprietor of the premises, who observed the design process.[12] White accessories Prada sent Thurman were dyed lavender. A logical move, it nonetheless "upset" Prada's publicist, to whom Tfank explained, "If Uma carried a white evening bag on the red carpet, when it's photographed, it will look like she's carrying a very large aspirin."[13]

The Sixty-seventh Academy Awards, March 27, 1995. Winsome Thurman, a-sparkle in liquid lavender silk, proved the long-stemmed rose on the Academy's red carpet next to so many weedy Hollywood women clad in tight black, navy, white, or red. Wrapped up in a gunmetal-gray-and-black, velvet, strapless Christian Lacroix, presenter Sigourney Weaver turned to Thurman, after overhearing her say to admiring reporters that her gown was from Prada.[14] "I didn't know Prada made evening dresses," said Weaver. "They don't," replied Thurman diplomatically. "They just made this one."[15]

"Bored-looking," wrote the *Los Angeles Times* describing Thurman's serious expression as she approached the Shrine, but actually an item beneath her plunge-back Prada had distracted her, as she confessed later: "I had the wrong bra on under my dress, so the bra kept riding up my back—that's what I spent most of the time worrying about."[16]

"Ladies and gentlemen, you must enter the theater now!" announced forecourt emcee Army Archerd. Thurman joined publicists, reporters, nominees, and presenters rushing the Shrine's entrance. "Make sure you have cameras ready for Uma Thurman and Oprah Winfrey," the ceremony's stage manager boomed from a walkie-talkie fixed to Gil

Cates, the show's director, seconds before ABC's production team began its countdown to host David Letterman's opening monologue.[17] Onstage facing Thurman, in a front-row seat next to Oprah Winfrey, Letterman delivered his first joke: "I've been dying to do something all day, and I think maybe I can take care of this. Oprah," he said, pointing to Winfrey as two thousand guests and eight hundred million viewers concentrated. "Oh, no! Oh, no!" thought Winfrey. "Uma," pronounced Letterman, turning to Thurman, who, gleaming in pastel Prada, flashed a pretty smile as she popped up on-screen. *"Uuuuma! Ooooprah!"*[18] Camera six focused on Susan Sarandon laughing. Camera four caught a smirking Jodie Foster as the host played on: "Oprah! Uma! Uma! Oprah! It's going to be one of those things I won't be able to stop doing all night long!"[19]

Ten minutes later, actor Tommy Lee Jones revealed that *Bullets over Broadway*'s Dianne Wiest had defeated Thurman for the supporting actress race. "*Gump* thumped *Pulp*," wrote Peter Biskind, summing up the outcome of the sixty-seventh Academy Awards, at which Paramount's feel-good movie *Forrest Gump* earned six Oscars, including the picture, actor, and director prizes, as well as another for adapted screenplay.[20] Quentin Tarantino and Roger Avary claimed the original-screenplay prize, the sole Academy Award *Pulp Fiction* received. But Thurman made a new friend. "Uma!" declared Oprah Winfrey, late into the ceremony spying Thurman backstage.[21] "Oprah!" effused Thurman.[22] Then Uma and Oprah both convulsed with glee.

Three months after the Oscars, the big-three names of Paris haute couture—Chanel's Karl Lagerfeld, Yves Saint Laurent, and Valentino—displayed on their runways shimmering variations of Thurman's Prada gown by Barbara Tfank. Later, as Prada became established as a "'name'—a dressmaking name as opposed to a bag and shoe making name," confirmed Elizabeth Saltzman, *Vanity Fair*'s fashion director, Susan Sarandon and Sharon Stone, front-runners competing for the Academy's sixty-eighth actress prize, hit the Oscar campaign trail, working ready-to-wear produced by designers whose special-event couture they also intended to display at the ceremony.[23]

Glamming it up at the Golden Globes and other annual award ceremonies, including a new one launched by the Screen Actors Guild, Sarandon and Stone dazzled onlookers, but as the traditionally tense countdown to the Academy Awards commenced, they realized their original ceremonial-wardrobe strategies were flawed.

Sarandon's sixty-eighth actress Oscar nomination acknowledged her immortalization of Sister Helen Prejean, the Catholic nun from New Orleans who opposed capital punishment. The film, based on her best-selling memoir *Dead Man Walking*, recounted her experience working for over a decade counseling death-row inmates at Louisiana State Penitentiary. Its screen adaptation, written and directed by Tim Robbins, Sarandon's partner, presented an objective view of the death penalty, chronicling a two-year period during which she as Sister Helen counsels Sean Penn's character, Matthew Poncelet, a convict on death row for rape and murder. For undertaking the role of Poncelet, a composite character based on two men Sister Helen actually advised, Penn placed as an actor Oscar contender, while the Academy acknowledged Robbins as one of five filmmakers competing for the director prize. *Dead Man Walking*, a critical hit, was labeled "exemplary" as well as "extraordinary," and as it became a commercial success, eventually grossing one hundred million dollars, its proceeds were donated to the Sisters of Saint Joseph of Medaille, Sister Helen's order.

Most critics conceded that *Dead Man Walking* was one of the year's best films, but also speculated that notoriously conservative Academy voters might shy away from casting their vote for Sarandon, considering the film a "downer," as Brian D. Johnson of Toronto's *Maclean's* magazine wrote, due to its controversial subject matter and somber tone.[24]

Further jeopardizing a possible victory for Sarandon and Robbins was their sideline as political activists. From their home, a brownstone in Chelsea, Manhattan, where they lived with their two young sons and Sarandon's daughter, they campaigned to raise awareness for an array of causes from AIDS to the fight against third-world political corruption. After an impassioned plea addressing the atrocity of Haitian internment camps, which the couple jointly delivered at the Oscar podium before bestowing the sixty-fifth editing prize, they were both banned for a year as presenters. "Susan deserves the Oscar, but her acting is far too subtle and the two of us are far too political for her to receive her due," said Robbins, concurring with the dire Oscar predictions for *Dead Man Walking*.[25]

Nevertheless, spirited, forty-nine-year-old Sarandon, a sharp intellect and regally beautiful redhead who refused to let her increasing years be a stumbling block in ageist Hollywood, was considered a heroine by her fans. Enhancing the believability of her characterization of Sister

Helen, she appeared makeup free before the camera, wore "funny clothes" and a "bad haircut."[26] She cried at *Dead Man Walking*'s late-summer 1995 preview because the fine lines and wrinkles on her plastic-surgery-free face were unattractively magnified once projected on-screen. "I'm vain to a certain extent," she admitted. "I felt very vulnerable and exposed."[27]

But as an Oscar nomination fell into place, Sarandon recovered. "She had a very confident sense of everything," confirmed New York designer Robert Danes, a Yale history graduate from San Antonio, Texas, whose evening dresses of silk-satin, layered chiffon, and folded organza were then sought after by an artsy Manhattan crowd and sold at Madison Avenue's boutique department store Barneys New York, where Nancy Seltzer, Sarandon's publicist, discovered his collection and then visited him in January 1996 on her client's behalf.[28] At the Soho studio Danes had operated from 1990, Seltzer selected versatile, day-to-night separates that Sarandon donned to promote *Dead Man Walking* on the TV talk-show circuit. A month later, Sarandon had three fittings with Danes, during which he tailored customized pieces she considered awards-show material—a corset-topped gown he cut from navy satin, which she modeled on NBC's telecast of the Screen Actors Guild awards, where on February 24 she accepted the organization's actor prize—an honor that seemed a positive step toward winning the actress Academy Award. For her Oscar-night look, Sarandon considered a "collage dress"—an intricate design Danes had pioneered as a signature piece. Approaching the traditional form of the bias-cut gown like an abstract painter, he messed with its shape, juxtaposing contrasting pieces of chiffon and satin, yielding a flattering, form-fitting patchwork silk frock. Sarandon's Danes collage was one of a kind, blending sixty pieces of lustrous and matte vivid blue silk pieces. "She picked up this really great one," confirmed Danes. "She had a really good idea of what kind of things worked for her figure. She knew what would show her off to her best advantage."[29]

So far, so Sarandon. Her approach to red-carpet dressing was decidedly more downtown cool than va-va-voom Hollywood. She often spiked her gala ensembles, with devil-may-care touches like wacky sunglasses. "Something in which I can relax and have a good time—something that has a sense of humor to it, looks contemporary, and has some dignity—something I won't trip and fall down in," she said, describing her ideal Oscar dress in 1982.[30] Back then, Sarandon first placed in the actress category, for *Atlantic City*, Louis Malle's gangster fable, but the nomination marked the beginning of a series of Oscar defeats, for performances in modern classics such as *Thelma & Louise*, Ridley Scott's feminist road movie, the family drama *Lorenzo's Oil*, and *The Client*, Joel Schumacher's courtroom thriller.

On the morning of her fifth competition for the actress prize, the sixty-eighth, Sarandon burned off ceremonial jitters playing ball with her family on the grounds of the Four Seasons Hotel in Beverly Hills, where they stayed. "There are two Susans," said Sarandon's hair colorist, Louis Licari, explaining his longtime client's nonchalant behavior on Oscar day. "There is the Susan of real life, the mother of three children, the Susan [who] is extremely low-key. And the other is the movie star."[31]

After *Dead Man Walking*, bicoastal Licari—proprietor of eponymous salons in Beverly Hills and Manhattan—dyed Sarandon's hair from the "understated" mousy brown he'd tinted it for *Dead Man Walking* to the vibrant shade of copper that defined her film-star-fabulous signature.[32] He also tended to her mane through Oscar season, turning its red shade up a notch just before the ceremony. "This was her big night. I knew it was going to be a major night," he reasoned. At the time, Licari was unaware of the impact his chemicals produced.[33]

Sarandon's distinctive hair color caught the eye of Stefano Gabbana, who, with Domenico Dolce, composes Dolce & Gabbana, the Milan luxury fashion label. Approximately two weeks before the Oscars, Sarandon accepted an offer from Dolce & Gabbana's Manhattan representative, who suggested that she wear their couture to the Oscars. "I had seen her a month before and I remembered the copper color of her hair, so I made a dress to match," recalled Stefano Gabbana. Sarandon concluded her Robert Danes collage was too similar to the navy satin Danes dress she'd worn to the SAG Awards. So consecutive Danes dresses might lessen the impact of her Oscar arrival. By contrast, Dolce & Gabbana's metallic gown was a breakthrough—the first Oscar piece ever produced by the thirtysomething design duo, who specialized in sexy evening gowns known as "movie star dresses," which they devised as a response to the women who served as sources of inspiration—feisty sixties Italian film stars Anna Magnani and Claudia Cardinale.[34]

Though Dolce & Gabbana's increasingly sophisticated signature seemed perfect for an Oscar dress, Gabbana shrugged his taut, suntanned shoulders at mention of the Academy Awards. He never followed the ceremony, and though a dress for the Oscars was an optimum publicity move, it in no way seemed a goal. "I don't like Oscar dresses," he divulged, then howled, "Oh my God! The styles are not modern. Not at all—I'm honest. I think that some people in Hollywood think it is elegant to wear an evening dress full of embroidery and really show off. But elegance is about attitude."[35]

According to Gabbana, Sarandon possessed the right kind. Her background was Italian like Dolce & Gabbana's muses supermodel Linda Evangelista, actress Isabella Rossellini, and Madonna, who displayed their corsetry in *The Girlie Show*, her televised 1993 concert world tour. Sarandon's shapely figure also evoked the "earthy" women the pair idealized. "Big breasts, well-defined waistline, and generous backside," explained Dolce of their preferred mannequin.[36]

So working full throttle, their atelier perfected in days not just Sarandon's Oscar dress but also synchronizing copper satin pieces including a wrap, handbag, and evening slippers. The total Oscar-night look was a gift from the boys as well as a leap of faith. "I wasn't sure if she was going to wear it," admitted Gabbana.[37] The Academy Awards edition of *Entertainment Weekly* and London's *Independent on Sunday* published on Oscar morning confirmed Robert Danes as the maker of Sarandon's Oscar dress, although by then the *New York Times* classified his collage as "plan B."

Midway through Oscar week Sharon Stone was totally uncertain about her ceremonial wardrobe plan, but with made-to-measure red-carpet entrance-makers by designer friends Valentino and Vera Wang, she seemed spoiled for choice, much like her Academy Award–nominated character, Ginger McKenna, a former prostitute and gaming-table chip hustler turned trophy wife in *Casino*, Martin Scorsese's Las Vegas gangster epic.

Casino's sole Oscar nomination went to gorgeous blonde Stone, a thirty-eight-year-old former beauty queen and Ford model from Meadville, a small northwestern Pennsylvania town. From 1980, she made twenty-two mostly forgettable Hollywood movies, as well as prime-time TV shows including *Magnum, P.I.*, until her beguiling portrayal as lesbian crime novelist Catherine Tramell in the 1992 sexual thriller *Basic Instinct* launched the ascent that culminated in her landing *Casino*'s coveted lead role. Recommended by Joe Pesci, who costarred in *Casino*, Stone won the part of Ginger over Nicole Kidman, Michelle Pfeiffer, and porn star Traci Lords (De Niro's first choice) and following

DOLCE & GABBANA

This copper satin gown for 1996 Academy Award nominee Susan Sarandon was the first piece of Oscar couture ever produced by Milan designers Dolce & Gabbana. (Dolce & Gabbana)

197

Casino's December 1995 premiere received unanimous critical acclaim, although her performance divided Academy members. Some "stomped" out of the pre-Oscar screenings of *Casino*, hosted by Universal, its producer, because they were put off by its graphic violence and prurient scenes.[38] However, *Variety* noted that on February 13, Oscar nomination day, as news of Stone's nomination went public, she intercepted "countless congratulatory phone calls," reporting one that "moved" her from prominent Academy member Lew Wasserman, the eighty-three-year-old Hollywood titan, former chairman and CEO of the Music Corporation of America.[39] "Everybody championed Sharon—she was one of those hardworking actresses who had hung in there for many, many years," confirmed Giorgio Armani's Wanda McDaniel.[40]

By Oscar week Thursday, McDaniel rescued her friend Stone, scheduling an eleventh-hour viewing of Armani's ceremonial shipment from Milan, because by then the actress front-runner was in a predicament. Stone classified her beige, beaded Valentino Oscar dress as "very Marilyn Monroe, very Marlene Dietrich."[41] As for her other ceremonial option— a dazzling navy, red, and gold Vera Wang—she daringly contemplated donning with it "some sort of Hindu head-wrap—sort of like Cole Porter goes to India on an acid trip," she said, explaining the exotic fusion she had planned as a perk.[42] But both numbers proved poor fits, frustrating faultlessly fashionable Stone. In the nick of time—merely eighteen hours before the ceremony—an ingenious solution materialized, enabling her to make a stroll along the Oscars red carpet seem like the walk in the park it had become for her as she'd established her reputation as one of its best dressed over three years leading up to the sixty-eighth Academy Awards.

Dominating the Oscars' spotlight in the early nineties, Stone upstaged prominent participants by alternating Wang and Valentino couture, evoking the retro-modern Old Hollywood brand of movie star glamour she'd revived after hitting it big. "It was fun in the beginning," reflected Stone of her first appearance at the Oscars in 1992. As nominees and presenters appeared in understated Armani, she elevated the standard of the ceremony's feminine dress code by "wearing gowns," she explained. "I just wanted to do my vision of what it would be like to go to the Oscars. Like out of a Carole Lombard movie, where everyone was dressed in ball gowns."[43] Establishing relationships with Van Cleef & Arpels as well as Martin Katz, the Beverly Hills estate jeweler, she resurrected the thirties Golden Era practice of flashing diamonds at the Academy Awards, reasoning, "If you're *gonna* go to the Oscars, you might as well go to the Oscars!"[44]

Twenty-four pieces from Valentino's spring 1996 couture collection came Stone's way as she prepared to tackle events dotting the calendar leading up to the sixty-eighth Oscars, including the European premiere of *Casino* and the fifty-third Golden Globes, at which she was considered the "long shot to win" in the Best Actress, Drama category. *W* noted that Stone, getting it all exactly right, "clogged" the fax machine at the Hôtel Ritz Paris, where Valentino's team were ensconced, delivering to them "specific directions" on how to alter her selections.[45]

Valentino's exuberant couture, typically executed in lush lipstick red, Mediterranean coral, and handmade lace, was long favored by crème de la crème jet-setters, including Her Royal Highness Princess Grace of Monaco, Jacqueline Kennedy Onassis, and Elizabeth Taylor. Intent on making an inroad in to modern Hollywood, he went all out wooing Stone, initially in 1992, dispatching to the set of *Sliver*, a thriller she was shooting in San Francisco, the head of his Rome atelier along with fifty couture dresses, merchandise worth about a million dollars, all Stone's to keep.[46] Valentino hoped she would wear something at a big event like the Globes or the Oscars. She obliged, modeling jet-black, beaded Valentino to the sixty-sixth Academy Awards in 1994. "It was the way you dream it would be—a real champagne event, not a greedy hustle," she recalled of his courtship.[47]

But two months before Stone's moment of truth at the sixty-eighth Oscars, Valentino's intention to gown his muse for her big moment took a wrong turn. At the January 1996 Golden Globes, a triumphant Stone clutched the actress prize in a black-on-white Vera Wang and declared, "Okay—it's a miracle."[48] Her sudden good fortune, considered a good omen for the Oscars, also marked another victory for Wang, who like Valentino banked on Stone wearing her design to the sixty-eighth Academy Awards. Stone made no promises, but betting on her was worth the risk to Wang. The *Los Angeles Times* claimed the publicity Stone generated wearing her first Wang—a white satin and chiffon ensemble— to the sixty-fifth Oscars in 1993 "launched" the career of the forty-seven-year-old designer, who after sixteen years as a *Vogue* fashion stylist had opened a couture and bridal salon in Manhattan's exclusive Carlyle Hotel in 1990.[49] Next Stone appeared at 1995's sixty-seventh Oscars in a platinum-satin, equestrain-style Wang two-piece. "I called it a blond dress for a blonde," remembered Wang. "Totally plain, very couture, yards and yards of Lafitte duchess satin, which is one hundred dollars a yard. Up until Sharon went out in my dress, Valentino thought she was wearing Valentino, and somebody else thought she was wearing something

else. But I knew she was wearing me."[50] A day later, the *Los Angeles Times* reported Valentino had "lost" Stone to Wang, classifying the move as a "definite setback" for the couturier Stone affectionately referred to as "V."[51] Two days before the sixty-eighth Academy Awards, togged up in a pin-striped trouser suit, an unusually subdued Stone arrived at the Oscars run-through picturing a big, black *X* in her mind ruling out her Wang and Valentino options as well as the sober Armani she had just viewed. "I don't know how many dresses I've tried on this week, and they all suck," confided Stone to actress Angela Bassett.[52]

Compounding the pressure? Surely it was the "Q," as Hollywood insiders referred to Quincy Jones, the sixty-three-year-old virtuoso composer who, as the producer of the sixty-eighth Academy Awards, planned a megaceremony, aimed to transmit a glossy Hollywood dignity. "It's just a different attitude," explained Jones. "We have got very, very talented people in front and behind the camera which will give the show an edge."[53]

Jones attempted to lure Princess Diana to the Oscars, offering to present her with a special humanitarian Academy Award, acknowledging her work as a roving ambassador for the British Red Cross.[54] Although the princess was friendly with Jones, she declined his invitation. Hollywood lothario Jack Nicholson also passed up the chance to emcee a high-concept Oscars fashion show planned to celebrate the screen wardrobes created by the five costume-design nominees. Coproducing the three-minute-twenty-five-second segment preceding the bestowal of the prize were Jamie King, the twenty-four-year-old host of MTV's dance program *The Grind*, and Los Angeles photographer Matthew Rolston, a multitalent whose aesthetic flair extended to album covers, music videos, TV commercials, and major fashion-magazine covers. "We handpicked every model," explained Rolston of the cast set to display the nominated screen costumes, including Tyra Banks, a two-time *Sports Illustrated* cover girl, Bridget Hall, the face of Ralph Lauren, and Veronica Webb, a muse of Azzedine Alaia's, along with hipster poster boys Tyson Beckford, Michael Bergin, and Marcus Schenkenberg.[55] Fifteen dancers Rolston considered "top"—nine from the cast of Paul Verhoeven's 1995 Vegas drama *Showgirls*—would jostle cameras, playing the paparazzi, while others would perch on gilt seats impersonating fashion critics. More wielded hairdryers and makeup brushes, pretending to be backstage fashion-beauty professionals.[56] James Bond star Pierce Brosnan as well as supermodels Naomi Campbell and Claudia Schiffer would announce the winner.

But on Saturday night of Oscar weekend, after thirty-three hours of

Dominating the Oscars' spotlight in the early nineties, Sharon Stone upstaged her colleagues by alternating Vera Wang and Valentino couture. (Corbis)

fittings and fashion-show rehearsals on a cold Hollywood soundstage, the energies of every supermodel waned. "I was militaristic," admitted Rolston of his practice sessions. "It had to run like clockwork. Every step had to fall on the right musical note. Dancers are used to that kind of rehearsals, but models aren't. So they were not thrilled. I just kept asking them, 'Do you want your parents to see you make a mistake on TV?'"[57]

Over at Sharon Stone's Benedict Canyon estate by eight P.M. that night, a support network composed of two assistants, her best friend, Mimi Craven, as well as family—her dad, Joseph; mother, Dorothy; and younger sister, Kelly—surrounded the nominee. But her ceremonial dressing dilemma remained unresolved. So Stone sent out a search party for a fashion expert she considered her last hope—costume designer Ellen Mirojnick.

Forty-seven-year-old Mirojnick had established her Hollywood reputation as an authority on contemporary design conceiving costumes

that defined modern epics, including Alan Flusser's bespoke power suits, which she'd placed upon Michael Douglas's corporate-raider character, Gordon Gekko, in Oliver Stone's *Wall Street*, as well as the tight, white, thigh-grazing dress she'd made to shape Stone's *Basic Instinct* she-devil character, Catherine Tramell.

Stone had no telephone number for Mirojnick. They lived close by, so spontaneously she sent for the costumer. "I just thought, 'I can't take it anymore—I don't like any of the dresses I have,'" remembered Stone.[58] Recounted Mirojnick: "I got a knock at the door and one of the people who worked for Sharon said, 'Sharon sent me to get you. She needs your help. Can you come to the house now? I'll take you. Can you come over?'" Instantly she obliged. "Here's a girl who is going to the Academy Awards. It is something she's dreamt of her entire life. She's at a moment in her career where it is everything a girl could dream of, and she doesn't have a dress to wear. That is not fun. I was in a desperate position myself. How do I make it okay?"[59]

A tough, two-hour session lay ahead. "It was quite a crowd, I have to say," quipped Mirojnick of the gathering at Stone's place, and though Valentino's gown never materialized, she immediately surveyed Vera Wang's. "It was a beautiful dress, but it [was] not an automatic fit. Sharon clearly needed a backup that she knew was going to be a slam dunk."[60] Stone spent thirty minutes bouncing around ideas, according to the costumer: "She was, 'What am I going to do? What *should* I do?' I needed to help her find a solution, so we went into her closet."[61]

Inside Stone's "closet," a palatial dressing room dominated by a sixteen-foot Louis XIV mirror, the actress recalled Mirojnick's manner as take-charge. "She said, 'Go get your five favorite things,'" recalled Stone of her marching orders.[62] "There was this skirt that was really good," reminisced Mirojnick, referring to a black, taffeta, floor-length Valentino trumpet skirt Stone sourced from her stash of couture and then slipped on.[63] "I took an Armani dress [and] wore [it] as a coat," continued Stone of an Armani black velvet coatdress, which went over her Valentino. She needed a third piece to cover her bare chest and complete the look.[64] "She tried on a couple of tops and they were not good," added Mirojnick. "There was not a dress in the lady's closet that she could cut and make into a top. Even if I called a dressmaker— what was she going to cut?"[65] As Stone saw out Oscar Saturday night from the closed quarters of her Benedict Canyon wardrobe, there was also no time to go out shopping on Rodeo Drive. "It wasn't a time that shops were open on Sunday," confirmed Mirojnick.[66]

But a T-shirt—Mirojnick's ten P.M. solution—was having a moment. The staple emerged as a unisex mainstay in the nineties. *Vogue* consistently dressed its cover girls in an array of pristine tops from tanks to starched men's shirts, while affordable cotton apparel flew off shelves at retail chain The Gap. Stone unearthed in her wardrobe the closest thing she had to a T-shirt—a black Gap mock turtleneck. "She put it on about three times—it made her more statuesque," recalled Mirojnick.[67] But Stone hesitated. Fearing critical reception to an Oscar-night look mixing chain-store merchandise with European eveningwear, she asked the costumer, "Do you think I could?"[68] Retorted Mirojnick to the movie star, "Who can say that it can't be right? Call me crazy, but I think it's you, and if nothing else, it will cause a stir. And I think she responded at that moment —'it will cause a stir,'" reflected Mirojnick. "Sharon just knew that she could throw out the word *Gap* [at the Oscars] and make it a sensation."[69]

Thumbs-up for a three-piece composed of the Valentino skirt, Armani's dressmaker's coat, and The Gap's T-shirt came from Stone's family and friends. "All agreed that it was a strange notion, but if anybody could pull it off, she could pull it off," added Mirojnick. "We all looked at one another—from her sister to her mother to her father to her best friend, and anyone else who was there. And I said, 'Sharon, it will either be the biggest hit or the biggest miss. But you look great in it.' The simplicity of those three pieces—the presentation was as beautiful as the Oscar."[70]

Before Stone and her father departed for the ceremony on Oscar Sunday, she telephoned Millard Drexler, The Gap's CEO, and struck a deal. On the Academy's red carpet she planned to plug her T-shirt as a piece of merchandise from The Gap, generating invaluable publicity for the retail chain, and in exchange for her doing so, Drexler agreed that the company would make a sizable donation to Planet Hope, a homeless charity Stone had cofounded and co-operated with Kelly, her sister. The style move seemed novel, but it harmonized with Stone's Old Hollywood fashion philosophy. From the late sixties, legendary movie stars like Barbara Stanwyck had spent thousands on Oscar dresses and then a day after the ceremony sent them to Cinema Glamour Shop, a Los Angeles boutique that contributed sale proceeds to the Motion Picture Television Fund, a charitable organization aiding financially challenged members of the film industry.

Vera Wang sympathized when on Oscar afternoon Stone explained her plan over the telephone. "It was too technically difficult—it combined so many different elements," claimed Wang of her dress design for Stone. "Since I have a relationship with Sharon as a friend, she can say to me, 'I'm not wearing you this year . . . I'm not okay that the dress didn't work out, but I'm okay that she could talk to me about it."[71] In Rome, an assistant alerted Valentino that his Oscar couture for Stone would remain unseen. "It got lost somewhere," he said later.

But hours before the Academy Awards, Stone had triumphed. There was just one hitch. "You can't wear that! You've got a huge hole in that shirt," said Dorothy Stone, noticing a rip in the underarm of her daughter's Gap mock turtleneck, just before she made tracks for the ceremony. "When I lifted my arm—sure enough, there was a huge tear," confirmed Stone. "My mother sewed it closed!"[72] Then Stone adorned her Armani coat with a homegrown corsage, recalling, "I took a gardenia from my garden and I was out the door."[73]

The Sixty-eighth Academy Awards, March 25, 1996. In the backseat of a limousine cruising toward the Dorothy Chandler Pavilion, Susan Sarandon experienced her final Oscar-season fashion mishap. "My earrings fell apart on the way—they just disintegrated off my ears," she remembered.[74] Decamping from the car with Tim Robbins, she emerged cool, collected, and copper-coated, from the tips of her Louis Licari freshly tinted crop to a glossed metallic pout by makeup artist Laura Mercier to the toes of her Dolce & Gabbana evening slippers, while an ABC-TV announcer gushed to a billion viewers, "There's Susan Sarandon in copper Dolce & Gabbana!" Wide-smiling Sarandon flashed a thumbs-up to the cameras, but she and Robbins bypassed fashion reporters camped out on the red carpet, making way for movie critic Roger Ebert. "It was a great film," said Ebert, congratulating the duo behind *Dead Man Walking.*

As ABC's preshow presenter, Oprah Winfrey, received final primping from her hairstylist, Joan Rivers described the red-carpet scene to her audience. "A madhouse!" said Rivers, who then questioned a lineup of supermodels about their dresses and beauty regimes, asking Ralph Lauren's slender model Bridget Hall, "Do you diet?" Catching sight of Gap-clad Sharon Stone, Rivers's head swiveled *Exorcist*-style. "She looks like a million bucks! Like a great actress!" she announced, hailing the contender's arrival. A nervous Stone babbled right back to Rivers, "I'm Cinderella! My Van Cleef diamonds go very well with my Gap T-shirt!"

Thirteen minutes and forty-five seconds into the ceremony, the costume fashion show began. "I was terrified—lots of opening-night jitters," admitted Matthew Rolston, who watched the proceedings from backstage.[75] All went smoothly as suave Pierce Brosnan announced, "Sixteen of the world's top models are with us to present the nominated costumes as you've never seen them before—now let's go to the runway for a supermodel fashion show!"

Throbbing techno music sent a tribe of supermodels bouncing through smoky clouds of dry ice. Period costumes and elaborate hairstyles ever so slightly clashed with their sensual swagger. A cannon blast showered the stage with gold confetti. Whoops and cheers from the film pros in the audience greeted Brosnan as he emerged at the foot of the runway flanked by Naomi Campbell and Claudia Schiffer as well the fashion show's model stars. Then he announced James Acheson as the winner of the costume design Academy Award for his work on the period drama *Restoration*. "I want to thank the wonderful team of people that cut and sew and print and dye the costumes that you see tonight," said Acheson graciously from the podium. Backstage, the miffed winner vented displeasure about the fashion show's proceedings. "There was no showing of the wigs we used—I was told that we would have some input, but we didn't."

Presenting two score awards—best original musical or comedy score and original drama—Quincy Jones came onstage with Sharon Stone, who had removed her Armani velvet frock coat, giving maximum exposure to her Gap mock turtleneck. But Stone was flustered. Accidentally she passed on the envelope with the result of the second score prize, for a drama, to the composer of *Pocahontas*, Stephen Schwartz, who shared the first prize, for best original musical or comedy score, with his partner, Alan Menken. Stone thought that she'd handed over to Schwartz the winning ballot as a memento. But it was the envelope concealing the result of the upcoming drama score Academy Award. "We have just blown it," thought Jones, realizing Stone had passed on the second ballot. So he dashed backstage to locate the Price Waterhouse representative charged with memorizing the Oscar-winning names. Alone at the podium, Stone comically ad-libbed channeling a higher power to reveal the recipient of the next prize: "I'd like us all to have a psychic moment. It's coming to me . . . *Oh*, you can do better than that . . ." Then Jones appeared, whispered the winner's name into Stone's ear, and she declared, "It's *Il Postino!*"

Backstage, Stone made way for the greenroom. Seemingly exhausted, she spied a catered buffet and wondered, "Is there anything here that'll help get me through tonight?"[76] An assistant offered a plate of melon, then Stone insisted, "I'm okay."[77] Seated in the audience, next to her dad, she laughed as presenter Tom Hanks announced her name as one of five actress nominees. Susan Sarandon closed her eyes after Hanks revealed that she'd won. Later she recalled the standing ovation greeting her victory as "completely surreal."[78]

"Oh, my!" said Sarandon, commencing her acceptance speech. "It was a great dance," she continued, thanking Sister Helen Prejean, publicist Nancy Seltzer, and Sean Penn, her costar, who was defeated by Nicolas Cage, the star of the drama *Leaving Las Vegas*. "This is yours as much as mine," said Sarandon to Robbins, who lost the director prize to *Braveheart*'s Mel Gibson.

Sarandon eventually relinquished her Dolce & Gabbana Oscar satin ensemble to the Costume Institute at New York's Metropolitan Museum of Art, personally delivering her bespoke pieces, where they remain a part of the institution's permanent collection. "People would ooh and aah," recalled a museum spokesperson of the reaction to the victory dress when it first went on display in April 2003. "They'd say, 'I remember that dress!'"[79]

Sharon Stone's eclectic three-piece and Uma Thurman's Prada respectively fetched $8,500 and $8,000 in March 1999 as Christie's auctioned them along with a group of fifty-six Academy Awards ceremonials as a part of its "Unforgettable: Fashion of the Oscars" fund-raiser, donating its $786,120 sale proceeds to the American Foundation for AIDS Research.[80] Thurman, Stone, and Sarandon's benevolent gestures were admirable, but they proved the last of their kind because by 1997 those actresses modeling Paris haute couture at the Oscars reaped their own handsome rewards.

Chapter Eleven

WHAT PRICE HOLLYWOOD?

New York Fashion Week kicked off the international round of annual ready-to-wear shows in March 1997, and from a privileged front-row seat, photographer Mario Testino recalled that supermodels, the adored troupe of beauties notoriously known for commanding ten-thousand-dollar-a-day salaries, remained the "biggest, hottest thing around. I was going to all the fashion shows," confirmed Testino, and then he listed the top five headline-generating runway attractions, using their first names, as their global fan base familiarly knew them: "Kate, Naomi, Claudia, Linda, and Nadja."[1] But within weeks as the shows progressed to Paris, supermodels were an endangered species and their earnings seemed like small change compared to the reported two million dollars that Nicole Kidman had just secured to display through 1997, at high-profile events, including the sixty-ninth Academy Awards, couture produced by John Galliano, recently appointed as designer in chief at Christian Dior. As fashion editors pondered the Dior Kidman would wear to the Oscars, more Hollywood news came to Paris, about Courtney Love. In Los Angeles, Oscar weekend had simultaneously launched into overdrive, and with it came scenes of fashion chaos surrounding rock-star-turned-actress Love, whom *Women's Wear Daily* had recently classified as "most sought after" by a long list of designers hoping to dress the ceremonial-bound.[2] Recalled a witness on the fringes of Love's entourage, "It was wild—one minute you'd see a publicist running through the Four Seasons screaming, 'Courtney's wearing Valentino!' Then you'd see another screaming, 'Courtney's wearing Versace!'"[3]

After Love displayed a style turnaround at the sixty-ninth Academy

Awards, she fronted an extensive fashion advertising campaign representing the designer who'd produced her Oscar couture. By 1998, executives representing big-league European luxury brands and American cosmetic giants turned their back on supermodels, scrutinizing the Academy Awards red carpet for potential celebrity muses. Designers also employed charming liaisons to court Oscar hopefuls year-round to secure their ceremonial commitment because Kidman's appearance at the Oscars in Dior exposed the venerable fashion label, beleaguered for over a decade by management upheaval, to a new audience of 54.5 million people, among them hordes of potential new customers.

The sixty-ninth Academy Awards is regarded as the momentous night that forged fashion's new alliance with Hollywood, as Love and Kidman fascinated millions witnessing the transformations they displayed on the red carpet. Deconstructed, their looks incorporated strikingly similar accoutrements, including couture first seen inside *Vogue*, precious jewels by Martin Katz of Beverly Hills, and costly satin Manolo Blahnik evening shoes. Meanwhile, dividing time on Oscar day between Kidman's Pacific Palisades compound and Love's West Hollywood home was Kevyn Aucoin, fashion's top makeup artist. And though Love, widow of suicide-victim rock star Kurt Cobain, and Kidman, the pampered Hollywood wife to heartthrob Tom Cruise, were two very different people, both recognized that making the scene at the Oscars could increase their prestige by establishing their reputations as fashion icons. So instantly they agreed to present Oscars, harboring no hurt feelings as they missed out on nominations, despite confident predictions that they'd rank within the Academy's roll call.

Attending the Academy Awards was Love's long-cherished dream. "I thought about going with long green hair and green fake fur and a green Bob Mackie gown—it was all based on Cher," she confided to Kevyn Aucoin, her friend, revealing a fantasy she'd conjured in 1980 as a rebellious sixteen-year-old growing up in Oregon.[4] Fifteen years later when Love reignited a brief acting career that had stalled in the late eighties, she attended *Vanity Fair*'s party celebrating the sixty-seventh Academy Awards. She wore white and generated headlines because a dollar-store tiara topping her bleached-blond hair and the twenties satin nightgown clinging to her wan frame complemented the getup of pretty blond British photographer Amanda de Cadenet, with whom she held hands and mischievously introduced as her "lesbian girlfriend."[5]

Love's *Vanity Fair* Oscar-party gown harked back to the time when she was a "fuck poor" struggling musician.[6] Back then she found her fancy dress—such as a vintage negligé she wore in February 1992 marrying grunge messiah Kurt Cobain, Nirvana's lead singer—at Pacific Northwest secondhand shops. Performing onstage with Hole, the successful rock band she fronted from 1990, Love made hip for adolescents such thrift-shop treasures, as well as baby dolls and Mary Janes. But after Cobain shot himself on the grounds of their Seattle estate in April 1994, they were painful memories and banished from the wardrobe inside her new King's Road, West Hollywood, home. But Love's old "girlie clothes" soon became the secret to a plan that resulted in her fashion triumph at the sixty-ninth Academy Awards. According to stylist Wendy Schecter, who devised it, vintage satin was a "nugget" linking Love's complex past to a new identity she'd forged in Hollywood as a conquering heroine.[7] So leading up to the Oscars, Schecter styled ensembles that sophisticated Love's penchant for retro-romantic and made seamless the performer's transition from grunge mascot to modern fashion legend. At crunch time during Oscar season, Love nearly sabotaged their successful collaboration, but when it commenced in September 1996, she was at her personal best.

She had kicked the toxic heroin habit she'd shared with Cobain and also completed a rehab stint to break her dependence on Valium. Love's once bloated figure was dramatically slimmed after she dropped twenty pounds to play Althea Leasure, the fourth wife of multimillionaire *Hustler* publisher Larry Flynt, in *The People vs. Larry Flynt*. The sweeping life story, directed by Czech filmmaker Milos Forman, concentrated on a fight against censorship by porn media magnate Flynt (Woody Harrelson), waged in a 1988 landmark legal battle with evangelist Jerry Falwell. Love perfected the role of Leasure, which required her to age sixteen years over the two-hour biopic. She first catches Flynt's eye as a nubile, barely legal stripper gyrating in a pastel pink, woven bikini and groovy gold go-go boots. Married to Flynt, she becomes hooked on heroin, contracts AIDS, and is last seen dead in her Jacuzzi bathtub at age thirty-three. *Larry Flynt* previewed at a late-August 1996 private Hollywood screening, and within days reliable trades including *Variety* tipped Love as a nominee for a sixty-ninth actress Oscar. It was five months before the Academy announced its nomination list. Up ahead for Love was a series of premieres, promotional events, and press interviews providing her with the opportunity to impress Oscar voters. Determined to please, she hired Pat Kingsley, the fierce founder of PMK, Hollywood's leading celebrity PR firm, representing superstars Tom Cruise, Jodie Foster, and Richard Gere. As shrewd Kingsley coached Love to meet the press, Schecter scoured Manhattan fashion showrooms for the modern movie-star clothes the Oscar hopeful would display with panache on her campaign trail.

Striking, blond, thirty-three-year-old Schecter operated from a Chelsea, Manhattan, loft, and her professional signature merged Manhattan cool with international sophisticated. For ten years from 1986, she styled editorials for *Interview* and Spanish *Vogue* and worked alongside gifted commercials director Tony Kaye as well as French fashion photographer Patrick Demarchelier. To create an "expensive" version of thrift-shopper Love, she received her customary day rate of three thousand five hundred dollars, but for the money she worked hard and in anonymity.[8] In today's Hollywood, stylists are as recognized as the celebrities they dress. But in 1997 comparatively few actresses relied on their services, and their skills went unrecognized. As Schecter explained, she was content toiling behind the scenes for Love, and though her discretion was commendable, it complicated matters as the Oscars drew near. "I always play down my role," said Schecter. "Celebrities are so attached to this illusion of people romanticizing them that they don't want anybody to know that they are real people who put their pants on one leg at a time. Everyone will admit they don't know how to do their own hair. Everyone will admit they don't know how to do their makeup. But nobody wants to fess up they can't pick out their own clothing."[9]

Courtney Love's *Vanity Fair* Oscar party gown became the secret to a plan that resulted in her fashion triumph at the sixty-ninth Academy Awards. (Alex Berliner)

On Love's behalf Schecter approached the task with chutzpah. "'Come on! It'll be *grrreat!* I won't have it out for very long,'" she continued, repeating the enthusiastic pitch she delivered through a first round of early-September 1996 telephone calls, attempting to source borrowed designer clothes from New York showroom executives for Love's trip to the world premiere of *Larry Flynt* at the upcoming New York Film Festival.[10] But Love, whose acting talent was unknown to the general public, was perceived to be hell perilously teetering upon a pair of secondhand Mary Janes. Looming large in the public's imagination was a recent one-hour ABC-TV special in which host Barbara Walters questioned Love about her troubled past with Cobain. Gossiped about, too, was Love's ABC-TV interview ensemble—a hot-pink Thierry Mugler miniskirt suit she later regretted having purchased at an Atlanta shopping mall. Fodder for "Page Six," the *New York Post*'s gossip column, were rumors of Love's other recent escapades, including rehab, a nose job, breast implants, and court time contesting assault charges pressed by Kathleen Hanna, the lead singer of Bikini Kill, Hole's rival. Hanna claimed Love roughed her up backstage at the Lollapalooza summer 1995 music festival. But Love's one-year jail sentence was lifted with her commitment to participate in anger-management classes and to refrain from fisticuffs for twenty-four months. "I clocked her," reflected Love of Hanna, upon whom she also showered fistfuls of Skittles, Tootsie Rolls, and tostadas.[11]

According to Schecter, no New York fashion PR would risk loaning expensive designer samples to Love, convinced that whatever went out would never safely arrive back in one piece. Schecter recalled, "People were, like, 'Courtney Love? *Whatever . . .*'"[12] But she pried from Prada a pewter satin Empire gown as well as a slim, black, sixties-inspired shift Love respectively donned for the New York Film Festival and *Larry Flynt*'s Hollywood premiere. The borrowed Prada looked so sleek on Love that Miuccia Prada sent her another dress for keeps. Next Schecter organized a fleet of Dolce & Gabbana Love showed off at her first film junket at the Beverly Hills Four Seasons Hotel. Then stories marveling at Love's new look appeared in January 1997 issues of every major fashion, film, and music magazine. "Toning down her bad girl image," noted *Rolling Stone*.[13] "Going Sharon Stone?" wondered *W*.[14] "Virtually unrecognizable," an anonymous source told *Los Angeles Magazine*, after spying Love at a West Hollywood nightclub.[15] "We've given her the *Vogue* "makeover,"" confirmed Anna Wintour, *Vogue*'s editor, revealing details to *Time* of an upcoming, six-page story showcasing Love.[16] At *Vogue*'s "makeover" shoot, Schecter, its original mastermind, stood by as Love met hairstylist Garren, a favorite of supermodels and young socialites, who composed the clientele at his Henri Bendel, Fifth Avenue, New York, salon. Garren reshaped Love's frazzled tresses into a soft platinum-blond bob, and with Aucoin's gloss it worked as the top note of her Oscar-night look.

By early February, Love realized her teenage fantasy—she received an invitation to the Academy Awards. That she was participating as a presenter, rather than an actress nominee, failed to trouble her. The Academy honored *Larry Flynt* with a pair of nominations—one recognized Woody Harrelson's lead role, the other, Milos Forman's direction. "I don't have a real body of work yet," said Love philosophically, reconciling her omission.[17] The diplomatic public statement increased her stature in Hollywood but disappointed die-hard Hole fans expecting Love to contest what some viewed as an Academy slight. Love, however, was hardly the Hollywood role model that typically qualifies as an Oscar nominee. Days after *Larry Flynt's* Christmas 1996 general release, she was outside Sunset Boulevard's Viper Room nightclub, brawling with thugs harassing actress Drew Barrymore, her friend. "Manhandling one punk, punching another," reported a witness.[18] By late January, as Hollywood's elite booked Rodeo Drive boutique appointments to survey potential Oscar couture, *Village Voice* columnist Michael Musto reported Love's trip to Meow Mix, the Lower East Side, Manhattan, lesbian bar, mentioning her purchase there of seven T-shirts emblazoned with its motto: DON'T FUCK WITH THE LADIES.[19]

Booking Love as an Oscar presenter was part of a ratings-boosting strategy exercised on behalf of the Academy by Gil Cates, its producer. Fearing that Middle America would tune out due to the Oscar-night competition of independent dramas, including *The English Patient, Breaking the Waves*, and *Fargo*, Cates figured Love's addition to the ceremony might attract a new audience from Hole's huge teen and twentysomething fan base. But word on the music scene was that Love's joining Hollywood's establishment for the Oscars would alienate her rock devotees, given that her slot was introducing the nominated song "For the First Time," the theme tune of the romance *One Fine Day*, performed by Kenny Loggins. Eighties pop star Loggins, famed for gold- and platinum-selling catchy hits, such as "Footloose," was the sort of successful commercial musician upon whom grunge-era Love would typically heap scorn. "Why would you not go?" asked an unrepentant Love.[20] By mid-February, at the Berlin Film Festival, the first stop on the European premiere tour of *Larry Flynt*, she already had her eye on a prize. "[The Oscars] isn't about who wins, it's about who wears the best dress!" she gushed, acknowledging her commitment to present.[21]

Up till Berlin, Love totally relied upon Wendy Schecter's style expertise. But soon after, she independently commissioned Valentino to make her Oscar dress and during a quick telephone call dismissed Schecter, who traces their falling-out back to preparations she made for Love's trip to Europe. Love had explained to Schecter she had enough clothes for Berlin, but asked if some red-carpet couture could arrive at her next destination—Paris, where she'd attend the French premiere of *Larry Flynt*. So Schecter dutifully visited Valentino's Madison Avenue showroom, selecting six dresses, but instead of sending them to Paris, Valentino's press office shipped the gowns to Berlin. According to Schecter, Love's manager—allegedly furious that his client was short on fancy clothes for the Berlin Film Festival—had shouted down his hotel phone to Valentino's press officer, "Where are the fucking dresses? We need these dresses! What's your fucking problem? If we don't get them, she's never wearing Valentino again!"[22]

Love, knocked sideways when Schecter's handpicked shipment of Valentino promptly arrived in Berlin, figured the couturier's team had assembled it on her behalf and granted him the task of creating her Oscar dress. "When Courtney asked [Valentino's press office], 'How did you know? These are the dresses I would have picked out myself. They are perfect!' [Valentino's press office said,] 'We could tell,' instead of 'Wendy picked these six dresses for you in New York,'" added Schecter.[23] Love had emerged as an important celebrity within Valentino's fold, thanks to Sharon Stone, his former muse. Love's new pal Stone loaned her a scoop-neck, midnight blue Valentino gown Love wore with Harry Winston diamonds and a polished Chanel navy manicure to the fifty-fourth Golden Globes in January 1997. A week later Amy M. Spindler, the all-important fashion editor of the *New York Times*, wrote that "Valentino's dressing of Courtney Love for the Golden Globes" was one of two "off-the-runway" style "coups" of the winter 1997 fashion season.[24] Number two? "Oscar de la Renta's dressing of Hillary Rodham Clinton for Inauguration Day."[25]

Back in L.A., Love replaced Schecter with Arianne Phillips, the thirty-two-year-old costume designer who'd orchestrated clever period costumes for *Larry Flynt*. Phillips says she and Love "bonded" on the film's Memphis set.[26] The hire may also have been prompted by "Great Costumes That Can't Win"—Amy Spindler's laudatory *New York Times* profile of Phillips, published on February 18, 1997, a week after the Academy announced its Oscar nominations. Hailing Phillips as a visionary, Spindler's story also lamented that she'd failed to qualify with *Larry Flynt* for an Oscar nomination. Because Love hoped her arrival at the Oscars would prove a zeitgeist defining moment, she enlisted Phillips, whose talent would ensure it. "I'm not a celebrity stylist, but if I have a relationship with someone, I will be there to help out," explained Phillips of working with Love. "It was [Courtney's] first time at the Oscars. She was healthy and in a great spiritual place. She felt like having a good time. It was like, 'Okay, I'll wear the diamonds. And I'll wear the dress.'"[27]

Monks advised Buddhist Love to incorporate gold into her Oscar ensemble, but she settled on a platinum and diamond Martin Katz lariat, which Phillips selected from the Beverly Hills jeweler. "The necklace was sassy and she's sassy—she loved it," said Katz of Love.[28] Though Love's Valentino Oscar couture was under way in Rome, upon Sharon Stone's recommendation she also visited the West Hollywood costume workshop operated by designer John David Ridge. From 1980 for six years, Ridge created the Halston collection, after Norton Simon, its parent company, ousted the designer from his own fashion label. "Courtney wanted a Halston," confirmed Ridge of the seventies-inspired, V-neck, matte black jersey dress he made for Love to consider for Oscar night. "It tied up at the back of the neck and was very slim."[29]

But in the Madison Avenue showroom of Gianni Versace, the Milanese designer famed for dressing rock stars Elton John and Madonna, as well as Diana, Princess of Wales, Schecter found what she considered a one in a million—a floor-length, shimmering white, bias-cut, sleeveless satin gown with tendrils floating from its back like angel wings. Canny Schecter recognized the creation as an "elegant" take on the "cheap, tacky" secondhand satin Love had worn to *Vanity Fair*'s Oscar party in 1995. "It was slightly romantic—in the vein of what we had been doing all along," Schecter remembered. "If you got out the checklist, it had every single thing Courtney needed to maintain her personality and still emerge anew. It was part of a bigger puzzle."[30]

Officially, Schecter was no longer Love's stylist. She went to Versace because she "pretended" never to have received the February call from her client explaining the appointment of Valentino as her Oscar-night couturier. "All I can think to myself is, 'Okay—I know that Valentino didn't pick out those dresses for Berlin—it's all going to be a disaster,'" said Schecter, explaining the thoughts in her mind during the conversation with Love. "I knew that I made Courtney more beautiful than she had ever looked in her life."[31]

The featherweight satin dress Schecter sourced was from Atelier, Versace's haute-couture collection, and in January 1997 it first appeared on his runway at the Paris Hôtel Ritz with diaphanous chiffon and satin eveningwear inspired by artist Alexander Calder's airy mobiles. Soon supermodel Shalom Harlow displayed it in *Vogue*'s March 1997 issue in a fourteen-page portfolio devoted to the best pieces that had debuted at the recent spring Paris couture shows. The dress appeared to be just a satin slip. But its tailoring was quintessentially figure-flattering Versace, although it was attractively bare of the baroque, gilt Medusa medallions that customarily adorned his couture. "Everything is so light," explained Versace, "all the collection could fit into one bag."[32]

By early March, Schecter, spying Versace's fresh take on spring in look-book photographs at his New York showroom, put a rush order on the white Atelier gown, then packed it in a duffel bag she carried as hand luggage boarding an Oscar-week flight from New York to Los Angeles.

Ten days before the Oscars Schecter had received a one A.M. telephone call from Love's frantic team explaining their leader had second thoughts about presenting in Valentino. Expecting it, Schecter had already booked her trip out to L.A. "'I have the perfect dress—this is when my flight gets in,'" she explained, went back to sleep, and later reflected, "I knew I had the situation under control."[33]

But arriving at Love's place on King's Road, Schecter was kept in a holding pattern. Already there were a team of Versace publicists, who'd traveled over from a temporary fashion headquarters set up inside a Four Seasons hotel suite. Learning that Love was considering the white Atelier gown, Versace's PRs brought more dresses for her consideration. "Courtney wasn't going to decide what she would wear until the day of the ceremony," affirmed John David Ridge.[34] "I pushed and then I realized she was leaning toward other dresses because I was pushing too hard," added Schecter. "It was one of those things—if it was anybody else's idea, purely on principle Courtney wasn't going to wear it, even if it was the best thing. It became a whole game of psychological espionage."[35]

By Friday of Oscar week, as Love contemplated an exhaustive couture supply, incessant calls from the fashion press about her clogged Schecter's cell phone. "Everyone wanted to put to print what [Courtney planned to] wear," she went on. "And then there was me, saying, 'You'll

The white satin Versace dress that stylist Wendy Schecter found for Courtney Love to wear to the sixty-ninth Academy Awards debuted as part of the Atelier Versace haute couture collection staged at the Paris Hotel Ritz in January 1997. (Chris Moore)

know when she's on the red carpet.'"[36]

As for Love, she busied herself with Oscar rehearsals. The Academy replaced her task from introducing Kenny Loggins to bestowing the makeup prize. Displeased with a presentation preamble she felt referenced her substance abuse, rehab stint, and formerly disheveled state, Love intended to read a poem by Emily Dickinson. "'Then Sunrise kissed my Chrysalis,'" said Love, concluding her recitation onstage at the Shrine Auditorium during a Sunday-afternoon run-through. "That's pretty vaginal for a girl from a band called Hole," cracked a scriptwriter standing nearby the podium.[37] Author Carrie Fisher, a member of the Academy's writing team, approached Love and patiently explained, "*Chrysalis* is too close to *clitoris* for comfort."[38] The Academy's writers retreated to their trailers and thrashed out a new script for Love. Adding urgency to their task was a phone call the Academy received from Milos Forman emphasizing Love's displeasure at reading their original material.

Meanwhile, the duty of presenting the thirteenth Academy Award—the editing prize—was granted to Nicole Kidman. Her latest film role, Isabel Archer, the tortured heroine in *Portrait of a Lady*, Jane Campion's 1996 adaptation of the Henry James novel, "stirred talk of an Oscar nomination," wrote *Vanity Fair*, but it also noted the putative view of the period drama as "an absurdly mannered indulgence."[39]

As Mrs. Tom Cruise, thirty-year-old Kidman maintained her position as Hollywood royalty. But while Cruise's smooth performance as a major-league sports agent, the title character of *Jerry Maguire*, Cameron Crowe's romantic box-office hit, earned him a shot competing for the sixty-ninth actor Academy Award, Kidman's critical beating for *Portrait* was an unexpected blow. Campion's film was the second phase of Kidman's careful career relaunch, which had started four years after she'd married Cruise in Telluride, Colorado, on Christmas Eve 1990. Their union, asserted *McCall's* magazine, was a "trade-off," orchestrated to halt rumors of Cruise's homosexuality, whereby his management at Creative Artists Agency would transform Kidman into a "movie star" in exchange for her commitment to wedlock.[40] There has never been any evidence to substantiate the rumours about Cruise or the so-called trade-off. After marrying Cruise, Kidman discovered a dearth of adequate Hollywood roles and in 1994 contemplated moving back home to Sydney, Australia. Reconsidering, she studied drama at the Actors Studio in New York, then graduated to her breakthrough role—Suzanne Stone, a ruthless TV weather girl at the center of a small-town sex scandal in *To Die For*, a critically acclaimed drama directed by Gus Van Sant, for which she earned a Golden Globe in January 1996. Mention that an Oscar nomination had eluded Kidman's *To Die For* comeback was said to spark Cruise off on "heated hour-long" diatribes.[41] During a June 1996 interview he calmly predicted that Kidman would emerge with *Portrait* as a contender for the sixty-ninth actress Oscar. "It's going to happen," said Cruise. "You don't want to say anything that could jinx it."[42]

After *Portrait*, an exhausted Kidman remained bedridden for two weeks. Wearing rigid corsets beneath her period costume, she thought, would heighten Isabel's suffering and confinement as a psychologically tormented, battered nineteenth-century wife. But the brittle apparatus bruised her body and left critics as well as the Academy unconvinced. Cruise considered "a damn miracle" a joint offer he and Kidman next accepted to star as married couple William and Alice Harford in *Eyes Wide Shut*, Stanley Kubrick's thriller.[43] For two decades reclusive Kubrick, who occupied a rambling estate in rural Hertfordshire, nurtured *Eyes Wide*

Shut as a screen adaptation of *Traumnovelle*, a tale of sexual obsession and matrimonial jealousy by Viennese playwright Arthur Schnitzler. Cruise and Kidman moved to London in autumn 1996, commencing *Eyes Wide Shut* in November. The details of the film remained top secret, as did a midwinter reception Christian Dior hosted at its avenue Montaigne headquarters so Kidman, on a rare break from shooting, could select an Oscar dress from John Galliano's debut couture collection.

Catching high-profile Kidman at her career crossroads was perceived as yet another conquest for Dior's impressive Galliano. But the thirty-three-year-old South Londoner was as much of a superstar in the fashion world, emerging as an esteemed player even before he established an independent eponymous label. In June 1984, Browns, the directional London boutique, purchased Les Incroyables, a deft collection recalling French revolutionary regalia that Galliano had produced to graduate from London's Central St. Martins College of Art and Design, the notoriously tough graduate fashion school. A decade later he turned fashion's tide from grunge to glamour by displaying Princess Lucretia— a spring 1994 collection inspired by a mythical monarch fleeing Russia. "With anything she can grab from her boudoir," explained Galliano, who interpreted the romantic notion with a collection of frock coats, slithery bias-cut satin dresses, and skirts made *Gone With the Wind*–sweeping by crinolines he constructed with electrical wire from BHV, the Paris department store.[44] Produced for his eponymous label at a tiny Bastille atelier kept afloat by Wall Street millions sourced by *Vogue*'s Anna Wintour, Galliano's unapologetic display of femininity contributed to his nabbing the coveted post helming Dior after a temporary stint running Hubert de Givenchy's couture house.[45] The private reception for Nicole Kidman, an abridged version of Galliano's January 1997 Dior couture debut extravaganza, began his mission to modernize the moribund fashion label.

"*Quelle extravagance! Quel succès fou!*" raved *Women's Wear Daily*, applauding the brio Galliano applied to his first Dior show.[46] To display the couture, fifty top models were hired instead of the customary twenty-five. Maximizing the drama of their parade, Dior secured the entire ground floor of the Paris Grand Hôtel (rival Valentino customarily made do with its ballroom). Decorated with four thousand pink roses, it became a bucolic paradise, and the audience was so star-studded that *Vogue* later summed up the guest list as "everybody."[47]

Kidman's jaw dropped at the sight of Galliano's Dior. She decided Absinthe—the twentieth couture piece in the lineup—was her ultimate

Oscar dress. "It was a spontaneous choice," she reflected. "I
. . . remember seeing the clothes
and thinking, '*This kind of
elegance and perfection just does not
happen.*'"[48] Inspired by decadent
Peking Opera costumes, mink
edged thigh-high slits of the
satin gown, and silk tassels
cascaded from its chenille mesh
back. Aqua and sapphire, hand-
stitched embroidery adorned its
upper bodice, a sparkling touch
to compliment Kidman's pale
blue eyes. Otherwise the shade
of Dior's Absinthe matched the
lime green color of Chartreuse,
the herbal liqueur regarded by
the French as the elixir of life.
Classically Gallic, chartreuse
was a Galliano signature and
best symbolized his mission to
energize Dior. "Beautiful,"
declared *Vogue* of Absinthe,

In January 1997 John Galliano was the fashion world's
superstar. (Peter Lindbergh/Courtesy of Christian Dior).

which was included in its March 1997 issue, while *WWD* splashed a
black-and-white snapshot of it across the cover of its Paris couture
edition.[49] Four Dior couture clients had already ordered the thirty-
thousand-dollar, handmade satin frock, but Kidman didn't mind. "She
just loved it and said, 'Let's do it,'" recalled Galliano.[50] But before she
could call Dior's Absinthe her very own, a couture custom dictated
that permission be granted from Anne Bass, the Upper Manhattan
blond socialite who, as the first client to order it, possessed the right
to sanction her successors. Kidman remained committed. "She was
prepared to put in the time," added Galliano.[51] Reached while skiing
in Aspen, Bass gave the go-ahead. Then Dior's tailors made two round-
trips to Kidman in London, where they fit the Oscar dress.[52]

Time, however, disdainfully labeled "harsh" and "poison green" its
chartreuse shade, after first noticing it amidst Galliano's January 1996
Givenchy couture show.[53] For a Dior Oscar dress, chartreuse was atyp-
ical. Rare were recent sightings of celebrities modeling Dior at the

219

Academy Awards. But when present in Dior, they wore white. Candice Bergen, for example, appeared in an ivory, off-the-shoulder Dior column at the fortieth Academy Awards in 1968. Twenty-two years later Isabelle Adjani competed for the actress prize at the sixty-second Academy Awards in a pretty, pallid Dior ruffled peasant blouse. "White is more beautiful than any color for evening," wrote Christian Dior in *Little Dictionary of Fashion*, his 1954 style bible containing rules observed with sanctity at 30 avenue Montaigne.[54] White also evoked lily of the valley, the delicate spring bloom Dior had made an emblem of his label by attaching its sprigs to lapels of late-forties New Look suit jackets, while its light, sweet bouquet became the dominant note of Diorissimo, his best-selling perfume. But as Galliano's tenure began at Dior, lily of the valley was relegated to the couture house archive. "I think if you are a shrinking violet, you wouldn't pass by Dior," said Galliano, reflecting upon the modern free spirits who favored his design daring, like Kidman.[55]

It was Kidman's adventurous streak that first intrigued Galliano. Three years before she agreed to represent Dior, she'd sought him out at his independent Bastille atelier and they became friends. His garretlike studio hovered high above a cobblestone alleyway found beneath a white arch. The bohemian enclave linked neon-lit rue de la Roquette with rue de Faubourg Saint-Antoine, where shops selling kitsch domestic fixtures were historic remnants. Back in 1789, a mob of furniture makers that operated in the Bastille had stormed the nearby prison, sparking the French Revolution. The locale was optimum for iconoclast Galliano, but Kidman's journey there removed her from Faubourg Saint-Honoré, the chichi street off the Champs-Élysées, upon which Hollywood's privileged traditionally window-shopped from the vantage point of passing stretch limousines. But she traversed Bastille cobblestones on foot, making her way up the winding staircase that led to Galliano's space. "She heard about me, came for a visit, and we hit it off," remembered Galliano. "At the time she was loving the bias-cut dresses and bought one. Then we kept up our relationship. Whenever she was in Europe, we would have lunch."[56] Over lunch, Kidman regaled Galliano with tales of skydiving with Tom Cruise. "Nic's a scream. She's a real tomboy—a laugh," he added. "She jumps out of helicopters with parachutes and stuff!"[57]

Conquering the klieg lights at the Academy Awards was "one of Cruise's favorite occupations," claimed Robert Sellers, his biographer.[58] But the red carpet remained for Cruise and Kidman Mount Everest—

"It was a spontaneous choice," reflected Nicole Kidman of Absinthe, the chartreuse satin dress she selected from John Galliano's 1997 début Christian Dior haute couture collection. "I . . . remember seeing the clothes and thinking, 'This kind of elegance and perfection just does not happen.'" (Courtesy of Christian Dior)

their insurmountable peak. Rangy, five-foot-eleven Kidman stood three inches taller than Cruise, and to lessen the discrepancy she perpetually wore flats. Her gesture worked in most situations—except at the Oscars. The sixty-second Academy Awards in 1990 was her first public appearance with Cruise. Competing for the actor trophy for his role as Vietnam War veteran Ron Kovic in *Born on the Fourth of July*, Oliver Stone's drama, Cruise appeared in mogul mode, neat in an Armani tuxedo. But Kidman ventured onto the Oscars red carpet in a footwear faux pas—silver, T-strap kitten heels. A year later, at the sixty-third Oscars in 1991, she trampled upon and ripped the train stemming from Anjelica Huston's Armani. "Tom kind of grabbed his face like 'My God, I can't believe you did that'—Anjelica looked not too pleased," revealed a TV reporter.[59] Then Cruise put his foot in it at the sixty-eighth Academy Awards. "Where did she get the necklace?" Joan Rivers asked Cruise of Kidman's eye-popping Fred Leighton diamond-and-opal choker.[60] "Umm, I really don't know," stammered a bewildered Cruise.[61] Catching sight of Kidman's Oscar dress, a long, lilac Prada, affable Oprah Winfrey announced, into her ABC-TV microphone, "To die for!" But its billowy fit suggested Kidman could do better, while its shade was a dead ringer for the lavender Prada Uma Thurman had worn a year earlier. "Turn around!" begged Joan Rivers of Prada-clad Kidman. "No!" replied Kidman. She grimaced, recoiled from Rivers's cameraman, but then obliged.

In 1995, Kidman told *Vogue* she needed help dressing for "big" events but said she'd "never hire a professional shopper."[62] She reasoned dressing to be "a creative thing. If someone else is dressing you, then it's their creative thing."[63] But impeccable red-carpet appearances were mandatory for Kidman as a Christian Dior representative. Just as Courtney Love prepared to meet the Oscar TV cameras with help from a talented costume designer, so did Kidman, appointing L'Wren Scott, a stylist who'd consulted on the wardrobe Marit Allen had produced for *Eyes Wide Shut*. At six foot three, Scott was well equipped to tackle Kidman's challenge of dressing tall. The former model had worked Chanel's Paris runway in the eighties, and back then couturier Thierry Mugler considered her a muse. By 1997, Scott played creative consultant to *Vogue* and *Vanity Fair* photographer Herb Ritts. Prepping Kidman, she sourced antique gold Indian earrings from a collection of rare jewels acquired by Martin Katz, as well as Manolo Blahnik pale blue silk pumps with Tom Cruise–friendly, three-inch heels. "I know sometimes she has to work with stylists," reflected Galliano of Kidman's preparations for the sixty-ninth Academy Awards. "But Nicole has an innate understanding of luxury and what looks good on her. She doesn't need a stylist. She loves fashion. She's a natural."[64]

On Oscar Monday, Kidman and Cruise both consulted with Sally Hershberger, the Los Angeles hairstylist famed for creating the "Meg Ryan"—a mod shag haircut that became widely copied after Ryan debuted it in *French Kiss*, the 1995 romantic comedy. After Hershberger blow-dried Cruise, she smoothed Kidman's strawberry-blond, waist-length curls into a neat, figure-eight chignon. Next, Kevyn Aucoin broke his steadfast rule that redheads should resist wearing red lipstick, painting Kidman's lips deep claret.

By noon that day, Courtney Love revealed her decision to wear the white satin Atelier Versace gown. "She wanted to emanate the positive side of her life," explained Arianne Phillips of Love's choice, which sent Wendy Schecter on a brisk expedition through the ladies' shoe department at Neiman Marcus on Wilshire Boulevard.[65] There she found Love's ashen satin Manolos, and at Gianni Versace's Four Seasons hotel suite she picked up a clutch purse. Delivering the last-minute accessories to Love, Schecter became an integral part of the Oscar presenter's titivating team. "Applying the fake tan to her breasts," said Schecter, recalling her exact duty on Oscar afternoon, adding, "I was in it for the day to day."[66] By three P.M., bronzed and immaculately clad Love slipped into the backseat of a rented limo. And as its chauffer departed for the Shrine, Schecter was bound for her boyfriend's house, where she planned to watch Love's anticipated Academy Awards arrival on TV. Navigating her Jeep rental car, she cranked up the stereo and in its driver's seat relaxed in a vintage bias-cut, black ball gown, something special she'd pulled from her wardrobe and packed in the duffel bag holding Love's Versace couture. "I stopped borrowing clothes when I was in grade twelve," reflected Schecter of her Oscar-night choice.[67]

The Sixty-ninth Academy Awards, March 24, 1997. On a typical Monday afternoon, it would take merely twenty minutes through freeway traffic to reach the Shrine Auditorium in downtown Los Angeles from the Cruise/Kidman Pacific Palisades compound. But on Oscar Monday, by three P.M. a lethal pile-up stretched crosstown, and for two hours Kidman, trapped in her limo, was rendered nearly motionless, fearful that she might crease Galliano's Dior satin. As she emerged from her Lincoln, barely a wrinkle marked it, so she joked to a nearby reporter about her trying journey, "You have to sit in a very odd position so as not to crush your dress!"[68] Next she confessed feeling a "little over the top" in Dior chartreuse.[69] Reaching the Shrine's entrance required journeying across six hundred feet of red carpet through a murky conga line clogged by tuxedoed players and black-clad box-office draws Kristin Scott Thomas, Sandra Bullock, and Winona Ryder. While Cruise progressed at a jaunty clip, Kidman's moves were equally sure-footed and made easy by her medium-heeled Manolos. "She looks fantastic— it takes guts to wear chartreuse to the Academy Awards," reporter Laurie Pike declared of Kidman into a KTLA-TV microphone. Kidman's sole detractor was *E!*'s Joan Rivers, who bellowed on air, "What an ugly dress!"

By then, Cruise and Kidman were safely ensconced within the Shrine, leaving the red carpet to the beacon in white, bias-cut Versace satin that was Courtney Love. Pundits heralded Love's Oscars red-carpet arrival as the second coming of a modern Jean Harlow. Meanwhile Love relied upon grunge-era performing skills and just let it rock. Flinging her yoga-toned arms into the air, she basked in the shower of 250 flashbulbs, twirling to an adulatory sound track provided by an appreciative press pack, who cried, "Courtney! Courtney! Courtney! Over here! Over here!" Showtime was minutes away, but ABC-TV's cameraman captured Love spinning round while an announcer professed, "Second only to the Oscars themselves is what the actresses are wearing!" Progressing to the Shrine, Love granted few interviews but made time for film critic Roger Ebert. "You just can't dive into the mosh pit after a certain age," she sighed. Next she sent a personal message to Valentino via *WWD*'s Merle Ginsberg: "I just want to apologize to Mr. Valentino. He's made me so many beautiful clothes, but in the end Versace was so accommodating."

Twenty minutes into the ceremony, Love faultlessly crossed the gleaming stage and then delivered the makeup prize without missing a beat. "The makeup artist has the power to transform from the cocoon of the dressing room to the butterfly of the film," she began, "giving the actor the confidence and inspiration to play that goddess or the extraterrestrial from deep space." But announcing as Oscar winner *The Nutty Professor*'s David Leroy Anderson, Love realized she'd made a critical error by omitting his collaborator, Rick Baker. She apologized to the pair as she walked them offstage and into the pressroom, "I fucked up. I'm so fucking sorry, you guys!"[70]

Next, as Kidman donned spectacles to introduce a performance by *Lord of the Dance* star Michael Flatley—part of a two-act presentation of the editing prize, which went to *The English Patient*'s Walter Murch— Carrie Fisher spotted Love backstage. "C'mon," announced Fisher to Love, and locking arms, they made tracks for a stage door to smoke cigarettes outside the Shrine.[71] "You were great," Fisher told a beaming Love as they crossed its threshold. "You were great."[72]

"I think we achieved our goal," reflected Schecter, recalling the front page of the *Los Angeles Times*' post-Oscars issue, on which was splashed a pinup-style snapshot of Love posing outside the Shrine. "There it was—a full-color photograph of Courtney above the fold."[73] Below it was a shot of Saul Zaentz, the picture-prize-winning producer behind *The English Patient*, which swept the Academy Awards, receiving nine Oscar trophies. Six months later, an arresting Patrick Demarchelier image of Love graced the cover of *Harper's Bazaar*, celebrating her fashion influence. "Courtney Love is the new American style," wrote Cathy Horyn in the accompanying September 1997 story, a who's who of modern style trailblazers, which recounted Love's exultant Oscar moment. "She is tough and chic," professed Horyn of Love, "a kind of corn-haired symbol of America's new fashion confidence."[74]

In the late nineties, the U.S. economy's fortuitous bull market saw retail sales figures skyrocket, providing leading luxury brands with the economic clout to pay actresses fronting ad campaigns film-industry-style wages. Advertising—once a realm avoided by actors fearing product endorsements might jeopardize their professional credibility—became viewed as a profitable sideline enabling them to carefully pick and choose future film projects. By 1998, fashion magazines, which formerly ran a few celebrity covers per year, upped the annual quantity to ten and twelve—a decision *Vogue*'s editor Anna Wintour attributed to a new enthrallment of "Oscar madness" among magazine readers. Representing Versace, Love appeared in a ten-page advertising campaign run worldwide in glossy magazines through autumn 1998. Her time as a trendsetter proved temporary, as did Kidman's alliance with Dior.

By 2003, Kidman had struck a seven-million-dollar deal with Chanel, agreeing to appear in TV commercials and print advertisements promoting its No. 5 perfume. Her contract with the venerable French fashion house also stipulated that she wear to gala events, including the Academy Awards, couture produced by Karl Lagerfeld, Chanel's designer in chief. Alongside Kidman, a new breed of supermodel-beautiful Oscar nominees heightened Hollywood's profile within the fashion world, but some resisted Oscar eveningwear that came with a corporate payoff.

Chapter Twelve
THE GREATEST SHOW ON EARTH

Vintage dresses and couture that harked back to Hollywood's Golden Era became the mode adopted by the Academy Awards' best dressed as the twentieth century gave way to the twenty-first. By now the Oscars fell at the tail end of a two-month-long awards season, and as fashion giants furnished nominees with a greatest-hits selection of gala eveningwear for nonstop fêtes such as the Golden Globes and the Screen Actors Guild Awards, most went vintage to the Oscars, having exhausted current style possibilities in the run-up to the affair. "Those dresses are dead," said Armani's Wanda McDaniel, dismissing with a wave of her Frédéric Fekkai manicure the thought that a contender would brave the Academy Awards' five hundred feet of red carpet in recent runway fashion, which could, thanks to the Internet be viewed moments after it debuted, on style.com.[1]

But the provenance of a hidden treasure—be it a dress plucked from a vault holding twentieth-century rarities or one preserved in a couture archive—would be impossible to immediately pinpoint. "Oooh, I'm special! I'm different! I'm wearing vintage," joked celebrity stylist Phillip Bloch, explaining that such finery lent mystique to an Oscar victory moment, ensuring that the Academy Awards' viewers witnessed an individual triumph rather than one eclipsed by a designer's current vision.[2]

Bygone glamour fit the late nineties as costume epics reminiscent of studio-era megaproductions such as *Shakespeare in Love* and *Moulin Rouge* hit the screen. Through a sobering economic and political climate that settled in after the turn of the new millennium, ladylike, retro-inspired fashion continued to predominate. Film production thrived in New

226

York, Toronto, Vancouver, and Chicago, and back in Hollywood nostalgia was rife for the good old days. In 2002, the Academy Awards returned to its original locale, Hollywood Boulevard. A new, high-tech venue, the Kodak Theater, towered above Grauman's Chinese Theatre, the landmark that had hosted forties ceremonies. The Kodak sat a block from the Roosevelt Hotel, where inside the Blossom Room, Louis B. Mayer had presided over the first Academy Awards in 1929.

The ruthlessness displayed at the eleventh hour, as painstakingly handcrafted Oscar couture was dispensed like Kleenex by new-millennium Oscar nominees and their stylists, would have prompted a reprimand from a studio mogul back in the day. So would the "tales" of "payola" changing hands, as well as "diva behavior" polluting perfumed hallways inside a network of five-star Beverly Hills hotels booked solid during Oscar week by designers, fine jewelers, and deluxe-accessory labels gifting contenders and presenters with pricey accoutrements. But the influence celebrities wielded over consumers kept the fashion industry catering to their whims. Long gone was the time when a contender found an Oscar dress after perusing a few. Some, like Halle Berry, considered hundreds. "Thirty or forty gowns," calculated the *Los Angeles Times*, estimating the average sent to front-runners, including two competing for the seventy-first actress prize in 1991—Gwyneth Paltrow and Cate Blanchett.[3]

Game for the style challenge posed by the extended awards season, Blanchett and Paltrow each moved toward the Oscars with a champion's zeal, swaggering as confidently as supermodels in eveningwear expressly tailored to detonate paparazzi flashbulbs. "Virtually every design house in the world" offered to make Blanchett's Oscar dress, according to Jessica Paster, her stylist.[4] Twenty-four hours before the ceremony, a designer encouraged to submit items for Paltrow's inspection arrived at Huvane Baum Halls, the PR firm representing her, and according to *WWD* "was almost stunned—a room awaited him stuffed with racks of *merch* but also large bags from Gucci and Prada."[5] Shipments of "garment bags filled with clothes" came regularly from Gucci's Tom Ford to the bicoastal class of 1990 Spence School graduate and *Vogue* cover girl after he met her at *Vanity Fair*'s Oscar party in 1996. By then Paltrow had soared to great heights at Miramax. She had been crowned "first lady" of the TriBeCa, New York, film studio whose founding cochairmen, brothers Bob and Harvey Weinstein, produced five out of the eighteen films she made from 1991, including blockbuster

Shakespeare in Love. "I'll do it!" said Paltrow, accepting the romantic comedy's starring role, which earned her an actress Oscar nomination. Viola de Lesseps, her character, is a "well-born" beauty who, posing as a boy, Thomas Kent, in 1593 London, wins a part in an unfinished Rose Theatre production penned by Joseph Fiennes's down-on-his-luck William Shakespeare. De Lesseps's seduction of the Bard provides the inspiration necessary for him to complete what evolves into the masterpiece *Romeo and Juliet*.[6] Paltrow refined her vocal cords, mastering a pitch-perfect British accent with the dialect coach Barbara Berkery, and also honed her theatrical skills with a Royal Shakespeare Company dramaturge. She veered effortlessly between Viola's opposite on-screen guises, commanding the Rose's floorboards in a mustache and wig and then tumbling naked between the sheets with Fiennes's besotted Will Shakespeare. As dastardly Lord Wessex complicated their three-week romance, she also translated genuine heartache through the brittle corsetry that nipped in close beneath her shimmering brocade gowns. "I worked my ass off," recalled Paltrow.[7] Her crisp comic timing and authentic British accent expertly played off *Shakespeare in Love*'s formidable Queen Elizabeth I, portrayed by thespian Judi Dench.[8] After the film's December 3, 1998, New York Ziegfeld Theater world premiere, Paltrow captivated critics on both sides of the Atlantic as well as Academy voters. "No coughing, no chatting, and, amazingly, no snoring," reported *Entertainment Weekly* after Miramax hosted Oscar-season screenings of *Shakespeare in Love*.[9]

Eschewing the services of a stylist, Paltrow prepped independently for the big night. "People were sending me sketches of what they thought I should look like," she recounted. "It was so funny because I really found most of their ideas had nothing to do with what I think I look like. I had a hard time because some designers actually made dresses and sent them to me. I got faxed articles about 'What is Gwyneth Paltrow going to wear?'"[10,]

Playing queen for a day probably proved a welcome distraction. "I had had a really difficult year," said Paltrow later of Oscar season.[11] On nomination day she set to work in Vancouver, Canada, on the offbeat comedy *Duets*, directed by Bruce Paltrow, her dad, who had recently undergone neck surgery and intense radiation therapy to halt the spread of cancer.[12] Compounding the Paltrow family crisis was news that Gywneth's grandfather had also contracted cancer. As *Duets* progressed through its eight-week shoot, Miramax waged an aggressive Oscar campaign from Los Angeles to guarantee supremacy for *Shakespeare in*

Love, which, placing in thirteen categories, emerged as the Academy's most nominated film.[13] But as publicists placed positive stories in newspapers and on television, and the number of promotional *Shakespeare* advertisements in *Variety* and the *Hollywood Reporter* climbed to a suspiciously high 118, Gramercy, producer of Shekhar Kapur's *Elizabeth*, a seven-times Oscar-nominated political thriller charting the early life of Elizabeth I, "upped" the promotion of its "best bet for a win," Cate Blanchett, due to her confident portrayal of the British monarch.[14]

Elizabeth was a career break for the twenty-nine-year-old Melbourne, Australian Blanchett. Graduating from Sydney's National Institute of Dramatic Art in 1992, she had won national awards performing in David Mamet's *Oleana* and Shakespeare's *Hamlet*. A month before the Oscars she was rehearsing an upcoming stage role, Susan Traherne, a World War II British freedom fighter, for the April 1999 London Albery Theatre production of David Hare's

Giorgio Armani lavished Gwyenth Paltrow with this sheer beaded column in which she posed next to First Lady Hillary Rodham Clinton and Miramax cochairman Harvey Weinstein at the November 1998 world premiere of *Shakespeare in Love*. (Corbis)

drama *Plenty*. With little spare time, she delegated the masterminding of her Oscar ensemble to Jessica Paster. At the seventieth Academy Awards, Paster, twenty-six, staged a double coup, rehabilitating supporting actress winner Kim Basinger's battered fashion reputation by faultlessly gowning her in Escada pistachio satin while the cherry red Halston jersey slip she simultaneously sourced for Minnie Driver "had style pundits dubbing it the Oscar dress of 1988," wrote Christa D'Souza in London's *Telegraph Magazine*.[15] "A piece of work but she has a vision," affirmed a prominent Melrose Avenue fashion retailer of Paster, who was notoriously known for hoarding red-carpet finery and toting twenty-five-thousand-dollar haute couture in tattered plastic grocery bags. But she

229

went all out in an effort to please her movie-star clients.[16] Take Basinger's Escada. Commissioned five days before the Oscars, Paster supervised eight takes at its remake over a crazed, forty-eight-hour period. Fed up with executing the alterations, a seamstress stationed at the Japanese-managed Hotel Nikko "finally lost her patience and ran screaming onto La Cienega Boulevard," reported *Variety*.[17] According to designer Randolph Duke, the "sitcom" situation concluded as Paster, a "PR person, and [the] hotel seamstress" finished it off.[18]

Three months before the seventy-first Academy Awards, Paster had already booked for Blanchett a cutting-edge Oscar grooming team composed of six-hundred-dollar-an-hour hairstylist Sally Hershberger and Jeanine Lobell, the makeup mogul behind avant-garde cosmetics brand Stila. Meanwhile, vying to produce Blanchett's Oscar couture were Europe's two preeminent couturiers, Christian Dior's John Galliano and Alexander McQueen. Dividing his time between an East London studio and Givenchy's Paris atelier, where he was its creative force, McQueen designed the gown Blanchett wore in 1997 marrying Australian film editor and scriptwriter Andrew Upton. Soon after she attended "The Overlook," McQueen's "Aspen meets East End" late-February 1999 London fashion show, they met at Monmouth Street's Covent Garden Hotel, Blanchett's preferred outpost where she resided while filming *Elizabeth*. "He sketched right in front of us one of the most beautiful dresses," recalled Paster, who was also on hand. "It was a strapless, light blue, fitted, beautiful—with some Asian motif on the bottom."[19]

But McQueen's handiwork was left on paper because John Galliano won the coveted assignment of gowning Blanchett for the Oscars. "The dress just blossomed," recalled Galliano's collaborator, production designer Michael Howells, recalling how the inventive couture that eventually proved Dior's second Academy Awards red-carpet master-stroke, topping Absinthe, Nicole Kidman's 1997 Oscar dress, evolved over a March 1999 midweek supper at Howells's Notting Hill, London, home. "John mentioned that he'd like to dress Cate for the Academy Awards, and you can go through the agents and publicists, but that can get political," added Howells. "So I said, 'Why don't we do it the old-fashioned way, over a bowl of spaghetti?'"[20]

"Some great things have happened over a dinner table," mused Howells, whose creative talent extends beyond fashion. He designs extravagant backdrops for Dior's Paris runway shows and feature films, including *An Ideal Husband*, director Oliver Parker's 1999 adaptation of the Oscar Wilde satire, where he met Blanchett, who was cast as its female lead, Lady Gertrude Chiltern. Recognizing her "individual beauty" as the perfect foil for the "theatricality" of Galliano's design, he invited her over. "But it was just supper," added Howells of the engagement. "Not an 'elegant' dinner party—it was one of those natural things. No one was selling anything."[21]

"I'm just not interested in that," continued Galliano, recalling the get-together over a coffee inside his Dior Paris atelier in June 2003. "It's nice to get to know an actress and discover their personality, so you are not feeling that what they are wearing [to the Oscars] is an alien creation. Instead, it's something that's made specifically for them."[22]

By March 1999, seven people relaxed around Howells's dining table, including Blanchett, Upton, Paster, Galliano, and two members of his team—design associate Steven Robinson and PR guru Mesh Chibber. "Completely informal," recollected Chibber of the supper party's ambience. "It wasn't about landing a celebrity endorsement. It was about producing beautiful clothes."[23] But first sparks flew. "I found her enchanting and her husband as well—they were gorgeous!" enthused Galliano of encountering Blanchett and Upton.[24] Typical of a meal shared among fashion professionals, nobody recalled exactly what was served, although Paster pronounced both the wine and the food "yummy."[25] Memorable to everyone was the postprandial confection concocted on Howells's black-and-red tartan drawing-room sofa, where Blanchett formed the threesome with Galliano and Paster. There, they conjured up the periwinkle silk knit column she soon described as her "fashion orgasm," due to an exuberant Garden of Eden scene complete with exotic flowers and fluttering hummingbirds conceived for a translucent tulle panel adorning its flip side.[26] Descending trellislike from Blanchett's shoulder blades to her coccyx, the reverse embellishment, a technique executed by Parisian embroidery specialists Lesage on behalf of Galliano, is often applied to his special-occasion couture, including the jade silk empire gown in which Kidman appeared at the 1996 premier of *Portrait of a Lady*. Blanchett spotted the delicate ornamentation plowing through look-books with which Chibber arrived at Howells's place. "I told them I wanted every look-book that John Galliano ever had, so he brought all of the look-books," said Paster.[27] "The hummingbirds, the embroidery, the color—it was her idea to put the embroidery on the back, and she was right. She was so precise, Cate," confirmed Galliano of Blanchett's input. "She knew exactly what she wanted. It was a true collaboration."[28]

Paster returned Galliano's initial attempt at the lavish Oscar sweater dress a few weeks before the Oscars. "The first color I didn't like," she remarked. "It was dark. It needed to be vibrant."[29] Oscar week brought no further Dior shipment to L.A. for Blanchett, who was by then said to be considering a "springy-looking vintage gown" and another by Oscar de la Renta.[30]

Meanwhile, Paltrow had checked into Santa Monica's cozy Shutters Hotel on the Beach. Though Kevyn Aucoin, her favorite makeup artist, was in "blinding pain," having recently slipped a disk, he was en route from Manhattan to beautify her for the event.[31] Meanwhile, she cut a swath around West Hollywood working the copious fashion freebies coming her way from every style capital, including cashmere evening-wear composed of a dress and fur-collared sweater. Sporting the sumptuous combo at a casual midweek gathering, Paltrow left Pamela Dennis, its designer, "crushed."[32] She had hoped her ensemble would touch down at the Oscars.

WWD charted the "bitter struggle" waged to secure a commitment from the five-foot-nine, flaxen-maned vision of loveliness by a host of fashion titans, including Giorgio Armani. Five months before the Oscars, Team Armani had courted Paltrow with passage to Milan, five-star-hotel accommodation, and front-row seats at the designer's October 1998 show. He lavished Paltrow with the sheer, beaded column in which she posed next to First Lady Hilary Rodham Clinton at the world premiere of *Shakespeare in Love*, as well as a sleek metallic Oscar dress. But competing with Armani was Donna Karan (whose autumn/winter 1996 collection Paltrow had modeled in Alfonso Cuarón's 1998 remake of *Great Expectations*), Donatella Versace, and Calvin Klein. "Calvin is my first and true love," confessed Paltrow of Klein, who earliest recognized her spare style as the ultimate receptacle for his unobtrusive luxe. From 1995, Paltrow appeared in Klein eveningwear at four successive Golden Globes ceremonies as well as the sixty-eighth Academy Awards. But as unexpected inclement weather engulfed the December 8 Los Angeles premiere of *Shakespeare in Love*, she replaced a skimpy, planned-on Klein with a twelve-ply, black cashmere evening sweater and crystal-drenched skirt by Celine, the formerly fusty Paris ready-to-wear label New Yorker Michael Kors had made feisty from 1997 as its designer in chief. So Kors factored in on the list of her potential Oscar couturiers, too.[33]

By Oscar-week Thursday, Paltrow was torn between the metallic Armani and an icy blue Celine two-piece, but she also visited Ralph Lauren's Rodeo Drive megaboutique to fit a full-skirted, rose-petal-pink gown she plotted out via fax and over the telephone with the all-American luxury king. "It was the two of them that made the decision about the type of dress and the style of dress," recounted Lauren's West Coast PR representative Crystal Moffett Lourd, who sparked the alliance, submitting for Paltrow's consideration dress sketches produced by Lauren's atelier soon after Oscar nomination day. "I got the call back saying she liked some of the sketches," continued Moffett Lourd. "And it was just a very simple process of working with her, pretty much—she and I—directly collaborating.

"Gwyneth wanted one-of-a-kind," she added. "Originally she was interested in a two-piece situation. Then she decided on a gown—to go even more formal. She saw fabric swatches and it was definitely all about pink."[34]

Powerful Hollywood connections were said to have been invaluable to Moffett Lourd as she wooed sought-after Paltrow on Lauren's behalf. Bryan Lourd, her brother-in-law, and Kevin Huvane, brother of Steven Huvane, Paltrow's publicist, operate as managing directors of Creative Artists Agency, the talent organization handling the nominee's career. Moffett Lourd refuted the notion that such associations granted her an in. She explained that even as Oscar weekend arrived, Paltrow juggled fittings with teams from Armani, Celine, and Lauren. "We would go to Shutters for fittings—many, many fittings—and run into representatives from Armani and Celine," confirmed Moffett Lourd. "It was really one of those things—you just did not know where it was going to go."[35]

Come Saturday afternoon, actress Ileana Douglas, presenter at Santa Monica's Independent Spirit Awards, joked that Miramax's Bob and Harvey Weinstein were "unavailable" at the beachfront ceremony because "they were pressing Gywnie's dress."[36] Over at Shutters, Paltrow was still fitting her final three amid a raucous slumber party happening inside her suite. "She had all of her girlfriends surrounding her and her family—it was really fun," reflected Moffett Lourd.[37] Recounted Paltrow, "When you're going through something like this, you want to rely on everyone you know and love to say, 'Hey, we're all normal. You're still normal. This isn't a big deal!' But everyone's going—'What are you going to wear?' And I'm just going, 'Oh, no!'"[38]

By early Saturday evening a plan conceived by luxury footwear label Jimmy Choo combusted, as three pairs of exorbitant evening shoes customized for Cate Blanchett proved tight fits. Though Jimmy Choo had established a novel ceremonial service, dying white satin pairs to match Oscar dresses, the company went further for Blanchett as its managing director, Tamara Yeardye, commissioned Craig Drake, the Philadelphia jeweler that had recently produced her engagement ring, to craft hundred-thousand-dollar, forty-carat diamond ankle straps for the nominee's satin evening slippers. After the Oscars, duplicates would be auctioned for charity, publicizing the new Jimmy Choo Beverly Hills boutique, because "one actress was worth a dozen ads," claimed a footwear expert.[39] But Blanchett couldn't budge in her customized, diamond-laden Choos. Or the "understudies." A late-breaking *WWD* story unfairly blamed Jessica Paster for incorrectly calculating her client's shoe size. At the time, Paster was styling Blanchett, Kim Basinger, Minnie Driver, Robert Duvall, as well as Brendan Fraser. Paster also conducted an Oscar-week interview with ABC's *20/20* and some wondered if she was "simply spreading herself too thin."[40] All week, however, the stylist walked on eggshells awaiting Blanchett's Dior. "The dress showed up literally the day of, or like, the day before [the Oscars]," said Paster.[41]

Because lists of actresses were furnished with free Jimmy Choos, its temporary headquarters inside L'Hermitage ran out of stock. But Yeardye dispatched Choo's Los Angeles PR Marilyn Heston to Saks, where, just before closing, purchased black satin Jimmy Choo sling-backs, tracked down Jacques Zatikian, proprietor of North Beverly Drive's Progressive Shoe Repair, and arrived on his doorstep by eleven P.M. "I'm standing at Jacques's house with a shoe box in my hands, begging him to open the front door. He was having a family dinner," recalled Heston.[42] But Zatikian accepted the all-night job of stripping off the sling-backs' black satin and then dying periwinkle a new white silk upper. "I said, 'Here's the shoe and here's a purple fabric swatch. When will these be ready?'" added Heston. "And he said, 'As soon as I finish dinner, I'll go back to my studio and get to work.'"[43]

Harry Winston provided Paltrow's Oscar-morning wake-up call. "I woke her up," admitted a mortified Carolyn Brodie, Winston's PR, who, viewing a TV report revealing Paltrow's intention to wear a necklace by a rival jeweler, checked in with the nominee just to ensure that Princess—a $160,000 strand of forty-carat, platinum-set diamonds especially fit to fall like a choker—would flash up on-screen. "She's never going to wear our jewelry now," concluded Brodie, putting down the receiver.

Paltrow spent Oscar day with her actress mom, Blythe Danner. "We just giggled and reveled in the whole thing," said Danner.[44] In less than an hour Kevyn Aucoin plucked Paltrow's brows and blushed her cheeks, while Orlando Pita smoothed her hair into a Grace Kelly–style chignon. Fastened on was Harry Winston's Princess choker, as well as a pair of the jeweler's floral cluster studs, a gift from Paltrow's ex-boyfriend Ben Affleck. Then she made a final choice about her frock, veering between Celine's two-piece and Ralph Lauren's gown. "When you are with your girlfriends, and you try on this pretty pink dress, you think it is so great, so pretty," said Paltrow of what ultimately sold her on the Lauren.[45] But left hanging up at Shutters was its bustier. Without it, Paltrow's dress fell slightly loose around her chest, but otherwise she looked just right. "She thought it was too structured," added Moffett Lourd of the underpinning. "She had a long night ahead of her and she wanted to be comfortable."[46]

To Blanchett's braided locks, hairstylist Sally Hershberger affixed jeweled barrettes made of an amalgamation of amethyst bracelets from the Daisy collection by Asprey & Garrard, the Bond Street, London, jeweler to Britain's monarchy. Slipping on Jimmy Choo sling-backs matching her Oscar Dior, Blanchett scooped up a thirty-five-thousand-dollar Elizabethan "crown" handbag and, according to Paster, "she was good to go."[47]

The Seventy-first Academy Awards, March 21, 1999. The evening sun setting outside the Chandler rendered Cate Blanchett's Oscar Dior a luscious sky purple. The "most fantastic Oscar dress ever," concluded *WWD* of Galliano's knockout Dior knitwear.[48] Blanchett made a thoroughly elegant package, but amid a scrum of two thousand Hollywood grandees and four hundred photographers, she was a bundle of nerves.[49] "This is all a bit surreal," she confessed. "I feel like I'm acting *and* playing me."[50] A relaxed Gywneth Paltrow breezed across the red carpet as though it were her front lawn, and after explaining Ralph Lauren's cloud of pink paper taffeta ("I just wanted to look very sweet"), and introducing her father ("My date!"), she extended best behavior to media professionals including Joan Rivers ("I'm honored to be a part of this big celebration," Paltrow told the *Hollywood Reporter*), then defended Miramax against continuing claims of overt Oscar

"The most fantastic Oscar dress ever," WWD described the periwinkle silk knit gown Cate Blanchett conceived with Christian Dior's John Galliano.
(David Downton)

campaigning.[51] "I think it's unfair to say that Miramax spent too much money. I think they just love their films and are being incredibly supportive," she told Roger Ebert. "It's show business," agreed Ebert. "You go out there and root for your team!"[52]

Shakespeare in Love was ahead with four Oscars to *Elizabeth*'s single as Jack Nicholson took the stage to present the actress prize, sighing,

At *Vanity Fair*'s Oscar party in 1999, ebullient winner Gwyneth Paltrow brandished her trophy and hugged her competitor Cate Blanchett. (Getty)

"I'm saying nothing because you've all exhausted every expression you've had . . ." Then he announced Paltrow as actress winner. "Holy shit!" she thought. Battling tears, Paltrow embraced her parents and was "out and out crying," ascending the podium. She wept through her two-and-a-half-minute acceptance speech. In a backstage greenroom her colleagues watched on a TV monitor. "Renée Zellweger got a little misty-eyed and Geena Davis applauded," noted *Premiere*. "Keep it down!" a publicist reprimanded heckling pressroom photographers.[53]

An "audible gasp" echoed through the Chandler after Harrison Ford announced *Shakespeare in Love* as recipient of the picture Oscar, instead of the expected winner, Steven Spielberg's *Saving Private Ryan*.[54] "I'm thrilled, shocked, overwhelmed," declared Paltrow at the Governor's Ball. "Like someone had let hundreds of balloons loose as she was floating in the air with them," said Blythe Danner, explaining her daughter's reaction. At *Vanity Fair*'s Oscar party, ebullient Paltrow brandished her Oscar as she worked the room. She also hugged Cate Blanchett, posed for her friend *Vogue*'s Mario Testino, and then bumping into Harry Winston's PR Carolyn Brodie screamed, "My daddy's buying me the necklace!"

By Friday of Oscar week 2000, teams of seamstresses trailing a flock of designer emissaries toting couture-laden garment bags came marching through the Hotel Bel-Air's breezeway. The last-minute delivery convoy shattered the serene ambience at the luxury Stone Canyon Road hacienda but aimed to please a VIP occupant—Hilary Swank, a frontrunner in the Academy's seventy-second actress race, who, as the countdown to the ceremony commenced, realized a nominee's worst fashion nightmare—her dream Oscar dress, a one-of-a-kind painstakingly produced in Paris, arrived in Los Angeles days before the ceremony, but it "wasn't put-it-on great. It was like—you know, when you turn your head sideways? It was one of those," said New York designer Randolph Duke, who eventually came to the rescue.[55]

Up till then, Swank's rise within a decade from her childhood home in a Bellingham, Washington, trailer park to actress Academy Award nominee was as much of a fairy tale as the view of a glassy swan pond she and her husband, actor Chad Lowe, shared from the Hotel Bel-Air bungalow they occupied over Oscar weekend. The former *Beverly Hills 90210* cast member who started out in Hollywood living in her aunt's '88 Oldsmobile, halted a three-year casting search in 1998, beating eight hundred actors to the lead role of Brandon Teena in *Boys Don't Cry*. The six-million-dollar independent feature dramatized the brutal rape and murder of Teena, a Lincoln, Nebraska, twenty-one-year-old, by a gang of ex-cons in 1993, after a local newspaper revealed Teena Brandon as his true female identity. The credible portrayal Swank delivered in the uncompromising and timely investigation of homophobia challenged the Academy's odds as she factored into its register of actress nominees. And though *Boys Don't Cry* flopped at the box office, earning merely three and half million dollars after an eighteen-week run following its October 8, 1999, release ("A total that is being made every few hours by *Scream 3*," commented its driving force, writer/director Kimberly Peirce), the low-budget drama struck a chord with urbane viewers as well as critics in Los Angeles, New York, Boston, and Toronto, from whom Swank received the first of a stratospheric total of nineteen actress prizes from January 2000 onward.[56]

Her Oscar weekend crisis resulted because a decision to collaborate with a famed couturier proved unwise, but Swank got caught up in a fashion frenzy surrounding her as she blossomed "into a movie star," recounted Peirce of the transformation her discovery experienced just prior to the Oscars. "I just pulled back and watched everyone fall in love with her. It was thrilling."[57]

Championing over veterans Meryl Streep, Sigourney Weaver, and Annette Bening through a spate of winter 2000 awards-season galas, Swank radiated megawatt charm, sporting a fetching pixie cut (a lengthened variation of her Brandon Teena barbershop crop), as well as a wardrobe plucked especially for her rake-thin frame from directional fashion runways of Manhattan, Paris, and Milan. "It's so weird—I get calls from designers: 'We'll send a look-book—just tell us what you want,'" recounted Swank of her sudden popularity. "Surreal," she described it. "Boxes arrive on my doorstep and I think, 'These are for me?'"[58]

Viewing *Boys Don't Cry*, Calvin Klein spotted its synergy with the message behind his advertising campaigns challenging gender politics and, inviting Swank to lunch, commenced their continuing liaison by providing her with casuals and formals in which she braved much of awards season. As guests of Italian designer Valentino, Swank and Chad Lowe flew first-class to Paris in January 2000 to view his couture presentation. Then later at a Hotel Costes after-party, Valentino was "overheard chatting her up about potential silhouettes for the [Oscars]," reported *WWD*.[59] So moved was Kevyn Aucoin by *Boys Don't Cry* that he waved his high hourly wage, gifting Swank with his service on Oscar day. "She was the new girl," confirmed stylist Jessica Paster, whom Swank hired to "navigate" her search for an Oscar dress because she "didn't really understand the process." "It was the film. It was her talent. She gave such a powerful performance and came out of nowhere."[60]

Swank emerged as number one on Must Dress lists compiled in advance of the Oscars by teams at Versace and Gucci. Her competitor, *Variety*'s "front-runner," forty-one-year-old Annette Bening, star of Sam Mendes's celebrated drama *American Beauty*, reached the nine-month mark during pregnancy with her fourth child just prior to the ceremony. So she abided by doctor's orders rather than fashion dictates and settled on an Oscar look composed of comfy "low heels" and a Giorgio Armani black tulle maternity gown.

Chanel courted twenty-five-year-old Chloë Sevigny, a supporting actress nominee for *Boys Don't Cry*, in which she portrayed Brandon Teena's girlfriend, nineteen-year-old factory worker Lana Tisdel. Aside from flashing a pair of Hello Kitty underwear during a Chanel dress fitting, she let Swank soak up the Oscar fashion spotlight, playing down her dress search after receiving news of her own Academy nod. The story goes that Sevigny was unaware of the honor until actress nominee Julianne Moore, with whom through Oscar season she worked on the drama *A Map of the World*, said, "Congratulations!" "On . . .?" replied Sevigny, who admitted, "I didn't really flip out. I've watched the Oscars my whole life but I never really agree on who they vote [for]." Considering Academy members "too old to choose someone like me," she told *Vanity Fair* she didn't care about winning the seventy-second supporting actress Oscar.[61] "I don't want to be a movie star or be famous," she explained to the *New York Times*. "I just want to do a few good movies and maybe move some people."[62]

Celebrated equally as her honest acting style was Sevigny's fearless sartorial flair, which she initially honed modeling for edgy magazines such as London's *i-D* as well as working at Liquid Sky, an ultramodern New York boutique famed for its club-kid clientele and for launching avant-garde Spanish designer Miguel Adrover's career. "The coolest girl in the world," novelist Jay McInerney labeled Sevigny in a 1995 *New Yorker* profile, when at nineteen she made an impressive screen debut as Jennie, an HIV-infected adolescent in *Kids*, Larry Clark's cinema verité take on Lower Manhattan youth culture.[63] Her Oscar fashion strategy incorporated the prophetic spin she always applied to fashion. Alber Elbaz designed the seventies-modern black halter Yves Saint Laurent gown she selected, and though today Elbaz produces fashion's most sought-after dresses on behalf of Jeanne Lanvin's Paris couture house, he became known in 2000 as a "lame duck" because a January management shake-up abruptly deposed him from the designer-in-chief position at the house of Saint Laurent after a short tenure.[64] *Vogue*'s editor Anna Wintour later described his misfortune as a "tumultuous fall."[65] But Sevigny, whose friendship with Elbaz furnished her with the best pieces from his YSL collections, saw to it that he made his departure from the couture house in a blaze of glory, reasoning. "He's been so good to me."

Two weeks before the ceremony, Swank returned to Paris for another view of Valentino, enjoying guest-of-honor treatment in the front row at the couturier's March autumn/winter ready-to-wear 2001 show, while Jessica Paster met with John Galliano's team to discuss a handmade silver satin crêpe chiffon that made the final cut. Integrating a delicate vintage piece of Lesage embroidery sourced by Swank after she and Paster had trawled through Paris's flea markets, as well as skill from top design teams (those stationed at the atelier producing Galliano's signature ready-to-wear line and Dior's couture specialists), it was meant to be the second two-way Oscar number produced by the modern master and his chosen nominee, following up the smashing success of Cate Blanchett's Dior silk knit at the seventy-first Academy Awards. "I think she's a great actress, of course," said Galliano of Swank.[66] But the 2000 effort remained unseen because days before the Oscars Swank received her Dior and concluded it "just wasn't the dress we had discussed."[67]

Complications transpired from the start of its making, and the process proved so costly that Galliano's atelier handed the dress over to Dior's, which customarily produces money-is-no-object couture. Recounted a professional involved in its conception, "What happened was, we were going to do it as a Galliano dress, but in terms of budget it was way too big so we had to hand it over to Dior. So it became a Dior credit, even though we worked on it, we put it together [at Galliano]. Dior had the beading passed by Jessica and Hilary. It was all done and dusted, but [Dior] delivered the dress with different beading on it. And Hilary didn't like the dress. The beads were changed at the last minute. So three days before the Oscars they had to find an alternative dress."[68]

Doing so got to Paster. On Oscar-week Friday, she rose at five A.M., and then, as a *Los Angeles Times* fashion reporter shadowed her trawling through Pamela Dennis's L'Hermitage suite, strain set in. Within forty-five minutes, Paster inspected "three rolling racks of clothes, memorized fabrics and colors, placated publicists, phoned Chad Lowe about the details of his tuxedo fitting" at Gucci, "rejected a special Dennis dress swathed in $1 million in diamonds, answered her beeper three times and returned two other calls."[69] Was she hunting around for Swank? "Oh, gosh, you know—we don't have to say if we don't want to," explained Paster. "But I do want a pair of pants for Cate Blanchett."[70]

"We'll make them specially," offered PR Piera Rossi Blodwell.[71] But the suggestion pushed the stylist's panic button or possibly revived the memory of the disappointing Dior as she snapped, "I don't want

241

anybody to make me anything because, you know what? Afterward, everyone goes crazy and says, 'Oh, she made us make something.' They offer and then . . . if you don't wear the designer, there's always a snide remark that you did something wrong, and you didn't."[72]

Zero hour arrived at the Hotel Bel-Air later that evening as Swank tossed aside like scraps of room-service toast innumerable gowns. "I had so many dresses going—I was overwhelmed," she confessed.[73] "It literally was, you know, the court running to the Bel-Air Hotel, lining up at the hotel suite door, and one by one bringing the dresses in," recollected Randolph Duke, who, inside quarters he occupied at West Hollywood's Le Montrose, answered his telephone by seven P.M. and listened to Paster on the other end "crying—and basically saying, you know [Hilary's] dress didn't come in right." Elaborating, he added, "The dress came and they started fiddling. And the more they fiddled, the more I think Hilary knew instinctively—the dress just didn't work."[74]

"I was devastated—bawling," admitted Paster. "I felt like I was letting Hilary down. I called everybody. All I wanted to do was find another dress."[75]

Duke made a smart port of call. After departing from a stint designing Halston ready-to-wear, he established a high-end, eponymous fashion label in 1999. To publicize his independent Seventh Avenue, Manhattan, venture, he debuted a capsule couture collection at the seventy-first Academy Awards in March. "Rita Wilson, Geena Davis, Lisa Kudrow, Kim Basinger," he said, naming four of six Hollywood women (including Minnie Driver and Laura Linney) who wore his ceremonial classics that year. "The fashion equivalent of Miramax—the little fish capturing the spotlight in the big pond," *Variety* classified Duke's sudden popularity at the Oscars, although vicious rumor attributed it to Paster, who in exchange for granting him access to her clientele allegedly accepted a few perks.[76] Duke, however, chalked up his popularity to ingenuity. His Oscar frocks were expertly fit (a forte he developed designing swimwear at Anne Cole and Jantzen in the late eighties) and imbued with an ageless romantic femininity. "You could come to a suite and try them on," he recalled of the personalized service he and his team of two laid on. "Or we would come to you with a group of dresses. And when you get the dress, it arrives in a beautiful gown bag, wrapped in tissue paper, and always [with] an orchid or, if she's a rose girl, a rose, pinned to the bag. And a good-luck note.

"Because it's not just about the dress," Duke went on. "There are millions of dresses out there—they don't need the dress. They need a confidant—they need the friend, they need to understand themselves a little bit better." After pausing, he cited an example: "Rita Wilson put a dress on and I said, 'Come on, let's do a little test, Rita. How do you normally stand on the red carpet?' And she said, 'What do you mean? I stand the way I stand. It's straightforward.' And I said, 'Hmmm. Let's take a Polaroid.' We took a Polaroid. She said, 'Oh my God! My hips look kind of wide.' I said, 'Okay. Do me a favor. Walk by the press line—*sideways*. Only turn your head and wave. Don't turn your body. Keep your hips sideways to them.' We did it. We took a Polaroid. Every time I see her now she says, 'Am I standing right? Look, I've got my hips sideways to the camera.'

"That's a confidant thing," concluded Duke. "Who's going to tell you that? Not a boss, not a publicist, not an agent. I always say, 'I'm part Dr. Phil and part designer.'"[77]

But Paster must have swallowed her pride pleading for Duke's help at the "very last minute," as a publicist representing a rival observed. Back in January, Swank "ran afoul" of Duke, reported *W*, when just before the Golden Globes she opted to wear a black, sequined Versace column instead of a crystal-dusted sheer slip of midnight tulle Duke had adapted especially from one of his risqué creations—a body skimmer Rene Russo had modeled seducing Pierce Brosnan in the steamy dance-floor-to-bedroom scene in John McTiernan's 1999 stylish remake of *The Thomas Crown Affair*.[78] "Too revealing," concluded Swank, realizing it was inappropriate for the Globes, and Duke concurred: "It had a splash of crystals down the front, *barely* covering the nipples and the crotch. The entire sides of the dress were sheer. It was a departure from Hilary playing a boy—let me tell you! It was like a whole new world!"

"Disappointed" by Swank's change of heart, Duke, however, was again at her service on the Friday night of Oscar weekend. "I want the best girl, in the best dress" was his mantra. Meeting Swank in January 2000 before the Globes, he was smitten. "These Russian tailors up on the top level of one of those drive-in malls," he said, recalling the spot of their initial rendezvous. "She was trying these dresses on and she came out with a towel wrapped around her, like a little minidress. It couldn't have been more coquettish and feminine and actually, flirty. And I was struck by how feminine she was. At the time she had a very gamine look."[79]

Duke's Le Montrose suite was bereft of a red-carpet conqueror as

'CREME DE MENTHE
DOUBLEFACE SILK
SATIN BALLGOWN.'

Randolph Duke's Oscar frocks were expertly
fit and imbued with a timeless romantic
femininity. (Randolph Duke)

the countdown to the seventy-second Academy Awards commenced. Loyal client Minnie Driver had already nabbed the best Duke—a white, strapless column appliquéd with midnight lace. So Duke dispatched to Swank a soufflé of fifties French bronze silk, which, with a bell-shaped, finely pleated skirt plummeting from a strapless, fitted bodice, recalled classic eveningwear pioneered during World War II by the American couturier Charles James. "I don't really do ball gowns like that," reflected Duke of the design. "I do softer dresses usually, probably sexier. It was the only dress like that that I had there with me, and it hung the entire time in a funny spot and I kept looking at it, thinking, 'That odd dress.'"

Tyra Banks had already tried on and rejected the Duke. "It wasn't a particularly popular dress," he added, but it made Swank's short list. "That's where it got a little gnarly," admitted Duke. "The problem was, the dress was maybe three sizes too big." His suggestion to personally fit the gown was rebuffed. "I was not allowed. When you have a designer present, the girl can feel committed," he explained. "It's a lot of pressure. Think about it. You are trying on dresses from many designers—the stylist is the middle ground. The designer being there—if you don't like the dress, you have to be polite. You are obligated to be nice. But it seems that once you pick it, you would want to have the designer there. Once it's yours, it's 'Okay, come on in.' And that has generally been the case. I get called in: 'Come on—let's do the magic. Let's make it perfect.'"[80]

Rejection made Duke "furious" and his temper could be fierce.[81] According to a 2000 *Telegraph Magazine* profile, he "flew into a rage when Angelina Jolie decided not to wear the Oscar gown he made for her" in 1999, and on another occasion he "dumped a dustbin" on a New York employee "while calling her a piece of 'white trash.'"[82] Of Swank's Oscar dress fitting, he explained, "Here I am [thinking]: 'How would this thing come out? What are they going to do to it?' You are leaving your fate in the hands of a stylist and a tailor, and the results aren't always great. You can't just zap [the dress] in on the side. It [was] all twisted and wrapped. It had a foundation. So an assistant of mine who was not a seamstress wound up taking the dress in."

By nine A.M. on Oscar Sunday morning it fit Swank. "My husband's jaw dropped," she recalled of the reaction that swayed her decision to wear Duke's strapless dress to the Oscars. "It made me feel comfortable. I didn't have to worry about my ass hanging out."[83]

★   ★   ★

The Seventy-second Academy Awards, March 26, 2000. Chloë Sevigny decamped from the front-row Shrine Auditorium seating reserved for *Boys Don't Cry* and headed for its vast, Moorish lobby. It was twenty minutes into the Oscars, and James Coburn had just announced that for *Girl, Interrupted* Angelina Jolie had trounced Sevigny's stake at the prize with *Boys Don't Cry.* "I knew I wasn't going to win. It was just a given that they were going to keep it in the family and give it Jolie," Sevigny told *Village Voice* columnist Michael Musto. "She was good— I mean, I'm not downplaying her performance at all."

Back in the Shrine's front row, Hilary Swank clutched Chad Lowe's hand. "Like a dream," she recalled of the three-hour telecast flashing by as *American Beauty* and blockbuster *The Matrix* divided up the prizes.[84] "Being shot out of a cannon," said Swank of the adrenaline rush she experienced after Roberto Benigni named her actress winner.[85] Reciting a prepared speech, she paid tribute to Brandon Teena before expressing gratitude to a list of associates including director Kimberly Peirce, Chloë Sevigny, and her mom. "It looks like living out of our car was worth it," said smiling Swank. Backstage, Gwyneth Paltrow hugged Swank before presenting the actor prize to *American Beauty*'s Kevin Spacey. Meanwhile, in the pressroom Swank referred to Chad Lowe as "my everything," making amends for omitting her husband from her onstage thank-you list.

Vanity Fair's Oscar party was filled cheek-by-implant with an Old/New Hollywood crowd including director Billy Wilder, mogul David Geffen, golden couple Brad Pitt and Lawrence Steele–clad Jennifer Aniston, as well as Hollywood first lady Nicole Kidman, wrapped in gold lamé Dior on her last trip to the Oscars with soon-to-be-ex-husband Tom Cruise. But Swank was the main attraction. "Sitting there with everyone coming to her," recounted Duke. "See, it all works out in the end," Swank told Duke. "I thought that was very cute," he reflected. "And that's how it is at the Oscars—you win some, you lose some."[86]

Surefire, like Elizabeth Taylor's expected coup at the thirty-third Academy Awards, was Julia Roberts's assumed victory in 2001, but with a short list of thirty Oscar dresses, she had over twice the choice of the twelve Diors perused by the all-time Hollywood great in 1961, as well as ten times the number of potentials Gwyneth Paltrow finally considered in 1999. Meanwhile as Roberts's Academy Awards vehicle, *Erin Brockovich*, premiered in March 2000, rather than in the traditional autumn slot reserved for features intended to qualify for competition, she enjoyed a heady, ten-month buildup to the seventy-third Academy Awards laced with glowing reviews for portraying its title character— a gutsy paralegal and former Miss Pacific Coast beauty-pageant queen who emerged as the brains behind the largest settlement from a direct-action lawsuit in American history, namely the $333 million paid in 1996 to the citizens of Hinkley, Southern California, by Pacific Gas and Electric, the corporation that had tainted their drinking water. Roberts's barely there *Erin Brockovich* wardrobe—a second-skin series of microminis, push-up bras peeping from cropped tops, and three-inch heels in which as a single mom on a mission she shimmied in and out of water wells contaminated with toxic chromium 6—accentuated her flawless figure but failed to distract from what was classified as a faultless performance. Critics unanimously championed her twenty-fifth film, including Philip French of London's *Observer*, who lauded it as a "towering achievement that never strikes a false note. It's Roberts's best—she'll be pushed to surpass it."[87]

Just for the kudos of being associated with the box-office force *Vanity Fair* classified as the "world's most mythic, inaccessible and intimidating," Los Angeles stylists volunteered to toil free of charge through Oscar season, although it was their most lucrative period. Fifty designers eventually vied to dress Roberts for the Oscars. All the while, she remained distant from the fervent competition enveloping her preparations. In the lead-up to the ceremony, she marked her own name on the Academy's actress ballot, completed the Billy Crystal comedy *America's Sweethearts* in Nevada, traveled up to Chicago to appear on *Oprah*, and then with her actor boyfriend Benjamin Bratt departed for a recuperative holiday in Mexico, scheduling Friday morning of Oscar week for dress fittings in Los Angeles. She viewed some Oscar dress sketches, but as she explained commandingly, "It's someone else's job to make sure I look the way I should."[88] So the task of vetting her couture fell to Debbi Mason, the stylist appointed by Marcy Engelman, Roberts's fierce publicist.

Mason, a thirtysomething Brit whose talent graced the pages of an international mix of magazines from *In Style* to *i-D*, had no contact with Roberts prior to Oscar weekend but counted among a clique of Manhattan beautifiers who'd rehabilitated the superstar's battered image after a series of surprise moves she'd made shocked fans, including hitching off her bra in 1996 while gyrating atop the bar inside the TriBeCa, New York, tavern Hogs and Heifers, a disastrous starring role that year as Dr. Jekyll and Mr. Hyde's housemaid in the fizzle-out horror thriller *Mary Reilly*, as well as flashing a hairy armpit to the horror of the British press at the May 1999 Leicester Square world premiere of *Notting Hill*, the hit comedy she next headlined. A new, improved Roberts emerged thanks to colorist Sharon Dorram, who regularly applied a chestnut sheen to Roberts's cascading mane. Hairstylist Serge Normant devised modern, sophisticated up-dos that tamed it for premieres and press junkets. "New hippie—very eclectic," said Mason, describing the characteristically relaxed approach she helped Roberts forge. "I had been working with Julia for some years," she added, recalling the Oscars assignment. "I ended up on a job by default—that was how it began—and we got on famously. I think there was a meeting of sensibilities somewhere."[89] Their mutual preference was informal—think black leather trousers for the February 23, 2001, red-carpet Los Angeles premiere of Roberts's box-office success *The Mexican*, while easy/breezy cashmere pashminas rather than Fifth Avenue jewels dripped from the highest-paid actress in Hollywood history because her legendary bright white, toothy smile seduced better than bling. "Julia really is a free spirit," added Mason. "She is true to herself and she just goes with what she feels."[90]

But the Oscars were an entirely different proposition. "Her appearance—particularly her dress—was of paramount importance," observed James Spada in his 2004 biography, *Julia, Her Life*. "It needed to be something really sleek and sophisticated," conceded Mason.[91] So from sketch to finished frock she supervised the production of a horde of couture to fill up a fashion heaven high up inside L'Ermitage. There, over Oscar weekend, in a sweeping suite serving as Roberts's private boudoir, rested her final count of thirty dresses. To get an edge on the competition, Vera Wang sent four. "Michael Kors, John Galliano, Calvin Klein, and Giorgio Armani—that was the list of potentials," confirmed Mason.[92] To tweak Roberts's fancy midway through Oscar week, Mason would also comb boutiques lining Rodeo Drive for more extraordinary pieces. "Beating the streets—my role was to be resourceful," said the stylist. "It looked as dead first as it could that Julia was going to get the Oscar. Everyone really had the strong feeling that she was going to win, and so the pressure was on to perform."[93]

Aside from heralding the long-awaited return of Julia Roberts, after a ten-year absence following her actress defeat with *Pretty Woman* in 1991, the seventy-third Academy Awards remain memorable not only for the red-carpet couture she eventually selected, but also for another four that made it a milestone. It was a rare event, at which ceremonial dress appeared defined by risk-taking. Bjork ambled along the red carpet in a tutu made to capture the look of a perishing swan. Stylish Angelina Jolie also cut through what the *Los Angeles Times* classified as an "almost gross display of wealth" in a sharp white pantsuit reminiscent of the dress mode of seventies actress contenders, but culled from the men's collection of Dolce & Gabbana. Hong Kong designer Barney Cheng produced a cheongsam, answering Academy presenter Michelle Yeoh's request for "one hundred and ten percent glamour."[94] His hand-beaded, traditional sheath included 187,000 smoky topaz crystals and weighed in at twenty-two pounds. "At the final fitting Michelle put it on and fell over because it was so heavy," recalled Cheng. But like some of the great Oscar gowns made through Hollywood's studio era, the cheongsam tastefully evoked, with its tiger stripes and hem-edging dragon appliqué, the spirit of the film Yeoh represented at the Oscars, *Crouching Tiger, Hidden Dragon*, Ang Lee's ten-times-nominated nine-teenth-century action masterpiece in which she starred as martial arts master Yu Shu Lien.

Like a great Old Hollywood Oscar gown, designer Barney Cheng's cheongsam for presenter Michelle Yeoh tastefully evoked, with its tiger stripes and hem-edging dragon appliqué, the spirit of the film she represented at the seventy-third Academy Awards, *Crouching Tiger, Hidden Dragon*. (Barney Cheng)

Accepting the chance to bestow the scientific and technical Oscars (held in advance of the ceremony and then incorporated into its telecast), thirty-two-year-old Texan blonde Renée Zellweger planned to utilize the Academy's red carpet and TV screen time to kick-start a publicity onslaught for the mid–April 2001 premiere of comedy *Bridget Jones's Diary*, her most anticipated feature since she'd appeared alongside Tom Cruise in the 1996 romantic drama *Jerry Maguire*. So in advance of the Oscars, off went the twenty pounds Zellweger had bulked on her willowy, five-foot-five, 110-pound frame to believably play British singleton Bridget Jones. Meanwhile, Nancy Ryder, her "best friend" and publicist, targeted Rita Watnick, the leading Los Angeles vintage couture expert, to stage Zellweger's critical Oscar moment.[95] Prepping for the Oscars proved an odyssey, starting in January, when Zellweger reported to Lily et Cie, Watnick's retail domain. "This really young thing came in and said, 'I'm going to the Oscars,' and I had no idea who [she] was," recalled Watnick of her initial encounter with Zellweger. "But one of the people in the store wrote me a note saying, 'I think *this* is Renée Zellweger.'"[96]

Watnick, a savvy Beverly Hills native with a background in fine jewelry sales at Van Cleef & Arpels, started a pioneering enterprise in 1978 opening Lily et Cie. Displaying vintage fashion amid a polished ambience rather than the tired surroundings in which secondhand clothes were once strictly sold, she laid the foundation of her mini-empire, which encompasses a world-renowned collection of five hundred thousand pieces of mint-condition period couture by the former leading lights of L.A.'s fashion scene, including Howard Greer, Edward Sebesta, Don Loper, and James Galanos, as well as European one-offs. Originally occupying a patch of West Hollywood's Third Avenue next to the Dance Academy, founded by forties choreographer Roland DuPree ("The most famous dance studio in the city, so we had this built-in megacelebrity clientele from DuPree," recalled Watnick), Lily et Cie transplanted its thriving trade in 1995 to a Beverly Hills show-place.[97] By then Watnick had gowned Demi Moore for the 1990 Academy Awards in a lace-appliqué, late-forties, lavender gown. "Forty thousand pieces of vintage clothing mostly from me," estimated Watnick of the "megacollection" Moore had amassed.[98] Watnick had also provided a spangled, sixties Sebesta cocktail frock for frequent customer Winona Ryder, who'd earned critical raves at the Oscars in 1994.

Anyone can ring the boutique's entry doorbell and splurge a few thousand on an immaculate eighties Azzedine Alaia, but for mere mortals Lily et Cie's evening gowns are as hard to score as invitations to *Vanity Fair*'s Oscar party. Oscar dresses never go out on loan from Lily et Cie. Carefully preserved in a backroom wardrobe space and an off-site vault, a five-figure cost covers the cost and custom-fitting of most, involving up to one hundred digital photographs to perfect manual reconstruction. "I think the thing about the girls who wear our clothes is that they relate to our sensibility about what glamour is," explained Watnick. "It's a commitment to a different aesthetic. You have to give up that kind of traditional 'of the moment' standard notion and rely more on your internal."[99]

While Zellweger browsed on the shop floor, Watnick's team quickly profiled the actress by downloading images displaying her recent public appearances. Watnick concluded Zellweger was far from an optimum candidate to model Lily et Cie at the Oscars. "She had a terrible—horrible—fashion history," recounted Watnick of Zellweger. "We very quickly looked at all of [Renée's] old clothes, and we were like, 'Okay, nightmare,'" added Watnick. "It was about frizzy hair and weird dresses. Very contrived, very trying hard. She was always everybody's worst dressed."[100]

But Watnick worked wonders with her new charge before the Oscars. Dressed in black Lily et Cie classics—a strapless, thigh-slit Galanos and a draped chiffon by MGM costumer Helen Rose, respectively—Zellweger accepted the actress prize at the Golden Globes, for her role as Betty Sizemore, a Kansas City waitress in Neil LaBute's black comedy *Nurse Betty*, then bestowed the Academy's scientific and technical honors. By February, Zellweger's Oscar dress was midway through five fittings and fifty-two hours of restoration. The fourteen-thousand-dollar vintage gown was made in 1959 by Egyptian Jean Dessès, the Paris couturier who in his midcentury heyday counted as clients Britain's Princess Margaret, sisters Eugenie Niarchos and Athina Onassis, as well as indomitable Simone Signoret (who in black Dessès won the thirty-second actress Academy Award in 1960). "My philosophy is that you can't give somebody with a bad history the yellow dress their first time out because people won't know how to read it," explained Watnick of the gradual-enhancement plan she devised for Zellweger before she made her crucial Oscar red-carpet crossing. "You can't go from bad to innovative. You have to go to from bad to good. And by the way, 'good' never lets anyone down."[101]

But Zellweger's circle of minders slighted the choice. "Nobody liked it," admitted Watnick of the Dessès. "Somebody who worked in that camp said she looked like Phyllis Diller in the dress."[102] So alternative plans were in the works. A phone call from Paris notified Watnick that Christian Dior's atelier had been asked to reproduce the Dessès in red, and Ralph Lauren's West Coast representative Crystal Moffett Lourd had purportedly arrived at Lily et Cie to take a peep at it. "She 'just wanted to see the color,' and then Ralph Lauren would make the dress," claimed Watnick. "And I'm like, 'How naïve do you think I am?'"[103] (Recalling no such encounter, Moffett Lourd confirmed,

"Renée's an acquaintance, but we didn't go down the road with anything to be made for her."[104])

Two weeks before the Oscars, *Vogue*'s André Leon Talley faxed to Nancy Ryder further possibilities after receiving a call from the publicist explaining, "We may not go down the road with the Dessès."[105] Zell-weger had bonded with Talley when *Vogues*'s April 2001 fashion-adventure cover story had chronicled her "debut" at the Paris haute couture shows. Talley had squired Zellweger through what he classified as a "marathon sweep of shows, parties, and fittings," and discussion about her "Oscar wardrobe went on and on," he wrote. "Would it be Chanel? Would it be vintage?"[106] But as word reached Watnick about Talley's faxes, work on the Dessès ground to a halt. "I was not going to finish the dress," admitted Watnick. "The whole thing was blowing up. It was the most gigantic, politicking thing all over the place. I felt really betrayed and I thought, 'I don't need to do this.'

"Someone's coming to me—they like the dress, they buy the dress. We do a good job," she added. "There needs to be a relationship between the person wearing the dress and the person doing the dress. And that's where an amazing thing comes from. If you look at Old Hollywood, [when] a costume designer did a dress for a celebrity, they had a relationship. There's a dialogue—not a last-minute scramble."[107]

Cristina Viera—Valentino's point person stationed at his Rodeo Drive boutique during Oscar season in 2001—went way back with the couturier. In the early seventies five-foot-eight Viera, a former top model from Rio de Janeiro, "walked all the international shows—Ossie Clark, Bill Gibb, Antony Price, Christian Dior, Yves Saint Laurent, Valentino, Kenzo," noted British *Vogue*.[108] Back then Viera's walk was no average runway sashay. According to a London fashion PR it had a "real swing," that put her in a "class of [her] own." At the start of Oscar week, after Valentino told Viera, "Get me Julia Roberts," his fine-boned Brazilian liaison was strutting her stuff around the Hollywood Hills home she shared with her husband, RCA Records executive vice president Ashley Newton, in what she described as her "Julia Roberts fantasy—the kind of dress in which she could really look like an Old Hollywood movie star."[109]

Viera had spotted it among a shipment of archive pieces Valentino sent from Rome to his Beverly Hills flagship as Oscar potentials. A tulle fishtail train accentuated with seven stripes of white satin finished the sumptuous flowing black velvet evening dress. "Very sophisticated, very forties movie star," explained Valentino of the one-of-a-kind's bygone inspiration.[110] After supermodel Helena Christensen debuted it as part of his autumn/winter 1992 Paris couture presentation, resurrecting an enticing hauteur reminding Valentino of thirties screen siren Hedy Lamarr, Christy Turlington displayed the frock in the October 1992 issue of *Harper's Bazaar*. "The most glamorous gown," the magazine described it.[111]

But Viera ensured that Valentino's was a flight of the imagination that could make the leap from the runway to the Oscars' red carpet. "I tried it on and I walked around in it," she admitted. "I went up and down the stairs wearing that dress. Before I sent anything out on behalf of Valentino, I always put it on. You have to make sure an actress can move in an Oscar dress. Valentino had said to me 'Come on—go out and get Julia Roberts.' So I had to be intelligent about it. I had to make sure the dress would work. Then I found out Debbi Mason was dressing Julia and I realized I had struck gold."[112]

The two fashion professionals became friends in the eighties, when Mason was a British *Elle* fashion editor and Viera was working as a public relations and marketing powerhouse for the London designer Jasper Conran. So, on Oscar week Monday, Viera rekindled her old contact by calling up Mason in Manhattan. "Her assistant answered the telephone and I said: 'My name is Cristina Viera. I know you are looking for an Oscar dress and I know for sure I have *the* dress.' I was gutsy."[113] But Oscar week Tuesday came and went without Mason returning Viera's phone call. Viera sat tight, reflecting: "The drums were beating. Every designer had made Julia Roberts an Oscar dress. But it was in the air—none of them worked. Nothing made her feel special."[114]

Valentino couture would also be a leap for the consistently casually clad Roberts, who planned to travel to the Shrine Auditorium via Ford Expedition sport utility vehicle. Up at L'Ermitage, as family and staffers surrounded her, a jubilant mood and Mexican suntan almost made the 1992 Valentino—which Mason presented after a brisk meeting with Viera at Valentino Beverly Hills—a glove fit. "Julia was ready for it— relaxed and bubbly—and it looked absolutely stunning," recounted Mason of the moment the black-and-white gown first went on.[115] "She said: 'I think this is the dress,'" added Viera.[116] "I just thought it was a pretty dress," remembered Roberts.[117]

But the corset beneath the sample-size Valentino nipped in too close, even around lithe Roberts. "It needed some tweaking," admitted Mason. "And there was the chance that the tweaking might not work."[118] So as Roberts selected a backup dress, what Mason classified as a "very good second, but somewhat less phenomenal" brown Michael Kors, Viera arranged a second fitting, to take place at L'Hermitage on the Saturday of Oscar weekend.[119] Conducting the session was Valentino's secret weapon, Levon, an Armenian tailor who had long worked with the couturier's Beverly Hills team. "Levon can make anything fit," explained Viera. "You ask him to give you an inch and somehow he just gives it to you."[120]

As the Saturday session concluded, Mason described Roberts as "perfection from every angle—one hundred percent perfect."[121] Then she boarded a plane bound for Manhattan. Before departing, Mason could deliver no guarantee to Valentino's team on behalf of her client. So she wished them well: "Good luck and let's see what happens."[122]

By ten P.M., Viera was at home rummaging through her own extensive wardrobe, looking for a wrap to send over to Roberts. "Marcy [Engelman], her publicist, called me and said 'She needs a wrap.' The boutique was closed. So I didn't have a choice. I had one that was made at Valentino for me to wear to the *Vanity Fair* party. I sent it over. It didn't matter if I felt cold on Oscar night."[123]

On Oscar morning, a call from Engelman interrupted Viera's breakfast. "Congratulations," Engelman told Viera. "Julia loves the dress. She's wearing Valentino to the Oscars."[124]

Serge Normant piled Roberts's hair up high in a topknot, and after he lacquered it unmovable, she made the trip by SUV to the Shrine with Benjamin Bratt, her sister, Lisa, and her brother-in-law, Tony Gillan. "The four of us just went into the night with such a sense of fun," remembered Roberts. "It was just so exciting."[125]

The Seventy-third Academy Awards, March 25, 2001. Julia Roberts's "coronation" commenced by four P.M. beneath sunny skies and against the fantastical backdrop of the Spanish-colonial Shrine Auditorium. Though she faced no competition in the actress category, Roberts's challenge proved to be making it through the night in her Valentino couture. Passing a quick security check, Roberts and Benjamin Bratt made way for Hilary Swank.[126] "Oh, wow, I tried on the dress Julia is wearing!" whispered Versace-clad Swank to husband Chad Lowe as they approached.[127] "I'm freaking out!" Roberts confessed to Swank.[128]

The seventy-third Academy Awards was a rare event at which ceremonial dress appeared defined by risk-taking, such as the Marjan Pejoski tutu in which Bjork captured the look of a perishing swan. (ChiChi for Marjan Pejoski)

"Breathe. Just try to breathe," suggested Swank, offering advice Lowe had delivered a year before.[129]

"Believe me, it isn't so easy in this dress!" Roberts next told a panting press scrum as Angelina Jolie nonchalantly explained the motivation behind her white Dolce & Gabbana pantsuit ("I just wanted to be comfortable"), and Renée Zellweger confessed what had finally sold her on Lily et Cie's Jean Dessès ("I loved the color and it fit").[130] From beneath her frilly Marjan Pejoski swan tutu, Bjork popped onto the red carpet a large, cream-colored egg sculpted by her artist boyfriend, Matthew Barney. As it lay by her white patent Balenciaga sandals, she "didn't seem to mind the sniggering," noted her biographer Mark Pytlik. But Bjork's date, Sindri, her fourteen-year-old son, cringed, looking on from behind his mum's shoulder.[131] "They didn't get it," said Bjork of the Hollywood press corps' missing the humor of her swan stunt. "They actually thought I was trying to look like Jennifer Aniston and got it wrong."[132]

Midway through the Oscars, host Steve Martin welcomed Roberts onstage to present the cinematography Academy Award. "She's one of the great movie starts of this generation, and there's nothing bad you can say about her," began Martin. "Here she is—Julia Roberts!" Approaching the podium from stage right, Roberts's determined gait across the colossal expanse of 194 feet of of glossy white stage seemed better fit for her permanent off-time uniform of jeans and cowboy boots than her sweeping Valentino. Pausing at the podium, she tugged on its train and then stumbled as she ad-libbed her presenter's speech. "Since I took so long to walk across that fine stage, I'm just gonna cut to the chase . . ." After a drum roll and a prerecorded announcement listing the five cinematographers competing for the prize, Roberts quipped of the winner, "Let's hope it's a name I can pronounce . . . in real life!" Tugging on the envelope, she produced the ballot and with a relieved sigh exhaled: "Peter Pau for *Crouching Tiger, Hidden Dragon!*"

Next, presenting visual effects were *Crouching Tiger*'s stars Chow Yun-Fat and Michelle Yeoh. And as Yeoh dazzled in Barney Cheng, Renée Zellweger, backstage, fretted about walking on in her strapless Jean Dessès. "I'm going to trip over my dress, I know it!" she told Goldie Hawn, although she dominated center stage.[133] So did Bjork, performing "I've Seen It All," although Bob Dylan's theme for comedy *Wonder Boys* ultimately received the original-song prize.

As 1999's best actor, Kevin Spacey, appeared to present the actress prize, *Erin Brockovich* had already suffered two defeats in the supporting actor and writing categories. "Julia practically held her breath," noted James Spada.[134] "Tonight, I'm sure that any of these ladies will be delighted to have the little golden guy around their house as well," began Spacey. "So the nominees for best performance by an actress in a leading role are . . ."

As soon as Spacey confirmed Roberts's victory, Benjamin Bratt prevented a Barbra Streisand–style tumble up the Academy's steps, scooping up his girlfriend after an empty water bottle got "stuck under her gown," tripping her as she bounded for the stage.[135] "Like falling down the rabbit hole but in high heels," said Roberts, reflecting on the moment.[136] "A thrill—I was out of my mind."[137] At the podium she gazed at the Oscar she clutched in her right hand, exclaiming, "I can't believe this! This, this is, um, this is quite pretty. I, uh, I want to acknowledge so many people who made *Erin Brockovich, Erin Brockovich*, but let me make my dress pretty," she said, smoothing the front

For the seventy-third
Academy Awards,
presenter Renée Zellweger
acquired this 1959 Jean
Dessès chiffon gown from
Rita Watnick's renowned
Beverly Hills vintage
boutique, Lily et Cie.
(David Downton)

of her Valentino. Halfway through a rambling, three-minute, unrehearsed speech, Roberts's heart was "pounding" as she chided Academy conductor Bill Conti for leading his orchestra through the theme from *2001: A Space Odyssey* to hasten her finish.[138] "Sir, you're doing a great job, but you're so quick with that stick. So why don't you just sit because I'll never be here again!" She named twenty-three people who'd helped her win the Oscar and got big laughs as well as torrents of applause as she threatened, "Stick man, I see you! Uh-huh, I love it up here. Ya, *anyway* . . ." Declaring love to the world, she wrapped it up, gushing, "I'm so happy! Thank you!"

Kevin Spacey escorted Roberts to the wings and she squealed, "My knees are weak!"[139] (Later she regretted omitting Erin Brockovich from her acceptance speech, explaining, "It doesn't bring out the Einstein moment that you hoped for.") As Roberts settled into a backstage seat, Spacey called out, "Julia needs a drink!"[140] After an Academy staffer pointed out the watercooler, Spacey declared, "Only champagne will do."[141]

At *Vanity Fair*'s bash, revelers cheered Roberts as she skipped the line to the ladies' room and made way for the men's. "I've never needed anything so much in my life," she said, heading in.[142] Over in the ladies' Courtney Love drew near to Renée Zellweger. "Lily?" asked Love of Zellweger's yellow Dessès, then expounded on Rita Watnick.[143] "You know what I hate? When you go in there and she says, 'You know, you're so much prettier than Kidman.' I mean, how big does she think our egos are? Don't tell me she never does it to you."[144] Zellweger remained mum, glossed her lips, and exited.

"I'll never be here again!" declared Julia Roberts, clutching her Oscar at the seventy-third Academy Awards. (Alex Berliner)

NOTES

Chapter One: Show Business

1. Frances Marion, *Off With Their Heads! A Serio-Comic Tale of Hollywood* (Macmillan, New York, 1972), page 161.
2. Roy Liebman, *From Silents to Sound: A Biographical Encyclopedia of Performers Who Made the Transition to Talking Pictures* (McFarland, Jefferson, NC, 1998).
3. Ephram Katz, *The Film Encyclopedia*, 4th ed. (Harper Resource, New York, 2001), page 518.
4. "distinguished": *Variety Film Reviews, 1907–1980* (Garland, New York, 1983), September 28, 1927. *Cahiers*: Katz, *Film Encyclopedia*, page 987.
5. Anthony Holden, *Behind the Oscar: The Secret History of the Academy Awards* (Simon & Schuster, New York, 1993), page 93.
6. Kevin Brownlow, *Hollywood: The Pioneers* (Collins, London, 1979), page 262.
7. "Fourth Premiere Enjoyed," *Los Angeles Times*, 9 June 1929, page 17.
8. "*Merriment in Star's Life Is All on Screen*," *Los Angeles Times*, 29 May 1929, page A7.
9. "I shall": Louella O. Parsons, "Triumphs, Trials, Tragedy in Awards," *Los Angeles Examiner*, 11 March 1956, page 11. See also Marion, *Off With Their Heads!*, page 161.
10. Eileen Callahan, "Two Best Dressed Women . . .," *Sunday News*, 30 November 1949, no page number on press cutting.
11. Parsons, "Triumphs, Trials, Tragedy," page 11.
12. Marion, *Off With Their Heads!*, page 162.
13. "Stephen Farber, "Janet Gaynor Recalls the First Awards," *New York Times*, 28 March 1982, page D19.
14. Ibid.
15. Ibid.
16. Marion, *Off With Their Heads!*, page 162.

17. Ibid.

18. Callahan, "Two Best Dressed Women . . .," no page number.

19. Robert Osborne, *Seventy Years of the Oscar: The Official History of the Academy Awards* (Abbeville Press, new York, 1999), page 20.

20. "helplessly feminine": Carolyn Hall, *The Twenties in Vogue* (Random House, New York, 1984). "Bank": Eileen Whitfield, *Pickford: The Woman Who Made Hollywood* (McFarlane, Walter & Ross, Toronto, 1997), page 146.

21. Whitfield, *Pickford*, page 228.

22. "Mary Pickford Gets Trunks," 20 June 1928, press clipping marked "unsourced" and "torn" by the Academy of Motion Picture Arts and Sciences.

23. "Pickford Gown Row Called a 'Mistake,'" International News Service, 19 June 1928, press clipping marked "unsourced" and "torn" by the Academy of Motion Picture Arts and Sciences.

24. Robert Windeler, *Sweetheart: The Story of Mary Pickford* (W. H. Allen, New York, 1973), pages 157, 158.

25. Kevin Brownlow, *Mary Pickford Rediscovered: Rare Pictures of a Hollywood Legend* (Abrams, New York, 1999), page 231.

26. Whitfield, *Pickford*, page 262.

27. Scott Eyman, *Mary Pickford, America's Sweetheart* (Donald I. Fine, New York, 1990), page 187.

28. Whitfield, *Pickford*, page 262.

29. Ibid.

30. Ibid.

31. Alexander Walker, *Stardom: The Hollywood Phenomenon* (Penguin, London, 1974), page 231.

32. "Rocher": Whitfield, *Pickford*, page 221. "gold": ibid., page 207.

33. Holden, *Behind the Oscar*, page 99.

34. "Film Art Winners Named," *Los Angeles Times*, 4 April 1930, page A12.

35. Mason Wiley and Damien Bona, *Inside Oscar: The Unofficial History of the Academy Awards* (Ballantine Books, New York, 1986), page 18.

36. Jim Tully, "Irving Thalberg," *Vanity Fair*, October 1927, page 71.

37. Ibid.

38. *MGM, British Film Institute Dossier, Number One* (British Film Institute, London, 1980), page 9; and Peter Hay, *MGM: When the Lion Roars* (Turner Publishing, Atlanta, Georgia, 1991), page 12.

39. Interview with Hamish Bowles, July 2003.

40. Anita Loos, *Cast of Thousands* (Grosset & Dunlap, New York, 1977), page 113.

41. Bob Thomas, *Thalberg, Life and Legend* (Doubleday, New York, 1969), page 164.

42. Mark A. Vieira, *Hurrell's Hollywood Portraits: The Chapman Collections* (Abrams, New York, 1992), page 18.

43. heavy: Gavin Lambert, *Norma Shearer: A Life* (Knopf, New York, 1990), page 60. "Torture": ibid., page 113. "bantam": Alma Whitaker, "Reformative Beauty," *Los Angeles Times*, 9 March 1930, page J15.

44. Lambert, *Norma Shearer*, page 60.

45. Ibid., page 45.

46. Vieira, *Hurrell's Hollywood Portraits*, page 18.

47. Elena Boland, "Gaudy Clothes Banished," *Los Angeles Times*, 16 November 1930, page B13.

48. John Kobal, *People Will Talk* (Alfred A. Knopf, New York, 1986), page 257.

49. Vieira, *Hurrell's Hollywood Portraits*, page 18.

50. Kobal, *People Will Talk*, page 401.

51. "Bushy": ibid., page 257. "forehead": Lambert, *Norma Shearer*, page 130.

52. Vieira, *Hurrell's Hollywood Portraits*, page 19.

53. Kobal, *People Will Talk*, page 259.

54. Vieira, *Hurrell's Hollywood Portraits*, page 19.

55. Jane E. Wayne, *The Golden Girls of MGM* (Robson, London, 2002), page 51.

56. Lambert, *Norma Shearer*, page 132.

57. Boland, "Gaudy Clothes Banished," page B13.

58. Mick LaSalle, *Complicated Women: Sex and Power in Pre-Code Hollywood* (St. Martin's Press, New York, 2000), page 72.

Chapter Two: The Getaway

1. Katharine Hepburn, *Me: Stories of My Life* (Knopf, New York, 1991), page 147.

2. Barbara Leaming, *Katharine Hepburn* (Crown, New York, 1995), page 294.

3. Ibid.

4. Ibid.

5. Ibid.

6. Hepburn, *Me*, page 158.

7. Leaming, *Hepburn*, page 293.

8. Robert La Vine, *In a Glamorous Fashion* (Charles Scribner's Sons, New York, 1980), page 27.

9. "The Truth About the Academy Awards," *Photoplay*, April 1949, page 100.

10. Frank Westmore and Muriel Davidson, *The Westmores of Hollywood* (JB Lippincott Company, New York, 1976), page 68.

11. Joseph McBride, *Frank Capra: The Catastrophe of Success* (Simon & Schuster, New York, 1992), page 306.

12. Amy Fine Collins, "A Perfect Star," *Vanity Fair*, January 1998, page 115.

13. Ibid.

14. Clive Hirschhorn, *The Columbia Story* (Pyramid Books, London, 1989), page 12.

15. Interview with Bob Mackie, January 2003.

16. Caroline Rennolds Milbank, *New York Fashion: The Evolution of American Style* (Abrams, New York, 1989), page 109.

17. McBride, *Capra*, page 308.

18. Ibid.

19. Ibid.

20. Collins, "Perfect Star," page 118.

21. McBride, *Capra*, page 106.

22. Bob Thomas, *King Cohn* (Bantam, New York, 1967), page 28.

23. Westmore and Davidson, *Westmores of Hollywood*, page 68.

24. McBride, *Capra*, page 307.

25. Robert Osborne, *Sixty-five Years of the Oscar: The Official History of the Academy Awards* (Abbeville, New York, 1989), page 36.

26. Lawrence J. Quirk, *Claudette Colbert* (Crown Publishers, New York, 1985), page 67.

27. Sylva Weaver, "Flashing Gowns of Latest Style . . .," *Los Angeles Times*, 3 March 1935, page B5.

28. Shirley Temple Black, *Child Star: An Autobiography* (McGraw Hill, New York, 1988), page 100.

29. Mason Wiley and Damien Bona, *Inside Oscar: The Unofficial History of the Academy Awards* (Ballantine Books, New York, 1986), page 56.

30. Ibid., page 56.

31. Collins, "Perfect Star," page 118.

32. Black, *Child Star*, page 100.

33. Wiley and Bona, *Inside Oscar*, page 57.

34. Ibid.

35. Black, *Child Star*, page 101.

36. James Spada, *More Than a Woman: An Intimate Biography of Bette Davis* (Little, Brown and Company, London, 1993), page 112.

37. Wiley and Bona, *Inside Oscar*, page 60.

38. Rudy Behlmer, *Inside Warner Brothers, 1935–1951* (Viking, New York, 1985), page 27.

39. Bob Thomas, *Clown Prince of Hollywood: The Antic Life and Times of Jack L. Warner* (McGraw Hill, New York, 1990), page 105.

40. Bette Davis, *The Lonely Life: An Autobiography* (MacDonald, London, 1963), page 149.

41. Anthony Holden, *The Oscars: The Secret History of Hollywood's Academy Awards* (Little, Brown and Company, London, 1993), page 128.

42. Frank Capra, *The Name Above the Title: An Autobiography* (Macmillan, New York, 1971), page 187.

43. "certain": Barbara Leaming, *Bette Davis: A Biography* (Weidenfeld & Nicolson, London, 1992), page 91.

44. Charles Higham, *Bette: A Biography of Bette Davis* (New English Library, London, 1981), page 67.

45. Whitney Stine, *Mother Goddam: The Story of the Career of Bette Davis* (Hawthorn Books, New York, 1974), page 75.

46. "servitude": Barbara Leaming, *Bette Davis* (Cooper Square Press, New York, 2003), page 101. "hired help": Spada, *More Than a Woman*, page 113.

47. Higham, *Bette*, page 67.

48. Davis, *Lonely Life*, page 149.

49. Leaming, *Bette Davis* (Weidenfeld & Nicolson), page 87.

50. Leaming, *Bette Davis* (Cooper Square Press), page 96.

51. Daniel Bubbeo, *The Women of Warner Brothers* (McFarland & Co., London, 2002), page 66.

52. Spada, *More Than a Woman*, page 108.

53. Higham, *Bette*, page 68.

54. Spada, *More Than a Woman*, page 108.

55. Lawrence J. Quirk, *Fasten Your Seatbelts: The Passionate Life of Bette Davis* (William Morrow and Company, New York, 1990), page 96.

56. Leaming, *Bette Davis* (Cooper Square Press), page 92.

57. Wiley and Bona, *Inside Oscar*, page 64.

58. Leaming, *Bette Davis* (Weidenfeld & Nicolson), page 92.

59. Wiley and Bona, *Inside Oscar*, page 65.

60. Ibid.

61. Spada, *More Than a Woman*, page 113.

62. Larry Swindell, *Screwball: The Life of Carole Lombard* (William Morrow and Company, New York, 1975), page 217.

63. Ibid.

64. Ibid., page 258.

65. Charles Francisco, *Gentleman: The William Powell Story* (St. Martin's Press, New York, 1985), page 168.

66. Warren G. Harris, *Clark Gable: A Biography* (Aurum Press, London, 2002), page 170.

67. Swindell, *Screwball*, page 105.

68. Ibid., page 112.

69. Larry Carr, *More Fabulous Faces* (Doubleday & Company, Garden City, NY, 1979), page 147.

70. David Chierichetti, *Hollywood Costume Design* (Harmony, New York, 1976), pages 49, 50.

71. Marie Brenner, "The Last Goddess," *Vanity Fair*, April 1998, page 399.

72. Margaret Brenman Gibson, *Clifford Odets, American Playwright: The Years from 1906–1940* Atheneum, New York, 1981), page 405.

73. *Variety Film Reviews, 1934–1937*, vol. 5 (Garland Publishing, New York and London, 1983).

74. James Kotsilibas-Davis and Myrna Loy, *Myrna Loy, Being and Becoming* (Bloomsbury, London, 1987), page 125.

75. Gibson, *Clifford Odets*, page 418.

76. Ibid., page 433.

77. Mel Gussow, "Revenge of a Studio Pawn: A Comeback, After 55 Years," *New York Times*, 12 August, 1999, page 5.

78. Interview with Luise Rainer, April 2003.

79. Wiley and Bona, *Inside Oscar*, page 72.

80. Harris, *Clark Gable*, page 171.

81. Swindell, *Screwball*, page 259.

82. Brenner, "Last Goddess," page 399.

83. Wiley and Bona, *Inside Oscar*, page 73.

84. Ibid.

85. Swindell, *Screwball*, page 259.

86. Interview with Luise Rainer, April 2003.

Chapter Three: Gone With the Wind

1. Anne Edwards, *Vivien Leigh: A Biography* (Simon & Schuster, New York, 1977), page 67.

2. Alexander Walker, *Vivien: The Life of Vivien Leigh* (Weidenfeld and Nicolson, London, 1987), page 112.

3. Edwards, *Vivien Leigh*, page 90.

4. Rudy Behlmer, ed., *Memo from David O. Selznick* (Viking, New York, 1972), page 180.

5. David Thomson, *Showman: The Life of David O. Selznick* (André Deutsch, London, 1993), page 296.

6. Roland Flamini, *Scarlett, Rhett and a Cast of Thousands* (Macmillan, New York, 1975), page 250.

7. Rick Fernandez, "Walter Plunkett, Designing for the Stars", unidentified clipping.

8. Evelyn Keyes, *Scarlett O'Hara's Younger Sister* (Lyle Stuart Inc., Secaucus, NJ, 1977), page 31.

9. Walker, *Vivien*, page 121.

10. Edwards, *Vivien Leigh*, page 96.

11. Walker, *Vivien*, page 126.

12. Ibid., 124.

13. Ibid., 127.

14. Ibid., 129.

15. Flamini, *Scarlett, Rhett*, page 292.

16. Keyes, *Scarlett O'Hara's Younger Sister*, page 31.
17. Frank Westmore and Muriel Davidson, *The Westmores of Hollywood* (J. B. Lippincott Company, New York, 1976), page 130.
18. Ibid., page 129.
19. Patrick McGilligan, *George Cukor, a Double Life: A Biography of the Gentleman Director* (St. Martin's Press, New York, 1991), page 144.
20. Jesse Lasky, *Love Scene* (Angus & Robertson, Brighton, 1978), page 95.
21. John Engstead, *Star Shots* (E. P. Dutton, New York, 1978), page 116.
22. Walker, *Vivien*, page 23.
23. Maureen Reilly, *California Couture* (Schiffer, Atglen, PA, 2000), page 71.
24. Thomson, *Showman*, page 326.
25. Robert Osborne, *Fifty Golden Years of Oscar: The Official History of the Academy of Motion Picture Arts and Sciences* (ESE, California, 1979).
26. Walker, *Vivien*, page 143.
27. Edwards, *Vivien Leigh*, page 117.
28. Hugo Vickers, *Vivien Leigh* (Hamish Hamilton, London, 1988), page 122.
29. Edwards, *Vivien Leigh*, page 117.
30. Walker, *Vivien*, page 143.
31. Anthony Holden, *Behind the Oscar; The Secret History of the Academy Awards* (Simon & Schuster, New York, 1993), page 144.
32. Tarquin Olivier, *My Father, Laurence Olivier* (Headline, London, 1992), page 86.
33. Hal Hall, "News About the Fourteenth Annual Academy Awards, for Immediate Release," Academy of Motion Picture Arts and Sciences Library, Beverly Hills, CA.
34. Ibid.

Chapter Four: Dark Victory

1. Amy Fine Collins, "Idol Sisters," *Vanity Fair*, April 1997, page 360.
2. Hedda Hopper, "Hedda Hopper's Hollywood," *Los Angeles Times*, 19 July 1942, page C3.
3. Ibid.
4. Joan Fontaine, *No Bed of Roses* (Berkley, New York, 1978), page 99.
5. Ibid., page 146.
6. Tom Milne, ed., *Time Out Film Guide* (Penguin Books, London, 1989), pages 687, 312.
7. Fontaine, *No Bed of Roses*, page 37.
8. Ibid., page 146.
9. W. Robert La Vine, *In a Glamorous Fashion: The Fabulous Years of Hollywood Costume Design* (Charles Scribner's Sons, New York, 1980), page 43.
10. Tony Thomas, *The Films of Olivia de Havilland* (Citadel Press, Secaucus, NJ, 1983), page 37.

11. Charles Higham, *Olivia and Joan* (New English Library, London, 1984), page 111.

12. Charles Higham, *Sisters: The Story of Olivia de Havilland and Joan Fontaine* (Coward-McCann, New York, 1984), page 135.

13. Louella Parsons, "Untold Stories of the Oscars," *Los Angeles Examiner*, dated 1956.

14. Higham, *Sisters*, page 135.

15. Fontaine, *No Bed of Roses*, page 147.

16. Parsons, "Untold Stories."

17. Hopper, "Hedda Hopper's Hollywood," page 4.

18. Fontaine, *No Bed of Roses*, page 147.

19. Higham, *Sisters*, page 136.

20. Fontaine, *No Bed of Roses*, page 148.

21. Ibid., pages 148, 149.

22. Ibid., page 148.

23. Higham, *Olivia and Joan*, page 115.

24. Daniel Bubbeo, *The Women of Warner Brothers* (McFarland & Co., London, 2002), page 62.

25. David Thomson, *Showman: The Life of David O. Selznick* (André Deutsch, London, 1993), page 410.

26. Isabella Rossellini, fax to Ms. Katell Le Bourhis, 11 December 1996, page 2, courtesy Christian Dior archive.

27. Joseph Henry Steele, *Ingrid Bergman: An Intimate Portrait* (David McKay Company, New York, 1959), page 68.

28. Ibid.

29. Aljean Harmetz, *The Making of Casablanca: Bogart, Bergman and World War II* (Hyperion, New York, 1992), page 91.

30. Donald Spoto, *Notorious: The Life of Ingrid Bergman* (HarperCollins, 1997), page 70.

31. Ibid.

32. Edith Head and Norma Lee Browning, "And Now, the Envelope, Please" (unpublished manuscript, the Academy of Motion Picture Arts and Sciences' Margaret Herrick Library).

33. Ibid.

34. Ibid.

35. Sydney Guilaroff, *Crowning Glory* (Sydney Guilaroff Enterprises, USA, 1996), page 249.

36. Ibid., pages 248, 249.

37. Ibid., page 249.

38. Jeffrey Meyers, *Gary Cooper, American Hero* (William Morrow, New York, 1998), page 183.

39. Head and Browning, "And Now, the Envelope, Please."

40. Joseph Henry Steele, *Ingrid Bergman*, page 68.

41. Edward Z. Epstein, *Portrait of Jennifer* (Simon & Schuster, New York, 1995), page 131.

42. Thomson, *Showman*, page 413.

43. Epstein, *Portrait of Jennifer*, page 109.

44. Thomson, *Showman*, page 414.

45. Bob Thomas, *Selznick* (Doubleday & Company, Garden City, NY, 1970), page 214.

46. Thomson, *Showman*, page 414.

47. Thomas, *Selznick*, page 214.

48. Robert Osborne, *Sixty-five Years of the Oscar: The Official History of the Academy Awards* (Abbeville Press, New York, 1989), page 78.

49. Shirley Temple Black, *Child Star* (McGraw Hill, New York, 1988), page 358.

50. Epstein, *Portrait of Jennifer*, page 135.

51. Ibid., page 136.

52. "Fearless: The Truth About the Academy Awards," *Photoplay*, April 1949, page 100.

53. Frances Scully, "Let's Take a Look at the Annual Academy Awards Presentation" (16 March 1945, radio transcripts, Academy of Motion Picture Arts and Sciences Library, Beverly Hills, California).

54. Howard Greer, *Designing Male* (Robert Hale, London, 1952), page 214.

55. Ibid.

Chapter Five: Applause

1. Alexander Walker, *Marlene Dietrich* (Applause Books, New York, 1999), page 116.

2. Ibid.

3. Barbara Leaming, *Orson Welles: A Biography* (Viking, New York, 1983), pages 268, 269.

4. *Life*, 9 August 1948, cover.

5. Patrick McGilligan, *Alfred Hitchcock: A Life in Darkness and Light* (Regan, New York, 2003), page 434.

6. Ibid., page 341.

7. Ibid.

8. Patrick O'Connor, Marlene Dietrich, *Style and Substance* (Dutton, New York, 1992), page 101.

9. "Dior Profile," *Collier's*, 10 June 1955, page 37.

10. Donald Spoto, *Blue Angel: The Life of Marlene Dietrich* (Doubleday, New York, 1992), page 219.

11. Maria Riva, *Marlene Dietrich, By Her Daughter* (Knopf, Toronto, 1992), page 117.

12. Steven Bach, *Marlene Dietrich, Life and Legend* (William Morrow, New York, 1992), page 340.

13. Ibid.

14. Riva, *Marlene Dietrich*, page 609.

15. Walker, *Marlene Dietrich*, page 116.

16. Bach, *Marlene Dietrich*, page 345.

17. Ibid.

18. Ibid.

19. Walker, *Marlene Dietrich*, page 116.

20. Edwin Schallert, "Judy Holliday, Jose Ferrer, Get Top Academy Oscars," *Los Angeles Times*, 30 March 1951, page 1.

21. Walker, *Marlene Dietrich*, page 116.

22. Lowell Redelings, "Marlene Applauded," *Los Angeles Citizen News*, 30 March 1951, page 22.

23. Philip Scheuer, "Fans Cheer Celebrities Arriving for Awards," *Los Angeles Times*, 30 March 1951, page 2.

24. Robert Osborne, *Fifty Golden Years of Oscar: The Official History of the Academy of Motion Picture Arts and Sciences* (ESE California, La Habra, CA, 1979), section 1950—this book lists no page numbers.

25. Jan Herman, *A Talent for Trouble: The Life of Hollywood's Most Acclaimed Director, William Wyler* (G. P. Putnam's Sons, New York, 1995), page 350.

26. Edith Head and Paddy Calistro, *Edith Head's Hollywood* (E. P. Dutton, New York, 1983), page 102.

27. Pauline Swanson, "Knee Deep in Stardust," *Photoplay*, April 1954, page 103.

28. Amy Fine Collins, "Anything for Oscar," *Vanity Fair*, March 1998, page 237.

29. Head and Calistro, *Edith Head's Hollywood*, page 104.

30. Audrey Hepburn, "The Costumes Make the Actors: A Personal View," extracted from *Fashion in Film*, Regine Engelmeier and Peter W. Engelmeier, eds. (Prestel Publishing, 1997), page 9.

31. Ibid.

32. Ed Sikov, *On Sunset Boulevard: The Life and Times of Billy Wilder* (Hyperion, New York, 1998), page 351.

33. Diana Maychick, *Audrey Hepburn: An Intimate Portrait* (Birch Lane, New York, 1993), page 100.

34. Sikov, *On Sunset Boulevard*, page 351.

35. Head and Calistro, *Edith Head's Hollywood*, page 104.

36. Barry Paris, *Audrey Hepburn* (Berkley, New York, 1996), page 79.

37. Sikov, *On Sunset Boulevard*, page 344.

38. Robert Riley, *Givenchy, Thirty Years* (F.I.T., New York, 1982), page 8.

39. Paris, *Audrey Hepburn*, page 97.

40. David Chierichetti, *Edith Head* (HarperCollins, New York, 2003), page 133.

41. Amy Fine Collins, "When Hubert Met Audrey," *Vanity Fair*, December 1995, page 173.

42. Ibid.

43. Ibid.

44. Alexander Walker, *Audrey, Her Real Story* (Orion, London, 1995), page 128.

45. Randall Riese, *Her Name Is Barbra* (Birch Lane, New York, 1993), page 38.

46. Ian Woodward, *Audrey Hepburn: An Intimate Portrait* (St. Martin's Press, New York, 1984), page 4.

47. Ibid.

48. Ibid.

49. Warren G. Harris, *Audrey Hepburn* (Simon & Schuster, New York, 1994), page 115.

Chapter Six: The Women

1. Gerald Clarke, *Get Happy: The Life of Judy Garland* (Random House, New York, 2000), page 325.

2. Jane Ellen Wayne, *Grace Kelly's Men* (St. Martin's, New York, 1991), page 172.

3. Sarah Bradford, *Princess Grace* (Panther, Glasgow, 1984), page 137.

4. Steven Englund, *Grace of Monaco: An Interpretive Biography* (Doubleday, Garden City, NY, 1984), page 77.

5. Joseph Latin, "Up in Edie's Room," *Collier's*, 2 September 1955, page 26.

6. Edith Head and Paddy Calistro, *Edith Head's Hollywood* (E. P. Dutton, New York, 1983), page 108.

7. Ibid., page 112.

8. Amy Fine Collins, "Anything for Oscar," *Vanity Fair*, March 1998, page 361.

9. Ibid.

10. James Spada, *Grace: An Intimate Biography of Grace Kelly* (Doubleday, Garden City, NY, 1987), page 103.

11. Wayne, *Grace Kelly's Men*, page 178.

12. Bradford, *Princess Grace*, page 138.

13. Englund, *Grace of Monaco*, page 90.

14. Thomas Schatz, *The Genius of the System* (Pantheon, New York, 1988), page 458.

15. "Hollywood's Hottest Property," *Life*, 26 April 1954, page 117.

16. "Now Starring the Gentle Women," *Vogue*, 1 October 1954, page 108.

17. Englund, *Grace of Monaco*, page 81.

18. Head and Calistro, *Edith Head's Hollywood*, page 109.

19. Spada, *Grace*, page 100.

20. Ibid., page 106.

21. Ibid., page 107.

22. Ibid.

23. Englund, *Grace of Monaco*, page 91.

24. Spada, *Grace*, page 107.

25. Peter H. Brown and Jim Pinkston, *Oscar Dearest* (Perennial, New York, 1987), page 112.

26. Gerold Frank, *Judy* (Harper & Row, New York, 1975), page 391.

27. Ronald Haver, *A Star Is Born: The Making of the 1954 Movie and Its 1983 Restoration*, (Knopf, New York, 1988), page 219.

28. Frank, *Judy*, page 394.

29. Emanuel Levy, *George Cukor, Master of Elegance* (William Morrow, New York, 1994), page 231.

30. Lauren Bacall, *By Myself and Then Some* (Harper Entertainment, London, 2005), page 247.

31. Haver, *A Star Is Born*, page 219.

32. Frank, *Judy*, page 393.

33. Haver, *A Star Is Born*, page 220.

34. Ibid.

35. "The Biggest Night for Oscar," *Life*, 18 April 1955, page 60.

36. Mason Wiley and Damien Bona, *Inside Oscar* (Ballantine Books, New York, 1986), page 252.

37. Ibid. page 250.

38. Robert Lacey, *Grace* (Pan, London, 1995), page 222.

39. Robert Osborne, *Sixty-five Years of the Oscar: The Official History of the Academy Awards* (Abbeville, New York, 1989), page 102.

40. Englund, *Grace of Monaco*, page 91.

41. Osborne, *Sixty-five Years of the Oscar*, page 102.

42. Haver, *A Star Is Born*, page 220.

43. Wiley and Bona, *Inside Oscar*, page 252.

44. Frank, *Judy*, page 394.

45. John Fricke, *Judy Garland: A Portrait in Art and Anecdote* (Bulfinch, Boston, 2003), page 203.

46. Frank, *Judy*, page 394.

47. Fricke, *Judy Garland*, page 203.

48. David Shimpman, *Judy Garland* (Fourth Estate, London, 1992), page 330.

49. Michael Troyan, *A Rose for Mrs Miniver: The Life of Greer Garson* (The University Press of Kentucky, Lexington, 1999), page 259.

50. "Marlon; Grace," *Life*, 11 April 1955, page 118.

51. Agnes Ash, "Film Queens Win Oscars for Fashions," *New York Times*, 27 March, 1958, page 43.

52. David Chierichetti, *Edith Head* (HarperCollins, New York, 2003), page 129.

53. Kitty Kelley, *Elizabeth Taylor: The Last Star* (Simon and Schuster, New York, 1988), page 138.

54. Joe Morella and Edward Z. Epstein, *Paul and Joanne: A Biography of Paul Newman and Joanne Woodward* (Delacorte Press, New York, 1988), page 67.

55. Brown and Pinkston, *Oscar Dearest*, page 112.

56. Patrick McGilligan, *George Cukor: A Double Life* (St. Martin's Press, New York, 1991), page 240.

57. Edward Dmytryk, *It's a Hell of a Life but Not a Bad Living* (Times Books, New York, 1978), page 210.

58. Ibid., page 213.

59. Kelley, *Elizabeth Taylor*, page 119.

60. Jerry Vermilye and Mark Ricci, *The Films of Elizabeth Taylor* (Citadel, Secaucus, NJ, 1976), page 129.

61. Ibid.

62. Kelley, *Elizabeth Taylor*, page 139.

63. Wiley and Bona, *Inside Oscar*, page 284.

64. C. David Heyman, *Liz: An Intimate Biography of Elizabeth Taylor* (Birch Lane, New York, 1995), page 150.

65. Ellis Amburn, *The Most Beautiful Woman in the World: The Obsessions, Passions and Courage of Elizabeth Taylor* (Clift Street Books, New York, 2000), pages 10, 11.

66. Head and Calistro, *Edith Head's Hollywood*, page 153.

67. Dick Shepherd, *The Life and Career of Elizabeth Taylor* (Doubleday, New York, 1974), page 139.

68. David Chierichetti, "Helen Rose Remembers," *Los Angeles Times*, 11 December 1981.

69. Kelley, *Elizabeth Taylor*, page 139.

70. Ibid., page 120.

71. Heyman, *Liz*, page 146.

72. Kelley, *Elizabeth Taylor*, page 124.

73. Helen Rose, *Just Make Them Beautiful* (Dennis-Landman, Santa Monica, CA, 1976), page 117.

74. David Chierichetti, *Hollywood Costume Design* (Harmony, New York, 1976), page 40.

75. Amburn, *Most Beautiful Woman*, page 99.

76. Kelley, *Elizabeth Taylor*, page 144.

77. Amburn, *Most Beautiful Woman*, page 146.

78. Ibid.

79. Kelley, *Elizabeth Taylor*, page 147.

80. Ibid., page 142.

81. Ibid., page 147.

82. Amburn, *Most Beautiful Woman*, page 107.

83. Kelley, *Elizabeth Taylor*, page 147.

84. Heyman, *Liz*, page 220.

85. Eddie Fisher, *My Life, My Loves*, (Harper & Row, New York, 1981), page 195.

86. "The Old Look," *Time*, 3 February 1961, page 72.

87. Ibid.

88. Ibid.

89. Telephone interview with Marc Bohan, May 2004.

90. Heyman, *Liz*, page 163.

91. Ibid., page 162.

92. Ibid., page 163.

93. Kelley, *Elizabeth Taylor*, page 174.

94. Heyman, *Liz*, page 219.

95. Gerald Clarke, *Capote: A Biography* (Simon and Schuster, New York, 1988), page 270.

96. Heyman, *Liz*, page 209.

97. Fisher, *My Life*, page 189.

98. Ibid.

99. Kelley, *Elizabeth Taylor*, page 183.

100. Ibid.

101. Troyan, *Rose for Mrs. Miniver*, page 293.

102. Wiley and Bona, *Inside Oscar*, page 326.

103. Ibid.

104. Ibid.

105. Sheppard, *Elizabeth*, page 268.

106. Fisher, *My Life*, page 198.

107. Ibid.

108. Wiley and Bona, *Inside Oscar*, page 329.

109. Paddy Calistro and Fred E. Basten, *Hollywood: The Hidden History of Hollywood in the Golden Age* (Universe, New York, 2000), page 150.

110. Sydney Guilaroff, *Crowning Glory* (W. Quay Hays, Santa Monica, CA, 1996), page 216.

111. Ibid.

112. Ibid.

113. Sheppard, *Elizabeth*, page 268.

114. Les Spindle, *Julie Andrews: A Bio-Bibliography* (Greenwood Press, New York, 1989), page 13.

115. Army Archerd, "Just for Variety," *Variety*, 17 March 1966.

116. Michael Feeney Callan, *Julie Christie* (St. Martin's Press, New York, 1984), page 89.

117. Aljean Harmetz, "Designer with an Affinity for the Past," *New York Times*, 13 March 1988, page 23.

118. Ibid.

119. Archerd, "Just for Variety."

120. Robert Windeler, *Julie Andrews: A Biography* (St. Martin's Press, New York, 1983), page 112.

121. Harmetz, "Designer with an Affinity," page 24.

122. Gloria Steinem, "Julie Andrews," *Vogue*, 15 March 1965, page 124.

123. Windeler, *Julie Andrews*, page 132.

124. Ibid., page 106.

125. Ibid., page 104.

126. Archerd, "Just for Variety."

127. Charles Champlin, "Recounting a Tale of Two Julies," *Los Angeles Times*, 20 March 1966, page B1.

128. Virginia Steele, "Julie Christie: A Wardrobe for London's Darling," *McCall's*, November 1966, page 96.

129. Callan, *Julie Christie*, page 89.

130. Windeler, *Julie Andrews*, page 112.

131. Callan, *Julie Christie*, page 89.

132. Windeler, *Julie Andrews*, page 112.

133. Kevin Brownlow, *David Lean: A Biography* (Wyatt, New York, 1996), page 542.

134. Callan, *Julie Christie*, page 89.

135. Ibid.

136. Ibid., page 90.

137. Windeler, *Julie Andrews*, page 112.

138. Interview with Theodora Van Runkle, December 2003.

139. John Parker, *Warren Beatty: The Last Great Lover of Hollywood* (Headline, London, 1993), page 134.

140. Ellis Amburn, *The Sexiest Man Alive: A Biography of Warren Beatty* (Harper Entertainment, New York, 2002), page 105.

141. W. Robert La Vine, *In a Glamorous Fashion: The Fabulous Years of Hollywood Costume Design* (Scribner's Sons, New York, 1980), page 148.

142. Faye Dunaway with betsy Sharkey, *Looking for Gatsby: My Life* (HarperCollins, London, 1995), page 117.

143. Ibid., page 143.

144. Doris Klein, "Miniskirts Will Be Dropped," *Hollywood Reporter*, 29 December 1967.

145. Jane Wilson, "Faye's Way," *Los Angeles Times*, 10 March 1968, page N18.

146. Amburn, *Sexiest Man Alive*, page 104.

147. Interview with Van Runkle.

148. Ibid.

149. Ibid.

150. Ibid.

151. Dunaway with Sharkey, *Looking for Gatsby*, page 166.

152. Ibid.

153. Gary Fishgall, *Gregory Peck: A Biography* (Scribner, New York, 2002), page 261.

154. Edith Head, Academy of Motion Picture Arts and Sciences letter, 25 March 1968.

155. Wiley and Bona, *Inside Oscar*, page 407.

156. Fishgall, *Gregory Peck*, page 261.

157. Interview with Van Runkle.

158. Ibid.

159. Ibid.

160. Dunaway with Sharkey, *Looking for Gatsby*, page 317.

161. Ibid., page 180.

162. Joyce Haber, "Academy Forecast Highlights Party," *Los Angeles Times*, 10 April 1968, page D17.

163. Shirley Paul, "The Mark of Elegance," *Citizen News/Valley Times*, Academy Awards Section, 11 April 1968, page 10.

164. Allan Hunter, *Faye Dunaway* (St. Martin's Press, New York, 1986), page 56.

165. Ibid., page 57.

166. Interview with Van Runkle.

Chapter Seven: Stepping Out

1. "Problems in Pants," *Time*, 18 April 1969, page 95.

2. Randall Riese, *Her Name Is Barbra* (Birch Lane, New York, 1993), page 328.

3. "Irene Sharaff," *Interview*, August 1989, page 129.

4. Interview with Tzetzi Ganev, 30 June 2005.

5. Riese, *Her Name Is Barbra* page 328.

6. Barbara Leaming, *Katharine Hepburn* (Crown Publishers, New York, 1995), page 499.

7. Corey Kilgannon, "Ray Stark," *New York Times*, 19 January 2004, page B7.

8. James Spada, "Becoming Barbra," *Vanity Fair*, September 1995, page 139.

9. Ibid., page 140.

10. Arnold Scaasi, *Women I Have Dressed (and Undressed!)* (Scribner, New York, 2004), page 97.

11. Bernadine Morris, *The Fashion Makers* (Random House, New York, 1978), page 196.

12. Bernadine Morris, *Scaasi: A Cut Above* (Rizzoli, New York, 1996), page 60.

13. Ibid.

14. Robert Sullivan, "Capitalist Tulle," *Vogue*, October 1996, page 148.

15. Scaasi, *Women I Have Dressed*, page 104.

16. Ibid., page 110.

17. Ibid.

18. Interview with Arnold Scaasi, June 2003.

19. Scaasi, *Women I Have Dressed*, page 110.

20. James Spada, *Streisand: The Intimate Biography* (Little, Brown, New York, 1995), page 281.

21. Ibid.

22. James Spada, *Streisand: The Woman and the Legend* (Doubleday, Garden City, NY, 1981), page 106.

23. Shaun Considine, *Barbra Streisand: The Woman, the Myth, the Music* (Delacorte, New York, 1985), pages 165, 166.

24. Ibid., page 166.

25. Spada, *Streisand: The Intimate Biography*, page 158.

26. Ibid., page 165.

27. Ibid.

28. Riese, *Her Name Is Barbra*, page 328.

29. Spada, *Streisand: The Intimate Biography*, page 280.

30. Anne Edwards, *Streisand: A Biography* (Little, Brown, New York, 1997), page 164.

31. "hated": Ibid. "nut": Riese, *Her Name Is Barbra*, page 148.

32. Scaasi, *Women I Have Dressed*, page 111.

33. Cecil Smith, "Oscars: The Good, Bad, Unexpected," *Los Angeles Times*, 29 March 1973, page G21.

34. Irene Sharaff, "Hollywood Dress Parade," *Good Housekeeping*, September 1976, page 84.

35. Edwards, *Streisand*, page 283.

36. Wayne Warga, "Old Excitement Lives—Oscar Finds New Home," *Los Angeles Times*, 15 April 1969, page 3.

37. Edwards, *Streisand*, page 283.

38. Ibid.

39. Considine, *Barbra Streisand*, page 167.

40. thirty million: "The Trade," *Time*, 25 April 1969, page 83. "ample": Riese, *Her Name Is Barbra*, page 329.

41. Joyce Haber, "Post Oscar Party Needs Revamping," *Los Angeles Times*, 16 April 1969, page G9.

42. Spada, *Streisand: The Intimate Biography*, page 281.

43. Scaasi, *Women I Have Dressed*, page 112.

44. Jane Fonda, *My Life So Far* (Random House, New York, 2005), page 279.

45. George Haddad-Garcia, *The Films of Jane Fonda* (Citadel, Secaucus, NJ, 1981), page 161.

46. Peter Biskind, *Easy Riders, Raging Bulls* (Simon & Schuster, New York, 1998), page 15.

47. Bill Davidson, *Jane Fonda: An Intimate Biography* (Dutton, New York, 1990), page 164.

48. Peter Collier, "The Fonda Factor," *Vanity Fair*, December 1990, page 169.

49. Peter Collier, *The Fondas* (G. P. Putnam's Sons, New York, 1991), page 119.

50. "The Flying Fondas," *Time*, 16 February 1970, page 62.

51. Christopher Andersen, *Citizen Jane* (Henry Holt, New York, 1990), page 132.

52. Haddad-Garcia, *Films of Jane Fonda*, page 142.

53. Fonda, *My Life So Far*, page 234.

54. Alice Rawsthorn, *Yves Saint Laurent* (Doubleday, New York, 1996), page 86.

55. Ibid., page 90.

56. Davidson, *Jane Fonda*, page 132.

57. Ibid., page 162.

58. Andersen, *Citizen Jane*, page 226.

59. Davidson, *Jane Fonda*, page 156.

60. Kenneth S. Lynn, *Charlie Chaplin and His Times* (Cooper Square Press, New York, 1997), page 526.

61. David Thomson, *Warren Beatty and Desert Eyes: A Life and a Story* (Doubleday, Garden City, NY, 1987), page 278.

62. David Robinson, *Chaplin: His Life and His Art* (McGraw Hill, New York, 1985), page 625.

63. Collier, *Fondas*, page 218.

64. Collier, "Fonda Factor," page 214.

65. Collier, *Fondas*, page 211.

66. Andersen, *Citizen Jane*, page 190.

67. Davidson, *Jane Fonda*, page 166.

68. Andersen, *Citizen Jane*, page 226.

69. Ibid., page 245.

70. Davidson, *Jane Fonda*, page 155.

71. Howard Teichmann, *Fonda: My Life* (New American Library, New York, 1981), page 301.

72. Fonda, *My Life So Far*, page 279.

73. Collier, *Fondas*.

74. Lynn, *Charlie Chaplin*, page 532.

75. Teichmann, Fonda, page 301.

76. Fonda, *My Life So Far*, page 279.

77. Rawsthorn, *Yves Saint Laurent*, page 101.

78. Fonda, *My Life So Far*, page 279.

79. Ibid.

80. Lynn, *Charlie Chaplin*, page 532.

81. Ibid. page 533.

82. Vincente Minnelli with Hector Arce, *I Remember It Well* (Doubleday, New York, 1974), page 373.

83. Gerald Posner, *Motown, Music, Money, Sex and Power* (Random House, New York, 2003), page 258.

84. Joyce Haber, "She Doesn't Have to Sing the Blues," *Los Angeles Times*, 11 February 1973, page Q19.

85. Kevin Boyd Grubb, *Razzle Dazzle: The Life and Work of Bob Fosse* (St. Martin's, New York, 1989), page 152.

86. Wendy Leigh, *Liza, Born a Star* (Dutton, New York, 1993), page 121.

87. Grubb, *Razzle Dazzle*, page 154.

88. Joyce Haber, "Joel Grey Talks," *Los Angeles Times*, 4 March 1973, page 19.

89. James Spada, *Judy and Liza* (Doubleday, New York, 1983), page 184.

90. Elaine Gross and Fred Rottman, *Halston; An American Original* (HarperCollins, New York, 1999), page 8.

91. "Throwaway Chic for Fall," *Newsweek*, 21 August 1972, page 48.

92. Grace Mirabella, *In and Out of Vogue* (Doubleday, New York, 1995), page 150.

93. Steven Gaines, *Simply Halston* (G.P. Putnam's Sons, New York, 1991), page 121.

94. Cindy Adams, "Halston," *Photoplay*, May 1976, page 37.

95. Gaines, *Simply Halston*, page 121.

96. Adams, "Halston," page 37.

97. Ibid.

98. Minnelli with Arce, *I Remember It Well*, page 374.

99. J. Randy Taraborrelli, *Diana* (Doubleday, Garden City, NY, 1983), page 147.

100. Ibid.

101. J. Randy Taraborrelli, *Call Her Miss Ross* (Birchlane, New York, 1989), page 292.

102. Beth Ann Krier, "From Aghayan and Mackie," *Los Angeles Times*, 18 March 1973, page D9.

103. Interview with Bob Mackie, 15 June 2005.

104. Ibid.

105. Krier, "From Aghayan and Mackie," page D9.

106. Interview with Mackie.

107. Ibid.

108. Minnelli with Arce, *I Remember It Well*, page 373.

109. Grubb, *Razzle Dazzle*, page 153.

110. Taraborrelli, *Diana*, page 147.

111. Interview with Bob Mackie, January 2003.

112. Dorothy Manners, "Diana Ross: 'New Found' Success," *Los Angeles Herald Examiner*, 25 February 1973, page D-3.

113. Taraborrelli, *Diana*, page 147.

114. Ibid.

115. Ibid.

116. Ibid.

117. Gregg Kilday, "Cheering Fans Stargaze," *Los Angeles Times*, 28 March 1973, page 3.

118. Cecil Smith, "Oscars," *Los Angeles Times*, 29 March 1973, page G21.

119. Ibid.

120. Minnelli with Arce, *I Remember It Well*, page 375.

121. Ibid.

122. Joyce Haber, "Evening of Solidarity," *Los Angeles Times*, 29 March 1973, page G18.

123. John Kander and Fred Ebb, *Cabaret, Vocal Score* (Hal Leonard Corp, Milwaukee, 1966), pages 189, 190.

124. Minnelli with Arce, *I Remember It Well*, page 375.

125. Taraborrelli, *Call Her Miss Ross*, page 293.

126. Posner, *Motown, Music, Money, Sex and Power*, page 265.

127. Spada, *Judy and Liza*, page 192.

128. Mason Wiley and Damien Bona, *Inside Oscar: The Unofficial History of the Academy Awards* (Ballantine Books, New York, 1996), page 477.

129. Faye Dunaway with Betsy Sharkey, *Looking for Gatsby: My Life* (Simon & Schuster, New York, 1995), page 317.

130. Bettijane Levine, "Timothy Hawkins, Academy Award-robes," *Los Angeles Times*, 31 March 1978, page 111.

131. Timothy Hawkins, "Dressing for a Date with Oscar," *Los Angeles Times*, 26 March 1982, page 17.

Chapter Eight: The Bad and the Beautiful

1. Interview with Nolan Miller, November 2003.

2. Ibid.

3. Ibid.

4. Ibid.

5. Ibid.

6. Interview with Cher, 9 January 2006.

7. John J. O'Connor, "The Academy Awards Ceremony," *New York Times*, 26 March 1986, page C22.

8. Interview with Nolan Miller, 1 July 2005.

9. Ibid.

10. Joan Juliet Buck, "Anjelica Huston," *Vogue*, September 1985, page 675.

11. Interview with Tzetzi Ganev, 30 June 2005.

12. Ibid.

13. Ibid.

14. Ibid.

15. Sheila Benson, "Oscars: They've Got to See It," *Los Angeles Times*, 9 February 1986, page 24.

16. "Cher," *Current Biography Yearbook* (HW Wilson, New York, 1991), page 142.

17. Cher and Jeff Coplon, *The First Time* (Simon & Schuster, New York, 1998), page 219.

18. Bruce Weber, "Cher's Next Act," *New York Times*, 18 October 1987, page 321.

19. Interview with Cher.

20. Ibid.

21. Ibid.

22. Ibid.

23. Ibid.

24. Interview with Bob Mackie, January 2003.

25. Ibid.

26. "Celebrity Style Secrets," *People*, 16 February 1998, page 144.

27. Interview with Cher.

28. E-mail from Roy Christopher, 15 December 2005.

29. *People*, 7 April 1986, page 104.

30. Interview with Nolan Miller, 1 July 2005.

31. Interview with Cher.

32. Ibid.

33. Ibid.

34. Ibid.

35. Ibid.

36. Frank DeCaro, *Unmistakably Mackie* (Rizzoli Universe, New York, 1999), page 65.

37. Interview with Cher.

38. Ibid.

39. Ibid.

40. Interview with Miller, November 2003.

41. Ibid.

42. Interview with Cher.

43. Ibid.

44. Ibid.

45. George Christy, "On Hollywood," *Interview*, May 1986, page 114.

46. Edward Douglas, *Jack: The Life and Many Loves of Jack Nicholson* (Harper Entertainment, New York, 2004), page 239.

47. Interview with Cher.

48. DeCaro, *Unmistakably Mackie*, page 64.

49. Interview with Cher.

50. Ibid.

51. Ibid.

52. Ibid.

53. Ibid.

54. Michael Musto, "Up the Academy," *Village Voice*, 8 April 1986, page 59.

55. "Oscar Night," *Women's Wear Daily*, 26 March 1986, page 34.

56. "Cher," *Current Biography Yearbook*, page 141.

57. Mary Rourke, "Mackie & Cher," *Los Angeles Times*, 8 April 1988, page 1.

58. Interview with Cher.

59. Ibid.

Chapter Nine: The Only Game in Town

1. Gaile Robinson, "Oscar de la Hayman," *Los Angeles Herald-Examiner*, 29 March 1989.

2. Interview with Giorgio Armani, June 2003.

3. Interview with Michael Chow, March 2006.

4. David Weddle, *Among the Mansions of Eden* (William Morrow, New York, 2003), page 173.

5. Leslie Bennetts, "Oscar Mire," *Vanity Fair*, April 1990, page 88.

6. Karen Stabiner, "Dressing Well Is the Best Revenge," *Los Angeles Times Magazine*, 11 December 1988, page 44.

7. Interview with Wanda McDaniel, 1 August 2005.

8. Ibid.

9. Ibid.

10. E. Graydon Carter, "Starface," *Vogue*, October 1989, page 419.

11. "Call It Dangerous Excess," *People*, 17 April 1989, page 137.

12. Todd Gold, "Personally Speaking," *Harper's Bazaar*, September 1989, page 158.

13. Interview with McDaniel.

14. Mark Ganem, Christina Lynch, and Glynis Costin, "Giorgio Armani's New Slouch Chic Dazzles Milan," *WWD*, 12 October 1989, page 1.

15. Ibid.

16. Interview with McDaniel.

17. Nandini D'Souza, "A Few Good Suits," *WWD*, 31 January 2005, page 10B.

18. Interview with Wanda McDaniel, November 2004.

19. Interview with McDaniel, 1 August 2005.

20. Ibid.

21. Ibid.

22. Paul Donnelley, *Julia Roberts Confidential* (Virgin Books, London, 2003), page 48.

23. Tom Christie, "Woman of Character," *Vogue*, April 1990, page 398.

24. David Ansen, "Star of the Nineties," *Newsweek*, 6 November 1989, page 3.

25. Ibid.

26. Interview with McDaniel, 1 August 2005.

27. Merle Ginsberg and Veronica Woolston, "Faces & Places," *Us*, 14 May 1990, page 12.

28. Interview with McDaniel, 1 August 2005.

29. Interview with Merle Ginsberg, 12 May 2006.

30. Ginsberg and Woolston, "Faces & Places," page 14.

31. Interview with McDaniel, 1 August 2005.

32. Ibid.

33. Mason Wiley and Damien Bona, *Inside Oscar: The Unofficial History of the Academy Awards* (Ballantine Books, New York, 1996), page 777.

34. Ibid., page 770.

35. Ibid., page 777.

Chapter Ten: A Foreign Affair

1. Interview with Giorgio Armani, June 2003.

2. Katherine Betts, "The Prada Principle," *Vogue*, August 1995, page 202.

3. Peter Biskind, *Miramax, Sundance and the Rise of Independent Film* (Simon & Schuster, New York, 2004), page 174.

4. Interview with Betsy Heimann, August 2005.

5. Interview with Barbara Tfank, November 2003.

6. Sarah Mower, "The Prada Habit," *Harper's Bazaar*, March 1995, page 360.

7. Interview with Tfank.

8. Alex Shoumatoff, "Numero Uma," *Vanity Fair*, January 1996, page 67.

9. Interview with Alberta Ferretti, July 2003.

10. Interview with Barbara Tfank, 12 August 2005.

11. David Colman, "What's in a Dress?" *Vogue*, March 1996, page 232.

12. Interview with John David Ridge, July 2005.

13. Interview with Tfank, November 2003.

14. Merle Ginsberg and Natalie Rooney, "The Fashion Shine," *Women's Wear Daily*, 29 March 1995, page 8.

15. Ibid.

16. Thomas Beller, "Uma!" *Harper's Bazaar*, June 1995, page 166.

17. Steve Pond, *The Big Show: High Times and Dirty Dealings Backstage at the Academy Awards* (Faber and Faber, New York, 2005), page 92.

18. Ibid.

19. Ibid.

20. Biskind, *Miramax, Sundance and the Rise*, page 206.

21. Greg Kilday, "Oscar '95: The Big Night," *Hollywood Reporter*, 7 April 1995, page 269.

22. Ibid.

23. Interview with Elizabeth Saltzman, July 2003.

24. Brian D. Johnson, "Is Oscar out of His Mind?" *Maclean's*, 18 March 1996, page 72.

25. Ibid.

26. Susan Sarandon, *Premiere*, January 1996, page 116.

27. Ibid.

28. Interview with Robert Danes, August 2005.

29. Ibid.

30. Timothy Hawkins, "Dressing for a Date with Oscar," *Los Angeles Times*, 26 March 1982, page 17.

31. Interview with Louis Licari, September 2005.

32. Ibid.

33. Ibid.

34. Katherine Betts, "Fashion's New Establishment," *Vogue*, July 1996, page 112.

35. Interview with Stefano Gabbana, June 2003.

36. Lisa Lockwood, "Dolce e Gabbana: Complice's New Accomplices," *Women's Wear Daily*, 20 November 1990, page 11.

37. Interview with Gabbana.

38. Johnson, "Is Oscar out of His Mind?" page 72.

39. "Just for Variety," *Variety*, 14 February 1996, no page number on press cut.

40. Interview with Wanda McDaniel, 1 August 2005.

41. Anne Slowey, "Shining Stars," *W*, June 1996, page 78.

42. Ibid.

43. Sharon Stone talked to Merle Ginsberg, 29 August 2005.

44. Ibid.

45. Unidientified clipping, *W*, March 1996.

46. Virginia Campbell, "Soft Like a Stone," *Premiere*, December 1994, page 60.

47. Ibid.

48. John Lahr, "The Big Picture," *New Yorker*, 25 March 1996, page 72.

49. Judith Michaelson, "Oscar Designers," *Los Angeles Times Magazine*, 26 March 1995, page 26.

50. Ibid., page 32.

51. Rose-Marie Turk, "Mostly Minimal Efforts," *Los Angeles Times*, 28 March 1995, page F3.

52. Pond, *Big Show*, page 116.

53. Quincy Jones, "Pushing the Envelope," *TV Times, Los Angeles Times*, 24 March 1996, page 5.

54. *People*, 4 March 1996.

55. Interview with Matthew Rolston, 6 September 2005.

56. Ibid.

57. Ibid.

58. Stone talked to Ginsberg.

59. Interview with Ellen Mirojnick, 4 December 2005

60. Ibid.

61. Ibid.

62. Stone talked to Ginsberg.

63. Interview with Mirojnick.

64. Stone talked to Ginsberg.

65. Interview with Mirojnick.

66. Ibid.

67. Ibid.

68. Ibid.

69. Ibid.

70. Ibid.

71. "too": Dana Wood, "Unveiling Vera," *W*, September 1988, page 238. "relationship": Eric Wilson, "On with the Show Business," *WWD*, 22 March 1999, page 28.

72. "Ouch!" *People*, 7 April 2003.

73. Stone talked to Ginsberg.

74. "Ouch!" *People*.

75. Interview with Rolston.

76. Pond, *Big Show*, page 127.

77. Ibid.

78. "Backstage at the Oscars," *Variety*, 26 March 1996.

79. "Where Are They Now?" *People*, 10 April 2000, page 102.

80. "Unforgettable": "The London Scene," *WWD*, 23 February 1999, page 16. $786, 120: James Barron, "Fame, and High Price Tags . . .," *New York Times*, 19 March 1999, page B1.

Chapter Eleven: What Price Hollywood?

1. Mario Testino, "That Day with Diana," *Vanity Fair*, December 2005, page 302.

2. Merle Ginsberg, "Oscar Mild," *Women's Wear Daily*, 26 March 1997, page 6.

3. Kimberley Ryan, "Oscar Fashion Frenzy," *Vogue*, May 1997, page 104.

4. Courtney Love, "The Makeup Shake Up," *Interview*, November 1997, page 44.

5. Michelle Green, "Oscars Classic Revival," *People*, 10 April 1995, page 36.

6. Charles R. Cross, *Heavier than Heaven: A Biography of Kurt Cobain* (Hyperion, New York, 2001), page 224.

7. Interview with Wendy Schecter, June 2005.

8. Ibid.

9. Ibid.

10. Ibid.

11. Poppy Z. Brite, *Courtney Love: The Real Story* (Simon & Schuster, New York, 1997), page 210.

12. Interview with Schecter.

13. *Rolling Stone*, 26 December 1996–January 9, 1997.

14. "Love in Bloom," *W*, January 1997.

15. "LA Raw," *Los Angeles Magazine*, February 1997.

16. "Out of Grunge and in Vogue," *Time*, 30 December 1996.

17. Fred Schruers, "Rebel Diva Labor's Lost," *Rolling Stone*, 3 April, 1997, page 50.

18. "Courtney Goes to Drew's Rescue," *Press Telegram*, 1 January 1997.

19. Michael Musto, "La Dolce," *Village Voice*, 21 January 1997.

20. Ann Powers, Courtney Love interview, *Us*, November 1997, page 62.

21. Schruers, "Rebel Diva Labor's Lost," page 50.

22. Interview with Schecter.

23. Ibid.

24. Amy M. Spindler, "Giving More Weight to Lightness," *New York Times*, 24 January 1997.

25. Ibid.

26. Interview with Arianne Phillips, January 2003.

27. Ibid.

28. Mark Erhman, "The Iceman Loaneth," *Los Angeles Times Magazine*, 21 March 1999.

29. Interview with John David Ridge, July 2005.

30. Interview with Schecter.

31. Ibid.

32. Katherine Betts, "Agents Provocateur," *Vogue*, March 1997, page 294.

33. Interview with Schecter.

34. Interview with Ridge.

35. Interview with Schecter.

36. Ibid.

37. "Backstage at the Oscars," *Variety*, 7 April 1997.

38. Steve Pond, "Behind the Oscar Curtain," *Premiere*, March 1998, page 91.

39. Michael Shnayerson, "Portrait of an Actress," *Vanity Fair*, October 1997, page 318.

40. Jennet Conant, "The Professional," *Vanity Fair*, June 1996, page 184.

41. Ibid.

42. Ibid.

43. Vincent Lobrutto, *Stanley Kubrick* (Donald I. Fine, New York, 1997), page 500.

44. Cathy Horyn, "Galliano, Cheri," *Vanity Fair*, February 1994, page 80.

45. Ibid.

46. "Dior's Golden Age," *Women's Wear Daily*, 21 January 1997, page 6.

47. Betts, "Agents Provocateurs," *Vogue*, April 1997, page 291.

48. Daisy Garnett, "Dramatic Leanings," *Harper's Bazaar*, September 2001, page 365.

49. Betts, "Agents Provocateurs," page 291.

50. Interview with John Galliano, June 2004.

51. Ibid.

52. Plum Sykes, "Fashion Ration," *Vogue*, September 1997, page 282.

53. Martha Duffy, "The New Kid in Town," *Time*, 5 February 1996, page 55.

54. *Christian Dior's Little Dictionary of Fashion* (Cassell, London, 1954), page 88.

55. Interview with Galliano.

56. Ibid.

57. Ibid.

58. Robert Sellers, *Tom Cruise* (Robert Hale, London, 1997), page 131.

59. Mason Wiley and Damien Bona, *Inside Oscar: The Unofficial History of the Academy Awards* (Ballantine Books, New York, 1996).

60. Damien Bona, *Inside Oscar 2* (Ballantine Books, New York, 2002), page 43.

61. Ibid.

62. Jamie Diamond, "Nicole Springs Forward," *Vogue*, February 1995, page 208.

63. Ibid.

64. Interview with Galliano.

65. Interview with Phillips.

66. Interview with Schecter.

67. Telephone interview with Wendy Schecter, 18 November 2005.

68. "Ouch!" *People*, 7 April 2003.

69. *TV Guide*, 12–18 April 1997, page 7.

70. Steve Pond, *The Big Show: High Times and Dirty Dealings Backstage at the Academy Awards* (Faber and Faber, New York, 2005), page 156.

71. Ibid.

72. Ibid.

73. Interview with Schecter, June 2005.

74. Cathy Horyn, "Courtney Love and the Coming of Age of American Style," *Harper's Bazaar*, September 1997, page 428.

Chapter Twelve: The Greatest Show on Earth

1. Interview with Wanda McDaniel, November 2003.

2. Interview with Phillip Bloch, January 2003.

3. Valli Herman-Cohen, "Hair, Makeup, a Titanic Event," *Los Angeles Times*, 19 March 1999.

4. Barbara Thomas, "Oscar Who?" *Los Angeles Times*, 19 March 1999, page E4.

5. Merle Ginsberg, "The Red Carpetbaggers," *Women's Wear Daily*, 22 March 1999, page 12.

6. *Parade*, 31 January 1999.

7. Alex Lewin, "*Shakespeare in Love*, Holiday Movies," *Premiere*, December 1998.

8. "Acting Up," *Times* (London), 21 January 1999.

9. "Soar Winner," *Entertainment Weekly*, 8 January 1999, page 26.

10. André Leon Talley, "Period Drama," *Vogue*, September 1999, page 606.

11. Kathy Bates, "Q&A," *Los Angeles Times*, 21 March 1999, page 93.

12. Michael Shnayerson, "Today Belongs to Gwyneth," *Vanity Fair*, September 2000, page 325.

13. "Miramax Fires Back," *Los Angeles Times*, 13 March 1999.

14. Bernard Weinraub, "Using the Hard Sell to Grab the Gold," *New York Times*, 7 March 1999, page one. 118: Kim Masters, "Moguls at Play," *Time*, 5 April 1999, page 9. "upped," "best": Nicole Campos, "*Gold Rush*," *L.A. Weekly*, 26 March 1999, page 47.

15. Ginsberg, "Red Carpetbaggers," page 12. "pundits": Christa D'Souza, "And the Winner Is . . .," *Telegraph Magazine*, June 2000, page 51.

16. Telephone interview with Mesh Chibber, July 2005.

17. "changing": Merle Ginsberg, "The Style Council: A Day in the Life of Four L.A. Stylists," *Los Angeles Magazine*, September 1998, page 66, "finally": Jan Lindstrom, "Glamorous Rogue," *Variety*, 19 March 1999, page 44.

18. Lindstrom, "Glamorous Rogue," page 44.

19. Telephone interview with Jessica Paster, August 2005.

20. Telephone interview with Michael Howells, 23 January 2006.

21. Ibid.

22. Interview with John Galliano, June 2003.

23. Interview with Chibber.

24. Interview with Howells.

25. Interview with Paster.

26. "Ladies of the Night," *Women's Wear Daily*, 22 March 1999, page 8.

27. Interview with Paster.

28. Interview with Galliano.

29. Interview with Paster.

30. Ginsberg, "Red Carpetbaggers," page 12.

31. Jessica Kerwin, "The Beauty Brigade," *Women's Wear Daily*, 22 March 1999, page 18.

32. Ginsberg, "Red Carpetbaggers," page 12.

33. Merle Ginsberg, "Much Ado About Gwyneth," *Women's Wear Daily*, 14 December 1998, page 4.

34. Telephone interview with Crystal Moffett Lourd, August 2005.

35. Ibid.

36. Damien Bona, *Inside Oscar 2* (Ballantine Books, New York, 2002), page 227.

37. Interview with Lourd.

38. Bates, "Q&A," page 93.

39. Booth Moore, "Shoe Designers Hope," *Los Angeles Times*, 23 March 2001, page E1.

40. Ginsberg, "Red Carpetbaggers," page 12.

41. Interview with Paster.

42. Debra J. Hotaling, "Making Sure Glamour Is a Shoe-in," *Los Angeles Times Magazine*, 26 March 2000.

43. Telephone interview with Marilyn Heston, August 2005.

44. Diane Clehane, "Jeanne Wolf, Star Style," *TV Guide*, 10 April 1999, page 10.

45. Talley, "Period Drama," page 606.

46. Interview with Lourd.

47. Interview with Paster.

48. "Ladies of the Night," *Women's Wear Daily*, page 8.

49. Ibid.

50. Ibid.

51. "sweet": Ibid. "date": Karen Heller, "Pretty in Pink," *Long Beach Press Telegram*, 22 March 1999, page C8. "honored": "In the Pink," *Hollywood Reporter*, 22 March 1999.

52. Bona, *Inside Oscar 2*, page 229.

53. Steve Pond, *The Big Show: High Times and Dirty Deals Backstage at the Academy Awards* (Faber & Faber, New York, 2005), page 219.

54. Amy Wallace, "'Shakespeare' Hit by Snipers," *Los Angeles Times*, 23 March 1999, page F5.

55. Telephone interview with Randolph Duke, July 2005.

56. Garth Pierce, "An Out of Body Experience," The Culture, *Sunday Times*, 27 February 2000, page 5.

57. Joanna Schneller, 288, "A Woman in Full," *In Style*, August 2001, page 244.

58. Barbara O'Dair, "Who's That Girl?" *Harper's Bazaar*, February 2000, page 256.

59. "Couture Scoop," *Women's Wear Daily*, 18 January 2000.

60. Telephone interview with Jessica Paster, 16 March 2006.

61. Stephen Dalton, "Agent Provocateur," Metro, *Times*, 25–31 March, 2000, page 8.

62. Dana Kennedy, "Who Says You Have to Struggle to Be a Star?" *New York Times*, 12 March 2000, page 26.

63. Ibid.

64. *Women's Wear Daily*, 29 February 2000, page 6.

65. Anna Wintour, "Forward Reach," *Vogue*, March 2006, page 100.

66. Interview with Galliano.

67. Hilary de Vries, "Seriously Swank," *W*, December 2000, page 360.

68. Telephone interview with Mesh Chibber, August 2005.

69. Valli Herman Cohen, "Oscars: The Ultimate Advertisement," *Los Angeles Times*, 24 March 2000, page E3.

70. Ibid.

71. Ibid.

72. Ibid.

73. Merle Ginsberg, "Seeing Stars," *Women's Wear Daily*, 27 March 2000, page 8.

74. Interview with Duke.

75. Interview with Paster, 16 March 2006.

76. Laurie Pike, "New Power Stylists Dress Up Showbiz," *Variety*, 21 April 1999, page A1.

77. Interview with Duke.

78. de Vries, "Seriously Swank," page 360.

79. Interview with Duke.

80. Ibid.

81. Ibid.

82. D'Souza, "And the Winner Is . . .," page 52.

83. de Vries, "Seriously Swank," page 360.

84. *TV Guide*, 22–28 April 2000.

85. Vicki Woods, "Fighting Spirit," *Vogue*, March 2005, page 210.

86. Interview with Duke.

87. Philip French, "And All Shall Have Prizes," *Observer*, 28 January 2001, page 9.

88. "Ain't Life Grand?" *In Style*, March 2001, page 440.

89. Interview with Debbi Mason, July 2005.

90. Ibid.

91. Ibid.

92. Ibid.

93. Ibid.

94. Interview with Barney Cheng, October 2005.

95. André Leon Talley, "Box Office Poison," *Vogue*, June 2001, page 60.

96. Telephone interview with Rita Watnick, May 2005.

97. Ibid.

98. Ibid.

99. Ibid.

100. Ibid.

101. Ibid.

102. Ibid.

103. Ibid.

104. Telephone interview with Crystal Moffett Lourd, July 2005.

105. Talley, "Box Office Poison," page 60.

106. Ibid.

107. Interview with Watnick.

108. Shane Watson, "Sister Act," British *Vogue*, March 1993, page 200.

109. Interview with Cristina Viera, July 14, 2006.

110. Sarah Mower, "Rocking the Ivory Tower," *Harper's Bazaar*, page 133.

111. Ibid., page 133.

112. Interview with Viera.

113. Ibid.

114. Ibid.

115. Interview with Debbi Mason, February 2006

116. Interview with Viera.

117. Beth Landman, Kate Coyne, and Jill Sieracki, "Julia Roberts, True Beauty," *Good Housekeeping*, September 2000, page 105.

118. Interview with Mason.

119. Ibid.

120. Interview with Viera.

121. Interview with Mason.

122. Interview with Viera.

123. Ibid.

124. Ibid.

125. James Spada, *Julia, Her Life*, (St. Martin's Press, New York, 2004), page 5.

126. Rachel Abramowitz, *Los Angeles Times*, 26 March 2001, page A1.

127. Spada, *Julia*, page 5.

128. Ibid.

129. Ibid.

130. "comfortable": "The Way They Wore," *People*, 9 April 2001, page 66. "Bought it": Jenny Rubinfeld, "The Best Dressed," *Us*, 16 April 2001, page 34.

131. Mark Pytlik, *Bjork, Womanflutter* (ECW Press, Toronto, 2005).

132. Emma Brockes, "Bjork," *Guardian*, 13 February 2006.

133. Pond, *Big Show*, page 276.

134. Spada, *Julia*, page 5.

135. Bona, *Inside Oscar 2*, page 373.

136. Billy Crystal, "Sitting on Top of the World," *Harper's Bazaar*, July 2001, page 101.

137. Liz Smith, "Julia Settles Down," *Good Housekeeping*, August 2001, page 98.

138. Ibid.

139. Pond, *Big Show*, page 279.

140. Ibid.

141. Ibid.
142. Bona, *Inside Oscar 2*, page 378.
143. Ginia Bellafante, "Hollywood Slips," *New York Times*, 27 March 2001, page B10.
144. Ibid.

ACKNOWLEDGMENTS

Special thanks to my family—especially to my mother, without whom this book would not be possible, and my father—Shevawn Barder, Simon Barder, Olivia Barder, George Barder, Roesheen Cosgrave, Bridget Cosgrave, Marc Humblet, and Oonagh Humblet. Thank you to my outstanding, indefatigable researcher Dean Rhys Morgan; and at Bloomsbury, my editor Kathy Belden as well as Alexandra Pringle, Karen Rinaldi, Katie Bond, Miles Doyle, Sara Mercurio, Mary Morris, Sarah Morris, Polly Napper, Eileen Pagan, and Greg Villepique. Many thanks to the BBC's Carla-Maria Lawson for giving me the chance to cover the Oscars and motivating the idea for this book. Thank you to Rebecca Smith at the BBC, my agent Janis Donnaud, Francis Sultana, and David Gill. At the Academy of Motion Picture Arts and Sciences I am grateful to the following experts for providing me with assistance: Barbara Hall, Kristine Krueger, Lawreen Loeser, Scott Miller, and Matt Severson. Thank you to everyone in the periodicals and performing arts departments at the Toronto Reference Library as well as Janine Button and Brett Crawford at the *Vogue* library in London. Thanks to all those who helped me in Los Angeles—Jonathan and Philippa Bender, Jason Byrne, Carol Brodie Gelles, Veronica Chambers, Merle Ginsberg, Marilyn Heston, Renee Horsch, Angela Kyle, Malerie Marder, Wanda McDaniel, Joe McFate, Arianne Phillips, Katy Sweet, Barbara Tfank, Theodora Van Runkle, Julia Stern, and Rita Watnick.

I am grateful to Jamie Kingham, David Friend at *Vanity Fair*, Brian Robinson at the NFT, David Downton, Nicky Haslam, Lizzy Kremer, Helen Scott Lidget, Alexandra Shulman, and John Sloss.

Thanks to all of my great friends Boris Bencic, Marina Chan, Jennifer

Cowan, Marie Creac'h, Madeleine Czigler, Julietta Dexter, Allegra Donn, Olivia Falcon, Nick Foulkes, Vanessa Friedman, Marcy Gerstein, Tanya Greiner, William Hall, Jenny-Lyn Hart, Emma Jordan, Stephania Kallos, Isabella Kullmann, Darian Leader, Matthew Lechtzier, Mary-Ann Metrick, Gigi Morin, Gillian Mosley, Dominic Palfreyman, Jasmin Pelham, Alejandro Pitashny, Rita Reichart, Mark Robert, Min Roman, Toby Rose, Rupert Sanderson, Vicki Sarge, Saskia Sissons, Desmond Smith, Kim Stringer, Richard Sutton, Glenn Scott Wright, Harriet Quick, Mallery Roberts Lane, Stephanie Theobald, Emily Tsingou and Henry Bond, Robert Violette, Andrea Wilson, and Thai Ping Wong.

At Giorgio Armani thanks to Victoria Gooder and Robert Triefus; at Christian Dior thank you to Tina Lignell and Soizic Pfaff; at Dolce & Gabbana many thanks to Paolo Locati; and at Alberta Ferretti thank you to Lisa Patten. Thank you to Angela Missoni and her fabulous team, including Gerlinde Hobel and Gai Pearl Marshall. A big, huge thank you to Sugar Ansari at Moschino.

Thanks to Sally Beames, Debbie Chin, Tara Ffrench Mullen, Dunstan King, Vinesh Nagawa at Corbis, Tiffney Sanford, Olivia Williams, Esme Wood, and Josh Wood.

INDEX

Note: Page numbers in *italics* refer to illustrations.

Academy Awards:
  (1929), 227; lead-in 1–4; costume, 4; ceremony, 4–6
  (1930/April), lead-in, 6–10, *9*; costume, 7, 10, *10*; ceremony, 10–11
  (1930/November), lead-in, 11–15, *13*; costume, 15, 16, *17*; ceremony, 16
  (1934), 18–19
  (1935), lead-in, 20–24, *22*; costume, 24, *25*; ceremony, 20, 24–26
  (1936), lead-in, 26–30, *29*; costume, 28, 30, *31*; ceremony, 30–31
  (1937), lead-in, 32–36, *35*; costumes, 33–34, 36, *37*; ceremony, 36–37
  (1938), 37
  (1940), 59; lead-in, 43–49, *40*; costume, 42–43, 45, *46*, *48*, 49; ceremony, 49–50
  (1941), 54; costume, 51, *52*; ceremony, 51
  (1942), lead-in, 53–56; costumes, 53–54, 55–56; ceremony, 56–57, *57*, *58*, 59
  (1944), lead-in, 59–64; costumes, 60–61, 63, *64*, 65; ceremony, 64–65, *66*, 67
  (1945), costume, 67–68, *67*; ceremony, 67–68
  (1949), 111; costume, 68, *69*; ceremony, 68
  (1951), lead-in, 70, 73–75; costume, 70, 74–75, *76*, 77; ceremony, 75–77
  (1954), lead-in, 78–83; costume, *81*, 83, 85; ceremony, 83–85
  (1955), lead-in, 87–93; costumes, 87–88, 90–91, 94, 95, *95*, 97; ceremony, 93–95
  (1957), costumes, 100, *102*
  (1958), lead-in, 97–101; costumes, 97–98, 99–100; ceremony, 101
  (1959), costume, *107*
  (1960), costumes, 95, *96*, 97, 251
  (1961), lead-in, 101–6, 246; costumes, 101–2, 103, *104*, *106*; ceremony, 106–8, *109*
  (1965), 140
  (1966), lead-in, 108–12; costumes, 110–11, 112, *113*, *114*, *115*; ceremony, 112–16
  (1967), costume, 120
  (1968), lead-in, 116–22; costumes, 118, 119–20, *121*, 122, 220; ceremony, 122–23
  (1969), 141; lead-in, 124–31; costumes, 124, 129–31, *132*, *133*, 133–35, *134*; ceremony, 131–35
  (1972), lead-in, 135–42; costumes, *138*, 142, *142*, *143*, 147; ceremony, 143–44, *143*
  (1973), lead-in, 144–51; costumes,

147–48, 149, *150*, 151, *152, 153,*
155, *157*; ceremony, 151–56, *157*
(1977), costume, 156
(1978), costume, 156
(1979), costume, 156
(1984), 163
(1986), lead-in, 158–67; costumes,
159, *160*, 161–63, 164–67, *168,*
169, 170–71, *171*, 172; ceremony,
167–73
(1988), costume, 172, *173*
(1989), 179
(1990), lead-in, 174–78, 180–82;
costumes, 175, 176–78, 180, 182,
182, 183–85, *183, 184, 185*, 220,
221, 250; ceremony, 182–85, *185*
(1992), 198
(1994), costumes, 199, 250
(1995), lead-in, 188–91; costumes,
188–91, *190*; ceremony, 191–92
(1996), 222; lead-in, 186, 192–204;
costumes, 186, *187*, 195–206, *197*,
232; ceremony, 204–6
(1997), lead-in, 207–23; costumes,
207–9, *210*, 213–15, *216*, 219–23,
221; ceremony, 223–25
(1999), lead-in, 227–35; costumes,
227, 228, 230–35, *236*, 245;
ceremony, 235–38
(2000), lead-in, 238–43, 245;
costumes, 189, 238–39, 241–43,
244, 245; ceremony, 246
(2001), lead-in, 246–54; costumes,
246, 248–56, *249*, 255, *257*;
ceremony, 254–58
cinematography, 2
creation of, 1
dress codes, 51, 53–54, 55, 68, 88,
110, 119–20, 122, 124, 142, 159,
164, 167, 171
extended season of, 227
fashion consultants for, 88, 158–61,
174, 176, 185, 232
first black winner, 50
first color telecast, 112
first fashion reporter to cover, 24
on the Internet, 226
new categories, 33, 79
Oscar, name of, 19, 31
publicity campaigns for, 9, 63, 98,
106, 119, 149–50, 209–10, 228–29
qualifications for, 9
satellite linkup for, 176

statuette, 5, 19, 43, *259*
stylists for, 210
televised, 70, 75, 88, 97, 110
"the envelope, please" introduced in,
57, 59
vintage couture for, 226–27
winners in a tie, 133
in World War II, 51–52, *53*, 55, 67,
142
Academy Bulletin, 5
Academy of Motion Picture Arts and
Sciences, 1, 31
Accused, The, 179
Acheson, James, 205
Actors Studio, 135, 163, 217
Adjani, Isabelle, 176, 220
Adrian, Gilbert, 6, 11, 12, 13–15, *13,*
17, 24, 33, 36, 53, 56
fashions by, *17*
Adrover, Miguel, 240
Adventures of Baron Munchausen, The, 189
Affleck, Ben, 235
Aghayan, Ray, 148, 149, 151
Aherne, Brian, 55, 56, *57*, 59
Alaia, Azzedine, 200, 250
Alberghetti, Anna Maria, 95
Aleandro, Norma, 163
Alice Adams, 27
Alice Doesn't Live Here Anymore, 179
All About Eve, 77
Allen, Marit, 222
Allen, Woody, 156
Allied Artists, 149
Allman, Gregg, 164
Ameche, Don, 171
American Beauty, 239, 246
American Gigolo, 174–75
American in Paris, An, 90, 145
America's Sweethearts, 247
Andersen, Christopher, 139
Anderson, David Leroy, 224
Andrews, Julie, 86, 108–16, *114*, 144
Ang Lee, 249
Aniston, Jennifer, 246, 255
Annie Hall, 156
Archerd, Army, 108, 166, 167, 191
Armani, Giorgio, 174–75, 177–85, *177,*
187, 198, 202–4, 205, 221, 226,
232, 233, 240, 248, 250
fashions by, *182, 183, 184, 185, 187, 229*
Arnaz, Desi Jr., 151, *153*
Around the World in Eighty Days, 98,
100, 102

Astaire, Fred, 45, 77, 159, 161
Astor, Brooke, 127
Atlantic City, 194
Aucoin, Kevyn, 208, 212, 222, 232, 235, 239
Avary, Roger, 192
Avedon, Richard, 129

Bacall, Lauren, 92, 99, 142
Bach, Steven, 74
Back to the Future, 159
Baker, Rick, 224
Bakst, Léon, 180
Balanchine, George, 61
Baldwin, Evelyn, 30
Balenciaga, 255
Bancroft, Anne, 116
Bankhead, Tallulah, 71
Banks, Tyra, 200, 245
Banton, Travis, 20–22, 22, 23, 24, 25, 33, 36, 43, 53, 60–61, 73, 79
fashions by, 22, 35
Barbarella, 136
Bardot, Brigitte, 103
Barker, Reginald, 12–13
Barney, Matthew, 255
Barrymore, Drew, 212
Baryshnikov, Mikhail, 159, 166
Basic Instinct, 196, 202
Basinger, Kim, 229–30, 234, 242
Bass, Anne, 219
Bassett, Angela, 200
Bavaria Studios, 145
Beatles, 118, 119
Beaton, Cecil, 38, 128
Beatty, Warren, 116–17, 120, 122, 139–40
Beckford, Tyson, 200
Beene, Geoffrey, 127, 156
Beery, Wallace, 133
Behind the Oscar (Holden), 2
Behrman, S. N., 41
Benigni, Roberto, 246
Bening, Annette, 239–40
Benny, Jack, 65
Benson, Sheila, 163
Benton, Robert, 117
Bergen, Candice, 139, 175, 220
Bergere, Ouida, 36, 55
Bergin, Michael, 200
Bergman, Ingrid, 54, 59–62, 65, 67, 67, 68, 131, 132–33, 134, 144
Berkery, Barbara, 228
Bernard, Jerry, 11

Berry, Halle, 227
Bessant, Don, 112, 114, *115*, 116
Bianchini-Férrier, 21, 34, 43
Big Five studios, 1, 27, 28, 68, 90
Birth of Venus (Botticelli), 120
Biskind, Peter, 135, 192
Bisset, Jacqueline, 175
Bjork, 249, 255, 256
Blanchett, Cate, 227, 229–32, 234, 235, *236, 237*, 238, 241
Blixen, Karen, 172
Bloch, Phillip, 226
Blodwell, Piera Rossi, 241
Bogart, Humphrey, 61, 78, 80, 92
Bogdanovich, Peter, 163
Bohan, Marc, 101–3
fashions by, *104, 107*
Bonnie and Clyde, 116–20, 122
Born on the Fourth of July, 184, 221
Borzage, Frank, 5
Bowles, Hamish, 11
Boys Don't Cry, 238, 239, 240, 246
Bracket, Charles, 77
Bradbury, Ray, 110
Bradford, Sarah, 89
Brando, Marlon, 154
"Brat Pack," 159
Bratt, Benjamin, 247, 254, 256
Braveheart, 206
Breaking the Waves, 212
Brice, Fanny, 124, 126, 130, 132
Bridges at Toko-Ri, The, 88
Bridget Jones's Diary, 249
Brigadoon, 145
Bright Eyes, 24
Brodie, Carolyn, 234–35, 238
Brodsky, Jack, 134
Brooks, Louise, 188
Brosnan, Pierce, 200, 205, 243
Brown, Christy, 176
Brown, Kay, 38
Brynner, Yul, 107–8
Buck, Joan Juliet, 161
Buck, Pearl S., 34
Bullets over Broadway, 192
Bullock, Sandra, 223
Burke, Billie, 34
Burnett, Carol, 149, 152
Butterfield 8, 101, 103, 105–6, 108

Cabaret, 145–46, 149, 154, 155–56
Cage, Nicolas, 206
Cagney, James, 26, 159

Cahiers du Cinéma, 2
Calder, Alexander, 215
Calistro, Paddy, 80
Camelot, 110, 122
Camille Claudel, 176
Campbell, Naomi, 200, 205
Campion, Jane, 217
Capote, Truman, 105
Capra, Frank, 20, 22–23, 27, 30, 32–33, 36
Captain and Tennille, 165
Cardinale, Claudia, 195
Carnegie, Hattie, 36, 55
Caron, Leslie, *160*, 161
Carr, Larry, 34
Carroll, Diahann, 131, 149
Carter, Graydon, 178
Casablanca, 61, 65
Casino, 196, 198
Cates, Gil, 176, 191–92, 212
Cat on a Hot Tin Roof, 99, 105, 108
Cavalcade, 18
Celine, 232–33, 235
Champion, Gower, 130–31
Chanel, Coco, 21, 43, 136, 140, 192, 213, 222, 225, 240
Chaplin, Charlie, 7, 140, 142, 143, 144
Charade, 159
Charisse, Cyd, 99, 161
Charisse, Nico, 145
Chase, Edna Woolman, 45
Cheng, Barney, 249, 256
fashions by, *249*
Cher, 149, 158–59, 163–72, *168*, *169*, *173*, 208
Chibber, Mesh, 231
Chierichetti, David, 34, 49, 82, 97, 99
Choo, Jimmy, 234, 235
Chow, Michael, 175, 180
Chow Yun-fat, 256
Christensen, Helena, 253
Christie, Julie, 110, 112, *113*, 114–16, *115*, 120, 135, 143, 144
Christopher, Roy, 166
Christy, George, 170
Cinema Glamour Shop, 203
Clark, Larry, 240
Clement, René, 77
Cleopatra, 20, 101, 103, 104, 105–6
Client, The, 195
Clinton, Hillary Rodham, 213, *229*, 232
Cobain, Kurt, 209, 211
Cobb, Irvin, 24, 25, 26

Coburn, James, 148, 152, 154, 246
Cocoon, 171
Cocteau, Jean, 72
Cohn, Harry, 21, 23, 25, 126
Colbert, Claudette, 19, 20, 21–26, *22*, 25, 43
Colby, Anita, 63–64
Collector, The, 114
Collier, Constance, 8
Collier, Peter, 136, 140
Collins, Pauline, 176–77
Color Purple, The, 159, 164, 172
Columbia Pictures, 21, 23, 105, 129, 149
Conran, Jasper, 253
Considine, Shaun, 129
Constant Nymph, The, 54, 55, 56
Conti, Bill, 258
Cooper, Gary, 61, 89
Cooper-Hecht, Gail, 172
Coppola, Francis Ford, 154
Coquette, 6, 7–9, *9*
Country Girl, The, 87–90, 94
Courrèges, André, 120
Coward, Noël, 18
Craven, Mimi, 201
Crawford, Joan, 4, 12, 14
Cream Princess, 27–28, 30
Creative Artists Agency, 217, 233
Crosby, Bing, 89
Crouching Tiger, Hidden Dragon, 249, 256
Crowe, Cameron, 217
Cruise, Tom, 164, 184, 208, 209, 217–18, 220–24, 246, 249
Crystal, Billy, 247
Cuarón, Alfonso, 232
Cukor, George, 32, 39, 40–42, 48, 87
Curtis, Tony, 96, 97, 131

Daddy Long Legs, 6
Dahl, Arlene, 89
Dandridge, Dorothy, 87
Danes, Robert, 194, 195, 196
Dangerous, 26, 31
Danner, Blythe, 235, 238
Dark Victory, 43
Darling, 110, 112, 114, 115
Davies, Marion, 4
Davis, Bette, 19, 23–24, 26–31, *29*, *31*, 37, 42–43, 55, 93
Davis, Geena, 237, 242
Davis, Ruth, 27
Davis, Sammy Jr., 143
Day-Lewis, Daniel, 184, 185

Dead, The, 162
Dead Man Walking, 193–95, 204
de Havilland, Olivia, 42, 54–59, *58,* 68,
    69, 103
de la Renta, Oscar, 127, 183, 213, 232
Del Rio, Dolores, 43
Demarchelier, Patrick, 210, 225
DeMille, Cecil B., 11, 20, 87, 93
deMille, William C., 10
Dench, Dame Judi, 228
De Niro, Robert, 196
Dennis, Pamela, 232, 241
Designing Woman, 99
Desire, 74
Dessès, Jean, 251, 252, 255, 256, 257
Dial M for Murder, 87
Diana, Princess, 200, 214
Dickens, Charles, 131
Dietrich, Marlene, 21, 43, 45, 70–71,
    72–77, *73, 76,* 80, 103, 122, 149,
    198
Dior, Christian, 70, 71–75, *72,* 77, 79,
    81, 93, 101–3, 104, 106, 208, 220,
    222, 225, 235, 241, 246, 251
    designers working with, 176, 207,
        218–20, 230–32
    fashions by, *76, 104, 221, 236*
    New Look, 81
Divorcée, The, 15
Dmytryk, Edward, 98
Dr. Jekyll and Mr. Hyde, 60
Doctor Zhivago, 110, 112
Dolce, Domenico, 195
Dolce & Gabbana, 186, 195–96, 204,
    206, 211, 249, 255
    fashions by, *197*
Donat, Robert, 50
Donen, Joshua, 164, 166, 167, *169*
Donen, Stanley, 158, 159, 166, 167
Dorram, Sharon, 248
Dorsey, Hebe, 103
Douglas, Ileana, 233
Douglas, Michael, 202
Drake, Craig, 234
Dream Lover, 189
Drexler, Millard, 203
Driver, Minnie, 229, 234, 242, 245
Driving Miss Daisy, 174
D'Souza, Christa, 229
Duets, 228
Dufy, Raoul, 21
Duke, Randolph, 230, 238, 242–45, 246
    fashions by, *244*

du Maurier, Daphne, 54
Dunaway, Faye, 86, 116–23, 156
Dunne, Irene, 32, 43
DuPree, Roland, 250
Durant, Alta, 49
Duvall, Robert, 234
Dylan, Bob, 119, 256

Eagels, Jeanne, 26
Eastern Silk Co., 191
Eastwood, Clint, 152
Easy Rider, 136
Ebb, Fred, 145
Ebert, Roger, 204, 224, 236
Edwards, Anne, 39, 50, 130, 131
Eggar, Samantha, 114
Elbaz, Alber, 240
Elizabeth, 229, 236
Enemies, A Love Story, 177
Engelman, Marcy, 247, 254
Engleman, Leonard, 166
English, Marla, 84
English Patient, The, 212, 224
Englund, Steven, 89, 91
Engstead, John, 43
Erin Brockovich, 247, 256
Eula, Joe, 146
Evangelista, Linda, 196
Evans, Bob, 154
Even Cowgirls Get the Blues, 188
Ex-Wife, 11–12, 14
Eyes Wide Shut, 217–18, 222

Fabulous Baker Boys, The, 181
Fahrenheit 451, 110
Fairbanks, Douglas, 1, 5, 7, 20
Falwell, Jerry, 209
Fargo, 212
Fekkai, Frédéric, 226
Fellini, Federico, 159, 166
Ferre, Gianfranco, 176
Ferrer, Mel, 83–85, *109*
Ferretti, Alberta, 189
Feury, Peggy, 170
Field, Ron, 166
Fiennes, Joseph, 228
Fisher, Carrie, 216, 224
Fisher, Eddie, 101, 104–8, *107*
Flatley, Michael, 224
Flatliners, 181
Fleming, Victor, 39–42
Flusser, Alan, 202
Flying Down to Rio, 161

Flynn, Errol, 26
Flynt, Larry, 209
Fonda, Henry, 136, 141–42
Fonda, Jane, 131, 135–44, *138, 142, 143,*
    156, 170
Fonda, Lily, 122
Fonda, Peter, 136
Fontaine, Joan, 54–59, *57, 58*
Ford, Harrison, 237
Ford, John, 30
Ford, Tom, 227
Forest, Jean-Claude, 136
Forman, Milos, 209, 212, 216
Forrest Gump, 192
For the Love of Mike, 23
For Whom the Bell Tolls, 59, 61–62, 65
Fosse, Bob, 145, 149, 154
Foster, Jodie, 179–80, 182, 184, 185,
    185, 192, 209
Fox, Michael J., 159
Fox Films, 1, 2–3, 6
Francis, Mme., 20
Franham, Joseph, 5
Frank, Gerold, 92
Fraser, Brendan, 234
French, Philip, 247
French Kiss, 222
French New Wave, 117, 136, 137
French Salon, 42, 43, 44, 56
From Here to Eternity, 85
Funny Face, 159
Funny Girl, 124–29, 131, 132, 134

Gabbana, Stefano, 195–96
Gable, Clark, 20, 25, 32, 33, 36, 41, 43,
    89
Galanos, James, 250, 251
Galliano, John, 207, 218–20, *219,* 222,
    223, 230–32, 235, 241, 248
    fashions by, *221, 236*
Ganev, Tzetzi, 125, 162, 170
    fashions by, *171*
Gang, Martin, 27
Gap, The, 203, 204, 205
Garbo, Greta, 42–43, 45, 131
Gardner, Ava, 99
Garland, Judy, 50, 87, 92–93, 94, 145,
    146, 155
Garr, Teri, 161, 170
Garren, 211
Garson, Greer, 43, 55, 65, 95, 106, 107,
    149
Gaslight, 61, 67

Gaynor, Janet, 2–6, *3,* 9
Geffen, David, 246
George, Gladys, 32, 36
George Washington Slept Here, 56
Gere, Richard, 174, 181, 209
Gershe, Leonard, 93, 94
Gibbons, Cedric, 1, 5, 43
Gibbons, Elliot, 43
Gibbons, Irene, 42, 56, 60
Gibson, Mel, 184, 206
Gigi, 80, 145
Gilliam, Terry, 189
Ginsberg, Merle, 183
Giraudoux, Jean, 83
Girl, Interrupted, 246
Givenchy, Hubert de, 70, 80–83, 88,
    218, 219, 230
    fashions by, *81*
Glaser, Frederick, 129–30
Gliddon, John, 38
Glory, 184
Goddard, Jean-Luc, 137
Godfather, The, 154, 178
Goetz, Edie, 43
Goetz, William, 63
Golden Arrow, 30
Goldman, James, 125
Goldwyn, Sam, 126
Gone With the Wind, 32, 38–42, *40,*
    43, 45, 48, 49, 50, 59, 61, 98,
    110, 218
Goodbye, Mr. Chips, 50
Goodbye to Berlin (Isherwood), 145
Good Earth, The, 34, 37
Gordy, Berry, 144–45, 148, 149–50,
    151, *152,* 155
Gould, Elliott, 130, 131, *132*
Grable, Betty, 79
Grace, Princess, 103, 120, 199
Graham, Sheilah, 92
Grant, Lawrence, 17
Great Expectations, 232
Great Ziegfeld, The, 32, 34, 36
Greer, Howard, 9, 67, 68, 250
Grey, Joel, 146, 154
Griffith, D. W., 7, 30, 31
Griffith, Melanie, 177
Gross, Elaine, 146
Gucci, 227, 239, 241
Guess Who's Coming to Dinner, 122–23
Guilaroff, Sydney, 62, 108
Guinness, Gloria, 102
Gunzburg, Baron Nicholas de, 126

Haber, Joyce, 122, 129, 134, 145, 151
Hackman, Gene, 155, *157*
Hall, Bridget, 200, 204
Halston, 146–48, 151, 155, 214, 229, 242
  fashions by, *153, 155*
Hammett, Dashiell, 29
Hanania, Stella (Miss Stella), 56
Hanks, Tom, 177, 206
Hanna, Kathleen, 211
Hare, David, 229
Harlow, Jean, 24, 33, 224
Harlow, Shalom, 215
Harper's Bazaar, 64, 72, 179, 225, 253
Harrelson, Woody, 209, 212
Harris, Jed, 18–19
Harris, Warren G., 33, 36
Harrison, Rex, 114–15
Hart, Gary, 140
Hart, Kitty Carlisle, 53
Hartman, Don, 87, 94
Harvey, Anthony, 133–34, *133*
Hauser, Gaylord, 45
Hawkins, Timothy, 156
Hawn, Goldie, 140, 256
Hay, Peter, 11
Hayman, Fred, 174, 175–77, *176*, 182, 185, 232
Hayward, Leland, 19
Hayworth, Rita, 149
Head, Edith, 97, 99, 106
  as Academy fashion consultant, 83, 88, 110, 119–20, 158
  fashions by, *95, 96*
  and Grace Kelly, 87–91, 93, 94, 95
  Oscars won by, *78*, 79, 84, 87–88
  and Paramount, 5, 21, 33, 43, 61, 62, 73–74, 79–80, 87–89, 91, 149, 158
  and Universal, 128
Hearst, Mrs. William Randolph Jr., 127
Hearst, William Randolph, 4
Heimann, Betsy, 188
Heiress, The, 68
Hello, Dolly!, 125, 128
Hemingway, Ernest, 59, 61, 62
Hepburn, Audrey, 70, 77–85, *81, 84*, 87, 88, 99, *109*, 116, 122, 131, 159, 172
Hepburn, Katharine, 8, 18–19, 27, 116, 120, 123, 125–26, 132, 133–34
Hermès, 21, 88–89
Hershberger, Sally, 222, 230, 235
Heston, Charlton, 152

Heston, Marilyn, 234
Higham, Charles, 28, 56–57, 59
High Noon, 90
Hilkevitch, Marie, 9
Hill, George, 34
Hirschhorn, Clive, 21
Hitchcock, Alfred, 54, 70, 71, 72–73, 74, 87, 88, 90
Hold Back the Dawn, 55
Holden, Anthony, 2
Holden, William, 78, 80, 89, 94
Holiday, Billie, 144, 145, 150
Hollywood Reporter, 150
Hollywood's Golden Age, 2, 12, 14, 15, 19, 21, 126, 226
Holman, Leigh, 41
Hope, Bob, 49–50, 92, 94, 107, 122, 130–31
Hopkins, Miriam, 21
Hopper, Hedda, 17, 20, 53, 57, 60, 74, 89, 100
Horyn, Cathy, 225
Housewife, 28, 30
Howells, Michael, 230–31
Hudson, Rock, 152, 154–55
Hughes, Howard, 54, 100
Hughes, John, 159
Hunt, Linda, 163
Hunter, Allan, 123
Hurrell, George, 12, 14–15
Huston, Anjelica, 111, 161–62, 166, 170, *171*, 177, 221–22
Huston, John, 82, 111, 159, 161–62, 166
Huston, Tony, 162
Huston, Walter, 162
Huvane, Kevin, 233
Huvane, Steven, 233
Huvane Baum Halls, 227

Ideal Husband, An, 230–31
Ihnen, Bill Wiard, 89
Il Postino, 205
Indiscretion of an American Wife, 77
Informer, The, 30
Inside Oscar (Wiley and Bona), 33
International Herald Tribune, 103
International News Service, 4
In the Good Old Summertime, 145, 155
In the Heat of the Night, 122
Irene, 42–47, *44*, 49, 71
  fashions by, *46, 47, 48, 52*
Isherwood, Christopher, 145
It Happened One Night, 20, 21–23, 25

Jackson, Glenda, 135
Jaffe, Steve, 139, 141
James, Charles, 245
James, Henry, 217
Jazz Singer, The, 5
Jeakins, Dorothy, 110–12, 118
  fashions by, *114*
Jean Louis, 149
Jerry Maguire, 217, 249
Jessel, George, 36–37
Jewison, Norman, 119
Joan of Arc, 111
John, Elton, 214
Johnson, Brian D., 193
Johnston, Leroy, 25
Jolie, Angelina, 159, 245, 246, 249, 255
Jolson, Al, 5
Jones, Jennifer, 54, 59, 62–65, *64, 66,*
  67, 144
Jones, Quincy, 200, 205
Jones, Shirley, 106
Jones, Tommy Lee, 192
Joyce, James, 162
Jurado, Katy, 93

Kael, Pauline, 135
Kahane, B. B., 18
Kander, John, 145
Kapur, Shekhar, 229
Karan, Donna, 232
Karinska, Barbara, 60
Katz, Ephram, 2
Katz, Martin, 208, 214, 222
Kaye, Tony, 210
Kazan, Elia, 94
Kazan, Nicholas, 189
Keaton, Diane, 156
Kelly, Gene, 159, 172
Kelly, Grace, 86, 87–92, 93–95, 97, 99,
  103, 120, 199
Kennedy, Jacqueline, 146, 199
Kerr, Deborah, 97, 99, 106, 107
Keyes, Evelyn, 40, 41
Kidman, Nicole, 196, 207, 208, 217–25,
  230, 231, 246
Kids, 240
Kilmer, Val, 164
King, Carole, 140
King, Jamie, 200
Kingsley, Pat, 209–10
Kiss of the Spider Woman, 159
Kitty Foyle, 51, 52
Klein, Calvin, 165, 186, 232, 239, 248

Klute, 135, 139
Koch, Howard W., 128, 129
Kors, Michael, 232–33, 248, 254
Kudrow, Lisa, 242
Kurosawa, Akira, 159

LaBute, Neil, 251
La Cava, Gregory, 32
Lacey, Robert, 93
Lacroix, Christian, 191
Ladies' Man, 33
Lady for a Day, 18
Lady Sings the Blues, 144–45, 148, 149,
  155
Lagerfeld, Karl, 192, 225
Lake, The, 18–19
LaLanne, Jack, 164
Lamarr, Hedy, 253
Lambert, Gavin, 15
Lamour, Dorothy, 163
Lancaster, Burt, 131
Lange, Jessica, 182, 185
Lansbury, Angela, 151
Lanvin, Jeanne, 10, 240
Lauren, Ralph, 165, 175, 200, 204, 233,
  235, 251
La Vine, W. Robert, 19, 117
Lazar, Swifty, 170, 182
Leaming, Barbara, 18, 19, 28, 30, 126
Lean, David, 110, 115
Leaving Las Vegas, 206
Le Bourhis, Katell, 137
Leigh, Janet, 95, *96*, 97, 106
Leigh, Vivien, 38–43, *40*, 45–46, 48–50,
  48
Leigh, Wendy, 146
Le Maire, Charles, 93
Lemmon, Jack, 116
Leonard, Robert Z., 15
Let's Make Love, 112
Letterman, David, 172, 192
Leuschner, Renata, 166
Levine, Beth, 147
Levon, 254
Licari, Louis, 195, 204
Liebman, Roy, 2
Lifeboat, 71
Lily et Cie, 250–51, 255
  fashions by, *257*
Linkletter, Art, 88
Linney, Laura, 242
Linton tweeds, 21
Lion in Winter, The, 125–26, 133

Little Annie Rooney, 6
Littlefeather, Sacheen, 154
Little Lord Fauntleroy, 6
Little Miss Marker, 24
Live from the Red Carpet (TV special), 186
Lobell, Jeanine, 230
Lockridge, Ross, 98
Loggins, Kenny, 212, 216
Lombard, Carole, 32–34, *35*, 36, 37, 43, 198
Loos, Anita, 12
Loper, Don, 106, 250
Lord of the Dance, 224
Lords, Traci, 196
Loren, Sophia, 95, 103
Lorenzo's Oil, 195
Los Angeles Times, 53, 224
Lourd, Bryan, 233
Love, Courtney, 207–16, *210*, 222, 223, 224–25, 258
Lowe, Chad, 238, 239, 241, 246, 254–55
Loy, Myrna, 34
Luft, Sid, 92, 94
Lynn, Kenneth S., 139
Lyon, Bill, 101

Mackie, Bob, 21, 148–49, 150, 151, 154–55, 159, 161, 163, 164–65, 166, 167, 170, 172, 177, 184, 208
fashions by, *150*, *152*, *168*, *169*, *173*
MacLaine, Shirley, 95, 106, 107, 113
Madonna, 196, 214
Magnani, Anna, 195
I. Magnin & Co., 56
Malle, Louis, 194
Maltese Falcon, The (Hammett), 29
Mamet, David, 229
Manchester, Melissa, 159
Mankiewicz, Joseph, 77
Mann, Daniel, 103
Manners, Dorothy, 125, 150
Manolo Blahnik, 189, 208, 222, 223
Map of the World, A, 240
March, Fredric, 85, 133
Marion, Frances, 2, 4, 5, 8
Martin, Steve, 256
Marx, Groucho, 144
Mary of Scotland, 27
Mary Poppins, 110, 112
Mary Reilly, 248
Mask, 163, 165
Mason, Debbi, 247–48, 253–54

Matrix, The, 246
Matthau, Walter, 131, 143
Maugham, Somerset, 23, 172
May, Elaine, 140
Maychick, Diana, 80
Mayer, Louis B., 1, 2, 5, 12–13, 15, 19, 32, 36, 37, 90, 99, 126, 227
McBride, Joseph, 22
McCombe, Leonard, 83–84
McDaniel, Hattie, 50, 59
McDaniel, Wanda, 177–82, *181*, 183–85, 198, 226
McGilligan, Patrick, 42, 71
McInerney, Jay, 240
McLaglen, Victor, 30, 36–37
McQueen, Alexander, 230
McTiernan, John, 243
Me (Hepburn), 18
Meet Me in Saint Louis, 145
Mele, Dreda, 82, 85
Mendes, Sam, 239
Mercier, Laura, 204
Mercouri, Melina, 107
Meredith, Burgess, 56, 59
Metro-Goldwyn-Mayer (MGM):
    and Academy Awards, 19, 32, 34, 36, 99
    in Big Five, 1
    costumers, 6, 11, 15, 56, 91, 100
    stars, 4, 13, 14, 15, 32, 34, 36, 45, 89–90, 99, 105, 160, 161
Metropolitan Museum of Art, Costume Institute, 206
Mexican, The, 248
Mighty Aphrodite, 186, 187
Milbank, Caroline Rennolds, 21
Milland, Ray, 89
Miller, Ann, *160*, 161, 166, 167
Miller, Nolan, 158–61, 164, 166, 167
    fashions by, *160*
Miller, Ron, 151
Minnelli, Liza, 144, 145–48, 151, *153*, 154–56, *157*
Minnelli, Vincente, 145, 149, 151, *153*, 154, 156
Mirabella, Grace, 147
Miramax, 227, 228, 233, 235–36
Mirojnick, Ellen, 201–3
Mitchell, Joni, 118
Mitchell, Margaret, 32, 38, 50
Moffett Lourd, Crystal, 233, 235, 251–52
Molyneux, Edward, 36

Monroe, Marilyn, 77, 79, 111–12, 149, 198
Monte Carlo Baby, 80
Montgomery, Robert, 15
Moonstruck, 172, 173
Moore, Demi, 250
Moore, Grace, 23
Moore, Julianne, 240
Morning Glory, 18
Morris, Bernadine, 127
Motown Records, 144, 150
Moulin Rouge, 226
Mugler, Thierry, 211, 222
Muni, Paul, 37
Murch, Walter, 224
Murnau, F. W., 2, 3
Music Box, 182
Musto, Michael, 172, 212, 246
My Fair Lady, 110, 114
My Left Foot, 176, 184
My Man Godfrey, 32, 33–34

National Velvet, 99
NBC, 92–93
Neal, Patricia, 132
Nelson, Harmon Oscar "Ham," 19, 27, 28, 30, 31
Network, 156
Newman, David, 117
Newman, Paul, 97, 101
Newman, Randy, 184
Newton, Ashley, 252
Newton, Helmut, 181
Newton, Huey P., 138, 139
New York Fashion Week, 207
Niagara, 111
Nichols, Mike, 140
Nicholson, Jack, 143, 162, 166, 170, 171, 200, 236
Niven, David, 85
No Highway, 74
Normant, Serge, 248, 254
Norton Simon, 214
Nothing Sacred, 32
Novarro, Ramon, 12
Nurse Betty, 251
Nutty Professor, The, 224

O'Connor, Donald, 85, 172
Odets, Clifford, 34–36, 87
Of Human Bondage, 23–24, 28, 31
O'Hara, John, 103
Oldman, Gary, 188

Oliver!, 131
Olivier, Laurence, 38, 41, 50
On a Clear Day You Can See Forever, 125, 128, 129
One Fine Day, 212
O'Neill, Oona, 140
On the Waterfront, 94
Orry-Kelly, 30, 53, 68
    fashions by, 31, 69
Osborne, Robert, 65, 77
Out of Africa, 159, 172
"Over the Rainbow," 50, 184

Pacific Heights, 177
Page, Geraldine, 172
Pakula, Alan, 135, 139, 141
Paley, Babe, 102
Paltrow, Bruce, 228
Paltrow, Gwyneth, 227–29, 229, 232–33, 234–38, 237, 246
Paramount Pictures:
    and Academy Awards, 23, 87–88, 91, 128, 154, 179
    in Big Five, 1
    stars, 21, 23, 32, 33, 43, 61–62, 71, 73–74, 78, 79, 80, 87–88, 90–91, 128, 144
    wardrobe department, 5, 20–21, 33, 43, 78, 88, 89, 90, 128, 149, 158
Parenthood, 184
Parker, Bonnie, 117, 118
Parker, Oliver, 230
Parsons, Estelle, 122
Parsons, Louella O., 4, 45, 56, 57, 106
Paster, Jessica, 227, 229–32, 234, 235, 239, 241–43
Pasteur, Louis, 37
Patou, Jean, 36
Pau, Peter, 256
Paul, Shirley, 122
Paxinou, Katina, 65
Peck, Gregory, 78, 79, 119–20, 122, 130
Peck, Veronique, 120
Peirce, Kimberley, 239, 246
Pejoski, Marjan, fashions by, 255
Penn, Arthur, 117, 118, 120
Penn, Irving, 136
Penn, Sean, 193, 206
People vs. Larry Flynt, The, 209, 211, 212, 213–14
Peretti, Elsa, 147
Perlberg, William, 88, 90
Pesci, Joe, 196

Peter, Paul, and Mary, 140
Pfeiffer, Michelle, 181–82, 183, *183*, 184–85, 196
Phillips, Arianne, 213–14, 223
Photoplay, 15, 19, 60
Pickfair, 7, 9
Pickford, Mary, 1, 2, 4, 6–10, *9*, *10*, 20, 65
Pickford-Fairbanks Studio, 8
Pike, Laurie, 223
Pita, Orlando, 235
Pitt, Brad, 246
Pleasure Mad, 12–13
Plummer, Christopher, 112
Plunkett, Walter, 39, 40
    fashions by, *40*
PMK, 209–10
Pocahontas, 205
Poitier, Sidney, 122–23, 131
Pollack, Sydney, 159, 172
Pollyanna, 6
Porter, Cole, 19
Portrait of a Lady, 217, 231
Powell, William, 24, 33, 34, 36
Prada, Miuccia, 186–87, 188–91, 192, 206, 211, 222
    fashions by, *190*
Prejean, Sister Helen, 193, 206
Pretty Woman, 181, 248
Price Waterhouse, 59, 77, 108, 205
Prime of Miss Jean Brodie, The, 141
Prizzi's Honor, 159, 162, 170
Pulp Fiction, 187–88, 192
Pytlik, Mark, 255

Quirk, Lawrence J., 30

Rachel, Rachel, 125
Radio-Keith-Orpheum (RKO), 1, 18, 27, 28
Rags, 6
Rainer, Luise, 19, 32, 34–37, *37*, 110
Rainier III, Prince, 97
Raintree County, 98, 100, 105
Rambert, Marie, 79
Rathbone, Basil, 36, 55
Rear Window, 87, 88, 90
Rebecca, 54
Rebecca of Sunnybrook Farm, 6
Redé, Baron Alexis de, 147
Redgrave, Vanessa, 132, 135
Reed, Rex, 141
Reva, James, 156

Reynolds, Debbie, 106, 166, 172
Richardson, Bob, 162
Richie, Lionel, 171–72
Ridge, John David, 191, 214, 215
Riese, Randall, 125, 133
Ringwald, Molly, 159
Ritt, Martin, 150
Ritts, Herb, 222
Riva, Maria, 71, 73, 74
Rivers, Joan, 186, 204, 222, 223, 235
Robbins, Jerome, 126
Robbins, Tim, 193, 204, 206
Robbins, Tom, 188
Roberts, Julia, 180–81, 182, 183–85, 246–48, 252–56, 258
Roberts, Nina, 9, 10
Robinson, Gaile, 174
Robinson, Steven, 231
Robson, May, 18
Rockefeller, Mary, 127
Rodin, Auguste, 176
Rogers, Ginger, 43, 45, 51, *52*, 57, 59, 161, 166
Rogers, Will, 18
Rolling Stones, 118, 119
Rolston, Matthew, 200–201, 205
Roman Holiday, 79, 81, 82, 83, 84, 85, 88
Romeo and Juliet, 32, 36, 228
Rose, Helen, 97, 99–101, 105, 251
Rosher, Charles, 8
Ross, Diana, 144–45, 148–52, *150*, *152*, 154–55, 184
Ross, Herb, 181
Rossellini, Isabella, 60, 196
Rottman, Fred, 146
Rourke, Mary, 172
Royal Shakespeare Company, 228
Ruddy, Albert S., 178, 182
Runaway Train, 159
Russell, Jane, 79
Russo, Rene, 243
Ruttenstein, Kal, 180
Ryan, Meg, 222
Ryder, Nancy, 250, 252
Ryder, Winona, 223, 250

Sabrina, 77–80, 82–83
Saint, Eva Marie, 95
Saint Laurent, Yves, 102, 124, 128–29, 136–37, 146, 179, 183, 192, 240
    fashions by, *138*, *142*, *143*
    Rive Gauche, 137, 138, 142, 144

Saltzman, Elizabeth, 192
Sarandon, Susan, 186, 192–96, 204, 206
Sartre, Jean-Paul, 181
Saving Private Ryan, 237
Scaasi, Arnold, 126–30, 131, 133, 134–35
    fashions by, *132, 133, 134*
Schary, Dore, 90, 91, 98
Schatz, Thomas, 90
Schatzberg, Jerry, 119, 122
Schecter, Wendy, 209, 210–11, 213,
    214–16, 223
Schenkenberg, Marcus, 200
Schiaparelli, Elsa, 21, 81
Schiffer, Claudia, 200, 205
Schiller, Lydia, 41
Schlesinger, John, 110, 115
Schmidt, Eddie, 33
Schneider, Bert, 139
Schnitzler, Arthur, 218
Schrader, Paul, 175
Schumacher, Joel, 181, 195
Schwartz, Stephen, 205
Scorsese, Martin, 179, 196
Scott, L'Wren, 222
Scott, Ridley, 195
Screen Actors Guild (SAG), 19, 24, 27,
    31, 33, 192, 194
Screen Directors Guild, 27
Screen Writers Guild, 27
Scully, Frances, 67
Seaton, George, 88
Sebesta, Edward, 250
Seger, Bob, 163
Sellers, Robert, 220
Seltzer, Nancy, 194, 206
Selznick, David O., 32, 38–40, 42, 43,
    49–50, 54, 57, 59–63, 65, 77
Selznick, Irene Mayer, 5, 32
Selznick, Myron, 32, 38, 41
Selznick Studios, 39, 59, 61, 62, 63
Seventh Heaven, 2, 5
Sevigny, Chloë, 240, 246
Shakespeare in Love, 226, 228–29, 232,
    236–37
Shall We Dance, 45
Shanghai Express, 21
Sharaff, Irene, 125, 131
Shearer, Norma, 2, 4, 11–17, *13*, 23, 32,
    36, 175
Sheedy, Ally, 159
Sheppard, Eugenia, 103
Sheridan, Jim, 176
Ship of Fools, 114

Shirley Valentine, 176
Show Boat, 90
Shute, Nevil, 74
Sign of the Cross, The, 20
Signoret, Simone, 114, 251
Sikov, Ed, 80
Silberstein, Bob, 148, 151, 152, 155
Silkwood, 163
Sinatra, Frank, 85, 92
Singin' in the Rain, 90, 159
Sliver, 199
Smith, Cecil, 152
Smith, Ludlow Ogden "Luddy," 19
Smith, Maggie, 141
Snow, Carmel, 72, 82
Somer, Enrica, 161
Song of Bernadette, The, 59, 62–63, 65
Sorvino, Mira, 186, *187*
Sounder, 150
Sound of Music, The, 109–10, 112–16
Spacey, Kevin, 246, 256, 258
Spada, James, 26, 28, 91, 126, 248, 256
Spensely, Dorothy, 7
Spielberg, Steven, 159, 164, 237
Spindler, Amy, 213–14
Spoto, Donald, 62, 73
Springsteen, Bruce, 163
Stage Fright, 70, 71, 72–74, 77
Stanwyck, Barbara, 88, 203
Star Is Born, A, 87, 92, 94
Stark, Fran, 130
Stark, Ray, 126, 130
Steele, Joseph Henry, 60, 62, 65
Steele, Lawrence, 246
Steel Magnolias, 180–81
Steelyard Blues, 140
Steiger, Rod, 122
Steinem, Gloria, 112
Stella, Miss, 55–56
Sternberg, Josef von, 21
Stevens, Fisher, 183
Stoltz, Eric, 164
Stone, Oliver, 202, 221
Stone, Sharon, 186, 192–93, 196, 198–206,
    201, 213, 214
Story of Louis Pasteur, The, 37
Stradling, Harry Sr., 125
Strasberg, Lee, 135, 136
Streep, Meryl, 239
Street Angel, 2
Streisand, Barbra, 124–35, *132, 133, 134*,
    140, 159, 170
Styne, Jule, 126

Suddenly, Last Summer, 105, 108
Sugar Babies, 161
Sunrise, 2–3
Supremes, 144, 148
Suspicion, 54–55, 59
Sutherland, Donald, 141, 142, *142*, 143
Sutherland, Kiefer, 180, 181
Suzman, Janet, 135, 143
Swank, Hilary, 238–43, 245–46, 254–55
Swanson, Pauline, 79
Swindell, Larry, 32, 33, 37
Sylvia, Madame, 12

Talley, André Leon, 252
Tall Story, 136
Tandy, Jessica, 174, 181
Taraborrelli, J. Randy, 150, 151
Tarantino, Quentin, 188, 192
Tarkington, Booth, 27
Taxi Driver, 179
Taylor, Elizabeth, 86, 97–108, *107*, *109*,
    158, 199, 246
Taylor, James, 140
Taylor, Sam, 8
Temple, Shirley, 24, *25*, 26
Ten Commandments, The, 152
Testino, Mario, 207, 238
Tfank, Barbara, 188–92
    fashions by, *190*
Thalberg, Irving, 11–12, 13, 15, 16, 32
Thelma & Louise, 195
Theodora Goes Wild, 32
They Shoot Horses, Don't They?, 141
Thomas, Bob, 17, 23, 26
Thomas, Kristin, 223
Thomas Crown Affair, The, 119, 120, 243
Thomson, David, 63
Three Faces of Eve, The, 97
Thurman, Uma, 186–92, *190*, 206, 222
Tierney, Gene, 84
To Catch a Thief, 87, 88, 90
Todd, Mike, 98–101, *102*, 105, 107
To Die For, 217
Total Recall, 178
Tout Va Bien, 137
Towne, Robert, 117
Tracy, Spencer, 49–50
Travolta, John, 188
Treasure of Sierra Madre, The, 162
Tree, Penelope, 129
Trigère, Pauline, 127
Trip to Bountiful, The, 172
Trittipe, James, 131

Truffaut, François, 110, 117
Truscott, John, 122
Turlington, Christy, 253
Turner, Lana, 97, 99
Turner, Tina, 180
Twentieth Century–Fox, 43, 59, 63, 71,
    106
Two for the Road, 159
Tyson, Cicely, 150

United Artists, 7
Universal Studios, 128, 163, 198
Upton, Andrew, 230, 231
U.S. Dress Institute, 6

Vadim, Roger, 135, 136
Valentina, 83
Valentino, 118, 186, 192, 196, 198, 199–
    204, 207, 213, 214, 215, 224, 239,
    241, 252–54, 256, 258
Valiant Is the Word for Carrie, 32
Van Cleef & Arpels, 250
van Heemstra, Ella, *84*, 85
Vanity Fair, 136, 217
Van Runkle, Theodora, 116, 117–22
    fashions by, *121*
Van Sant, Gus, 188, 217
Van Throtha, Trude, 145
Variety, 2, 34, 97, 120, 150, 198
Verhoeven, Paul, 200
Versace, Donatella, 232
Versace, Gianni, 214–15, 223, 224, 225,
    239, 243
    fashions by, *216*
Vespuci, Simonetta de, 120
Vidal, Gore, 105
Viera, Cristina, 252–54
Vietnam War, 117, 139, 140
Virgin Queen, The, 93
Vogue, 7, 11, 20, 21, 38, 55–56, 72, 74,
    136, 181, 208, 215, 218, 252
Voight, Jon, 159
Vreeland, Diana, 118
Vuitton, Louis, 140, 147

Walker, Alexander, 8, 38, 46, 70, 75, 83
Walker, Alice, 164
Walls of Malapaga, 77
Wall Street, 202
Walt Disney Productions, 110, 112
Walters, Barbara, 211
Wang, Vera, 196, 198, 199–204, 248
Wanger, Walter, 20, 54, 59

Warhol, Andy, 158
Warner, Jack, 23, 26–30, 31, 55, 71, 72, 117, 119
Warner Bros., 1, 5, 23, 26–28, 30, 54, 55, 56, 71, 116, 119, 136
Warwick, Dionne, 140
Washington, Denzel, 184
Wasserman, Lew, 198
Waterbury, Ruth, 31
Watnick, Rita, 250–52, 257, 258
Wayne, John, 101
Weaver, Sigourney, 191, 239
Weaver, Sylva, 24
Webb, Veronica, 200
Weinstein, Bob, 227, 233
Weinstein, Harvey, 227, *229*, 233
Weir, Peter, 159
Welch, Raquel, 155, *157*, 175
Wellman, William, 87
Wells, George, 99
Werfel, Franz, 59
Western Costume, 122, 125, 162
Westmore, Mont, 42
Westmore, Wally, 20, 23, 61
Whitaker, Alma, 12
White Nights, 172
Whitfield, Eileen, 7
Wiest, Dianne, 192
Wilde, Oscar, 231
Wilder, Audrey, 78, 79, 80, 81
Wilder, Billy, 78, 79, 80–81, 83, 159, 246
Wilding, Michael, *73*, 74
Williams, Esther, 99, *160*, 161
Williams, Tennessee, 99, 105
Wilson, Henry, *64*

Wilson, Rita, 177, 242, 243
Windsor, Duchess of, 102
Winfrey, Oprah, 191–92, 204, 222
Winston, Harry, diamonds by, 63, 64, 189, 213, 234, 235
Wintour, Anna, 211, 218, 225, 240
Wise, Robert, 114
Witness, 159
Wizard of Oz, The, 50, 184
Wonder Boys, 256
Wood, Natalie, 131, 149
Wood, Sam, 42, 62
Woodward, Joanne, 97–98, 101, 125, 132
World War II, 51–52, 53, 55, 61, 68, 70, 72, 142
Woulfe, Michael, 92
Wright, Tenny, 28
Wuthering Heights, 41, 50
WWD/Women's Wear Daily, 185, 199, 207, 218, 219, 224, 232, 234, 239
Wyler, William, 77–78, 81, 124, 129
Wyman, Jane, 74, 87, 95
Wynyard, Diana, 18

Yearde, Tamara, 234
Yeoh, Michelle, 249, 256
Young, Loretta, 14, 36, 88, 175

Zaentz, Saul, 224
Zaitikian, Jacques, 234
Zellweger, Renée, 237, 249–52, 255–58, *257*
Ziegfeld, Florenz, 34
Zinnemann, Fred, 90
Zorina, Vera, 61

A NOTE ON THE AUTHOR

Bronwyn Cosgrave covered the Academy Awards for BBC TV. In addition to working as the London correspondent for the internationally syndicated weekly television program *Fashion File*, she contributes features on fashion, film, contemporary art, and interior design to the UK editions of *Harper's Bazaar* and *House & Garden* as well as *How to Spend It*, the monthly glossy magazine published by the *Financial Times*. She recently edited *Sample: Cuttings from Contemporary Fashion*, which the *Guardian* named one of 2005's best books. She is the author of *Costume and Fashion: A Complete History* and is the former features editor of British *Vogue*. She lives in London.

A NOTE ON THE TYPE

The text of this book is set in Bembo. This type was first used in 1495 by the Venetian printer Aldus Manutius for Cardinal Bembo's *De Aetna*, and was cut for Manutius by Francesco Griffo. It was one of the types used by Claude Garamond (1480–1561) as a model for his Romain de L'Universite, and so it was the forerunner of what became standard European type for the following two centuries. Its modern form follows the original types and was designed for Monotype in 1929.